Educating a
New Majority

Laura I. Rendón, Richard O. Hope
and Associates

Foreword by Donald M. Stewart

Educating a New Majority

Transforming America's Educational System for Diversity

Jossey-Bass Publishers • San Francisco

Substantial discounts on bulk quantities of Jossey-Bass books are available
to corporations, professional associations, and other organizations. For
details and discount information, contact the special sales department at
Jossey-Bass Inc., Publishers. (415) 433-1740; Fax (415) 433-0499.

For international orders, please contact your local Simon & Schuster
International office.

 Manufactured in the United States of America on Lyons Falls Pathfinder
Tradebook. This paper is acid-free and 100 percent chlorine-free.

Library of Congress Cataloging-in-Publication Data

Rendón, Laura I.
　　Educating a new majority : transforming America's educational
system for diversity / Laura I. Rendón, Richard O. Hope, and
associates. — 1st ed.
　　　　p.　　cm. — (A joint publication in the Jossey-Bass higher and
adult education series and education series)
　　Includes bibliographical references and index.
　　ISBN 0-7879-0130-X (alk. paper)
　　1. Socially handicapped children—Education—Social aspects—
United States.　　2. Poor children—Education—Social aspects—United
States.　　3. Children of minorities—Education—Social aspects—
United States.　　4. Educational sociology—United States.
5. Educational change—United States.　　I. Hope, Richard O.
II. Title.　　III. Series: Jossey-Bass higher and adult education
series.　　IV. Series: Jossey-Bass education series.
LC4091.R42　　　1996
371.96'7'0973—dc20　　　　　　　　　　　　　　　　　　　95-18537

FIRST EDITION
HB Printing　　10 9 8 7 6 5 4 3 2 1

Contents

Foreword

In a period of considerable skepticism, if not hostility, toward many social programs, yet with a concomitant rise in the problems of an increasingly diverse population, we sorely need the counsel of sound research results translated into effective educational practices. At a time when sloppy social science can resurrect long-discredited notions of intelligence in the service of dangerous social policies, we need systematic deliberation over what obstacles our schools and colleges face. We need to widely disseminate programs that do offer great promise. Fortunately, Laura I. Rendón and Richard O. Hope describe in this volume the programs, findings, and recommendations of a wide spectrum of experienced educators, providing an essential contribution to a reasoned and research-informed public discussion of educational change. Estrella M. Triana and Shirley M. Malcom, for example, contribute to that effort when they note the work of the National Urban League's Preschool Science Collaborative and the National Council of La Raza's Project EXCEL. Vinetta C. Jones and Rochelle Clemson do likewise in describing the College Board's Equity 2000 initiative, as do Tony Cipollone, Michael K. Grady, and Warren Simmons when they tell the story of the Annie E. Casey Foundation's Urban Education Reform Initiative.

This volume also reveals the complexity of the reform task, and the need to carefully define the problems faced by minority students as well as to spell out specific solutions. Several currents are converging to change the demands placed on schools and colleges. Government policies at both state and federal levels, discussed in Dewayne Matthews's chapter, present historically unprecedented challenges and opportunities to educational institutions, and especially to their ability to provide equitable academic preparation to all students. The family structure and economy have changed dramatically, the demographics of the student body continue to shift in age and ethnicity, and tight government and institutional budgets threaten to circumscribe our collective dreams. José A. Cárdenas and Shirley Vining Brown argue in their respective chapters that the challenges of poverty, language deficiencies, and unequal resources combine with a deadening systemwide inertia to frustrate the needs of "nonmainstream" populations. Yet the labor market's new demands for higher levels of education, as described in Ray Marshall and Robert W. Glover's chapter, create economic as well as moral imperatives for educational reform, and for building the broad alliances and coalitions that requires.

With its fluid demographics, this nation will always have a "new majority," as Rendón and Hope point out in their chapter, and this presents one of the most fundamental changes that our educational systems will experience. This is also our great strength, though we must know how to build on it, especially in our schools. We will always need to build and reassert core values, adapt and tap emerging technologies, and build and rebuild a broad consensus about how our schools and colleges should contribute to this nation's growth. We are not a people fixed in time, and if this volume can help bring about a more equitable and therefore richer educational system, it will help to call us back to the fundamental purposes of this republic.

We do well perhaps to recall the vision and challenge of an American deeply committed to educational equity, W.E.B. Du Bois. Speaking to the universal longing to "soar in the dim blue air above the smoke" in these "times that try . . . souls," Du Bois evoked a richly transcendent image of educational access:

I sit with Shakespeare and he winces not. Across the color line I move arm in arm with Balzac and Dumas, where smiling men and welcoming women glide in gilded halls. From out the caves of evening that swing between the strong-limbed earth, the tracery of the stars, I summon Aristotle and Aurelius and what would I will, and they come all graciously with no scorn nor condescension. So, wed the Truth, I dwell above the Veil. Is this the life you grudge us, O knightly America? Is this the life you long to change into the dull red hideousness of Georgia? [Du Bois, 1989, p. 76].

We are a long way from the "red hideousness of Georgia," but we simply cannot accept the outrageous educational inequities that tear at this nation's body politic as would any chronic and debilitating disease. The schools do not stand alone in this; years before students enter resource-rich or paint-chipped classrooms, long before schools have the chance to sort and track in the insidious ways that Jeannie Oakes and Martin Lipton describe in their chapter, we as a society sort and track large segments of our population into dead-end lives and desperate communities. As educators, we cannot hide behind the promises of a new assessment format, a new set of standards, or even a new set of structures. We must not, as we have so often done, hide behind the robes of court judges to bring about reasonable opportunities for all of our youth. We cannot stand idly by as need-based aid is weakened and only give polite lip service to the equal opportunity to learn for every citizen. When an estimated 76 percent of high-income students complete their bachelor's degrees versus 4 percent of their low-income classmates, we cannot stand by silently, nor shrug off the responsibility because the problem is wider than the classroom.

In spite of the distance between our professed goals and current educational system, we live in a time of exciting possibilities and opportunities for renewal. We learn more every day regarding new theories of cognition, new technologies of teaching and learning, and improved approaches to how schools and colleges can work best with families and communities. We continue to see the importance of cultivating dynamic and responsive leadership for our schools and colleges, an argument forcefully put forward here by Blandina Cárdenas Ramírez.

It is my hope that this volume, in collaboration with its readers, may contribute to the achievement of all our students' potential, both our youth and our fellow adults, and to the more complete realization of this fine nation of promise. Through dialogue and action informed by the educators featured here, we can indeed begin to accompany all our students as they "glide in gilded halls," as they lead us at last toward a just society beyond all veils.

Donald M. Stewart
President
The College Board

Reference

Du Bois, W.E.B. "Of the Training of Black Men." In W.E.B. Du Bois, *The Souls of Black Folk*. New York: Bantam, 1989.

Preface

A new student majority is on the rise—one that will shape the American political, social, and economic future for a long time to come. However, this new student majority also constitutes the bulk of the nation's most imperiled students—new immigrants, native-born ethnic and racial minorities, low-income and language-minority children. And the future of these students appears to be in jeopardy. In the 1990s, educators who work with at-risk students maintain that the nation's destiny is being threatened by a significant educational gap between white and minority children. Minority students, especially African Americans and Latinos, still trail whites, despite gains in high school completion rates, pointing to the need to address many factors behind this phenomenon, including immigration, poverty, and the uneven quality of education between urban and suburban schools. Test scores for minorities have gone up, but scores of African American, Mexican American, and Puerto Rican students continue to lag behind those of white students. Progress has also been seen in college participation, but American Indians, Hispanics, and African Americans are still less likely than whites to participate in postsecondary study. To make matters worse, students most at risk appear to be getting the least of what American education has to offer—schools with the fewest resources, the least experienced teachers, the least challenging curriculum, and the lowest expectations. Reversing the educational gap between whites and students of color remains a key imperative in the years ahead—an imperative that challenges educators and policy makers alike.

This book emerges during a highly critical, politically explosive time. Different political, socioeconomic, and cultural forces appear to be having a detrimental impact on at-risk students. In terms of educational policy, the 1990s have offered some of the most interesting developments in American history. The overhaul of policies enacted during the 1980s and early 1990s by two Republican presidents, Ronald Reagan and George Bush, began in 1993, when Bill Clinton was sworn in as president. Espousing his Democratic Party's values, President Clinton promised a new government that reflected the changing face of America—one that was multicultural, multilingual, and multi-life-style oriented. The new president also offered hope to educators, many of whom believed that important strides in areas such as civil rights and educational reform that benefited students from impoverished backgrounds had suffered significantly during the long Republican administration.

But as 1994 came to a close, a dramatic political development occurred, the effects of which may last well into the next century. Overwhelming Republican victories in the November 1994 election that included a well-publicized shakeup in Congress and pickups in several governors' offices and state legislatures laid the groundwork for a big shift in state and federal educational policy. The next century may see a continuing emphasis on less government, schools that work without additional funding, school choice, and charter schools (which win freedom from state regulations by signing a performance contract with the state). Federal policy shifts also propel concern about the elimination of many provisions created by Democrats under the Goals 2000: Educate America Act and the Elementary and Secondary Education Act, as well as the closing down of the federal Education Department.

The mid 1990s brought about another significant development bound to impact immigrant and language-minority children and parents. In California voters passed controversial Proposition 187, designed to restrict public schooling, welfare, and nonemergency medical services to persons that were unable to prove their legal immigration or nationality status. Proposition 187 was adopted even in the face of *Plyler* v. *Doe,* the 1982 Supreme Court decision that made it unconstitutional to prohibit educational services to undocumented students. The constitutionality of this new law is still in question. However, in the future an increasing number of states could consider placing a similar proposition on the ballot. Whether this marks the beginning of a campaign to overturn the Supreme Court decision remains to be seen, but it is apparent that the next century may see public sentiment growing in favor of reducing or eliminating services to undocumented aliens.

Some political developments may hurt immigrant, low-income, and minority students, but so do ill-fated efforts at school reform, as well as social unrest, racial tensions, and increased poverty. Moreover, the reduced availability of financial aid has diminished opportunities for low-income students, a high percentage of whom are ethnic and racial minorities, to pursue a college education. In colleges and universities, students of color frequently encounter social isolation, racism, and hostile climates in predominantly white institutions. These conditions have resulted in an educational crisis, particularly in urban areas. Piecemeal strategies that focus on one educational sector have attained some positive results, but now it appears that more is warranted. One sector, acting independently, cannot solve the issues related to the education of at-risk students.

A new vision of educating diverse peoples is needed in order to tap all the country's human potential so that the nation can continue to prosper and compete in the global arena. The educational crisis demands an action-oriented approach to reform the entire educational pathway—from kindergarten through high school, and from community colleges to universities. A holistic approach to educational reform is needed to involve all key partners and stakeholders in an effort to connect schools with two- and four-year institutions and to allow schools and colleges to forge partnerships with external constituencies. The nation's educational institutions, in partnership with community-based organizations and social service providers, need to work in unison to galvanize action that will help clear the pathway of barriers that preclude at-risk students from experiencing academic success. Americans, whether they want more or less government, have to provide a series of workable, field-tested solutions that can narrow the gap between the haves and have-nots.

Audience

Educating a New Majority is intended for anyone wishing to contribute to the success of at-risk, low-income, and minority students. At the K–12 level, the book will be particularly useful to superintendents, principals, teachers, and counselors who work in cities where minorities already are, or are rapidly becoming, a new majority. Similarly, it will be of interest to college presidents, chief academic officers, academic administrators, faculty members, college students, and student affairs professionals in two- and four-year colleges with large and increasing numbers of culturally diverse students. In addition, the book is targeted at state and federal policy makers, as well as community leaders in the nation's urban centers. For these audiences, it provides essential information needed to understand and address the complex issues that surround the education of an emerging new student majority. Moreover, the book proposes action-oriented solutions—new proposals to galvanize action throughout the entire educational system. In the end, *Educating a New Majority* should be a useful tool to help educational leaders respond to the changing face of a new America—indeed to help them refashion an educational system that works not just for some, but for *all* students.

Overview of the Contents

The introductory chapter provides an overview of the multiple issues related to educating a diverse constellation of students throughout the educational pipeline and serves as a backdrop for the chapters that follow. Part One begins by introducing current challenges to minority education in the twenty-first century. We address issues related to the nation's changing labor market and the training that will be required of workers in the future. We also outline obstacles students confront as they follow the educational pathway, and conclude the section by discussing contemporary state and federal policy issues related to the education of low-income and minority students.

In Part Two we probe deeper into the issues and reforms needed to make the K–12 system more responsive to culturally diverse students. In particular, we explore issues and reform strategies related to school restructuring, teaching, tracking and assessment, mathematics education, parental involvement, and the education of Alaska Native and American Indian students.

In Part Three we turn our attention to the nation's higher education system. We focus on curricular transformation, as well as on models and strategies needed to increase the participation, retention, transfer, assessment, and degree completion rates of minority students in two- and four-year colleges and universities. We also explore the role of foundations in supporting efforts targeted at students at risk and discuss the contributions, future, and status of African American, Hispanic, and tribal colleges.

In Part Four we focus on leadership needed to redesign the nation's educational system. Special attention is given to leadership needed to create schools for all learners and to leadership imperatives in higher education. The concluding chapter brings the issues raised in the book into a forward-looking context, emphasizing new ways of thinking about student diversity and new policies and practices that can serve to better educate a new student majority.

The authors' contributions, prepared for this book by invitation, do not represent a consensus.

Acknowledgments

We wish to thank all of the contributing authors for making this book possible. In addition, we thank our editor, Gale Erlandson, who supported the idea for this book from the very beginning. Finally, we thank our families, friends, and colleagues who share our concern, caring, and commitment for culturally diverse students and for transforming our educational system so that it embraces and promotes the development of the full potential of the diversity of students it serves.

September 1995   Laura I. Rendón
                                                     Tempe, Arizona

                                                     Richard O. Hope
                                                     Princeton, New Jersey

The Authors

LAURA I. RENDÓN is professor in the Division of Educational Leadership and Policy Studies at Arizona State University, where her teaching and research focus on K–16 educational partnerships, minorities in two- and four-year colleges, and student diversity issues in education. Rendón is also director of evaluation of the National Center for Urban Partnerships, funded by the Ford Foundation. The project involves the evaluation of citywide alliances in sixteen U.S. urban centers, where partnerships among schools, colleges, business and industry, and community-based organizations have been formed to improve the condition of education for at-risk students. Rendón is also a senior research scientist with the National Center for Postsecondary Teaching Learning and Assessment, funded by the U.S. Department of Education. The center involves a six-university consortium that is examining student learning in two- and four-year colleges. In addition, she is affiliated with the Hispanic Research Center at Arizona State University.

Rendón is the author of numerous articles. In addition, she is associate editor of the *Journal of Women and Minorities in Science and Engineering* and serves on the editorial boards of the *Community College Review*, the *Journal of Planning for Higher Education*, and the *Teaching and Learning Forum*. She has been a member of the National Board of Directors of the American Association for Higher Education, the National Advisory Board of the Woodrow Wilson Fellowship Foundation, the National

Advisory Board of the Center for the Freshman Year Experience, and the Technical Advisory Board of the Quality Education for Minorities Network.

Rendón received her A.A. degree (1968) from San Antonio College in English, her B.A. degree (1970) from the University of Houston in English and journalism, her M.A. degree (1975) from Texas A&I University in Kingsville in counseling and guidance and psychology, and her Ph.D. degree (1982) from the University of Michigan in higher education.

RICHARD O. HOPE is vice president and director of the Woodrow Wilson Program in Public Policy and International Affairs at the Woodrow Wilson National Fellowship Foundation. He received his B.A. degree (1961) from Morehouse College in sociology and his M.A. degree (1967) and Ph.D. degree (1969) from Maxwell School, Syracuse University, in sociology. In 1990, Hope attended the Institute for Educational Management (Postgraduate School) at Harvard University. He has been executive director of the Quality Education for Minorities Project (later the Quality Education for Minorities Network) at the Massachusetts Institute of Technology (1988–1990); has served as director of the Intercultural Studies Center and professor, Department of Sociology, Indiana University of Indianapolis (1986–1988); and was chairperson and professor at the Department of Sociology at Indiana University in Indianapolis. Hope was honored with a distinguished award given by the Center for Leadership Development at Indianapolis, Indiana; has received numerous grants; and has been noted in *Who's Who in the United States*. He has authored or coauthored numerous publications, including *African-Americans and the Doctoral Experience* (1991, with others), and *Education That Works: An Action Plan for the Education of Minorities* (1990, with others). Hope has been a past member of numerous advisory boards. He is presently on the advisory board for the Morehouse Research and on the advisory council for the Department of Sociology, Princeton University. He is a member of the New Jersey Committee for the Humanities; on the Board of Directors for the Millhill Family Center, Trenton, New Jersey; and on the Advisory Panel on Minority Concerns for the College Board in Washington, D.C.

BEVERLY J. ANDERSON is dean of the College of Arts and Sciences at the University of the District of Columbia (UDC). She served on the faculty of mathematics at UDC (formerly Federal City College) from 1969 to 1994. She returned to UDC in 1992 after a three-and-one-half-year appointment as director of the Office of Minority Affairs at the National Research Council's Mathematical Sciences Education Board. In her position at the National Research Council, she was director of the national program "Making Mathematics Work for Minorities," whose goal was to mobilize the country to meet the challenge of reversing long-standing trends of underachievement and underrepresentation of minorities in the mathematical sciences. She also directed the Alliance to Involve Minorities in Mathematics, a group of fifty national organizations whose charge was to plan, develop, coordinate, and implement action programs to correct the underachievement and underrepresentation of minorities in the mathematical sciences. She was also an educational columnist for the *Prince Georges News,* a monthly newspaper in Prince Georges County, Maryland.

SHIRLEY VINING BROWN is senior research scientist at the Educational Testing Service in Princeton, N.J. Brown received her A.B. degree (1958), her M.S. degree (1973), and her Ph.D. degree (1975) in sociology from the University of Michigan. From 1975 through 1993, she taught at the University of Maryland. Brown has published numerous articles and has been project director for various research projects during the past decade. These projects have included (1) Project Directory for the Nature of Public Social Services for Pregnant Teenagers, (2) Increasing Minority Faculty, (3) the Postgraduate Status and Field Mobility of Minority Doctorates, and most recently, (4) the Underrepresentation of Minority Women in Science and Engineering Education. In 1984, Brown received a postdoctoral fellowship award from the Department of Social Relations and Center for Social Organization of Schools at Johns Hopkins University. From 1981 through 1983, she was included in *Who's Who in the East,* and in 1981, in the *Directory of Distinguished Americans.* Brown is a member of the National Advisory Board, Myerhoff Scholarship Program, University of Maryland. She has also been a grant reviewer, consultant, and member of various other boards.

JOSÉ A. CÁRDENAS is founder and director emeritus of the Intercultural Development Research Association of San Antonio, Texas, a nonprofit organization dedicated to equity and excellence in education for all children. Nationally recognized as an education expert and civil rights advocate, Cárdenas has served as a source of technical information to the Texas legislature, U.S. Congressional representatives, the U.S. Department of Justice, the Mexican American Legal Defense and Educational Fund, the Harvard Center for Law and Education, the National Urban Coalition, the Hearst Foundation, the Rockefeller Foundation, the Ford Foundation, the U.S. Department of Education, and the U.S. Department of Health and Human Services. He has served as superintendent of an urban school district, chair of the education department at an institute of higher education, director of a research and development center, and at all levels of the education professional hierarchy. Cárdenas has published extensively in the areas of bilingual education training and evaluation, desegregation, school finance, and the needs of America's forgotten children. He coauthored *The Theory of Incompatibilities,* a new paradigm of minority education, and has written or contributed to over fifty other publications. He is currently working on a four-volume series on a broad range of major educational topics.

TONY CIPOLLONE is an associate director of the Annie E. Casey Foundation in Greenwich, Connecticut, and has primary responsibility for managing the foundation's research, evaluation, and education policy initiatives. He has been with the foundation full time since 1989 and was previously director of its New Futures Initiative. Prior to coming to the foundation, Cipollone spent fifteen years working directly with at-risk youth and influencing issues affecting them. As a senior research associate at Education Matters, Inc., a research and consulting firm in Cambridge, Massachusetts, he provided consultation to numerous foundations, school districts, state agencies, and youth organizations, including the Children's Defense Fund, Public/

Private Ventures, the Connecticut and Massachusetts Departments of Education, the Edna McConnell Clark Foundation, and the Carnegie Corporation. He has researched, evaluated, and written extensively on issues surrounding school dropouts, school improvement, teacher working conditions, collaborative service delivery systems for at-risk youth, and school-business partnerships, including the Boston Compact. Before Joining Education Matters, Cipollone worked with at-risk youth as a teacher, school administrator, group home houseparent, and counselor in residential treatment centers. He was also on the adjunct faculty of the College of New Rochelle, South Bronx Campus, and Bank Street College. He holds a doctorate in Administration, Planning, and Social Policy from Harvard University, a master's degree in special education, and a bachelor's degree in urban education from the State University of New York at Buffalo.

ROCHELLE CLEMSON is Assistant State Superintendent of Certification and Accreditation at the Maryland State Department of Education. She formerly held positions as chief of the Teacher Education and Certification Branch and specialist in teacher recruitment and teacher education for that agency. Her background includes experience as an administrator and faculty member in higher education. She was director of the University of Maryland's Office of Laboratory Experiences and coordinator of Teacher Education Centers in Charles and Howard Counties. Clemson's background includes teaching in urban, suburban, and rural school systems. She has given many presentations at national conferences and has published articles and book chapters on topics related to teacher education. As a consultant to colleges, universities, school systems, and a private corporation, she has served as a staff developer, workshop facilitator, and keynoter. Clemson serves on a number of advisory committees within and outside Maryland. She has recently completed a three-year term on the American Association of Colleges for Teacher Education's Committee on Multicultural Education, and she serves on the Unit Accreditation Board of the National Council for the Accreditation of Teacher Education.

WILLIAM G. DEMMERT, JR., has been a visiting professor in anthropology at Western Washington University since 1992. He received his B.A. degree (1961) from Seattle Pacific College, his Ed.M. degree (1968) from the University of Alaska, and his Ed.D. degree (1973) from Harvard University. From 1990 to 1992, he was an Irvine Scholar and visiting professor at the School of Education, Stanford University. In Alaska, Demmert was Commissioner of Education (1987–1990), professor of education and dean (1984–1987) as well as acting dean (1983–1984), director for the Center for Teacher Education (1982–1983), and deputy commissioner for the Department of Fish and Game (1980–1982). He has been author, coauthor, and editor for numerous publications. Demmert has also served as consultant and member of numerous boards, panels, councils, delegations, and committees. He has been honored as the Indian Educator of the Year (1984), has received the Distinguished Early Childhood Education of Year Award (1977), and has received the (Honorary) Doctor of Laws (1977).

MILDRED GARCÍA is assistant vice president for Academic Affairs at Montclair State College in Upper Montclair, New Jersey. She received her Ed.D. and M.A. degrees in higher education administration from Columbia University Teachers College. Prior to her current position, she was dean of students at Hostos Community College in New York. García also attended Harvard University's Institute for Educational Management and was a visiting summer scholar/research associate in the National Center for the Study of Higher Education at Pennsylvania State University. She has served as associate editor of the *Foundations of America Higher Education*, which is part of the *ASHE Reader Series*. Other works have been published in the *Journal for Higher Education Management* and in the book *The Effect of Assessment on Minority Student Achievement*, edited by Michael Nettles. She has also delivered a number of presentations and keynote addresses, covering such issues as organizational structure and the socialization of women and minorities in higher education.

HÉCTOR GARZA is director of the Office of Minorities in Higher Education at the American Council on Education. During the

1980s, at twenty-five years of age, Garza became one of a very few Mexican Americans to assume the post of assistant graduate dean in the United States. During his twelve years of service at the graduate school of Eastern Michigan University, he was promoted to the rank of associate graduate dean and special assistant to the provost. In 1985, he was tapped by then–Michigan Governor James J. Blanchard to serve as the executive director of the Commission on Spanish Speaking Affairs. His long-term service and numerous achievements in academe have earned him many awards, including those from the University of Michigan, Eastern Michigan University, the National Hispanic University, George Mason University, the American Association for Higher Education, the Council of Graduate Schools, and the State of Michigan. Garza holds a bachelor's degree in general studies and a master's degree in public health from the University of Michigan. He is currently completing his doctorate in higher education administration at the University of Michigan. He has published several book chapters relating to graduate education, minorities in higher education, and Chicano cinema.

ROBERT W. GLOVER is a research scientist in the Study of Human Resources, Lyndon B. Johnson School of Public Affairs, the University of Texas at Austin, where he has specialized in studies of various aspects of learning and work for more than two decades. Glover has authored or coauthored more than fifty publications and has visited various nations—including Germany, Denmark, Sweden, Hong Kong, China, and Japan—to examine approaches to workforce preparation and development. He is one of the nation's leading authorities on apprenticeship and school-to-work transition. He served as chair of the Federal Committee on Apprenticeship from 1978 to 1982. Glover is deeply involved in school-to-work activities, such as the Austin Project, where he chairs the Task Force on Paths into the Workplace and Professional Life. He is a founding member of the School-to-Work Transition Committee of the Greater Austin Chamber of Commerce as well as a member of the Capital Area Tech Prep Consortium and the Capital Area Workforce Alliance and its planning subcommittee to research and select priority occupations for vocational training. He is also a member of the Austin Mayor's Literacy

Task Force, the Mayor's Task Force on Apprenticeships and Career Pathways for Austin Youth, and the Education Advisory Committee of the Austin/Travis County Private Industry Council. With his wife, Toni Falbo, he served as co-chair of the Austin Independent School District Strategic Action Team on Student Achievement and Motivation. He is coauthor of *Bridging the Gap: Implementing School-to-Work Transition in Austin, Texas* (1993).

MICHAEL K. GRADY joined the Annie E. Casey Foundation in 1991 to help manage the foundation's portfolio of research and evaluation grants. His current responsibilities include evaluations of Casey's large-scale systems reform initiatives in the areas of family foster care, children's mental health, juvenile justice, and teenage pregnancy prevention. Additional responsibilities will emerge from the foundation's funded research and evaluation agendas that are currently being formulated. These investigations will complement the foundation's major investment strategies by studying both the processes and outcomes of other national efforts to reform human service systems. Prior to joining the foundation, Grady was director of research and evaluation for the Prince George's County Public Schools (Maryland) from 1988 to 1991. While in Prince George's County, he supervised research studies on the academic achievement of African American males, magnet schools, school-based management, and the Comer school development process. From 1986 to 1988, Grady served as research associate to the Magnet Review Committee in St. Louis, providing support to a panel of experts appointed by the federal court there to develop a long-range plan for magnet schools for city schools. In 1984–85, he assisted Charles V. Willie in a Danforth Foundation–sponsored evaluation of St. Louis's interdistrict desegregation program, resulting in the publication of *Metropolitan School Desegregation* (with Willie). Other publications include *African Americans and the Doctoral Experience* (with Willie and Richard Hope), "The Function of Education in American Society" (with Faith Sandler), and "The Comer School Development Program: A Theoretical Analysis" (with A. Anson, T. Cook, J. Comer, and N. Haynes). Grady graduated from the Harvard Graduate School of Education, where he earned his master's and doctoral degrees in education.

SHANETTE M. HARRIS is currently assistant professor of clinical psychology in the Department of Psychology at the University of Rhode Island. Previously, she served as assistant professor in the Department of Educational and Counseling Psychology at the University of Tennessee at Knoxville. She received her B.S. degree (1982) from Howard University in psychology and her M.A. degree (1984) from Western Carolina University in clinical psychology. She received her Ph.D. degree (1989) from Virginia Polytechnic Institute and State University in clinical psychology. Her research interests focus on culture and mental and physical health, gender-role behavior, and minority retention in higher education. She is coeditor of *Multicultural Needs Assessment for College and University Populations* (1994, with S. Stabb and J. E. Talley).

RUTH S. JOHNSON is associate professor of educational administration at California State University at Los Angeles and received her Ed.D. degree from Rutgers University. Prior to her current position, she held a variety of positions in K–12 education, including those of classroom teacher and consultant, assistant superintendent in curriculum and business administration, and superintendent of schools. Her major research emphasis is on processes related to changing the academic culture of urban schools. While directing the California-based Achievement Council's comprehensive urban school improvement initiative, she developed instruments to measure qualitative indicators of change in underachieving schools. She has coauthored two reports for the Independent Analysis Unit of the Los Angeles School District: one on achievement patterns in elementary schools and the other on actual college-going rates by ethnicity. Johnson serves on national, state, and local advisory boards and committees, makes frequent presentations, and serves as a consultant to schools and districts throughout the nation.

VINETTA C. JONES is the national director of EQUITY 2000, a national school reform initiative of the College Board that has been featured in the *New York Times Sunday Magazine,* the American Association of School Administrators' *Leadership News,* the U.S. Department of Education's *Dwight D. Eisenhower Mathematics and*

Science Education, and *Education Week,* among other publications. EQUITY 2000 represents a partnership between the College Board, urban school districts at six sites nationwide, higher education institutions, and numerous private foundations. The goal of the program is to close the gap in the college-going and success rates between minority and nonminority, disadvantaged and advantaged students. Prior to joining the College Board in 1991, Jones was dean of the School of Education and Urban Studies at Morgan State University in Baltimore, where she developed effective models for preparing teachers for diverse student populations. She served as the first statewide director of the Mathematics and Science Education Network at the University of North Carolina at Chapel Hill, where she developed and managed a program to strengthen math and science education in the state's public schools. This followed her pioneering work as statewide director of the Mathematics, Engineering, Science Achievement (MESA) Pre-College Programs at the University of California at Berkeley. She holds a doctorate in human development and learning from the University of California at Berkeley, and a bachelor's degree from the University of Michigan.

MARTIN LIPTON is an English teacher at Calabasas High School, Calabasas, California. He received his B.A. degree (1965) from California State University at Long Beach in English and has been teaching for over twenty-five years. Lipton has served as a consultant to research projects and as an instructor and presenter at various inservices and seminars. He is coauthor (with Jeannie Oakes) of *Making the Best of Schools: A Handbook for Parents, Teachers, and Policymakers* (1990) and has coauthored numerous articles as well.

SHIRLEY M. MALCOM is head of the Directorate for Education and Human Resources Programs of the American Association for the Advancement of Science (AAAS). The directorate includes AAAS programs in education, activities for underrepresented groups, and public understanding of science and technology. Malcom was head of the AAAS Office of Opportunities in Science from 1979 to 1989. Between 1977 and 1979, she served as program officer in the Science Education Directorate of the National Science Foundation. Prior to this, she was assistant professor of biology at the University of North Carolina at Wilmington. Other work experience includes two years as a high school science teacher. Malcom serves as a member of the board of the National Center on Education and the Economy, as vice chair of the executive committee, and as a member of the governing board of the New Standards Project. She is also a member of the Smithsonian Advisory Council. She has been nationally recognized for her efforts and those of the Office of Opportunities in Science to improve the education of young women and minority young people by involving community organizations and parents in educational reform. Malcom served on the Clinton-Gore transition team, chairing the task group on vocational/technical education for the Departments of Education and Labor, looking at programs for training as well as school-to-work transition. She received her doctorate in ecology from Pennsylvania State University, her master's degree in zoology from the University of California at Los Angeles, and her bachelor's degree with distinction in zoology from the University of Washington. In addition, she holds honorary degrees from the College of St. Catherine, New Jersey Institute of Technology, and St. Joseph's College.

LIONEL A. MALDONADO is professor of ethnic studies at California State University at San Marcos and has published on race and ethnic relations in American society. His main research focus has been on Chicanos in the United States, principally labor force participation issues. Prior to joining the faculty at California State University at San Marcos, he was deputy executive officer and director of the Minority Fellowship Program at the American Sociological Association. He earned his Ph.D. degree (1971) at the University of Oregon in sociology.

RAY MARSHALL holds the Audre and Bernard Rapoport Centennial Chair in Economics and Public Affairs at the University of Texas at Austin. From 1962 to 1981, he served as professor and chair for the Department of Economics and director and founder for the Center for the Study of Human Resources. Marshall received his B.A. degree (1949) from Millsaps College; his

M.A. degree (1950) from Louisiana State University, and his Ph.D. degree (1954) from the University of California at Berkeley in economics. From 1977 to 1981, while on leave from the University of Texas, he served as U.S. Secretary of Labor in the Carter administration. Throughout his career, Marshall has served as chair, co-chair, board member, president, director, adviser, or consultant for numerous organizations. Current activities include: co-chair, Commission on Skills of the American Workforce; member of the Commission on the Future of Worker/ Management Relations; and director and founding economist, Economic Policy Institute, Washington, D.C.

Marshall was a Fulbright Research Scholar to Finland (1955–56), a Wertheim Fellow at Harvard University (1959–60), a Ford Foundation Faculty Fellow (1964–65); a Phi Beta Kappa Visiting Scholar (1982–89), and holder of the Wayne Morse Chair in Law and Public Policy at the University of Oregon (1991–92). He has received the Veblin-Commons Award from the Association for Evolutionary Economics (1993), Sydney Hillman Book Award (1993), Lewis-Murray-Reuther Social Justice Award from the AFL-CIO Industrial Union Department (1992), Outstanding Alumni Award at Hinds Community College (1992), Outstanding Economist Award from the Kentucky Economic Association (1992), Alumni Hall of Distinction Award from Louisiana State University (1985), and Order of Achievement Award from Lambda Chi Alpha (1982).

Marshall has authored or coauthored over 30 books and monographs and approximately 175 articles and book chapters.

DEWAYNE MATTHEWS is the senior program director for Student Exchange Programs at the Western Interstate Commission for Higher Education (WICHE) in Boulder, Colorado. Matthews began his career in education as a first-grade teacher in a four-room schoolhouse in rural northern New Mexico and later administered a facility for neglected and abused children. After working as an educational policy analyst with the New Mexico legislature, he joined the staff of the New Mexico Commission on Higher Education and became its executive director in 1985. While in New Mexico, Matthews was a commissioner to both the Education Commission of the States and WICHE and was active in the State Higher Education Executive Officers' national organization. More recently, Matthews completed a Ph.D. in educational leadership and policy studies at Arizona State University. His major research interest has been the effect of state policy on the practices of universities, particularly as they relate to the enrollment, retention, and graduation of minority students.

MICHAEL T. NETTLES is professor of education and public policy in the Center for the Study of Higher and Postsecondary Education at the University of Michigan. He directs several research projects. The following topics are included among his present projects: equity and educational testing and assessment, computerized performance tasks to help all students meet higher standards in mathematics and science, and evaluating distance learning via university humanities courses offered using telecommunications and computer technologies. He serves as a member of the National Assessment Governing Board and is on the editorial boards of the *Review of Higher Education,* the *Journal of Negro Education,* and the *Journal of Higher Education.* He received his B.A. degree (1976) from the University of Tennessee in political science and his M.S. degree (1977) in higher education, his M.A. degree (1978) in political science, and his Ph.D. degree (1980) in higher education from Iowa State University. His publications and presentations reflect his broad interest in public policy, minority access, student achievement, and educational assessment in education at both the K–12 and higher education levels.

JEANNIE OAKES is professor of education at the University of California at Los Angeles. She received her B.A. degree (1964) from San Diego State University, her M.A. degree (1969) in American studies from California State University at Los Angeles, and her Ph.D. degree (1980) from the University of California at Los Angeles in education. Oakes's research and writing focus on how state, district, and school-level policies affect curriculum content, teaching practices, and classroom processes, and on the effects of educational policies on the schooling opportunities of minority and disadvantaged students. Among her research projects is one study that investigates whether and how the activities supported by the Carnegie Corporation's Middle Grade Schools State Policy Initiative generate commitment and provide capacity for the reforms identified in *Turning Points*. Another study, funded by the Lilly Endowment, is an effort to identify creative alternatives to tracking in racially mixed secondary schools.

In 1990, Oakes was awarded the Raymond B. Cattell Award for programmatic research by the American Educational Research Association. Her publications include *Keeping Track: How Schools Structure Inequality* (named one of ten "Must-Read Books for 1985" by the National School Boards Association), *Multiplying Inequalities* (1990), and *Making the Best of Schools: A Handbook for Parents, Teachers, and Policymakers* (with Martin Lipton, 1990), as well as numerous articles, including a series in the *Phi Delta Kappan* that was awarded a 1986 Distinguished Achievement Award by the Educational Press Association of America.

BLANDINA CÁRDENAS RAMÍREZ is professor of education at Southwest Texas State University. Previously, Cárdenas Ramírez served as director of the Office of Minorities in Higher Education for the American Council on Education in Washington, D.C.

WARREN SIMMONS is a senior associate at the Annie E. Casey Foundation, where he is leading the development of an urban education reform initiative. Prior to joining the Casey Foundation, he was director of equity initiatives for the New Standards Project, a coalition of eighteen states and six school districts that is developing a performance assessment system that will incorporate world-class standards in several subject areas. While at the center, Simmons served as acting co-director of the National Alliance for School Restructuring, one of eleven groups funded by the New American Schools Development Corporation to develop models for comprehensive school reform. He is a graduate of Macalester College in St. Paul, Minnesota, and has a doctorate in psychology from Cornell University. Simmons has led several research programs focused on disadvantaged youth through his work in the early 1980s with the National Institute of Education, the Center for Children and Technology at the Bank Street College of Education, and the Office of Bilingual

Education and Minority Languages Affairs. He has worked directly with schools to improve curriculum and instruction, serving as director of equity programs for Prince George's County Public Schools in Maryland and as director of race equity programming for the Mid-Atlantic Equity Center at American University.

DARYL G. SMITH is associate professor of education and psychology at the Claremont Graduate School. She received her B.A. degree (1965) in mathematics from Cornell University, her M.A. degree (1966) in education from Stanford University, and both her M.A. degree (1966) in psychology and her Ph.D. degree (1975) in psychology and higher education from the Claremont Graduate School. Her current research interests have been focused on the organizational implications of diversity in higher education, the role and impact of women's colleges, and the lessons of special purpose institutions (such as women's colleges and historically black colleges and universities) for higher education. Her writings include two monographs on issues of diversity, *The Challenge of Diversity: Involvement or Alienation in the Academy?* (1989) and *Studying Diversity in Higher Education* (1994).

ESTRELLA M. TRIANA previously directed the Hispanic Initiative Program for the Directorate for Education and Human Resources Programs of the American Association for the Advancement of Science (AAAS). With funding from the Carnegie Corporation of New York, Triana brought together eight leading national Hispanic community- and science-based organizations to begin discussions on improving science and mathematics education for Hispanics. She has produced two publications: *Making Mathematics and Science Work for Hispanics* and *United-Unidos: Mathematics and Science for Hispanics*. Triana managed AAAS Proyecto Futuro, a multiyear project she helped to develop, which is designed to build local capacity for excellence in K–8 mathematics and science education for Hispanic students. In addition, she serves on a number of advisory councils, including Humboldt State University Professors Rethinking Options in mathematics for Preservice Teachers (PROMPT), National Council of La Raza Excellence in Community Educational Leadership

Math and Science (EXCEL-MAS), and National Urban League Project PRISM. Prior to joining AAAS, she conducted educational and developmental research studies for George Washington University and George Mason University. She has published in a number of scientific journals, including *Infant Behavior and Development*. She is a graduate of George Mason University.

CHARLES V. WILLIE received his B.A. degree (1948) from Morehouse College in sociology, his M.A. degree (1949) from Atlanta University, and his Ph.D. degree (1957) from Syracuse University in sociology. Since 1974, he has been professor of education and urban studies at the Graduate School of Education at Harvard University. Previously, Willie was a sociology professor, department chair, and university vice president at Syracuse University. He has served as president of the Eastern Sociology Society, member of the American Sociological Association's Council, member of the board of directors of the Social Science Research Council, member of the President's Commission on Mental Health (by appointment of President Jimmy Carter), member of the technical advisory board of the Maurice Falk Medical Fund, and an overseer of the Boston Science Museum.

The Society for the Study of Social Problems awarded Willie the Lee Founders Award in 1983 for effectively combining social research and social action. The Committee on the Role and Status of Minorities of the American Educational Research Association designated him the recipient of its Distinguished Career Contribution Award in 1990. *Ms. Magazine* named Willie a male hero—along with forty other men—for taking courageous action on behalf of women, since he had participated as a lay preacher in the irregular service of ordination for the first eleven women priests in the Episcopal Church of the United States.

Willie has authored or edited 23 books and more than 100 articles and book chapters. He has also served as host of a weekly national public affairs television program, *Inner City Beat,* on the Monitor Channel. He has appeared on *NBC Today, CBS This Morning, ABC Good Morning America,* and the *MacNeil/Lehrer News Hour.* He is a frequent lecturer for corporations, voluntary associations, and colleges and universities.

L. STEVEN ZWERLING is a program officer in the Division of Education and Culture at the Ford Foundation. He was formerly associate dean of New York University's School of Continuing Education. Prior to that, he was director of Staten Island Community College's Division of Special and Experimenting Programs. He is the author of *Second Best: The Crisis of the Community College* (1976), *The Community College and Its Critics* (1986), and *First-Generation Students: Confronting the Cultural Issues* (1992, with Howard B. London). He has been a consultant to The Fund for the Improvement of Postsecondary Education (FIPSE), the National Endowment for the Humanities (NEH), and the National Institute of Education (NIE). In addition, he is a part-time professor of continuing education at New York University's Graduate School of Education.

Chapter 1

An Educational System in Crisis

Laura I. Rendón, Richard O. Hope

The 1990s are an electric time, for the era appears right for shaping the debate about America's future as a multicultural society. It is also a time ripe with hope if the American people choose to confront their demographic reality and respond to a clarion call about making a truly significant difference for students who have for so long been the victims of extreme neglect. The American people are facing one of the most dramatic cultural transformations in history. Americans are becoming more nonwhite and more diverse than ever before. Immigration, coupled with births from recent immigrants and the fact that native-born American minorities have high fertility rates, have contributed to this enormous diversity. In their book *American Renaissance,* Cetron and Davies (1989) state that the most fundamental change of the 1990s is in who the American people are. The spillover of these population shifts is being acutely felt in the nation's schools and colleges. Correspondingly, the most fundamental change witnessed in the nation's educational system is in who the students are *becoming*.

Students of color are expected to make up 24 percent of the under-eighteen population by 2012, a 5 percent increase from 1990. By 2010, these students will represent more than half the population eighteen years of age and younger in seven states, including California, Florida, Texas, and New York. States such as Mississippi, New Jersey, and Illinois are projected to have a youth population more than 40 percent minority (Carter and Wilson, 1994; Hodgkinson, 1991). Thus, the term *minority* is losing its statistical meaning, as a new student majority rapidly emerges, comprised collectively of African Americans, Latinos, Asians, American Indians, and Alaska Natives. In twenty-two out of the twenty-five largest urban school districts and in some two- and four-year colleges, they are already the majority. While some of these students come from well-to-do families and have attained the American Dream, many are poor and have lost faith in what America has to offer.

This chapter highlights the profiles of peoples who are transforming the United States into a new, multicultural America, reviews the issues that schools and colleges must confront as they reorganize for diversity, and outlines the consequences if our nation's educational system fails a new student majority.

America's Changing Demographic Profile

The American people are now the most diverse ever. Two trends characterize the nation's demographic profile: Americans are getting older and they are becoming more differentiated. As America grays, so does it add color. In 1970, the median age of the American population was less than thirty, but today it is nearing thirty-three, and by the year 2000, it is expected to top thirty-six. However, there is another side to this graying photo of America. New waves of immigrants are flocking to the United States. In the 1980s about twice as many immigrants as in the previous decade migrated into the United States. About 84 percent were from Asia, the Caribbean, and Latin America. Immigrants arrive at the rate of one million a year, and foreign-born residents (legal and illegal) represent 8.5 percent of the U.S. population, nearly twice the percentage in 1970. Fully 40 percent of recent immigrants settle in California, where 22 percent of the population was born outside the United States (Topolnicki, 1995). Consequently, immigration is becoming one of the most important state and federal policy issues. For example, California's Proposition 187 would restrict education to undocumented students, and educators are concerned that teachers would be forced to become de facto border patrol agents who would turn in students suspected to be illegal aliens.

These new Americans are younger than mainstream white America and have high fertility rates. The same is true for native-born minorities. The birth rate among African Americans is double the national average and for Hispanics it quadruples the national average. Immigration and high birth rates, as well as the movement of Anglos from cities to suburbs, are the main reasons that in 1990 minorities were the majority in 51 of 200 cities with 100,000 or more residents. Most of the cities where minorities are now the majority are in the South and West. These groups are so diverse that generic classifications obscure differences in culture, language, country of origin, and traditions. Just as the term *European* would not do justice to Old World immigrants, labels such as *Hispanic, Asian,* and *African American* fail to capture the full diversity within each racial and ethnic group. Indeed, because of this diversity, ethnic and racial minorities often do not act as a group. They remain separated by geographic location, national origin, immigrant status, and socioeconomic level. Therefore, their political influence is not as clear as what their numbers indicate.

These new people are being met by both those who praise diversity and those who harbor xenophobic views. Nativists, who are partial to native-born people and unaccepting toward immigrants, believe that U.S. immigration procedures are too lax and that immigrants cost more in welfare, health, and educational services than they pay in taxes. Some native-born minorities are concerned that new immigrants could take away the few jobs for which they qualify. Antiassimilationists argue that diversity is an inherent good, that this country benefits from different communities, and that immigrants constitute a net addition to the country's wealth, given that they come from an environment of poverty and are willing to work hard in a new country. The vast majority of today's immigrants (legal and illegal) are doing well. Those who arrived in the United States before 1980 actually boast higher average household incomes ($40,900) than all native-born Americans (Topolnicki, 1995). The xenophobia of today is reminiscent of what happened in the late eighteenth century, when German immigrants were characterized as unassimilable because of their language and Catholicism. Irish immigrants on the East Coast and Chinese on the West Coast were also greeted with religious and racial prejudice. Still, new people of color, combined with native-born minorities, are altering the nation's ethnic and cultural balance either to the dismay or the enthusiasm of white and nonwhite Americans. The next section highlights the heterogeneous elements of the different groups that are fast becoming new majorities.

African Americans

African Americans, often referred to as blacks, are the largest minority group in the United States, at nearly thirty million people or about 12.1 percent of the population. African Americans are drawn from a diverse range of cultures and countries in Africa, the Caribbean, and Central and South America. Half of all African Americans live in the South, but large proportions now reside in urban areas, especially Detroit, New York, Chicago, and Atlanta. African Americans have suffered a long history of oppression, including racism and poverty. They were unwillingly brought to the New World from Africa only to become oppressed people with no civil rights. Although African Americans now enjoy civil rights won at great cost by black leaders such as Martin Luther King, Jr., and many others, racial unrest still permeates American society. The unlawful beating of African American motorist Rodney King in the streets of Los Angeles and attacks in Bensonhurst and Howard Beach in New York are testimony to the notion that racism has survived the civil rights movement of the 1960s and is still a looming threat to millions of African Americans and other minority groups (Quality Education for Minorities Project, 1990; Quality Education for Minorities Network, 1993).

Alaska Natives/American Indians

Alaska Natives constitute about 14 percent of Alaska's population. Together, Alaska Natives and American Indians represent

0.8 percent of the total U.S. population. The heavy in-migration of non-Native groups has reduced the Alaska Native population since 1930, when it accounted for 50 percent of the total. Alaska is home to three distinct Native groups: Eskimos, Aleuts, and American Indians. Alaska Natives are not a monolithic group. There are twenty Alaska Native languages and more than 200 Native villages, with about 60 percent living in the state's rural areas. Alaska Natives have suffered rampant attempts to destroy the Native culture, particularly from Russians and Americans, who have wanted to "civilize" them by moving them away from their basic culture. They have experienced the banning of their languages, games, and dances and have suffered the consequences of having their children removed from families and placed in boarding schools. Nonetheless, Alaska Natives have sought to restore their villages and control over education (Quality Education for Minorities Project, 1990; Quality Education for Minorities Network, 1993).

American Indians are characterized by diversity, with at least 100 Native languages still spoken today by more than 300 tribes. Still, it is not always easy to determine just who is Indian due to problems in data collection, recording, and processing. Self-reporting in the category of "race" and "ancestry" on the U.S. census form has revealed great discrepancies. Additional complicating factors include whether the tribe is federally recognized, residence, adoption of life-styles, and percentage of Indian blood. In 1990, the largest numbers of Alaska Native/American Indians were found in Oklahoma, California, Arizona, New Mexico, Alaska, Washington, and North Carolina. American Indians strongly believe in self-determination and tribal sovereignty and enjoy a unique legal status with the federal government. They suffered attempts by the Europeans who colonized this country to assimilate them, eliminate their "barbarian" nature, and turn them into Christians (Quality Education for Minorities Project, 1990; Quality Education for Minorities Network, 1993). American Indians, like Alaska Natives, balk at the notion that the United States is a land of immigrants, for their history is such that they lived in what is now known as America many years before the arrival of Columbus in 1492.

Asians

Since the removal of discriminatory immigration policies in 1965, Asians have become one of the nation's fastest-growing minority groups. In 1990, Asian/Pacific Islanders numbered some seven million, or 2.9 percent of the U.S. population. Most of the Asian American population (outside the state of Hawaii) is found in the West, where they represent 7.7 percent of the area's population. The six largest Asian subgroups are Chinese, 23.8 percent of the Asian-American population; Filipino, 20.4 percent; Southeast Asian (those of Vietnamese, Laotian, Cambodian, or Hmong origin), 14.5 percent; Japanese, 12.2 percent; Asian Indian, 11.8 percent; and Korean, 11.6 percent. In the 1980s, nearly 900,000 refugees arrived from Vietnam, Laos, and Kampuchea (Cambodia) as they fled Southeast Asia for safety and opportunity in America. About 800,000 Hmong tribespeople driven from Laos by the Pathet Lao after the United States abandoned its military commitment to Southeast Asia have also settled here. California alone has hosted nearly half a million Vietnamese, to the point that Orange County now has an area called Little Saigon. Other Southeast Asians have settled in Long Beach, Modesto, Stockton, Fresno, and San Francisco (Cetron and Davies, 1989; Quality Education for Minorities Network, 1993).

Asians come from affluent as well as poor socioeconomic backgrounds. Roughly one million are North Koreans who escaped the communists in the 1950s. The Koreans, like the Japanese of previous generations, are the elite of Asia—well educated, entrepreneurial, and wealthy. Their energetic nature has helped them to own 85 percent of the green grocery business in New York City, some 300 grocery stores in Atlanta, most of the liquor and convenience stores in Los Angeles, and a growing number of service businesses in Anchorage. Similarly, the Vietnamese that escaped communist takeover just after the fall of Saigon were the upper tier of South Vietnamese society. Most male adults were college educated and many spoke English fluently, having worked with Americans during the war. They were able to overcome initial problems in America to build a major American success story. The second wave of Vietnamese that followed in the late 1970s—ethnic Chinese expelled by the Communist regime—have also done well (Cetron and Davies, 1989).

More unsettled are the third wave of Vietnamese immigrants, the "boat people" of the 1980s. They are largely illiterate and poor, and many are emotionally troubled due to the oppression they experienced in their homeland and the trauma of escape from their country. Another problem-plagued group that has settled in California is the Khmer of Kampuchea, nearly all of whom are poor, on welfare, and emotionally troubled due to the destruction of their country and loss of their relatives. The Hmong of northern Laos also find life in America a difficult process. They too have suffered at the hands of oppressors. Few can read and write their own language, but their farming skills have allowed them to carve out their own communities in rural areas of Minnesota, Nebraska, North Carolina, Texas, and Washington (Cetron and Davies, 1989).

Latinos

Latinos, often referred to as Hispanics, vary greatly in socioeconomic background and cultural traditions. Some, like the first immigrant wave of wealthy Cubans, have found success in America. Others, like newly arrived Mexicans, Central and South Americans, and Puerto Ricans, often live below the poverty line. Nonetheless, Latinos are proud of their culture, and many resent the "English Only" movement that they feel would do away with their freedom to express themselves in Spanish, the language that connects the Latino culture. Yet most Latinos recognize the importance of learning English as a means to participate fully in American society.

Immigrants from Mexico continue to arrive in the United States each year, mainly crossing through the porous U.S.-Mexico border that stretches some 2,000 miles from California to Texas. But not all Hispanics are recent immigrants. The Mexican-origin population, sometimes referred to as Chicanos, *mexicanos,* or Mexican Americans, consists partly of individuals who have roots in the United States extending back more than ten generations, even before the establishment of Jamestown. Texas, New Mexico, Arizona, Colorado, and California were once

a part of Mexico but had to be given up when U.S. forces over-
took Mexican troops in the U.S.-Mexican War. In a historical
account of the U.S. Southwest, Gloria Anzaldúa (1987, p. 7)
points out that "the border fence that divides the Mexican people was born on February 2, 1848 with the signing of the Treaty
of Guadalupe-Hidalgo. It left 100,000 Mexican citizens on this
side, annexed by conquest along with the land. The land established by the treaty as belonging to Mexicans was soon swindled
away from its owners. The treaty was never honored and resti-
tution, to this day, has never been made."

Other Mexican-origin communities are those whose residents applied for legalization (amnesty) under the Immigration
Reform and Control Act of 1986 to become permanent U.S. citizens. Today, people of Mexican origin number over thirteen
million and constitute 61.2 percent of the persons of Hispanic
origin living in the United States. Most live in the Southwest and
West, especially in California and Texas (Quality Education for
Minorities Network, 1993).

However, other Latino subgroups are growing even faster
than those of Mexican origin. These include Central Americans,
especially those from El Salvador, who now represent 6 percent
of the Latino population in the United States. South Americans
and "other" Latinos such as those from the Caribbean have also
settled in America. About 300,000 immigrants from the Dominican Republic have settled in New York City. Immigrants from
Spain and Portugal have also come to the United States (Quality
Education for Minorities Project, 1990; Quality Education for
Minorities Network, 1993; Cetron and Davies, 1989).

Another group of Latinos is Puerto Ricans, who are engaged in a circular migration between the island and the mainland. This is because Puerto Ricans are U.S. citizens with strong
ties to the island. In constant migration, Puerto Ricans cross cultural boundaries, languages, and school systems. The 2.3 million
Puerto Ricans on the mainland account for about 12 percent of
Latinos in the United States. High birth rates and continued
immigration will ensure that Puerto Ricans represent an increasing share of the American population in the years ahead, not
only in New York and New Jersey, where they are most heavily
concentrated, but in other mid-Atlantic states (Quality Educa-

tion for Minorities Project, 1990; Quality Education for Minorities Network, 1993).

Among Latinos the ones considered most successful are Cuban Americans, who number over one million and constitute 4.8 percent of the U.S. Latino population. Most have settled in Florida, especially Miami. There have been three waves of Cuban immigrants. The first consisted of well-to-do Cuban families who fled the Castro revolution in the early 1960s. The second arrived in the Mariel boatlift in 1980. While the first wave consisted mainly of the upper crust of Cuban society, the second wave was more diverse. Many were poor and illiterate. Others were well educated, but their economic and social success in Cuba had been quite limited. While the first wave was able to attain success in America, a large proportion of the second remains impoverished (Cetron and Davies, 1989). A third wave arrived in 1994, as Cubans again tried to escape economic hardship and political oppression in makeshift boats.

As a new century dawns, the task of dealing with the explosion of multiculturalism is one of the most critical issues facing the United States. A cultural revolution is slowly reshaping the country, and trends are readily apparent. California is expected to become the first "minority majority" state in the continental United States, and Texas and New Mexico are poised to follow. The University of California at Berkeley's freshman class is now over 50 percent minority. Overall, more than 30 percent of students in public schools—about twelve million and growing—are now minority. In Los Angeles alone, about ninety different languages are spoken. Interracial marriages have tripled. Non-Western religious cultures are also penetrating American society, and Islam is gaining increased popularity.

This country does not appear prepared to cope with the ultimate reality: a new majority and a new minority are rapidly emerging. By the last quarter of the twenty-first century, people who are today considered minorities will be the majority population. And the nation is clearly not ready for mediating the effects of unprecedented diversity in language, culture, religion, and life-style. Tensions between whites and nonwhites appear to be escalating. Hate crimes have increased, resulting not only in civil unrest but in the killings of nonwhites by individuals who preach white supremacy. Equally disturbing is that as resources, jobs, and opportunities for advancement shrink, minority groups begin to confront each other for what little there is. In the Los Angeles riots of 1992, Korean businesses, as well as black and Latino neighborhoods, were hard hit, partly due to intraethnic tensions and to economic competition among groups and individuals living in resource-poor areas (Pastor, 1993). The challenge for a new American society is as clear as it is complex: how to build communities that respect and value difference, how to foster interracial harmony, and how to connect different groups in an effort to grant them equal access to economic and educational opportunities.

Nowhere in America's infrastructures are these issues becoming more glaring than in the educational system. The school of today is nothing like before. Take Hollywood High, for instance, known for its distinguished alumni, which include some of the nation's foremost entertainers. At this high school some fifty-seven languages are now spoken, and 92 percent of the students count English as their second language. Students go through a daily weapons search, and the school has hired two full-time police officers. Many students are single parents and find they must work part time, leaving them precious little time to attend to their studies. How do children learn and how do faculty teach in a school where there is no common language and no common culture? How do students interact with each other in unsafe schools? What are the consequences to students in schools where everyone appears to be at risk? The next section discusses the issues the nation's K–12 school system and higher education institutions must confront as they attempt to address the needs and strengths of an emerging student majority.

Crisis in the K–12 School System

Poor and minority children are the most underserved in America. They come from the poorest families, have the worst health care, are more likely to be attacked, killed, or shot at as they walk to school, attend the most underfunded schools, and are taught by the least prepared teachers. The *New York Times* called children who live in bleak worlds "children of the shadows." In a series of articles that attracted national attention, the *Times* referred to these children as "impoverished youth who live in tumble-down neighborhoods of the American inner city; the children of often desperate and broken families, where meals are sometimes cereal three times a day; the young people who daily face the lures of drugs, sex, fast money and guns; the unnoticed youths who operate in a maddening universe where things always seem to go wrong" (Wilkerson, 1993, p. 1).

While not all minority children live in such dark worlds, more and more are doing so. The proportion of children living in poverty is increasing, school performance is declining, and juvenile crime has exploded and turned more violent. According to a report issued by the Commission on Chapter 1 (1992) that called for fundamental changes in the federal Chapter 1 program targeted at educationally disadvantaged children, these are the very children that deserve the best the nation's educational system can offer. But as the commission said, "Instead, to those who need the best . . . we give the least. The least well trained teachers. The lowest-level curriculum. The oldest books. The least instructional time. Our lowest expectations. Less, indeed, of everything we believe makes a difference" (p. 4).

Overall, children at risk have made some considerable achievement gains over the past twenty-five years. According to the Commission on Chapter 1 (1992), almost all poor and minority children today master rudimentary skills. Between 1972 and 1991, the high school dropout rate for whites decreased from 12.3 percent to 8.9 percent, and the dropout rate for African Americans also declined from 21.3 to 13.6 percent during the same time span. However, the dropout rate for Hispanics increased from 34.3 percent to 35.3 percent (Ramírez, 1993). Achievement gaps that have long separated poor and minority children from other youngsters in reading, as measured by the National Assessment of Educational Progress, have declined by nearly half, although there are ominous signs that the trend is now reversing. SAT scores have also improved. The largest gain in SAT average score from 1976 to 1993 was for African

Americans, a gain of 21 points in the verbal score and 34 points in the math score. Still, gaps between whites and nonwhites remain, with whites scoring higher on the verbal SAT score than all other groups and Asians scoring higher on the math score.

America's schools have largely failed poor and minority youngsters. About fifty years since *Mendez* v. *Westminister School District* (1945), forty-seven years after *Delgado* v. *Bastrop Independent School District* (1948), and about forty-one years since *Brown* v. *Board of Education* (1954)—the major cases that declared segregated schools unconstitutional—minority children continue to attend segregated and underfunded schools. According to a report issued by the Quality Education for Minorities Project (1990), minority children attend separate and decidedly unequal schools. These schools operate with outmoded curricula and structures based on the assumption that only a few students will be successful. Further, the problems students face in and out of the classroom, such as racism, poverty, language differences, and cultural barriers, are not addressed in the typical school. Students attend schools where their teachers do not expect them to amount to much. They attend crowded classrooms with fewer resources than predominantly white suburban schools have. Often, their teachers are inexperienced, engage students in mundane tasks such as circling letters on dittos, and fail to challenge children. The predominant mode of instruction is drill and practice. Keeping order in class takes precedence over engaging students in active learning and higher-order thinking skills. It is not surprising that so many of these students leave school before they graduate and that those who persevere often wonder what their education is worth, since they still find themselves unprepared for college or the work world.

Key Educational Issues

Educational reform has become one of the top federal and state policy issues of the day. Congress and the Supreme Court have played a major role in shaping educational policy over the past twenty-five years. Below is a sampling of some of the most critical educational issues related to the education of poor and minority students today.

School Restructuring and Systemic Change. The problems of inner-city schools are so perverse that many believe there are only two solutions: radically restructure schools or let schools compete for students in the marketplace of education. Those who believe in school restructuring argue that special "add-on" programs have done little or nothing to help poor and minority youngsters. The Commission on Chapter 1 (1992, p. 7) explains: "No matter how wonderful the staff in special programs or how terrific their materials and equipment, they cannot compensate in 25 minutes per day for the effects of watered-down instruction the rest of the school day and school year. And watered-down instruction is precisely what most poor children get." Instead of special programs that contribute next to nothing to the mainstream academic program, restructuring advocates argue that nothing short of total reform is needed—fundamental changes in traditional school organization, governance, policies, programs, and practices. Restructured schools are those that make fundamental changes in the rules, roles, and relationships in schools. They make student achievement the main criterion against which teachers, principals, and administrators are judged and rewarded. They decentralize decision making and increase the involvement of teachers and principals in policy discussions. They focus on site-based management where decisions about how to achieve objectives established by policy makers are made by teachers, principals, parents, child development professionals, and other school and community leaders. Restructured schools are guided by professional standards based on knowledge and skills developed through research and experience (Quality Education for Minorities Project, 1990).

National efforts such as the Ford Foundation's National Center for Urban Partnerships, the National Science Foundation's Urban Systemic Initiative, the U.S. Department of Education's Educational Partnerships Project, as well as the Pew Charitable Trust's Community Compacts Project focus on systemic change. The projects involve entire cities, including schools, community colleges, four-year institutions, business and industry, and community-based organizations, in an all-out effort to reduce the barriers to academic achievement and progress for at-risk students. Focusing on systemic change from the earliest grades to the baccalaureate degree level, these projects aim at restructuring the entire system by involving key stakeholders, allowing for shared decision making, encouraging teacher collaboration, fostering site-based management, focusing on student support and development, involving parents, and building in accountability through assessment and evaluation, among other measures. Systemic change is focused on making every school a school of choice. Yet creating systemic change takes time, is often met with resistance, is subject to political maneuvering, and can be costly.

School Choice. Advocates for what has become known as "school choice" believe that schools will change only when they know they must compete with each other. The state of Minnesota enacted one of the earliest choice plans in 1985. The plan allowed parents to send their children to any school in the state, so long as the school had room for them. When students moved from one school to another, the state tuition money that paid for their education went with them. The theory behind choice is that schools perceived to offer the best education will flourish, while those perceived to be of lesser quality will lose students and go bankrupt. Consequently, it is to every school's advantage to undertake reform strategies. But critics believe that this allows already good schools to get even better, while underfunded schools could get even worse. The scenario for poor and minority kids might well be that they would be attending even worse schools than before choice plans were enacted.

Standards. Ever since President George Bush convened an Education Summit with the governors of fifty states in 1989, setting national goals and standards has been central to the agenda of educational reform. Those who believe in instituting national content and world-class performance standards, such as those found in Japan and Great Britain, want U.S. students to be competitive. Proponents believe that national standards are needed in math, science, history, the arts, civics, geography, and English to identify what students need to know to live and work in the twenty-first century. President Bush's America 2000 Plan was based on the notion that by the year 2000 all American students would demonstrate competency in challenging subjects. In 1991 Congress established the National Council on Education Standards and Testing, a bipartisan panel that recommended the creation of voluntary national standards and a voluntary national system of student assessment based on world-class standards. Opponents argue that getting universal agreement on what constitutes a basic education is almost impossible. They also charge that standards do little or nothing about the issue of equalizing educational opportunities, such as improving teacher preparation and curricula to ensure that poor and minority students can meet agreed-on standards. Still others argue that setting national standards amounts to little if there is no local discussion about what children should learn, and that setting national standards may lead to a national curriculum and to national testing.

School Finance. Funding inequities have long divided "good" and "bad" schools. Reform advocates argue that true educational opportunities for all children can only come through equalized school funding. Disproportionate numbers of poor and minority students attend schools that have few resources, the most crowded classrooms, and the lowest per-pupil expenditures. These inequalities perpetuate the economic gap between minority and nonminority families. In 1968 Demetrio Rodriguez and parents of children who attended schools in the Edgewood district in San Antonio, Texas—a district that was poor and 96 percent nonwhite—filed an important school finance case. The Mexican American Legal and Education Defense Fund (MALDEF) represented Rodriguez and argued funding disparities between wealthy and poor school districts. While the Texas federal district court held that Texas was in violation of the equal protection clause of the U.S. Constitution, the decision was reversed by the Supreme Court in *San Antonio Independent School District* v. *Rodriguez* (1973). In the words of Jonathan Kozol, author of *Savage Inequalities* (1991, p. 229), "Twenty-three years after Demetrio Rodriguez went to court, the children of the poorest people in the state of Texas are still waiting for an equal chance at education." So are the rest of the children attending underfunded inner-city schools throughout America.

Computer-Aided Learning. Teaching children with computers holds the promise for greater gains in student achievement through individualized learning. Yet children who attend poorly funded schools that lack computers and whose families cannot afford computers at home or whose homes are not electronically wired for computers will likely be unable to learn skills needed to gain employment in a technological society.

School-to-Work Transition. Schools of today have allowed students in non–college preparatory programs to flounder by taking a general education course core that does little or nothing to prepare them for the world of work. Many students find high school boring, underachieve, and graduate with no preparation for the work world. Consequently, experimental programs such as Boston's Project Pro Tech, funded partly by the U.S. Labor Department, are being created. The Boston project links three high schools with the city's health care industry. The school curriculum for students in this program is developed using real-life applications. Students are involved in youth apprenticeship programs that help them gain employable skills, a work income, and an academic education.

Drug and Sex Education. For many inner-city children, especially "latchkey" children and those who come from broken homes, their role models are dropouts and drug dealers. These kids find it easy to gain acceptance by having children or doing drugs. With the AIDS epidemic looming in schools and with an unprecedented number of children having children, drug education and sex education are becoming integral parts of the school curriculum. But this is not happening without opposition from conservative groups, who argue that these forms of education, as well as condom distribution, actually encourage sexual promiscuity and drug abuse. In 1993, the chancellor of the New York City schools was dismissed in part because of his support for condom distribution and tolerance of homosexuals. These concerns give rise to the following questions: To what extent should schools become social service agencies? To what extent should schools replace the role of parents in instilling values?

School Safety. Minority children are largely attending schools embedded in violent neighborhoods and are becoming victims of attack in school. One in three Latinos, one in five African Americans, and one in eight whites reported that gangs operated in their schools in 1989 (Ramírez, 1993). Inner-city schools face the challenge of creating safe learning environments. Yet these are the very schools that lack the resources to create and maintain campus safety.

Year-Round Schools and Extended School Days. The basic premise of year-round schools and extended school days is that American students have too much time off. Japan's school year consists of 240 eight-hour days, while American schools average 180 days of about six and a half hours. Many educators feel the longer hours explain why Japanese schoolchildren score two or three years ahead on standardized achievement tests. In America, many minority educators believe that students should be exposed to academically reinforcing activities such as Saturday academies and after-school and summer programs. More important, the quality of education available to poor and minority youngsters needs great improvement.

Tracking. Considered one of the most pernicious barriers to minority student progress, tracking occurs early on in schooling, when children are classified as advanced, average, or behind. This judgment, often made without formal assessment, can seal a child's fate for life. "Slow" students almost never catch up, since they are made to engage in mundane activities while advanced students engage in higher-order thinking skills. Minority children, as well as those for whom English is a second language, are often misdiagnosed as slow learners or as having learning disabilities. Yet tracking persists because many teachers are unequipped to develop strategies that help all children achieve and harbor the belief that minority children have low levels of learning ability.

Teacher Preparation. Instead of inner-city schools getting the best-prepared teachers, most get the opposite. Having few resources, poor school districts are unable to attract outstanding teachers, who tend to be lured by wealthier schools paying higher salaries. Consequently, minority children often have the least-qualified and least-experienced teachers. Moreover, teacher preparation programs in colleges and universities have largely been lax in preparing teachers to work with multicultural students in urban settings.

Lack of Minority Teachers. At a time when almost one in three students in America's public schools belongs to a minority group, only 8 percent of teachers are African American, 3 percent are Hispanic, and 1.4 percent are Asian (Ramírez, 1993). The minority student population in schools will exceed 30 percent and approach 50 percent in most urban areas, but minority teachers are expected to decline from the current 10 percent of the teacher workforce to only 5 percent. Fewer than 8 percent of the students in teacher preparation programs are minority, and this pool is likely to shrink if candidates fail to pass teacher competency tests required for licensing in most states (Quality Education for Minorities Project, 1990). What will be the effects on minority children if they are taught by a largely white teacher workforce?

Student Assessment. With the growing trend toward developing performance standards, the issue of assessing student learning is becoming paramount. Yet it is well known that although some minority students do well on standardized tests, many do not. Explanations for this situation include the following: some of these tests incorporate questions that are culturally biased, minority students are likely to attend inferior schools that give them a poor-quality education, and they are less likely to have access to courses and computer software that could help them prepare for standardized tests.

Multicultural Education. With America being a multicultural nation, many educators believe that the curriculum should include multicultural education. Proponents argue that students should be exposed to and helped to understand diverse cultures and ways of knowing in order to help them function in a multicultural society. Opponents believe that multiculturalism focuses too much on difference, and that what students need is a common perspective about American life. Distorted views about multicultural education have led to divisiveness between those who argue for particularistic approaches, where separate courses emphasize each of the primary racial and ethnic groups in America, and those who advocate a pluralistic or infusion approach that calls for all courses to include content that is more representative of the pluralistic nature of this country.

Bilingual Education and English as a Second Language. With such a wide range of languages spoken in some schools today, there has been a dramatic growth in limited-English-proficiency (LEP) students. Between 1979 and 1989, public school enrollment of children who spoke a language other than English at home increased by 41 percent. Bilingual and ESL instruction are considered essential to help students make the successful transition into an English-driven curriculum. Bilingual education, which builds on the students' first language and moves them toward the development of English proficiency, is seen as the vehicle to facilitate this transition. Yet there is a shortage of qualified teachers, counselors, and other school personnel prepared to work with LEP students. Bilingual education also continues to be under attack from some educators, who believe that a common language is needed for national unity and that non-English instruction impedes assimilation. In any case, schools will need to be prepared to provide ESL instruction to the millions of adults who emigrate to this country.

Parental Involvement. Almost all educators believe parental involvement is essential to student achievement. The problem is that many minority parents do not feel empowered to participate in school functions, especially those who speak little or no

English or who have not graduated from high school. Yet there is evidence that minority parents do care about their children getting the best education, and schools need to do a better job of helping parents get involved in school management and academic activities.

Revitalization of Minority Communities. Education is a process that occurs within the context of the total community environment. Yet according to the report issued by the Quality Education for Minorities (QEM) Network in 1993, a significant percentage of the nation's low-income minority population is concentrated in low-income public housing and other impoverished communities. Many of the residents of these communities have been denied a high-quality education. Consequently, these communities are characterized by high rates of joblessness, deteriorating housing conditions, violence and other crime, substance abuse, and a lack of access to adequate health care and social services. Improving schools will resolve only part of the problem. What is needed is the revitalization of minority communities through a comprehensive, coordinated approach that connects the various educational and social services of the community. The Quality Education for Minorities Network initiated pilot sites for campus-based community service centers in six cities that link the resources of participating colleges and universities to the needs of neighboring low-income public housing.

In summary, poor and minority children constitute the nation's most imperiled resource. They deserve the best but are likely to receive the worst. It is no wonder that so many students have lost faith in the American system of education, drop out before high school graduation, and believe that a college education is beyond their reach. Consequently, few minorities are earning college degrees, even though gains have been made during the past ten years. According to Hodgkinson (1991), a large segment of the baby "boomlet" that occurred mostly in Florida, Texas, and California faces the prospect of childhood poverty, along with limited educational opportunities. Without support, these children risk school failure and may not guarantee more enrollments for higher education.

The next section examines the issues institutions of higher education must confront as they work with a new student majority.

A New Student Majority in Higher Education

The future of higher education is already here. All that the children of immigrant and native-born Americans have to do is get older, for they constitute the next generation of potential college students. Higher education is not well prepared for this reality. As the pool of potential white college students shrinks, the pool of students of color expands, especially the number of college-age Hispanics. The sharp decrease in the number of college-age youths that began in the mid 1980s continued through 1993. This was due primarily to a continuing decline of whites age eighteen to twenty-four. Interestingly, African Americans also followed this trend, with a college-age population that declined by 9 percent over the same period. Conversely, the number of Hispanics in this age group increased by 37 percent between 1983 and 1993. Nonetheless, college enrollments for African American, Asian, American Indian, and Latino students increased by 57.6 percent from 1983 to 1993. The highest increases were seen for Hispanics, American Indians, and Asian Americans and the smallest for African Americans (Carter and Wilson, 1995).

The share of bachelor's degrees awarded to minority students is another bright spot in higher education. Between 1991 and 1992, the share of bachelor's degrees earned by minorities increased by 11.4 percent. The share of master's degrees earned during that same period increased by 12.4 percent. At the first professional degree level, degrees among students of color rose by 9.5 percent, and increased at the associate degree level by 8.3 percent. In all four degree categories, the increase for students of color was above the progress of white students (Carter and Wilson, 1995).

Yet all is not well in higher education. Educators are concerned that only small numbers of minority high school graduates are choosing to go to college, especially those in inner cities.

Many have lost faith in higher education. Despite enrollment growths during the 1980s, African Americans, Latinos, and American Indians continued to be underrepresented at many of the nation's two- and four-year colleges and universities. While students of color represented 23 percent of all undergraduate students in 1992, their representation among degree recipients remained far below their share of undergraduate enrollments (Carter and Wilson, 1995). Despite the concentration of minorities in community colleges, few complete the transfer process to four-year institutions where they can pursue bachelor's and graduate degrees. College entrance exams are still being used as the sole criterion or the most important criterion to determine college admission by many college and university programs, thereby excluding many talented minorities who have the potential to succeed in college. The underrepresentation of minority students in fields requiring a math and science background persists. And evolving financial aid policy threatens access, since most minority students simply find it difficult to sustain their families and still have enough financial resources to attend college.

In addition, students of color are likely to be the victims of racist attitudes and behaviors on many predominantly white college campuses. Tensions on college campuses today mirror those in the larger society. Growing student diversity and intense competition for student aid and admissions have fueled many of these tensions. Intergroup hostility has occurred when minorities have called for the establishment of separate dormitories and cultural centers, and when administrators have been thought to overreact to the demands of minority students on campus. Some students have used acute measures to press college administrators to respond to their demands. To cite but two out of many examples, in 1993 Chicano students effectively used a fasting strategy and not-so-peaceful demonstrations to pressure the University of California at Los Angeles to create the César Chávez Center for Interdisciplinary Instruction in Chicana and Chicano Studies. In 1992, African American students staged two days of sit-in demonstrations at Georgia State University to protest a climate of racial tension and to lobby for an African American Studies department, which they ultimately got.

Key Educational Issues in Higher Education
As higher education prepares to educate a new student majority, it will find that it must confront issues such as those sketched
in the following paragraphs.

Curriculum Transformation. The influx of faculty and students
of color is having an impact on the curriculum in higher education. Minorities and women are demanding a more inclusive
curriculum that integrates issues of gender, race and ethnicity,
class, sexuality, and culture. But moving away from the traditional canon has created great controversy, as some argue that
ethnic and women's studies are uprooting the classic Eurocentric curriculum that predominates in the academy. Moreover, as
gays and lesbians seek to augment the curriculum with gay studies, many minorities feel that ethnic studies will suffer since limited resources are available to support different study emphases.

Higher Education Finance. Today, almost every state in the
union has some form of funding crisis. As a result, cutbacks in
state funding have impacted faculty salaries, student fees, and
enrollments, as well as programs and services for students. The
impact on access to college for students of color can be felt in
admissions (as colleges decide they can only enroll just so many
students), financial aid, and student services. Lack of funding
also affects minority faculty recruitment at a time when more
faculty of color are needed to work with college students.

An important higher education finance case in Texas highlighted inequities in educational opportunities for minorities.
In *LULAC* v. *Richards* (1992), a group of Mexican American
plaintiffs, represented by MALDEF, which had argued the *San
Antonio Independent School District* v. *Rodriguez* (1973) school finance case, charged that the Texas higher education system was
unconstitutional and unenforceable. MALDEF pointed out that
few resources—in terms of both funding and academic programs, especially graduate programs—were being afforded to
students who resided along the Texas-Mexico border, which is
about two-thirds Mexican American and the poorest area in
Texas. In January 1992, State District Judge Benjamin Euresti,

Jr., ruled that the Texas higher education system discriminated against Hispanic citizens. The court ruled that the Texas higher education system was unconstitutional and unenforceable because it did not provide Hispanic citizens equal rights and equal opportunity under the law. As a result, the state of Texas moved toward correcting inequities in funding formulas and ensuring equal treatment for six four-year colleges and universities in south Texas. Nonetheless, the Texas Supreme Court later ruled that the disparities in the state's higher education institutions between border and nonborder schools were not the result of intentional discrimination against Mexican Americans. MALDEF continued litigation in phase two of the lawsuit, which alleged that the state discriminated against Mexican Americans and African Americans throughout the state in the areas of admissions, recruitment and retention, scholarships, and the use of standardized testing (Rodríguez, 1993).

Student Aid. Access to college for minorities is linked to financial aid. Under the Bush administration, minority scholarships were attacked as discriminatory because they were thought to make less money available to white students. While President Clinton's administration appeared to have saved minority scholarships, in 1994 race-based scholarships were once again struck down. A federal court ruled that the University of Maryland could not award race-based scholarships, invalidating the university's Benjamin Banneker Scholarship Program for outstanding African American Students.

Faculty Diversification. Few minority faculty are available to work with students in higher education. In the fall of 1987, black faculty constituted 3.2 percent of the total faculty in higher education, Latinos represented 2.4 percent, Asians, 3.9 percent, and American Indians, 0.8 percent (Quality Education for Minorities Network, 1993). However, affirmative action efforts have come under attack from those who believe that they engender reverse racism and promote the hiring of unqualified persons simply to fill a quota. Nonetheless, minority faculty object to what they often feel are racist institutional environments that devalue their research interests, expect them to be "superstars," relegate them to the bottom tier of the professoriate, and expect them to fulfill their scholarly demands while working extensively with students and their communities, something white male faculty members are rarely expected to do.

Transfer Rates from Two- to Four-Year Colleges. While minority students, especially Latinos and American Indians, are disproportionately enrolled in two-year colleges, the minority rate of transfer is so low that many question the viability of two-year colleges as conduits toward the baccalaureate. There is also concern that a mission shift from college preparatory to vocational education may steer minorities away from careers that ensure long-term prosperity and upward mobility.

Admissions Standards. College admissions policies have been at the center of controversy since the Supreme Court considered the merits of Affirmative Action in *Regents of the University of California* v. *Bakke* (1978). In the *Bakke* decision, a five-to-four majority agreed that Bakke, a white medical student applicant to the University of California at Davis, had been wrongly excluded due to the university's affirmative action policy. However, the Court affirmed that race and gender could be taken into account when considering an applicant's qualifications in order to bring diversity and racial parity to American higher education. Critics have charged that colleges and universities have gone too far in overlooking deficiencies when making admissions decisions involving minorities and that preferential treatment implies quotas. Consequently, these institutions struggle with providing access and educational opportunities to underrepresented groups, while trying to avoid reverse discrimination.

Education Collaboratives. Both research and practice efforts over the past twenty years have concluded that one sector, working alone, is insufficient to address the multitude of issues that plague poor and minority students. Postsecondary educators are beginning to realize that education is a continuous pathway, where every tier has some connection to the other. Consequently, partnerships involving corporations, foundations, churches, law enforcement and social service agencies, and schools and higher education institutions are being formed to link business and industry with educational institutions as well as with the community, in an effort to create an integrated system of education that works for all students.

Diversification of Instructional Strategies. Educating a new student majority requires rethinking the way instruction is delivered. College classes tend to be competitive as opposed to collaborative in nature, and faculty tend to use lecture as opposed to active learning techniques. However, the most used practices may have a detrimental effect on students with divergent ways of learning. While more research is needed to assess how students of color learn best, active learning strategies and group activities such as collaborative learning and learning communities are having a positive impact on students of color (Tinto, 1994).

Campus Climate. Many minority students at predominantly white colleges encounter a hostile campus climate. The number of racial incidents has increased, and many minorities find themselves the victims of hateful acts such as caricatures, jokes, and stereotyping by both students and faculty. American Indians have responded to culturally insensitive college mascots, logos, and chants at athletic events. According to the National Institute Against Prejudice and Violence, which has been monitoring acts of hostility against minorities on college campuses, up to 25 percent of minority students on campus now experience slurs, harassment, or assaults each year. That calculation does not include acts of group defamation such as graffiti or the burning of crosses. Nor does it count hostile acts against gays and lesbians or gender violence (Winbush, 1992). Some universities have responded by creating codes of speech and conduct. However, student speech and conduct codes are coming under fire from groups who argue that they infringe on First Amendment rights. While pressure has been placed on institutions to set up appropriate policies, practices, and organizational structures that are sensitive and supportive toward increased participation and achievement of people of color, resentment and resistance may harden as more and more minorities enroll in predominantly white colleges.

Graduate Opportunities. Despite modest gains in the 1980s, a shortage of minorities earning master's and doctoral degrees remains. Minority educators are calling on graduate schools to affirm their commitment to diversity by designing a plan of action to improve the representation of minorities in graduate and professional schools. In 1986–87, minority students represented about 11.5 percent of the graduate enrollment, yet earned only 10.4 percent of the master's degrees and 8.8 percent of the doctorates. In fact, nonresidents earned more doctorates (19.4 percent) than all minority students combined (Quality Education for Minorities Project, 1990).

Desegregation. Although the Supreme Court declared racial segregation at the college level unconstitutional at the same time it decided *Brown* v. *Board of Education* in 1954, policies such as admissions requirements and hiring practices could still foster segregation. In the June 26, 1992, *U.S.* v. *Fordice* decision involving higher education systems in the South, the Supreme Court ruled that states should eliminate policies that foster segregation. The case is crucial given that some eighteen years ago a group of black plaintiffs sued the state of Mississippi for operating one system of universities for whites and a less desirable one for blacks. The Supreme Court ordered the district court to review all policies that "substantially restrict a person's choice of which institution to enter" and that "contribute to the racial identifiability" of the state's colleges and universities. The district court was also ordered to remove unjustifiable policies. The policies under review included admissions standards for historically white and historically black institutions, duplication of "non-essential or non-core" programs between historically white and historically black institutions, and even whether "retention of all eight institutions itself affects student choice and perpetuates the segregated higher education system," and if so, whether one or more should be closed or merged. The *Fordice* decision is bound to have a major impact on the survival of historically black institutions, as well as on admissions, curricular, faculty hiring, and financial resource policies in institutions of higher education (Division of Governmental Relations, 1993).

In summary, higher education is not immune to the issues surrounding ethnic and racial minorities. Nor does it operate in a vacuum. Increasingly, what happens in schools will touch every facet of higher education. Society charges two- and four-year colleges with a key responsibility: educating and training the next generation of leaders so that they can sustain the nation's world eminence, as well as its economic, technological, and scientific competitiveness. The consequences of failing to meet this imperative are enormous, both for students and for the nation as a whole. The concluding section underscores why schools and colleges must not fail an emerging student majority.

Conclusion

In the past, issues involving minority students were considered unique to only a small group and were ignored in favor of the concerns of the white students making up the majority of the student population. However, it is now clear that this nation can no longer discuss educational reform without considering the issues that surround ethnic and racial minorities. A group that by the year 2000 will account for 60 percent of total population growth and that currently is or will be the majority population in many urban cities and some states cannot be ignored or treated as unimportant. To continue to neglect the issues pertaining to this emerging student majority is to ignore the demographic reality that confronts this country. Ethnic and racial minorities are America's future. America cannot succeed without them. The education of racial and ethnic minorities constitutes an investment in human capital that will be necessary to sustain the nation's economic strength. Take health and pension requirements, for instance. As the baby boom generation starts reaching retirement age in the year 2010, resources derived from a younger workforce will be needed to sustain costs of health care and social security benefits (Quality Education for Minorities Project, 1990).

A quality workforce demands a highly trained citizenry. Minorities, white women, and immigrants will constitute over 90 percent of the net growth of the nation's workforce in the near future. In fact, it is expected that white males will constitute less than 10 percent of the net growth of the workforce between now and the year 2000. Consequently, developing the talents of this new, emerging workforce necessitates a high-quality educational system.

Work requirements are also changing as higher levels of skill are needed to remain competitive in the world economy. A high school diploma is no longer the ticket to the future. The real ticket is having the highest level of education possible as well as the specific skills required by a changing society. According to the Hudson Institute's 1987 publication *Workforce 2000*, between now and the year 2000, for the first time in history, a majority of all new jobs will require some form of postsecondary education (Johnston and Arnold, 1987). Consequently, minorities cannot afford to end their education in high school. They must continue to further their education in two- and four-year colleges. The pay-off for advanced education is clear. In 1990, persons with a bachelor's degree earned an average of $2,116 per month, twice as much as high school graduates ($1,077) and four times as much as high school graduates ($492).

Clearly, the education of minorities is synonymous with the success of America. But America cannot succeed if the door to educational opportunities is shut for all but a few students. Nor can it succeed if it wastes the talents of new Americans. This nation has made significant strides in granting civil rights, allowing for equal protection, desegregating schools, and making financial aid available to needy students. But all these strides are now in jeopardy. The chances of minorities getting an equal chance to succeed become nil as civil unrest escalates and minorities continue to attend poorly funded segregated schools. Other threats to parity are budget cutbacks resulting in tuition increases that restrict college enrollment, as well as uncertainties about the future of financial aid and affirmative action.

To fail this imperiled generation is to allow America to continue to become a divided society along the lines of race, ethnicity, and socioeconomic status. If Americans fail to understand that all of us face a common destiny dictated by whether one or more groups fails or succeeds, this nation will become fragmented and weak. Yet if Americans learn to harness as well as develop the strengths of all citizens and incorporate them into our economy, this nation will prosper. The American vision for the future must allow ethnic and racial minorities to have equal access to economic and educational opportunities. This will require putting an end to the educational neglect of children at risk and keeping the door of opportunity open in higher education so that these students have the tools necessary to be fully functioning citizens who contribute to the success of our society. It will require the coordination of federal, state, and local resources to families and children. And it will require the end of educating poor and minority students in "bits and pieces," resulting in piecemeal delivery of services. Instead, a highly coordinated, systemwide effort that involves the K–12 school system, two- and four-year colleges, business and industry, community-based organizations, religious organizations, and law enforcement and social service agencies, among others, will be needed to truly make a dent in a disjointed educational system that has for so long been fraught with neglect.

In short, the education of an emerging student minority is inextricably tied to the future of this nation. We can view the challenge before this nation as an economic or a moral one. But whether we believe that bargain-basement schools will produce a dime store economy or that the education of ethnic and racial minorities is a moral responsibility, the consequences of failing to meet this challenge are readily apparent. This country simply cannot afford the consequences of neglect, nor can it ignore the fact that within a relatively short period, people of color will constitute the nation's greatest resource. In the end the choice is clear: America can be resource rich or resource poor. The victims of neglect call yet again for America's response.

References

Anzaldúa, G. *Borderlands la Frontera: The New Mestiza.* San Francisco: Spinsters/Aunt Lute Book Company, 1987.

Carter, D. J., and Wilson, R. *Minorities in Higher Education.* Washington, D.C.: American Council on Education 1994.

Carter, D. J., and Wilson, R. *Minorities in Higher Education.* Washington, D.C.: American Council on Education, 1995.

Cetron, M., and Davies, O. *American Renaissance.* New York: St. Martin's Press, 1989.

Commission on Chapter 1. *Making Schools Work for Children in Poverty.* Washington, D.C.: American Association for Higher Education, 1992.

Division of Governmental Relations. "ACE Legal Report: Implications of Mississippi Higher Education Desegregation." *Educational Record,* 1993, *74*(2), 56–57.

Hodgkinson, H. *Higher Education 1990–2010: A Demographic View.* Washington, D.C.: Institute for Educational Leadership, 1991.

Johnston, W. B., and Arnold, H. P. *Workforce 2000: Work and Workers for the 21st Century.* Indianapolis, Ind.: Hudson Institute, 1987.

Kozol, J. *Savage Inequalities: Children in America's Schools.* New York: Crown Publishers, 1991.

Pastor, M. *Latinos and the Los Angeles Uprising: The Economic Context.* Claremont, Calif.: Tomás Rivera Center, 1993.

Quality Education for Minorities Network. *Acting for Tomorrow —Now: A Summit on Quality Education for Minorities.* Washington, D.C.: Quality Education for Minorities Network, 1993a.

Quality Education for Minorities Network. *Opening Unlocked Doors.* Washington, D.C.: Quality Education for Minorities Network, 1993b.

Quality Education for Minorities Project. *Education That Works: An Action Plan for the Education of Minorities.* Cambridge: Massachusetts Institute of Technology, 1990.

Ramírez, W. R. *Facing the Facts: The State of Hispanic Education.* Washington, D.C.: ASPIRA, 1993.

Rodríguez, R. "Court Rules No Discrimination Against Texas Border Colleges." *Black Issues in Higher Education,* 1993, *10* (18), 16–17.

Tinto, V. "Learning Communities: Building Supportive Learning Environments in Urban Settings." Paper presented at the conference of the Association for the Study of Higher Education, Tuscon, Ariz., Nov. 1994.

Topolnicki, D. M. "The Real Immigrant Story: Making It Big in America." *Money,* 1995, *24*(1), 128–138.

Wilkerson, I. "Children of the Shadows." *New York Times,* Apr. 1993, pp. 1–16.

Winbush, D. E. "Georgia State Racial Confrontations Typify National Problem." *Black Issues in Higher Education,* 1992, *9* (20), 16–18.

Current Challenges to Minority Education in the Twenty-First Century

In the introductory chapter, Laura I. Rendón and Richard O. Hope depicted the changing profile of America's population and the spillover effects in the nation's K–12 and higher education system. They argued that unless systemic efforts are undertaken to assist schools and colleges in reorganizing for diversity and addressing the factors having a detrimental effect on minorities, the nation's future will be imperiled. Part One elaborates on both the crisis and the challenges facing schools and colleges in the context of an evolving economy.

In Chapter Two, Ray Marshall and Robert W. Glover connect education to the nation's economy. Given that women and minorities are playing an increasingly important role in our competitive and technologically sophisticated world, the authors focus on the nation's economic imperative: that education and training must be improved for *all* Americans. They argue that the future requires more learning and that more sophisticated skills will be needed for front-line workers to participate and survive in consumer-driven markets and in technology.

In Chapter Three, José A. Cárdenas outlines how entrenched

policies, practices, and attitudes have created a crisis in the K–12 system, with poor and minority children bearing the disproportionate impact of neglect.

In Chapter Four, Shirley Vining Brown veers into the next stage of the educational pathway: higher education. The author focuses on access patterns and barriers to academic success, degree trends, and the importance of financial aid as a means to broaden access for minorities.

In the concluding chapter, Dewayne Matthews outlines the critical role that state legislatures and the federal government can play with regard to issues of educational equity.

Chapter 2

Education, the Economy, and Tomorrow's Workforce

Ray Marshall, Robert W. Glover

This chapter provides an overview of the economic, technological, and demographic changes that make quality education for all such an important national problem. Both our schools and our businesses are being forced to adjust to a much more competitive and technologically sophisticated world—a world that requires different policies, structures, and institutions than in the past.

Women and minorities will constitute almost all of the growth of the workforce in the 1990s. White men will constitute the slowest-growing group, increasing only 8.5 percent between 1988 and 2000, compared with 19.9 percent for white women, 24.6 percent for all African Americans, 13.6 percent for all whites, 21.4 percent for African American men, and 28 percent for African American women.

Looked at another way, minorities comprised about 16 percent of the U.S. labor force in 1976 and 21 percent in 1988 and are projected to be about 25 percent by the year 2000. Similarly, minorities constituted 39 percent of the *growth* of the U.S. labor force between 1976 and 1988 and are projected to account for more than 52 percent of the labor force growth between

1988 and 2000. Men's proportion of the workforce will decline from 55 percent in 1988 to 52.7 percent in 2000 (Marshall and Tucker, 1992).

African Americans and Hispanics constituted 19 percent of the U.S. population in 1984 but are expected to increase to 34 percent by 2020. Making conservative assumptions about immigration, the non-Hispanic white proportion of the U.S. population would drop to just under 50 percent by 2080 and the proportion of various groups would be: Asians, 12 percent; Hispanics, 23 percent (they would surpass African Americans in 2010); and African Americans, 15 percent. Of course, these population changes would be reflected in school enrollments much earlier—minorities are already a majority of the school population in California and Texas (Marshall, 1991b, pp. 13–16).

America faces only two options to compete in the new world economy: either to lower wages or to increase skills. In a world in which 80 percent of workers make less than $1 per hour, the first choice is neither viable nor a contest we could win without severe costs. Most other industrial countries have rejected the low-wage option because the resulting unequal incomes pose significant threats to their political, social, and economic health. Not only does the low-wage option imply lower and more unequal wages, it also limits improvements in incomes to those that can be achieved by working harder—which is essentially what we have been doing in the United States since the early 1970s.

In the new global information economy under conditions of free trade with high mobility of capital and technology, the quality of a nation's human resources becomes a key factor in determining the strength of its economy. The primary theme of this chapter is that education and training must be improved for *all* Americans—not as a moral obligation but as an economic imperative. While all our learning systems, including workplace training and learning within families, must be upgraded, improvements in formal schooling at every level are fundamental to the changes that need to be made. In terms of dropout rates, test scores, and other indicators, schools generally have demonstrated marginal improvements with minority students over time.

However, recent profound changes in the economy call for much more radical improvements, and existing demographic trends give us a relatively short time to accomplish such changes.

Problems in Adjusting to a More Competitive World

A major determinant of a country's economic performance is its speed in adapting to new economic conditions. Because America has not adjusted as fast as some of its competitors, its economy is losing its relative position, as measured by market shares, productivity growth, and real incomes. America's losses have not been restricted to any one sector—since 1981, we have experienced trade deficits even in high-tech industries like communications equipment, scientific instruments, and engines. Productivity growth in America has slowed from an annual average increase of 2.9 percent in the period 1960 through 1973 to just over 1 percent since 1973. As a consequence, real average weekly earnings in the United States dropped more than 12 percent from 1969 through 1989 (Commission on Skills of the American Workforce, 1990, p. 19). If we do not improve our rate of productivity growth, we are going to have great trouble maintaining high real family incomes. Hourly compensation for U.S. production workers ranked tenth among industrial countries in 1993. This change has occurred rapidly. As recently as 1985, no country in the world had higher real wages than the United States.

How have we been adjusting to this decline in real wages? In short, we have tried to maintain our living standards by working more and by going into debt. In 1973, 40 percent of Americans worked. By 1990, more than 50 percent of the population was employed. Some American families have been able to sustain their real incomes only because more women now work more hours than ever. Because of declining real wages, the average American worker worked about one month longer in the 1980s than in the 1960s for about the same compensation (Schor, 1991). Unfortunately, there are limitations to this strategy. Families do not have more than one wife to contribute to the labor force. Further, this option is not available to families with single household heads. Thus poverty rates have risen substantially among single-parent families. Similarly, the slowdown in productivity growth means that it took three times as much labor in the 1980s to achieve the same increase in output as in the 1950s and 1960s.

Reasons the Future Will Require More Learning

To understand better why stronger intellectual tools are necessary, we need to examine the impact of technological innovations and international competition, two forces that have profoundly changed economic activity, skill requirements, and America's standing in the global economy.

Decline of Traditional Mass Production Systems

The American economy was enormously successful through the first two-thirds of the twentieth century due to abundant natural resources, economies of scale created by a large internal market, and supportive policies and institutions. Mass production techniques were implemented under a hierarchical organizational structure influenced heavily by the "scientific management" ideas of Frederick Winslow Taylor. According to Taylor and his colleagues, engineers and professional staff using time-and-motion studies were to find the "one best way" to produce things, which was then implemented through close supervision of the production workforce. Typically, this resulted in jobs being divided into narrow tasks, which were repeated hundreds of times per day. The tasks were often simple so that they commonly required no more than a week of orientation and training. Schools were organized using similar principles to mass produce literates who could perform most of the work. The system led to greatly increased productivity and living standards. Workers with literacy and minimal skills could earn good wages to support their families.

Technology and international competition have changed all this. A factory organized along such traditional lines can be established anywhere in the world, attracting employees who can work competently at that system for one-eighth of American wages—or less. As a result, jobs that require minimal skills and pay high wages are simply becoming obsolete in America. In short, the status quo is no longer viable.

Demands of Technology

Technological innovations have had a monumental impact on the workplace and the economy. Information technology, for example, has diminished the need for many managers, inspectors, and unskilled workers and has made smaller producing units more efficient. This technology has, in addition, caused much of the direct labor to be done by machines, while humans increasingly are involved in indirect work, mainly with knowledge and information. To be used most effectively, these technological changes require workers to have more *higher-order thinking skills* than when most workers were involved in direct, routine manual labor. A major consequence of the new technology, for instance, is to make more data available to everybody. A premium therefore attaches to the *ability to impose order on chaotic data* (that is, to see patterns and causal relationships that permit the data to be used to solve problems, improve technology, and increase the value of products). In essence, productivity is improved by substituting ideas, skills, and knowledge for physical resources and labor. Nobel laureate Theodore Schultz (1981) discovered this process at work in American agriculture. Great increases in U.S. agricultural output were achieved despite the fact that there have been no increases in labor and physical resources since the 1920s. Output was increased significantly by *knowledge*, not by increased quantities of land, labor, and capital. Schultz argued that economic progress depended heavily on the development of human resources, not primarily, as many economists had emphasized, on the accumulation of physical capital, or on natural resources, a traditional American advantage.

Need for Competitiveness

Internationalization of the American economy interacts with technology to change traditional work practices and skill requirements. Standardized mass production, the system largely responsible for America's economic success, depended heavily on U.S.

companies' virtual control of the large American market, an advantage no longer available to them. The new main requirement for economic viability and power is *competitiveness*. A more competitive environment forces companies to pay greater attention to factors that were less important to mass production companies. One of these is *quality*, which essentially means meeting customers' needs. Mass production companies could pay less attention to quality because that system was more producer driven; competitive systems, by contrast, are more consumer driven. Competitive companies also derive their main advantage from improving productivity by using *all* factors more efficiently, not just through economies of scale. Mass production companies stressed *stability* through price controls, orderly technological change, and detailed regulation; more market-driven companies must stress *flexibility* in order to adjust to changing markets and technologies. Variety, customization, convenience, and timeliness have all become more important in a consumer-driven world (Carnevale, 1991, pp. 44–51).

Competitiveness can be achieved in only two ways: by reducing wages or by paying more attention to productivity, quality, and flexibility. A country that wants to maintain and improve income must stress measures to increase productivity. Productivity improvements within a company depend on the effectiveness of management systems and on a firm's ability to develop and use leading-edge technology. Experience during the 1970s and 1980s has shown America's traditional authoritarian and bureaucratic mass production management systems to be extremely vulnerable to more efficient systems used in countries such as Japan and Germany and in a few American companies. These systems stress fewer layers of management, a high degree of employee involvement in production decisions, heavy investments in on-the-job learning systems, employment security, and positive incentive systems that relate monetary and nonmonetary rewards directly to productivity and quality. In essence, high-performance organizations substitute positive incentives and productivity and quality goals for rules, regulations, and layers of supervision. More participatory management systems are as important in schools as they are in companies—

and for the same reasons: schools, like companies, must now be more concerned about productivity, flexibility, and quality or excellence. Schools also must produce higher-order thinking skills for all students, not, as in the mass production system, just for the elites.

Competitive enterprises develop and use technology in very different ways from their less competitive predecessors. The mass production system attempted to combine standardized technology and unskilled labor. Since standardized technology can be used anywhere, in a competitive global economy it is unlikely to be economical in high-wage countries. Leading-edge technologies that have not been standardized enable their owners and users to have higher incomes. We should note, however, that standardized technology can be very sophisticated, or "high tech." Three technology-skill combinations are possible: (1) standardized or "low technology" and unskilled workers, which implies low wages and weak competitiveness; (2) high technology and unskilled workers, which implies somewhat higher wages but a limited ability to innovate or apply higher-order thinking skills; and (3) high technology and highly skilled workers, which is more competitive because highly skilled workers can develop and use the technology more effectively. If America wants to be a high-wage country, it must develop a highly skilled workforce and give high priority to the development and use of leading-edge technology. This has become an even greater challenge because the United States no longer has the broad technological lead that we enjoyed in the 1970s.

Changes in the Way Work Is Organized for High Performance

Another force driving the skill demand placed on all workers is new ways to organize work to achieve higher productivity, quality, and adaptability. The Commission on Skills of the American Workforce reported in 1990 that relative to our international competitors, 95 percent of major U.S. companies were clinging to traditional patterns of organizing work. Most globally successful firms are organizing for high performance. These "high-performance work organizations" share several common characteristics:

- They are quality driven, strongly geared to customer satisfaction, and emphasize more cooperative relations with unions and suppliers. Traditional mass production systems are producer driven and have more adversarial relations with suppliers and unions, emphasizing price competition and wage concessions.
- They have lean management structures and decentralized decision making and responsibilities to the point of production or sale. Computer technology puts information in the hands of front-line workers, who can now handle many tasks formerly performed by indirect workers, including quality control and parts inventory.
- High-performance organizations adjust quickly to change, in contrast to mass production systems, which seek stability through rules, regulations, and rigid contractual relationships.
- Positive incentives are used to reward desired outcomes. By contrast, negative, or even perverse, incentives are characteristic of mass production systems. For example, workers are often laid off with the introduction of new technology.
- Investing in educating and training all workers, especially front-line workers, is a high priority.

Increasing Importance of Front-Line Workers

The decline of traditional mass production and the rise of new forms of work organization have placed new and increasing skill demands on front-line workers. The pace of change in consumer-driven markets and in technology has increased, requiring front-line workers to be adaptable. This emphasizes multiskilling and continuous learning, which in turn require strong foundation skills. Decentralization of decision making and responsibilities has also meant changes for front-line workers. They can no longer rely on supervisors to think for them. They must be able to make good use of the computer and the information it provides them. They must be able to organize information and make sense of it for decision making. They must have a high capacity for abstract, conceptual thinking and the ability to apply knowledge to real-world problems. They must work well in teams, communicate well orally and in writing, and be able to assume responsibility without requiring much supervision. Above all, they must be efficient learners. Many of these are skills that our schools either have neglected or never taught.

Several groups have studied the skills needed in the modern workplace and produced elaborate lists, the details of which need not be repeated here (Carnevale, Garner, and Meltzer, 1990; Secretary's Commission on Achieving Necessary Skills, 1991). What is clear from all the evidence is that skill requirements are rising, especially at the level of the front-line worker.

Uneven Quality of America's Workforce
Unfortunately, no good measures of workforce quality are available. The customary measure of quality has been years of schooling, an area where the United States ranks high. However, average years of schooling is not a good measure because school years vary significantly across countries. The United States has a relatively short school year, and our high school students spend about a fourth less time on homework than the Japanese and take a third less math. According to one estimate, the typical American senior high school student spends an average of one-half hour per day on homework, while Japanese students average two hours; Japanese students are required to take three years of mathematics to one for the Americans; and Japanese students average six years of foreign language to the Americans' zero to two years (*Japan Update,* 1988, p. 6). It is not surprising, therefore, that American students rank near the bottom on most international math and science tests while Japanese students rank near the top.

Furthermore, schooling, while pivotal, is an imperfect measure of workforce quality because other learning systems play important roles, especially families, work, the media, community organizations, and political processes. Schooling does provide the foundation on which other skills are built.

There seems to be an emerging consensus that America's higher-level professional, technical, and scientific workers are world class, but that, with few exceptions, those without post-secondary training are not. Several factors account for the high quality of our best workers. Some of our colleges and universities are world class and are net exporters of educational services to the rest of the world. Some of our largest companies in export markets have world-class learning systems and, while accurate data are not available, according to one estimate American firms spend over $30 billion a year on formal education and training (Carnevale, 1986). Many legal immigrants to the United States have higher levels of education than native-born Americans and therefore enrich our human capital pool (Marshall, 1991a). Finally, although we do not do a very good job of translating science into products, the United States clearly has the world's leading scientific research system.

Why do we have serious problems with our least-skilled workers? There are several answers, but the common theme is that our learning systems are inferior. First, we tolerate much higher percentages of our children living in poverty, and with some remarkable exceptions, poor families are not good learning systems (Marshall and Tucker, 1992; Marshall 1991b; Comer, 1980; Grubb and Lazerson, 1982). Second, our elementary and secondary schools are not world class. Third, we have the worst school-to-work transition system in the industrialized world. Finally, we invest less than other countries in training for workers after they enter jobs.

America has a much higher proportion of its children in poverty than any other major industrial country. In 1988, an Urban Institute study found that 17.1 percent of American children were below the poverty line compared with 8.2 percent in Germany, 5.1 percent in Sweden, 10.7 percent in the United Kingdom, 9.6 percent in Canada, and 16.9 percent in Australia. Almost a fourth of America's children are now born into poor households, and children constitute about 40 percent of the poor. Among all groups, the age category with the highest rates of poverty is 0–6 years old. Poverty is a particularly serious problem for minority households, especially those headed by women.

With a few remarkable exceptions, poor households do not give children the kinds of knowledge and skills they will need to succeed in school. This is one reason that family income is such a strong predictor of educational achievement. This also is why the Committee for Economic Development (1987), a leading business policy organization, found that early childhood programs and health care for mothers and babies yield such high returns.

America's elementary and secondary schools are not world class and probably serve less than 20 percent of our students very well. According to the National Assessment of Educational Progress (NAEP) (1986), only 20 percent of high school graduates can write a decent letter, only 12 percent can arrange fractions in rank order, and less than 5 percent can read a train or bus schedule. Contrary to popular myth and political rhetoric, the United States ranks near the bottom among industrial countries on expenditures on K–12 education (Rasell and Mishel, 1990).

As noted earlier, the United States has the worst school-to-work transition system of any major industrialized country. We offer little or no help to the half of our sixteen- to twenty-four-year-olds who are not college bound (William T. Grant Foundation Commission on Work, Family, and Citizenship, 1988). Employers in other industrialized nations take responsibility jointly with schools for the professional formation of adolescent youth. In sharp contrast, most American employers in a position to pick and choose among job applicants for career positions choose *against* youth, preferring to hire and train more mature and experienced applicants in their mid twenties. Japanese and German employers make early connections with youths, hiring them in their teenage years and placing them in rich learning environments with access to structured experiential learning on the job and to related classroom instruction. Skills are certified and recognized by the industry. As a result, the expectations and incentives for performance are clearer and the paths to careers are more formal and transparent under such systems.

The consequences for Americans are serious. The delay in hiring provides German and Japanese youths a five- to ten-year head start in gaining access to significant occupational skill training. American employers are largely disengaged from the process of instructing and socializing their future workers. Employers who delay hiring job entrants until they are "mature" young adults in their mid twenties miss significant opportunities to communicate with schools and to feed back important information about the quality of education and the skills needed in modern workplaces. Perhaps most important, effort and achievement in school are disconnected from rewards in the workplace, undermining student incentives to work and achieve in school.

Our economy includes a considerable number of low-wage jobs at which little learning takes place. Unlike our principal competitors, we have had no national policy with respect to job quality. While America experienced relatively rapid job growth during the 1970s and early 1980s, many of these jobs paid low wages and provided limited learning opportunities. We therefore have perpetuated jobs that would be unacceptable to other high-wage countries.

The United States also invests relatively little in employment and training either in the public sector or the private sector. In 1991, for example, the United States spent 0.85 percent of its gross domestic product on public sector labor market programs, compared with 2.7 percent in France or 2.7 percent in Germany (Organization for Economic Cooperation and Development, 1992).

On average, American companies spend 1 to 2 percent of payroll on training. However, a closer examination reveals that two-thirds of it goes to train managers and professionals. Fewer than 10 percent of America's front-line workers without a college education have received any significant formal job training. Further, most of the training is highly concentrated among a few companies. According to the American Society for Training and Development, fully 90 percent of the $30 billion spent on formal training in 1985 was paid by 15,000 employers, or one-half of 1 percent of all American employers. Moreover, only 100 to 200 companies—the largest firms with many managerial and professional staff—spent more than 2 percent of their payroll on formal training.

Demographic Trends That Add Urgency to Our Tasks

The crises in our economy and schools are exacerbated by a combination of demographic developments that should create a sense of urgency about improving the performance of both systems. Two aspects of demographic trends raise special concerns about America's future. The first concerns the growth of minority populations who generally have not been well served by either our economy or our schools, and the second relates to the aging of the American population.

Population growth in the United States is occurring almost exclusively among minorities. Whites will become a minority of the U.S. population sometime in the twenty-first century because minority populations are growing much faster. Indeed, in some areas, the term *minority* already has lost its statistical meaning, for minorities are already in the majority. Alaska Natives, American Indians, African Americans, and Hispanics presently constitute about 20 percent of our population; by 2020 or so, one-third of the nation will be minority, including Asian Americans. By about 2080, minority Americans are projected to be in the majority.

In our schools, the future has already arrived. Between 1968 and 1986, the number of white students fell by 16 percent, the number of African Americans increased by 5 percent, and the number of Hispanics rose by 100 percent. More than 30 percent of students in public schools—some twelve million—are minority. Several states, including Mississippi, New Mexico, California, and Texas, have "majority minority" public schools. Today, minorities constitute a majority of the enrollments in twenty-three of the nation's twenty-five largest school districts. The demographics make it clear that the country cannot develop a world-class educational system without addressing the needs and perspectives of minority Americans.

A second demographic factor is the aging of the American workforce. The large baby boom generation of over seventy-five million will start reaching retirement age by the year 2010. Substantial improvements are needed in the economy over the next fifteen years. Otherwise, the health and pension requirements of an aging population will greatly restrict the resources available for investment and other uses, and inadequate investment in physical and human capital will be a major deterrent to our economic strength.

The first of seventy-seven million baby boomers will turn fifty-five in the year 2000 and by 2010 will be retiring in significant numbers. In 1989, programs for the elderly accounted for approximately 28 percent of the federal budget. This proportion will probably be closer to 40 percent of the federal budget after 2010. Retirement and health care costs could place a substantial burden on our resources unless we turn the American economy around and make it possible for the baby boomers to be more productive over the next twenty years.

The graying of the baby boom generation may be the most visible trend, but our entire population is aging. Fertility rates began to drop in the 1960s and Americans are living longer. A much larger proportion of our population is now over age eighty-five than ever before, and that trend is likely to continue. Because of the "baby bust" that started in the 1960s, fewer young workers entered the workforce during the 1980s than in the 1970s. This, combined with the fact that women are entering the workforce at a slower rate, will cause substantially reduced growth in the workforce throughout the 1990s.

Thus, America is faced with a large aging population that is primarily white, and a large and growing minority population that has traditionally been badly served by our economy and our schools. The potential for explosive conflict that such a situation yields in an economy of relative decline is alarming. This situation should create a sense of urgency, because the window of opportunity for dealing with the problem extends only for about the next twenty years.

The good news is that the American economy, despite its problems, remains strong. With the proper policies, the well-educated baby boomers and highly motivated minorities and women could be the source of substantial improvements in productivity and economic performance—provided, of course, that we adopt the proper social and economic policies and give all of our people, especially minorities, the kind of intellectual tools they will need to function effectively in the internationalized information world.

Conclusion

It is in the schools—increasingly minority schools—where the economic future of the United States will be determined. The world economy is driven by powerful new technologies and competitive forces, and our schools, as they are presently structured, will not provide the skilled workforce the nation will need to sustain our economic competitiveness.

No subject is more important to the provision of quality education for minorities than school restructuring. School restructuring is needed for a very basic reason: the traditional hierarchical factory school model is obsolete and unsustainable. The first overarching principle around which restructured schools need to be designed is high expectations for everyone. Second and equally important, schools must be responsive to the needs of minority children. A third overarching principle that must drive education for minority youth is the need to keep educational options open throughout the learning life cycle that begins in early childhood and continues throughout life.

References

Carnevale, A. P. "The Learning Enterprise." *Training and Development Journal,* 1986, *40*(1), 18–26.

Carnevale, A. P. *America and the New Economy: How New Competitive Standards Are Radically Changing American Workplaces.* San Francisco: Jossey-Bass, 1991.

Carnevale, A. P., Gainer, L. J., and Meltzer, A. S. *Workplace Basics: The Essential Skills Employers Want.* San Francisco: Jossey-Bass, 1990.

Comer, J. *School Power.* New York: Free Press, 1980.

Commission on Skills of the American Workforce. *America's Choice: High Skills or Low Wages!* Rochester, N.Y.: National Center on Education and the Economy, 1990.

Committee for Economic Development. *Children in Need: Investment Strategies for the Educationally Disadvantaged.* Statement by the Research and Policy Committee. New York: Committee for Economic Development, 1987.

Organization for Economic Cooperation and Development. *Employment Outlook.* Paris: Organization for Economic Cooperation and Development, 1992.

Grubb, N., and Lazerson, M. *Broken Promises: How Americans Fail Their Children.* New York: Basic Books, 1982.

Japan Update, Summer, 1988, whole issue.

Marshall, R. "Immigrants." In D. W. Hornbeck and L. M. Salamon (eds.), *Human Capital and America's Future* (pp. 95–138). Baltimore, Md.: Johns Hopkins University Press, 1991a.

Marshall, R. *The State of Families, 3: Losing Direction.* Milwaukee, Wis.: Family Service of America, 1991b.

Marshall, R., and Tucker, M. *Thinking for a Living: Education and the Wealth of Nations.* New York: Basic Books, 1992.

National Assessment of Educational Progress. *Literacy: Profiles of America's Young Adults.* Princeton, N.J.: Educational Testing Service, 1986.

Rasell, M. E., and Mishel, L. *Shortchanging Education: How U.S. Spending on Grades K–12 Lags Behind Other Industrial Nations.* Briefing paper. Washington, D.C.: Economic Policy Institute, 1990.

Schor, J. L. *Overworked Americans.* New York: Basic Books, 1991.

Schultz, T. W. *Investing in People: The Economics of Population Quality.* Berkeley: University of California Press, 1981.

Secretary's Commission on Achieving Necessary Skills. *What Work Requires of Schools.* Washington, D.C.: U.S. Government Printing Office, 1991.

William T. Grant Foundation Commission on Work, Family, and Citizenship. *The Forgotten Half: Pathways to Success for America's Youth and Young Families.* Washington, D.C.: William T. Grant Foundation Commission on Work, Family, and Citizenship, 1988.

—————————— Chapter 3 ——————————

Ending the Crisis in the K–12 System

José A. Cárdenas

One of the most severe crises facing America today is the performance of the nation's educational system, particularly in dealing with the education of non-mainstream populations: minorities, the economically disadvantaged, the limited English proficient, immigrants and migrants. Participation in school for these populations is so precarious that they are currently being lumped into a common category called "at-risk" students because of the high risk of not being able to complete a high school education.

This chapter discusses key issues affecting at-risk students, identifying existing barriers to the education of children in American schools and providing direction for subsequent efforts at change, reform, improvement, and success.

Limited Impact of Successful Programs

Reviews of educational literature show an extensive array of successful school programs in every sector of the country and for every segment of the population. During the past decade we have been encouraged by reports of school success among students

51

deemed uneducable in the traditional school. The Committee for Economic Development's *Children in Need: Investment Strategies for the Education of the Disadvantaged* (1987), Lizbeth Schorr's *Within Our Reach* (1988), and very recently the Quality Education for Minorities (QEM) Project's report, *Education That Works: An Action Plan for the Education of Minorities* (1990), are three efforts at documenting the success of pilot, model, and innovative programs. It is important to note, however, the observation of former Secretary of Labor Ray Marshall, who chaired the QEM effort: though QEM found an abundance of successful *projects* in their nationwide effort, they did not identify one single successful educational *system*.

Three elements found in all successful projects provide important clues in addressing educational reform. In most of the successful projects, children are valued in ways not commonly found in regular and traditional schools; students are provided support services not commonly provided in regular and traditional schools; there are unique relationships among the school, the community, and the family not commonly found in regular and traditional schools.

However, transporting the success of innovative programs to the traditional school program has been difficult. Neither the valuing of students, nor the supportive structures, nor the unique school/community/home relationships characteristic of successful programs have transferred to nonparticipating classes or nonparticipating schools. Below are key issues educators must confront as they attempt to address at-risk students.

Devaluation of Children by Educators

To a great extent, the lack of value placed on children in the schools reflects the lack of value placed on children in the larger society. Social scientists view children as the greatest resource available in our society, but the country fails to address the needs of children in proportion to their importance. For some reason, it has been difficult to grasp that the educational problems of a large segment of the population should receive the same attention, personnel, money, mobilization, and support given in Operation Desert Storm or to the oil crisis in the Middle East.

There is no better example of the negative value assigned to children in schools than the history of the 1992 federal court case *Doe* v. *Plylar.* The Texas legislature enacted an amendment to the Texas Education Code that contained a sleeper modification of school enrollment. The new law required legal status for tuition-free enrollment in the public schools. Nonresident children were required to pay tuition, but since few had the money to do so, they were prevented from enrolling in school.

The denial of educational opportunity to undocumented children was challenged in the courts in *Doe* v. *Plylar* and the 1992 *Multiple District Litigation.* The educational establishment vigorously fought through two federal district courts, an appellate court, and the Supreme Court in continuous attempts to exclude nonresident children from the public schools of Texas.

Though educational experts at trial estimated the number of eligible undocumented children at less than 20,000, the Texas Education Agency (TEA) maintained that Texas schools would be flooded with at least 200,000 undocumented children if the law were to be changed. To prove its estimate of the unusually large number of undocumented alien children in Texas, TEA commissioned a study by Dallas professors who "identified" at least 100,000 such children on the basis of the following rationale: undocumented alien children are not enrolled in school; there are at least 100,000 children in Texas not enrolled in school; therefore, there are at least 100,000 undocumented alien children in Texas.

Federal district Judge Woodrow Seals provided an opposing view, by stating that "to assume that children not enrolled in school are undocumented is simply unsound." The court further criticized the TEA study for using poor methodology and being illogical, unsound, and unreliable. Judge Seals pointed out to the TEA that using the same methodology on other populations could lead to the rather bizarre and untenable conclusion that there were a similar number of undocumented black children in Texas. Following the Supreme Court's repeal of the

Texas law, school districts reported the enrollment of some 8,000 undocumented children statewide.

The TEA argument based on the financial impact of educating these children with state and local resources fared even worse in the courts. The plaintiffs' support for the court case was partly based on information from the Immigration and Naturalization Service that most of the undocumented children in question were eligible for U.S. citizenship and would eventually become citizens. It is interesting that all participants in the court case except the educational leadership were aware of the future implications of not educating the children, in terms of the eventual cost of social services that the state will have to provide to these subsequent citizens.

The final argument presented by the Texas educational leadership concerning the impact of undocumented alien children on the quality of minority education in Texas was similarly dismissed by the courts. The courts simply noted that the quality of education for minority children in Texas was so bad that doubts could be raised about education becoming any worse with the addition of undocumented alien children.

It was ironic to see the diverse participants in *Doe* v. *Plylar*—including the Immigration and Naturalization Service, whose policies are designed to limit immigration—arguing on behalf of children's rights and children's needs, while the educators to whom the state entrusted its children for the provision of educational services left no stone unturned in attempts to exclude undocumented children from schools.

Treating children as if they have no intrinsic value causes them to develop a negative self-image; it also alienates them and their parents from schools. Devaluing children also leads to poor performance and increased dropout rates. Moreover, when children are devalued, any attempt to implement change in order to accommodate unique characteristics of atypical populations is precluded.

One of the most pernicious ways of devaluing children is to assume that they cannot learn and/or do not want to learn. This myth has guided the thinking of far too many educators, many of whom have given up on children of color. This misguided belief manifests itself in the setting of low expectations for children most at risk. Instead of benefiting from a challenging curriculum, these children are often given menial tasks, including circling ditto sheets and doing other boring, repetitive work. Often, these children are pulled out of regular classes to do remedial work that is unchallenging. The results are staggering. Children begin to fall farther and farther behind in their academic work, ending up in nonacademic programs of study because no one believes they can or want to ever enroll in college, and many students simply never make it even to high school (Quality Education for Minorities Project, 1990).

Language Development in Children

Truth is not stranger than fiction, as subsequent educational developments have indicated. It took nine justices of the U.S. Supreme Court to point out to certified educational personnel and responsible board members in the 1974 *Lau* v. *Nichols* decision that if the school system had 1,800 Chinese children who did not speak English being taught by school teachers who did not speak any Chinese, the makings of an educational problem were clearly evident. When the school district in question acceded in court to the existence of a problem, it argued that the problem rested with the students, not with the schools. The school conducted its affairs in the English language and advocated that it was up to the parents of the Chinese students to prepare them adequately by teaching them English. The Supreme Court explained to the school officials that the parents did not speak English and their main interest in sending their children to school was for them to learn English.

The special attention required by limited-English-proficient children is seldom available to them. *Lau* v. *Nichols* is an example in which language-minority children were being offered the same instructional program presented to English-proficient children. The inevitable failure produced by the incompatibility between the language of the classroom and the language of the student may be viewed as leading to a lack of student readiness and to the creation of rationalizations for the lack of success.

One such rationalization is the myth that the use of the primary language interferes with the acquisition of a second language. Language-minority children in American schools were prevented for generations from speaking their native language lest it impede the learning of English. Research in linguistics has challenged this myth, though educators have been known to continue educational practices based on erroneous assumptions for many years after the assumptions have been found faulty. Thus, Spanish-speaking children in this country are still perceived by educators as the only ethnic group in the world unable to cope with two languages, even though demographic information indicates that more people in the world speak two or more languages, than speak only one language.

One would assume that once a child has been found lacking proficiency in English, the school would provide ample opportunity for English language development in the classroom. However, this is not the case. Studies conducted by the Department of Education confirm what Hispanic educators have long observed. The less proficiency in English on the part of the student, the less language development activity is provided in the instructional program. Limited-English-proficient children spend more time on desk work and less time on language-utilizing activities than their more English-proficient counterparts. An early school response to the English language limitations of language-minority children was to place them in a special program dedicated to the development of English language skills prior to initiating traditional instruction in the various areas of the school curriculum. Though this methodology was preferable to the prior sink-or-swim approach, it did produce an undesirable by-product. Spending a year or two on the development of English language skills led to a postponement of instruction in the regular curriculum, making the children overage for a grade during the rest of their years in school. Being overage is associated with an increased likelihood of dropping out.

Bilingual Education

During the 1960s, a strong movement emerged in the United States that encouraged bilingual education as a way of addressing the needs of language-minority children. This approach was intended to remedy the problems faced by children who lost a year or two of instruction in the traditional curriculum areas while they were learning English. Bilingual education utilizes the native language of the student for instructional purposes while English is being learned as a second language. When student mastery of English is sufficient for instructional purposes, a transition is made to English language instruction.

Proposals for bilingual instruction received extensive acceptance and support when initially introduced in 1968. Not only did the rationale sound logical, but at that time there was a strong federal commitment to the Cuban American population that had recently fled from Cuba. There was great interest among the Cuban population in maintaining their children's Spanish language skills pending a return to Cuba. Mexican Americans and Puerto Ricans provided the grassroots support for bilingual education; Cuban Americans provided the political clout for federal support.

Though the rationale of bilingual education is pedagogically sound and limited-English-proficient children perform better through participation in a bilingual program, the benefits of such programs have been severely limited due to the following factors:

- The funding for bilingual education from federal, state, and local sources has been meager.
- Only a small fraction of eligible language-minority children have participated in bilingual education programs.
- The number of trained personnel for the implementation of bilingual instruction has been limited. In an evaluation of bilingual education conducted by the Department of Education, over half of the "bilingual" teachers spoke no language other than English.
- Bilingual programs have been plagued by inadequate materials. Textbook companies have been reluctant to develop textbooks and materials that can be marketed to a small segment of the school population.
- Students are placed in bilingual programs for only a portion of the school day. Successes in the bilingual program

are offset by the traditional failure and frustration during the rest of the school day.

- There is a lack of native language utilization in the bilingual program.
- Students are prematurely transitioned into the English language instructional program on the basis of student capability to utilize English in a social context, rather than on the basis of capability to utilize English in an academic setting.
- Students are often prematurely released from the bilingual program and into an all-English instructional program.
- Instruments and techniques for measuring language proficiency are inadequate.
- Local and state administrative support for bilingual education programs is inadequate.
- Mainstream America continues to harbor xenophobic attitudes.

Developmental Patterns in Disadvantaged Children

An analysis of the performance of preschool-age, economically disadvantaged children in 1969 (Edgewood Independent School District, 1972) indicated a marked deviation in developmental patterns, as compared with the patterns of middle-class children. One such deviation was an unusually low level of auditory discrimination ability. This finding was considered important because of its impact on the subsequent development of visual discrimination ability as a necessary prerequisite skill for learning to read.

A review of the literature revealed that a low level of auditory discrimination was characteristic of economically disadvantaged children. The educational literature attributed this problem to characteristics of disadvantaged homes, such as high child-to-adult ratios, large numbers of persons in small areas, the location of the home in noisy and congested neighborhoods, and so on. Psychologists believed that when brought up in a noisy environment, children tended to block out sound, rather than learning to make fine auditory discriminations, as do children in less noisy middle-class homes.

In typical instructional programs, auditory discrimination is a necessary prerequisite for visual discrimination, which in turn is a necessary prerequisite for learning to read. The absence of auditory discrimination ability at school entry could be the cause of a reading disability. Compounded over the elementary school years, it could account for the poor performance of disadvantaged children in reading. On the other hand, a few weeks of intensive instruction in auditory discrimination brought the preschoolers to a middle-class level of auditory discrimination and facilitated the development of visual discrimination skills as prerequisite skills for learning to read.

Though the low level of auditory discrimination was recognized as characteristic of economically disadvantaged children, the basal reading program in schools did not address this characteristic. This failure stems from a basic fallacy in school instructional programs—the assumption that the student comes from a middle-class home and has a middle-class pattern of educational development. The incompatibility between student socioeconomic background and the school's instructional program accounts for the poor performance of disadvantaged children. The unique developmental pattern of the disadvantaged is a characteristic over which the child has no control, and in most cases, neither does the family. It is the responsibility of the school, as established in *Lau* v. *Nichols,* to adapt the instructional program to the unusual characteristics of the child.

Homework and Disadvantaged Children

An educational example of the failure of conventional methods in the education of atypical children is homework. Homework is a middle-class institution that has been very successful in providing reinforcement for school learning and in expanding the temporal and geographic horizons of the school. In keeping with the proven impact of homework, early school reform efforts focused on increasing the amount of homework assigned in order to improve student performance.

Unfortunately, homework is not a very successful method in poverty homes. Such environments seldom can provide space, time, privacy, isolation, or proper assistance in doing the homework. There is often no children's room where homework is to be done. Parents may not even speak the language used in the school or have an extensive academic background, and may not have the skills to provide assistance to the student. Instead of providing reinforcement for schoolwork or expanding temporal and geographic impacts of the school, homework can be difficult, frustrating and dysfunctional, and even counterproductive if the student repeats the incorrect way of doing long division fifty times.

This does not mean that school instruction cannot be reinforced or expanded; it means that the school should opt for alternative ways to do it. Tutors, individualized assistance, and adequately staffed study periods may be much more effective than assigning massive amounts of homework for students facing constraints with this type of educational methodology.

School Finance Disparities

Implementing a comprehensive reform effort aimed at improving educational opportunities for minority and disadvantaged children in American schools would require extensive resources. One of the major problems in minority education is the inequitable distribution of existing resources, as evidenced in a host of state school finance court cases following the U.S. Supreme Court's reversal of the 1971 *San Antonio ISD* v. *Rodriguez.* School finance cases in California, Texas, New York, New Jersey, Colorado, Kentucky, and about half the other states have demonstrated the inadequacies of state systems of school finance. Even in states where school finance suits have failed, the failure in the courts is usually attributed to the constitutionality of the existing system, rather than to the failure of plaintiffs to prove the existence of an inequitable system.

Without exception, minority and disadvantaged children have been the recipients of low levels of funding in each of the contested state systems. Though the absence of adequate resources affects all aspects of education, there are few areas of education in which the performance of the haves and have-nots is as disparate as in science and mathematics.

The most dramatic point in the original court trial of the 1987 Texas school finance equity case, *Edgewood* v. *Kirby*, was testimony presented by Superintendent Alan Boyd of the San Elizario Independent School District in the El Paso area. Boyd testified about the absence of high school subjects due to the financial limitations of the school district. Activities such as football, music, and choir, taken for granted in most schools, were not available to students in the low-wealth school district. But there was an audible gasp from participants and audience alike when Boyd testified to a limited science and mathematics offering due to lack of resources and the inability of the school district to afford or attract qualified teachers of geometry, calculus, chemistry, physics, and other subjects commonly deemed essential in American schools but not available in his school district.

Access to Programs

Quality science and math instruction is not accessible to minority and disadvantaged children in poorly funded schools due to three exclusionary mechanisms: lack of enrollment in college preparatory classes, the low quality of science and math instruction in classes in which they are enrolled, and the subsequent effect of nonenrollment in gatekeeping classes.

The high-socioeconomic-status schools with few minority and disadvantaged students were found to have the best science and math programs. The reason for the quality programs found in high-socioeconomic-status schools is the quality and extent of science and math program offerings, the quality of the instructional staff, and the availability of resources in support of high-quality programs. Although little research exists on the performance of the few minority and disadvantaged students enrolled in high-status schools, in a RAND study conducted by Oakes (1990), it was found that even low-capability minority and disadvantaged students enrolled in high-status schools performed better in science and math than high-capability minority and disadvantaged students in lower-status schools.

Though the quality of science and math programs in mixed schools was superior to that of low-socioeconomic-status central city schools, minority and disadvantaged students seldom benefited from such programs. For the most part, these students are excluded from participation in higher-quality classes by two exclusionary practices at the mixed schools: ability grouping and gatekeeping courses.

Access to Qualified Teachers

The RAND study (Oakes, 1990) found significant differences between the quality of science and math teachers available to high- and low-socioeconomic-status students. Schools with large proportions of minority and disadvantaged students have poorer-quality science and math teachers than schools enrolling mixed or large proportions of minority and disadvantaged students. The schools with lower-socioeconomic-status students had fewer financial resources for attracting and hiring highly qualified teachers, and in cases where financial resources were adequate, highly qualified teachers did not opt to teach in such schools.

Science and math teachers who taught large numbers of minority and disadvantaged students indicated a lack of interest in the student population, inadequate preparation for the teaching of science and math, and less confidence in their ability to teach science and math.

Comparisons of science and math teachers in the various types of schools and in varying tracks in mixed schools indicated that minority and disadvantaged students consistently had the teachers with the least advanced degrees, the lowest certification status, the least extensive academic background in science and math, and the least teaching experience.

Access to Resources

The RAND study (Oakes, 1990) compared resources other than teachers available to students in schools of different socioeconomic status. In general, the study found large discrepancies in facilities and equipment in the elementary schools and even larger discrepancies in the secondary schools. Schools enrolling high-socioeconomic-status students invariably had better access to resources deemed necessary for the teaching of science and mathematics. Significant differences were found in the availability of computers to students, in the availability of specialized computer staff, laboratories, and equipment, and even in the quality of science and math textbooks available to the students. Instructional staff in schools enrolling low-socioeconomic-level students more frequently identified the lack of instructional resources as a critical problem in the teaching of science and math.

The RAND study concluded that differences in performance of high- and low-socioeconomic-status students in science and math were attributed to significantly different educational opportunities available to the two groups. Inferior opportunities are afforded to low-socioeconomic-status students from minority groups in the inner cities. The inequality is initiated by common and extensive misclassification of low-socioeconomic-status students as being limited in academic skills, and the inequality is continued by inferior and inadequate instruction in elementary school and by limited access to quality science and math programs, teachers, and instructional resources in the remaining school years. The poor performance of minority and disadvantaged students in science and math occurs in a context of diminished resources and low expectations.

Reallocation of Funds

There is little possibility that existing school resources can be channeled toward the improvement of educational opportunities for minority and disadvantaged children. School budgets are highly institutionalized in support of highly institutionalized activities. Since there is little accountability for the success or failure of these activities, the highly ineffective school programs continue making a heavy demand on school funds year after year. The absence of zero-based budgeting in education precludes the funding of alternative and innovative programs from state and local allocations. Any new initiatives stemming from government, foundation, or corporate efforts must be accompanied by new funds. Old funds are so committed to educational practices that do not work that new sources of funding are required for trying other practices that might work. Even when special allocations of funds are made in support of minority and disadvantaged children, the new funds are commonly channeled to the extension of unsuccessful practices. If left entirely up to local initiatives, new funds are invariably allocated to doing the wrong things better, doing the wrong things longer, and doing the wrong things more often.

This has been the experience of the influx of massive amounts of federal dollars in support of education for minorities and the disadvantaged since the inception of the Elementary and Secondary Education Act of 1964. The bulk of the federal assistance has gone for the establishment of remedial classes to which the target population is erroneously assigned as lacking in mental capacity and subjected to a slow-paced instructional program destined to make the erroneous diagnosis into a self-fulfilling prophecy.

Proceeds from the California lottery, which were initially assigned to the schools as a windfall in support of innovation, have become so institutionalized that they have become indistinguishable from traditional state allocations. In Texas, state legislation adding a requirement that bilingual education funds be used in support of bilingual program activities resulted in a massive protest from school district personnel, who testified to the imposition the new requirements created by diverting the bilingual funds away from their prior use as general school support.

Training and Retraining of Educational Personnel

According to the U.S. Census Bureau, within the next few decades there could be as many as 70 million Hispanics throughout the nation. In California, which is home to nearly 40 percent of the nation's estimated 2.4 million non-English-speaking students, officials have declared a shortage of 20,000 accredited bilingual teachers. That number represents a 40 percent jump from several years ago. Nationwide, educators expect that more than 150,000 more teachers certified in bilingual instruction are needed. Yet not all needing bilingual instruction are immigrants. Native Americans who have lived on this continent for thousands of years maintain their own languages and cultures, as do Latinos who have lived here for generations (Manzo, 1994).

The Bilingual Education Act (Title VII of the Improving America's Schools Act) passed by Congress in 1994 provided $215 million annually through the year 2000 to schools, colleges, and community-based organizations to establish, implement, and sustain programs for children and youth of limited English proficiency. The legislation also responded to the need for trained teachers by offering grants to colleges and universities to develop or expand bilingual education programs. The idea was to better prepare educators such as counselors, teachers, principals, and specialists to be effective with diverse student populations and to build a mindset that views these students as resources rather than liabilities (Manzo, 1994).

A major barrier to the improvement of educational opportunities for minority children is the need for massive training and retraining of educational personnel. School personnel's present level of understanding of cultural, social, economic, and other characteristics of atypical populations can be summarized by testimony presented in the 1973 *Keyes* v. *Denver* desegregation court case: "In general, schools are unaware of the cultural characteristics of minority populations. When they are aware of the cultural characteristics they generally do nothing about it, and when they do something about it, they inevitably do the wrong thing."

The biggest failure in American education has been the failure of schools to recognize and accept cultural characteristics of atypical students. For the most part, schools perceive just two types of culture, the American culture and the wrong one. During the 1960s and the 1970s there was an increased awareness of this country's cultural diversity, and American education even made an attempt to incorporate culture into the school curriculum (Cárdenas and Cárdenas, 1973). Unfortunately, an early attempt to provide cultural relevance in education by relating instruction to the cultural background of children gave way to ethnic studies, in which the objective and content were geared to learning and appreciating cultural characteristics of minority groups rather than relating these characteristics to instructional practice.

Ethnic studies can provide three major benefits: (1) for minority students, an understanding and appreciation of their own ethnic group, leading to a positive perception of self; (2) for educational personnel, an understanding and appreciation of the minority ethnic group, leading to a positive perception of minority students; and (3) for school personnel, adapting instructional practice to minority characteristics. Since participation in ethnic studies courses has usually been limited to members of the ethnic group under study, ethnic studies has successfully addressed the need for a better understanding of self but has provided limited mainstream understanding and appreciation of minority populations. It has done nothing for the adaptation of instructional practice.

A major concern in the implementation of a massive pre-service and inservice training program is the source of the training. Institutions of higher education have not made noticeable progress in revamping their teacher education training programs so as to become a resource for educational reform. Preservice teacher training programs for the most part are preparing teachers for a career of teaching Anglo, English-speaking middle-class students, though the graduates of such programs are having great difficulty finding such children to teach.

Staffing patterns at most colleges and universities fall far short of having a culturally diverse faculty that mirrors the population diversity their graduates will be teaching. Programs addressing cultural diversity are usually found at the graduate level and are not available in the basic teacher preparation program. Similar constraints surface in the massive retraining of educational practitioners. It is difficult to find the necessary funds to address the cost of retraining, time in which this training is to be provided, and personnel capable of providing the training.

Why Preschool Programs Often Fail

Early interventions in the preparation of atypical children for school can easily become dysfunctional and even counterproductive. The extensive implementation of preschool-age programs in Texas is an example.

Extensive evaluation of children in Head Start and other types of early childhood programs substantiate the value of this early intervention. The investment in the early development of children prior to regular school enrollment has produced sufficient dividends to justify the investment. The payoff in improved subsequent performance has been big enough to lead a number of states to provide early schooling for five-, four-, and even three-year-olds in the public schools. In Texas, half of the school districts are providing prekindergarten education to low-income and limited-English-proficient four-year-olds.

Texas recently completed an evaluation study of preschool programs in its public schools (Texas Education Agency, 1991). The results of the preliminary report are not encouraging (Cárdenas, 1992). Although student performance data are not yet available, it is generally recognized that the Texas preschool programs differ considerably from traditional early childhood programs. The difference is explained in the TEA evaluation report as the implementation of a "pushdown" model. Instead of the preschool program focusing on the development of the child's physical, intellectual, social, and emotional development in order to prepare the child for the academic curriculum of the first grade, Texas programs have pushed down the academic curriculum of the first grade to the kindergarten and the preschool level. As a result of this early focus on academic skills, the failure previously experienced in the first grade is being encountered at the age of four or five.

The TEA compared early childhood programs to standards established by the National Association for the Education of Young Children (NAEYC) (1992). The following is based on the "Comments and Conclusions" section of the TEA report. Although administrators and teachers in prekindergarten programs in Texas are receptive to the concept of developmentally appropriate practices, little evidence of their implementation was apparent. Several barriers currently impede the implementation of these practices. First, prekindergarten programs did not appear to be grounded on sound beliefs or theories about how young children learn, nor did a framework exist at the state level to identify program quality standards. Second, staff typically did not receive the training in early childhood development and education necessary to implement developmentally appropriate programs. In programs with teacher assistants, training in early childhood was minimal or nonexistent. Third, in many classrooms the adult-child ratio of 1:22—which exceeded the NAEYC-recommended 1:8 adult-child ratio—did not support individualized instruction and adequate supervision of children. Fourth, the programs for limited-English-proficient students appeared to focus on moving children into English, rather than ensuring that children first had a strong foundation in their native language. Finally, parents, although strongly supportive of prekindergarten, did not appear to have a partnership relationship with the districts.

Much of the proven value of early interventions has been lost in its transition to the school. What had always been an appropriate response for disadvantaged and limited-English-proficient children has become dysfunctional and somewhat counterproductive in that the "pushdown" curriculum in preschool programs has produced frustration and failure for the target population at an earlier age.

Short of an extensive reform effort in the schools, even sophisticated responses can become dysfunctional. Simplistic responses such as raising standards, increased retentions in grade, no-pass-no-play, increased homework, and expanded testing programs will continue to be dysfunctional at best and counterproductive at worst.

Conclusion

The ideal characteristic of a reform effort for atypical school populations is the creation and implementation of a "culturally democratic learning environment." This environment is one in which adaptive responses to the unique characteristics of the students will lead to the elimination of barriers to effective schooling, with the performance of each of the participants being dependent on the level of interest, motivation, effort, and capability of the individual students rather than on ethnicity, language spoken at home, economic class, gender, or residential characteristics. School restructuring efforts must include the components of culturally democratic learning environments, including language development and aural learning development.

The ideal school for minority and disadvantaged children will parallel America's ideal: a democratic society in which freedom is exercised by freedom of choice, and freedom of choice is made a reality by the existence of feasible alternatives from which to choose. The creation of a culturally democratic learning environment should be based on the school's commitment to the identification, reduction, and eventual elimination of the incompatibilities between the characteristics of the atypical school populations and the characteristics of the schools.

References

Cárdenas, J. A. "Early Childhood Education in the Public Schools: The Texas Education Agency Evaluation." *Intercultural Development Research Association (IDRA) Newsletter* (San Antonio, Tex.), Jan. 1992, pp. 1–3.

Cárdenas, J. A., and Cárdenas, B. *The Theory of Incompatibilities.* San Antonio, Tex.: Intercultural Development Research Association, 1973.

Committee for Economic Development. *Children in Need: Investment Strategies for the Educationally Disadvantaged.* New York: Committee for Economic Development, 1987.

Edgewood Independent School District. *Evaluation of the Model Cities Early Childhood Education Program.* San Antonio, Tex.: Edgewood Independent School District, 1972.

Manzo, K. K. "Meeting the Needs of Many." *Black Issues in Higher Education,* 1994, *11*(19), 28–31.

National Association for the Education of Young Children. *Accreditation Criteria and Procedures of the National Academy of Early Programs, Revised.* Washington, D.C.: National Association for the Education of Young Children, 1992.

Oakes, J. *Multiplying Inequalities: The Effects of Race, Social Class, and Tracking on Opportunities.* Santa Monica, Calif.: RAND Corporation, 1990.

Quality Education for Minorities Project. *Education That Works:*

An Action Plan for the Education of Minorities. Cambridge: Massachusetts Institute of Technology, 1990.

Schorr, L. *Within Our Reach.* New York: Doubleday, 1988.

Texas Education Agency. *Texas Evaluation Study of Prekindergarten Programs: Preliminary Findings.* Austin: Texas Education Agency, 1991.

Chapter 4

Responding to the New Demographics in Higher Education

Shirley Vining Brown

Before the Civil War, historians described students on American college and university campuses as predominantly white Protestant men from affluent family backgrounds. It was not until after World War II, when the GI Bill increased the college participation rates of working-class students, that the first step was taken toward the democratization of higher education. The second step resulted from the pivotal decision of the U.S. Supreme Court in the *Brown* v. *Board of Education* case, which officially ended imposed segregation in public education in 1954. The intent of this decision was to increase student access to all colleges and universities regardless of race, ethnicity, or gender. Nearly four decades later, there is evidence that changes in the identity and composition of the higher educational community have occurred slowly. What progress has been made toward multicultural campuses, and what is the make-up of U.S. college campuses today?

Statistics show that formerly all-male institutions and many degree fields that were once the primary domain of white men have been markedly expanded to include women, particularly at the undergraduate level. Today, women account for the majority of students in higher education and, even at the doctoral level, their numbers and proportions are increasing almost yearly. By 1992, 37 percent of all doctorates were awarded to women, compared to almost 20 percent three decades ago. Another encouraging sign is that women are making significant progress in traditionally male-dominated fields like the physical sciences, life sciences, and engineering (Brown, 1992; Thurgood and Weinman, 1991).

Minorities also increased their presence on traditionally white campuses, but the early advances made by minorities suffered serious setbacks during the Reagan and Bush administrations because of various policy changes and other developments that chipped away at their gains in higher education. Not only are minority participation rates becoming static; in some groups they have declined.

Why revisit this topic? Lessons learned from the past reveal that the undereducation of minority citizens could be taken as a sign that the United States is of two minds about constructive educational reforms. For instance, there is considerable talk about revitalizing the educational system to prepare U.S. citizens for a new world economy. Yet Chapter Three describes how the winnowing processes of an inferior education take a tremendous toll on minority students during the formative years of their education. Moreover, the principles of equity and diversity and strategies for implementing them are the subject of continual debate.

Because these unyielding trends are troublesome and lay the foundation for later educational attainment, the lagging attainment of minority citizens increases and follows them into higher education, where the disparities grow wider. Thus, the "cybernetic effect" of an inadequate precollege education results in huge losses before minority students enter college, and the wastage is compounded by even greater losses by the time these students reach graduate education.

The information in this chapter is familiar to educational researchers but is less well known to policy makers, rank-and-file educators, and administrators. It is even less familiar to the public. The first section of the chapter reviews the representation of minorities among U.S. college students, the trends in minority educational attainment, and the barriers associated with their setbacks over two decades. The second section responds to the needs raised by the current status of minorities in higher education. It suggests fundamental changes in public policy and institutional adjustments that might strengthen the structure and promote democracy in American higher education.

Access Patterns: Who Goes to College

We begin by looking at the access patterns of minority and majority students.

Family Income

As social changes took place during and after the civil rights movement, the press toward egalitarianism in American society somewhat weakened the elitist bases of student selection procedures and gradually altered the demographic profile of students on U.S. college campuses. But a closer look at the personal profiles of entering college freshmen shows that little has changed over the years (Table 4.1). The typical college student is still a white student from a relatively advantaged family background.

For example, if we ignore the discounting of the U.S. dollar, Table 4.2 shows that as family income rose, the relative family income differences between minority and white entering freshmen remained fairly constant between 1975 and 1990. Although income differences diminished somewhat among students from families with incomes of $40,000 or more, almost two-thirds of white entering freshmen came from families in this income bracket in 1990 compared to 44 percent of American Indian, slightly better than a third of Hispanic, and less than a third of the black freshmen. At the other extreme are families earning less than $20,000 a year, where the minority representation was two to three and a half times that of whites in 1990. Asian American freshmen came from families with annual incomes that most closely approximated the incomes of whites, but they were also overrepresented among low-income families and were 10 percentage points behind whites in the higher income bracket. Later, we will see how family income is linked to falling minority enrollment and degree rates over the past two decades.

Table 4.1. Distributions of Entering Freshmen in Four-Year Institutions
by Race or Ethnic Group, 1975, 1980, 1985, 1990.

Race or Ethnic Group	1975	1980	1985	1990
Asian Pacific Islander	0.8%	1.2%	1.5%	1.5%
American Indian/ Aleut	0.8	0.8	1.4	1.6
Black	11.9	13.5	14.1	15.7
Hispanic[a]	1.7	1.8	1.4	2.0
White	85.3	82.7	82.3	79.0
Other	1.5	1.9	1.3	1.7

[a]Percentages do not add up to 100 because Hispanics may be of any race.

Source: Cooperative Institutional Research Program, University of California at Los Angeles, 1975, 1980, 1985, 1990.

Parents' Educational Attainment

Family income is generally associated with the educational attainment of parents. Although the parents of 1990 freshmen are somewhat better educated in 1990 than were the parents of freshmen in 1975, more than a third of the fathers had only a high school education or less (Table 4.2).

Asian American fathers are better educated than the fathers of other freshmen. Seventy-two percent of the Asian American fathers attended college and 61 percent earned college degrees. This is 6 percent higher than the percentage of white fathers (65 percent) who attended college and 11 percent higher than white fathers who earned a college degree (50 percent). The educational attainment of both Asian American and white fathers surpassed the educational attainment of non-Asian minority fathers in 1990. Only 43 and 42 percent, respectively, of the black and Hispanic fathers attended college, and just over a quarter of each group (26 percent) earned undergraduate and graduate degrees. The number of American Indians who attend college is quite small, but of this group, over half of the fathers attended college and more than a third earned college degrees.

The educational attainment of the mothers of college

Table 4.2. Personal Profile of Entering Freshmen in Four-Year Institutions, 1975 and 1990.

Family Background Characteristics	All Freshmen		Race or Ethnic Group									
			Asian American		American Indian		Black		Hispanic		White	
	1975	1990	1975	1990	1975	1990	1975	1990	1975	1990	1975	1990
Family Income												
$19,000 or less	52%	16%	66%	20%	71%	24%	89%	35%	84%	31%	55%	9%
$20–39,999	28	31	26	27	24	32	10	34	11	35	34	28
$40,000 or above	8	53	8	53	5	44	1	31	5	34	11	63
Parent Education[a]												
Fathers												
High School or less	46	37	41	26	51	43	72	52	70	55	38	30
Some college	4	16	11	11	15	17	12	17	10	16	15	15
B.A. degree	14	22	18	28	14	21	7	16	7	14	20	28
Graduate degree	14	18	8	33	12	14	6	10	9	12	18	22
Mothers												
High School or less	54	40	52	37	58	41	67	43	78	59	49	36
Some college	15	18	13	10	16	24	13	21	8	16	16	18
B.A. degree	16	20	20	30	10	20	9	18	7	13	18	26
Graduate degree	6	10	22	17	7	10	6	11	3	7	6	12

[a]Percentages do not add up to 100 because they exclude percentage with postsecondary education (not college).

freshmen has also improved, although their educational attainment is generally lower than that of fathers. American Indian and black mothers tend to be somewhat better educated than fathers. Although the differences between the educational attainment of fathers and mothers are not striking, the same pattern exists between the educational attainment of minority and majority mothers, and minority and majority fathers.

Student Performance on Achievement Tests

Uneven and lower student performance on the SAT has caused growing concern that the quality of students entering college is declining. Record lows in 1991 fueled these fears as students nationwide dropped an average of 2 points on the SAT. But if high school grade-point averages (GPA) are used as a measure, Table 4.3 indicates that the quality of entering freshmen remained fairly stable between 1975 and 1990.

There were persistent differences between the GPAs of non-Asian minority and of Asian American and white college freshmen, however. For example, Asian Americans stood apart from everyone else because of the high proportions (46–48 percent) who entered college with A-average high school GPAs. This was considerably higher than the percentage of white freshmen with GPAs in this range (28–32 percent), and both groups had higher percentages of A-average students than American Indian (24–27 percent), Hispanic (22–28 percent), and black (8–11 percent) freshmen. However, most college freshmen were not A-average students; rather, they were solid B-average students when they entered college. Only a few—primarily black—students entered with weak GPAs in the C+-average or below category.

Why do high school graduates choose to attend college? What is their primary motivation? In spite of highly disparate minority and white background characteristics, educational preparation, test performance scores, and entrance rates, most students entered college for the same reasons (Table 4.3). They wanted to (1) learn more, (2) get a better job, and (3) get a general education. The number one reason given by black students has always been to get a better job but, in 1990, this answer was the number one reason given by all entering freshmen, perhaps

Table 4.3. High School Grade-Point Average and Reasons for Going to College, Four-Year Institutions, 1975 and 1990.

| | All Freshmen | | Race or Ethnic Group | | | | | | | | | |
| | | | Asian American | | American Indian | | Black | | Hispanic | | White | |
GPA and Reason	1975	1990	1975	1990	1975	1990	1975	1990	1975	1990	1975	1990
GPA												
A− to A+	21%	24%	46%	48%	24%	27%	8%	11%	22%	28%	28%	32%
B− to B+	63	58	49	46	60	56	58	57	60	58	60	57
C+ and below	16	17	5	6	16	17	34	32	18	14	12	11
Top Three Reasons for Going to College	1980	1990	1980	1990	1980	1990	1980	1990	1980	1990	1980	1990
Learn more		73	79	78	81	76	80	78	84	79	75	73
Better job		77	73	71	73	77	83	83	73	76	74	7
Gain general education		65	75	72	71	66	78	75	79	72	68	63

Source: Cooperative Institutional Research Program, University of California at Los Angeles, 1975, 1990.

because of the economic recession and the increased awareness that changing technologies lead to changing skill needs.

Enrollment Trends

From 1970 to 1991, the total college participation rate increased from 26 to 31 percent among eighteen- to twenty-four-year-olds but there was little change in the share of minority and majority enrollments (Levine and Associates, 1989). As Table 4.4 shows, minority enrollment in U.S. institutions increased by just over 5 percent. Asian American and Hispanic students were the prime beneficiaries of this enrollment increase, although most Hispanics are enrolled in two-year institutions. While the enrollment of other minorities increased or remained constant, the participation of black students in higher education began to taper off in 1976 and, by 1990, enrollment had declined. More recent figures are encouraging in that they indicate an interruption of this trend and a slight upturn in black enrollment in 1990 and 1991 (Carter and Wilson, 1992; National Center for Education Statistics, U.S. Department of Education, 1993). The proportion of American Indians enrolled in higher education has barely changed even though their numbers have increased. They still represent only 0.8 percent of the total enrollment, and 54 percent are enrolled in two-year institutions (O'Brien, 1992).

Whether one looks at undergraduate or graduate enrollments, the patterns are similar. Minority enrollment grew by less than 3 percent at the undergraduate and graduate levels. The primary breakthrough was in the first professional degree programs, where the minority share increased by almost 6 percent. Except for American Indians, all minority groups made progress, especially Asian Americans, who more than doubled their enrollment share, from 1.7 to 5.3 percent.

Almost a quarter (23 percent) of all students enrolled in two-year institutions are minorities, and these proportions are growing. The rise in minority enrollment in two-year institutions reflects the high participation of minority part-time students, particularly Hispanics and American Indians, who are overconcentrated in two-year institutions. Most minority students attending two-year institutions have low transfer rates to four-year

Table 4.4. Total U.S. Enrollment in Higher Education by Race or
Ethnic Group, 1976 and 1988.

Race or Ethnic Group	1976	1988
American Indian	0.7%	0.7%
Asian American	1.8	3.9
Black	9.6	8.9
Hispanic	8.6	5.4
White	84.3	83.6

Source: National Center for Education Statistics, U.S. Department of Education, 1989.

institutions, and even lower graduation rates from these institutions. This roundabout pathway to a college education accounts for some of the large disparity between the undergraduate and graduate degree attainment rates of non-Asian minority and of white and Asian American students.

Degree Trends

Minority and majority students differ in their degree attainment rates, but a poignant, long-standing phenomenon is that minority students have higher educational aspirations than white students.

Table 4.5 shows that, in 1990, the percentage of non-Asian minority freshmen planning to earn a doctorate or professional degree (for example, law or medicine) was about 3 to 4 percent higher than of white freshmen, even though their aspirations go unfulfilled when measured by their degree attainment rates. For example, the minority share of bachelor's degrees rose only 2 percent between 1976 and 1987 (Brown, 1992; Levine and Associates, 1989). This small increase occurred against the background of decreases in the absolute number of black students who received degrees. In other words, the gains of Asian Americans offset the 1 percent decline of black baccalaureate recipients, the lack of progress of American Indian recipients, and the less than 1 percent growth rate of Hispanic baccalaureate recipients. In contrast,

Table 4.5. Highest Degree Planned Anywhere of Entering College Freshmen, 1975 and 1990.

Degree Aspiration	Race or Ethnic Group											
	All Freshmen		Asian American		American Indian		Black		Hispanic		White	
	1975	1990	1975	1990	1975	1990	1975	1990	1975	1990	1975	1990
Highest Degree Planned												
B.A.	35%	30%	18%	14%	29%	28%	25%	23%	26%	23%	36%	29%
M.A.	33	41	32	35	26	33	35	39	27	38	31	41
Ph.D/Ed.D	11	14	19	23	16	17	17	17	15	18	11	14

Source: Cooperative Institutional Research Programs, University of California at Los Angeles, 1975, 1990.

foreign students gained 1.3 percent more of all baccalaureates awarded during this period, a percentage higher than the combined growth of American Indian, black, and Hispanic baccalaureate recipients.

Not only do non-Asian minorities earn relatively fewer baccalaureate degrees, but it takes them longer to complete their degrees. Based on the National Longitudinal Survey (NLS) of high school seniors, 56 percent of Asian Americans and 29 percent of white high school seniors finished a four-year college program after fourteen years out of high school (Figure 4.1). But only 19 percent of the black, 18 percent of the American Indian, and 11 percent of the Hispanic high school seniors completed a four-year college degree in the same amount of time. This trend holds up when comparing the completion rates of the High School and Beyond seniors as well (Brown, 1992).

At the graduate level, the drop in the share of master's degrees earned by black students whittled away their gains in the mid 1970s (Table 4.6). However, the proportion of master's degrees awarded to Asian Americans and Hispanics grew steadily between 1976 and 1991. The largest gain, though, was made by foreign students, who more than doubled their share of master's degrees during this period.

In the late 1970s, the number of U.S. citizens earning Ph.D.'s began to decline. By 1990, there were 12 percent (2,892) fewer Ph.D.'s produced by U.S. institutions. Pointing out this trend is important because it confirms that, even with a shrinking pool, the growth of minority doctorates is almost at a standstill. Table 4.7 reveals that the combined share of minorities increased by nearly 3 percent over a fifteen-year period, which provides some insight into the enormity of the problem of producing minority doctorates. Again, the increase merely reflects how the gains of Asian American and, to a lesser extent, Hispanic Ph.D.'s balanced out the loss of 165 black Ph.D.'s since 1977.

It is interesting that, except for Asian Americans and American Indians, most minority gains are accounted for by women doctorates (Brown, 1992). Women are taking advantage of the expanding opportunities for women and minorities by increasing their participation in doctoral degree programs traditionally open

Figure 4.1. Cumulative Percent of 1972 High School Seniors Who Completed
a Bachelor's Degree by Race or Ethnic Groups, 1976–1986.

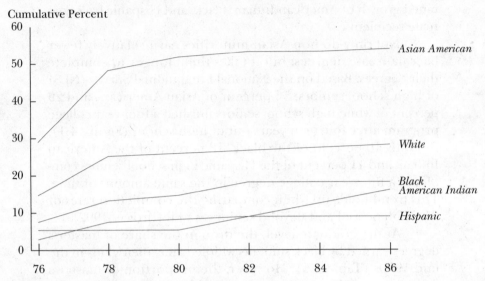

Note: Data corrected for American Indians and Asians.

Source: National Center for Education Statistics, U.S. Department of Education, 1989.

to women but also in the natural sciences and engineering. In all, American Indian women Ph.D.'s grew by 23 percent, black women Ph.D.'s by 25 percent, Hispanic women Ph.D.'s by 27 percent, and Asian American women Ph.D.'s by 11 percent. The comparable growth among white women Ph.D.'s was 20 percent. Most of the gains made by minority women took place in the late 1970s and early 1980s (Brown, 1992). But, similar to the trend for black men, a reversal for black women dropped their numbers by 3 percent from the number of Ph.D.'s they earned in 1983.

Because degree trends follow enrollment trends, minorities made more progress in the professions. American Indians earned about the same percentage of degrees in medicine, law, and dentistry (Table 4.8). Blacks, Asian Americans, and Hispanics earned relatively more degrees in medicine and dentistry than in law. Even though minorities made more progress in the professions, they are still underrepresented in these fields. Out of all first professional

Table 4.6. Percent Master's Degrees by Race or
Ethnic Group, 1976 and 1986–87.

Race or Ethnic Group	1976	1986–87
American Indian	0.3%	0.4%
Asian American	1.6	2.9
Black	6.6	4.8
Hispanic	1.9	2.4
White	84.0	79.1
Nonresident Aliens	5.4	10.3

Source: National Center for Education Statistics, U.S. Department of Education, 1989.

Table 4.7. Percent Doctoral Degrees by Race or
Ethnic Group, U.S. Citizens, 1977 and 1990.

Race or Ethnic Group	1977	1990
American Indian	0.3%	0.4%
Asian American	1.3	2.6
Black	4.5	3.5
Hispanic	1.7	2.9
White	92.2	90.6

Source: National Research Council, 1988.

degrees awarded to U.S. citizens during the 1990–91 academic year, the total share awarded to non-Asian minority citizens was only 12.8 percent in dentistry, 10.2 percent in medicine, and 8.9 percent in law (National Center for Education Statistics, U.S. Department of Education, 1993).

College Degree Field Choices

Many freshmen identify in broad terms the field in which they think they will major. Business and the professions are still the fields of choice for most freshmen. About 40 percent of the

Table 4.8. Percent First Professional Degrees by Race or
Ethnic Group and Selected Fields, 1986–87.

Race or Ethnic Group	Dentistry	Law	Medicine
American Indian	0.3%	0.4%	0.4%
Asian American	6.9	1.9	5.3
Black	5.7	4.8	3.1
Hispanic	3.6	2.9	5.1
White	83.0	89.9	85.1

Source: National Center for Education Statistics, U.S. Department of Education, 1989.

1990 black entering freshmen chose business as their intended major, which was higher than any other group. Intended majors may change, but as Figure 4.2 shows, 18 to 26 percent of undergraduates do go on to earn a bachelor's degree in business fields. Another large percentage of minorities choose majors in science and engineering fields at the undergraduate level. Nevertheless, choosing science and engineering as a career path is scarcely a viable option for non-Asian minorities, who clearly shift to education at the graduate level. The field distributions for most groups are remarkably similar, but the shift is most apparent among black master's degree recipients (38 percent). Asian Americans, who are the exception, earn almost half of their baccalaureate and master's degrees in the natural sciences and engineering.

Degree field differences are even more striking at the doctoral level, where Asian Americans and blacks stand out from other Ph.D.'s. Two-thirds of all 1990 Asian American Ph.D.'s earned doctorates in the natural sciences and engineering, while only 10 percent earned education doctorates. In contrast, over half (51 percent) of all black Ph.D.'s earned education doctorates, and only 14 percent earned doctorates in the natural sciences and engineering. From the standpoint of field switching and field losses, this means that potential black doctorates in the natural sciences and engineering fell 12 percent between the

Figure 4.2. Percent Bachelor's, Master's, and Doctoral Degrees Earned Within Race or Ethnic Group by Broad Field, U.S. Citizens, 1986.

Percent Bachelor's Degrees Earned Within Race or Ethnic Group by Broad Field, U.S. Citizens, 1986.

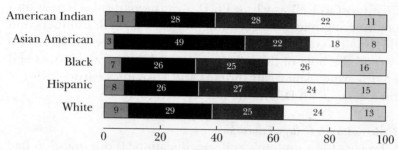

Percent Master's Degrees Earned Within Race or Ethnic Group by Broad Field, U.S. Citizens, 1986.

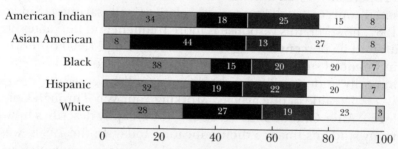

Percent Doctoral Degrees Earned Within Race or Ethnic Group by Broad Field, U.S. Citizens, 1986.

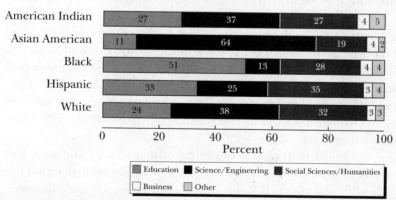

Source: National Research Council, 1988.

baccalaureate and doctoral levels, while the percentage of Asian Americans increased in these fields.

The field distributions of the other groups are quite similar, but the fact that American Indians and Hispanics seem to do almost as well as white Ph.D.'s in the natural sciences and engineering may be misleading because of small numbers and the way the data are aggregated. Unlike white Ph.D.'s, who earned the bulk of their doctorates in the natural sciences and engineering, American Indians and Hispanics earned most of their science Ph.D.'s in the life sciences.

Underwriting a College Education

Who pays for a student's college education? If this question had been put to the average college student in 1980, less than half (41 percent) would have said that financial aid comes from personal sources (such as parents, relatives, self, savings). Since 1987, however, this response is more frequent and fluctuates at around 65 percent among freshmen receiving $1,500 or more in financial support. Based on their family incomes, how can minority students afford today's soaring college costs?

The title of one article, "Working Your Way Through College—After Graduation" (Rasbery, 1992), aptly describes how many students finance their education today. In the 1980s, we saw the soaring growth in educational loans as federal cutbacks reduced grants to finance college costs. A parallel trend was a notable loss in minority student enrollments, even in fields where minorities had previously concentrated (for example, education or the humanities). The high cost of education has taken its greatest toll on black students and is reflected in the federal guaranteed loan rates for black freshmen that climbed from almost 4 to over 18 percent between 1978 and 1990, a period of reversal in black enrollment and graduation rates (National Research Council, 1990). The trends are similar for other student groups.

In addition to skyrocketing educational expenses, the sources, amount, type, and duration of financial assistance decide who will succeed in graduate education. One of the basic differences in the principles and assumptions that govern financial aid is that society expects parents to pay for their children's undergraduate education; this expectation diminishes once the children graduate from college (Hauptman, 1986). At the graduate level, students are expected to be financially self-sufficient and responsible for their own educational expenses.

However, the cost of graduate education is outside the reach of most graduate students, and available financial aid is typically based on academic merit regardless of need. This may be a barrier to some minority students who, because of earlier educational disadvantages, are qualified but less competitive than Asian American and white students for merit-based financial support. It is not surprising that in 1990, as in prior years, American Indian, Hispanic, and black Ph.D.'s graduated with the highest debt burden of all doctorates.

In short, the cumulative disadvantages of a less affluent family background, inadequate educational preparation, and heavier reliance on self-support are closing the door to higher education for thousands of minority citizens. Because this situation places more than the future of minorities on the line, we must find workable solutions to eliminate the barriers and unlock the gates to higher education.

Opening the Gateway to Higher Education

Few people would deny that education is the gateway to America's marketplace or that swings in the marketplace have a clear impact on higher education participation rates (Brown and Clewell, 1991; Reich, 1991, Halberstam, 1991). But whether the U.S. economy is in a state of boom or bust, non-Asian minorities (except for newer Asian immigrants) continue to live on the margin of America's social and economic order precisely because of inadequate education and training opportunities. Reich (1990) and Halberstam (1991) look to the future and point out that although America is in need of a well-educated and highly trained workforce, the federal government's position on crucial educational reforms is the shortsighted view that "we cannot pay for it." But Brown and Clewell (1991) point out two questions that must be continually raised in connection with America's

workforce needs: What can we afford? What institutional adjustments are needed to develop America's human resources? This
section looks squarely at these issues. Specific strategies are suggested for changing unacceptable policies and practices that
affect all segments of American society.

New Challenges, New Demands

Institutional and policy changes to improve higher education
require more than empty promises during election-year politics.
Simply put, educational leadership requires long-term vision and
a collective investment in excellence by government and academic officials. A reasonable strategy to improve America's educational system is to fix what does not work. But before this can
be done, the problem must be clearly identified and stated. The
real barriers to access in American higher education are twofold.
First, although America's educational philosophy is genuinely
democratic, democratizing higher education has never been a
national priority. Second, until recently, there was no (perceived)
return on investing in educational democracy.

This is no longer the case. As an outgrowth of the nation's
diminishing leadership in the world economy, the United States
must rethink the benefits that accrue to a nation and its citizens
from investing in across-the-board education and training programs. This investment involves two key issues: a national resolve
to (1) shore up America's competitive strength by human capital
development, and (2) incorporate all groups into the technological fabric of American society. Without these two goals, diversification in higher education and the workforce is highly unlikely.

National Investment in Human Capital

What can the government do? The role of the nation is to provide leadership to meet anticipated workforce needs. In the
1950s, the United States demonstrated its ability to offset the
nation's relative imbalance in the international community of
scientists and engineers by infusing massive funds in fellowship
and trainee programs. Even in the 1950s, there was a call to draw
on the scientific talent of minority citizens to preserve the
strength of the nation (Branson, 1955). The problem we faced

in 1950 is the same problem we face today: the accepted notion that human talent is innate, limited, and invariant. The failure to acknowledge that human talent is variable in the nation's population and can be nurtured and shaped has led to a whole body of literature devoted to the nature-nurture controversy over the determinants of human ability (Jensen, 1969, 1970; Shockley, 1970; Herrnstein, 1971; Eysenck, 1971). This controversy continues even though the quality of the data and methodology supporting the heritability argument is said to be flawed (Taylor, 1980).

Many institutions, policies, and programs assume extant between-group ability differences that disadvantage minorities. Take, for instance, the concern over the anticipated population shift that will increase minority and decrease white students in the college-age population. The expressed concern is that there will be insufficient talent among the future college-age population to go into the physical science and engineering fields. This is one way of saying that minorities and women, who will make up larger proportions of the college-age population, cannot fill the talent void left by majority-group men.

The indifference to minority talent also shows up in structured programmatic efforts to meet future workforce needs. For example, the minority fellowship programs developed in the 1970s and 1980s paralleled existing fellowship programs that ostensibly were open to all students. Minority fellowship programs operate under the premise that minorities cannot or should not compete with students in the regular applicant pool. In general, this may be true because of the built-in inequalities in public education. But for a growing segment of the minority population, American Indian, black, and Hispanic students can compete with the best students in the nation but are unofficially restricted to financial resources designated for minorities, which, by themselves, advance only a few minorities in the pipeline. Past administrations have attempted to ban race-specific scholarships, and even the programs that have had a modest impact on the access problems for minorities are in jeopardy.

Leadership for positive programmatic change must come from the federal government. Cutting grant programs and increasing the loan limits of many Guaranteed Student Loan (GSL) programs is not an expedient long-term solution to minority access and retention problems. Nor does it reflect unprecedented federal support for education. Contrary to the intent, loan programs ensure continued low-level minority participation in higher education by forcing many minority students to reluctantly borrow money for college expenses. Many minority students become overwhelmed by debt burdens and fail to pay back the loan. This is reflected in spiraling loan default rates in institutions that primarily serve minority students and are faced with expulsion from the program. In spite of valid arguments against loans versus grants, expulsion would exclude more minority students from higher education. GSL programs would better serve minority students by providing forgivable loans that require students to provide service in return for financial aid. Until the relative socioeconomic status of minorities is brought into line with the rest of society, serious initiatives by the government should make a major investment in grants as an entitlement to low-income students rather than forcing them to borrow against their future in the form of loans.

This is particularly true at the graduate level, where doctoral study is often drawn out and occurs during an individual's most productive years. In the past five years, the number one source of minority financial support for doctoral education has been self-supporting efforts (for example, self, loans, family, spouse). It may be one of the reasons minorities shift from the physical sciences and engineering to the field of education between the bachelor's and doctoral degrees. Doctoral programs in education permit minority students to go to school and hold down full-time jobs, even though the time to degree is considerably longer. Other degree fields are not as accommodating or flexible for protracted study. Thus, it is no surprise that at their highest level, non-Asian minorities make up less than 3 percent of the Ph.D.'s in the physical sciences and engineering.

The federal government can increase and diversify the pool of minority doctorates by renewing portable grants and fellowship programs that will permit full-time study for the duration of graduate education (four to six years depending on the program). Fully funded grant programs are important for attracting and raising the number of minority male doctoral candidates who, on average, have more dependents than other Ph.D. students. At the very least, a program of forgivable government loans would boost the number of minority doctorates in all degree fields.

Institutional Adjustments

Although national leadership and reformed federal funding policies are crucial, at the operational level the responsibility for minority access to higher education rests with academic institutions. Colleges and universities cannot continue to ignore the changing population shifts. Not only will minorities comprise one-third of the nation by the turn of the century, but in eleven states, minority students are expected to comprise from 29 to 49 percent of the high school graduates.

How can academic administrators respond to student population changes? The first step is for college and university presidents to set high institutional goals to diversify their campuses. The top administrator is the key to institutional change. Just as one expects leadership from the president of a nation, institutional adjustments to accommodate a different mix of students must be initiated by the heads of college campuses. They are responsible for setting the tone, expectation, mission, and climate for change. In the past, institutions that earned a reputation for excellence not only made changes, they were in the forefront of change. In the early 1990s, this class of leadership was exemplified in the decision made by the president of Georgia Tech University establishing the goal that this institution will become the nation's top producer of minority science and engineering Ph.D.'s. This goal was set during a time of retrenchment, yet Georgia Tech is well on its way to reaching its goal, with forty-five Ph.D. black engineering candidates in 1989 and fifty-six in 1990).

Second, leadership goes beyond goal setting. It requires the designation of funds to ensure real follow-through to reach intended goals. This may mean diverting university funds from one budget line item to another to achieve diversity in their institutions. For example, graduate programs across the United States fund many foreign nationals with university funds. In the physical sciences and engineering, up to 70 percent of foreign Ph.D.'s receive support from university funds (Brown and Clewell, 1991). While university funds should continue to be used for the support of foreign students who seek education in U.S. institutions, the proportional amount should be adjusted in light of the comparatively smaller share of university funds received by minority students in the same degree programs and the drastic cuts in federal funds for U.S. students.

Third, institutions should engage in self-assessment studies to track minority students who drop out. Information gained from students who leave before graduation could provide important insights and evidence of problems other than financial problems that, if corrected, could retain many minority students in college until they graduate.

Fourth, colleges and universities are ineffective in marketing the material benefits of higher education to minority students. Although government agencies and large corporations employ students with graduate degrees in foreign languages, mathematics, and engineering, potential positions have little or no visibility to minority students. As a part of its public service mission, each school and department in the university should go into elementary, middle, and senior high schools to acquaint students with the variety of "real" jobs and careers long before these students are ready for college. Too often the career options of students are foreclosed before they enter college because they do not have the prerequisite coursework to enter fields in the physical sciences and engineering.

Fifth, isolation is a major problem for minority students on predominantly white campuses. This is particularly true at the graduate level, where group study is often a factor in who succeeds and who does not. Because minority students may frequently be excluded from study groups, one of the most important steps a graduate program serious about recruiting and retaining minority students could take is mentioned in the advice of a recent minority graduate of an engineering program: "Send [minority] students to graduate school in threes; then you will get graduates" (Bozeman, 1989). Uri Treisman's (1992) research on the benefits of group study confirms the wisdom in this statement, and it is wisdom that institutions can draw on to develop a substantial minority talent pool.

Finally, as the largest producer of black college undergraduates, historically black colleges and universities are a major source of potential master's- and doctoral-level students in all fields, particularly the sciences and engineering. An important role in the educational enterprise of diversifying students and faculty is to build strong linkages between major research institutions and institutions with large concentrations of minority students that can serve as feeder schools to research institutions. Georgia Tech and Ohio State Universities have effectively maintained linkages with historically black colleges and universities to facilitate the flow of minorities into their graduate programs. Moreover, faculty exchanges between major research institutions and institutions that serve minority students (such as Native American tribal colleges, although there are few native American faculty, or colleges with large Hispanic populations) could facilitate and increase the flow of minorities into undergraduate and graduate education. Faculty exchange programs could benefit minority students by providing white and minority faculty role models in both institutions. This is particularly important in predominantly white institutions that have low recruitment and retention rates for minority students and faculty.

Conclusion

Making institutional adjustments requires vision, the ability to galvanize the attention of educational administrators and government policy makers around this issue, and timing. The time for prudent change is now. The anticipated tight labor market provides the federal government and the American educational system with a remarkable opportunity to put in place educational reforms that will benefit all citizens. In turn, the United States will be better able to meet the challenges of a changing world marketplace. Our future national wealth depends on the skills, training, and education of the nation's citizens. It also depends on the extent to which we renew, strengthen, and live by the meaning of a term embodied in our national ethos: *e pluribus unum*—"out of many one."

References

Bozeman, S. "Black Women Mathematicians: In Short Supply." *Sage: Scholarly Journal on Black Women*, 1989, *6*(2), 18–23.

Branson, H. R. "The Negro Scientist." In J. H. Taylor (ed.), *The Negro in Science*. Baltimore, Md.: Morgan State College Press, 1995.

Brown, S. V. "Minorities in the Graduate Education Pipeline: An Update." In S. V. Brown (ed.), *Minorities in Graduate Education: Pipeline, Policy, and Practice*. Princeton, N.J.: Graduate Record Examinations Board, Educational Testing Service, 1992.

Brown, S. V., and Clewell, B. C. *Building the Nation's Work Force from the Inside Out: Educating Minorities for the Twenty-First Century*. Norman: University of Oklahoma, 1991.

Carter, D. J., and Wilson, R. *Ninth Annual Status Report on Minorities in Higher Education*. Washington, D.C.: American Council on Education, 1992.

Cooperative Institutional Research Program, University of California at Los Angeles. *The American Freshman: National Norms*. Los Angeles: Cooperative Institutional Research Program, University of California at Los Angeles, 1975.

Cooperative Institutional Research Program, University of California at Los Angeles. *The American Freshman: National Norms*. Los Angeles: Cooperative Institutional Research Program, University of California at Los Angeles, 1980.

Cooperative Institutional Research Program, University of California at Los Angeles. *The American Freshman: National Norms*. Los Angeles: Cooperative Institutional Research Program, University of California at Los Angeles, 1985.

Cooperative Institutional Research Program, University of California at Los Angeles. Los Angeles: Cooperative Institutional Research Program, University of California at Los Angeles, 1990.

Eysenck, H. J. *The IQ Argument.* New York: Library Press, 1971.

Halberstam, D. *The Next Century.* New York: Morrow, 1991.

Hauptman, A. M. *Students in Graduate and Professional Education: What We Know and Need to Know.* Washington, D.C.: Association of American Universities, 1986.

Herrnstein, R. "IQ." *Atlantic,* 1971, pp. 43–64.

Jensen, A. R. "How Much Can We Boost IQ and Scholastic Achievement?" *Harvard Educational Review,* 1969, *39,* 1–123.

Jensen, A. R. "Can We and Should We Study Race Differences?" In J. Hellmuth (ed.), *Disadvantaged Child: Compensatory Education, a National Debate* (pp. 124–157). New York: Brunner/Mazel, 1970.

Levine, A., and Associates. *Shaping Higher Education's Future: Demographic Realities and Opportunities, 1990–2000.* San Francisco: Jossey-Bass, 1989.

National Center for Education Statistics, U.S. Department of Education. *Digest of Education Statistics, 1989.* Washington, D.C.: U.S. Government Printing Office, 1989.

National Center for Education Statistics, U.S. Department of Education. *Digest of Education Statistics, 1993.* Washington, D.C.: U.S. Government Printing Office, 1993.

National Research Council. *Survey of Earned Doctorates.* Washington, D.C.: U.S. Government Printing Office, 1988.

National Research Council. *Digest of Education Statistics, 1990. Summary Report. Doctorate Recipients from U.S. Universities.* Washington, D.C.: National Research Council, 1990.

O'Brien, E. M. "American Indians in Higher Education." *Research Briefs* (American Council on Education), 1992, *3*(3).

Rasbery, W. "Working Your Way Through College—After Graduation." *Washington Post,* Feb. 22, 1992, p. A-19.

Reich, R. B. *The Work of Nations: Preparing Ourselves for 21st Century Capitalism.* New York: Knopf, 1991.

Shockley, W. "New Methodology to Reduce the Environment-Heredity Uncertainty About Dysgenics." Paper presented at the National Academy of Sciences, Rice University, Houston, Tex., 1970.

Taylor, H. F. *The IQ Game: A Methodological Inquiry into the Heredity-Environment Controversy.* New Brunswick, N.J.: Rutgers University Press, 1980.

Thurgood, L., and Weinman, J. M. *Summary Report 1990: Doctorate Recipients from United States Universities.* Washington, D.C.: National Academy Press, 1991.

Treisman, U. "Studying Students Studying Calculus: A Look at the Lives of Minority Mathematics Students in College." *College Mathematics Journal,* 1992, *23*(5), 314–316, 318, 320, 322.

Chapter 5

Changing State and Federal Roles in Improving Minority Education

Dewayne Matthews

By all measures, minority students are less well served by the educational system than nonminority students. Levels of academic achievement, high school graduation, and college enrollment are all lower for minority students. This chronic national problem has been well documented in numerous national reports going back over forty years (Quality Education for Minorities Project, 1990).

In an attempt to improve the quality of education for minority students in both K–12 schools and higher education, numerous policy initiatives at both the state and federal levels have been advanced over the past several decades. This chapter reviews the highlights of state and federal policy activity related to minority education from the 1960s to the present. The nature of the policy concerns about minority education has shifted over the decades from a preoccupation with equity to one with performance and quality, driven perhaps by changing economic concerns. Whatever has caused the shift, it is clear that minority education concerns tend to be seen today as a result of perceived shortcomings in the entire educational system.

Likewise, policy makers increasingly look for solutions to

the educational problems of minority students in wholesale change in the educational system. In contrast to the 1960s and 1970s, minority students are less frequently the specific target of policy interventions. This changing nature of the policy environment for minority education, as reflected in current policies for K–12 schools and higher education, is described later in the chapter.

Is it good that concerns about minority education now tend to be subsumed in a broader policy debate about education generally, or has the relative lack of a clear policy focus on minority education weakened progress toward the improvement of education for minority students? A definitive answer to this question is beyond the scope of this chapter; however, it suggests a way to begin to address such questions. The chapter concludes with a discussion of an approach for analyzing the respective roles of various types of state and federal policies related to minority education. The approach suggests that both targeted interventions and more systematic change have their place in improving education for minority students.

State and Federal Policies Toward Minority Education

State and federal policies toward minority education have had an interesting history. The next section examines these policies and their impact on minority students.

The 1960s and 1970s: A Focus on Equity

Federal and state policies to address the problem of education for minority students were first driven by the national movement toward the desegregation of society epitomized by the landmark Supreme Court decision in the case of *Brown* v. *Board of Education* of Topeka, Kansas, in 1954. Through the 1960s and early 1970s, numerous federal programs were enacted that were designed, among other things, to improve the educational performance of minority students. These programs included the landmark provisions of the Elementary and Secondary Education Act of 1964, such as Title VII bilingual education programs.

To understand the effect of these policies, it is necessary to consider the underlying policy assumptions that guided their development. First, the policies were based on a deficit model of minority education. Minority students were assumed to be lacking in the background, skills, motivation, or talent necessary to be successful in school, which accounted for their relative lack of success. This assumption did not necessarily blame the student for the deficits; they were in fact usually seen as the inevitable product of a segregated society. Second, the policies were based on the assumption that a segregated society created numerous barriers to school success, including barriers that were financial, cultural, social, and legal in nature. Minority student success in education was seen as dependent on the elimination of these barriers. Finally, the policies were based on the assumption that local control of education placed the basic managerial and organizational dynamics of schools and colleges beyond the reach of policy makers.

These assumptions determined the development of federal policies toward minority education in both K–12 schools and higher education through the 1960s and most of the 1970s. Title I of the Elementary and Secondary Education Act of 1964 demonstrates the deficit model at work in a program targeted to elementary and secondary schools. The various financial aid programs of the Higher Education Act of 1965 show the barrier reduction strategy directed toward higher education institutions. Both programs reflect the assumption that the underlying organizational structure of educational institutions need not change to accommodate minority students.

Judicial activity remained a significant influence on minority education policy. In 1970, the Supreme Court in the case of *Adams* v. *Richardson* ruled that several states with historically black institutions were practicing de facto discrimination in the way state support was distributed. A number of large metropolitan areas were subjected to court-ordered public school desegregation, including court-ordered busing, during the 1970s and early 1980s. In these and other states where court-mandated desegregation plans were enacted, state policies were driven by the need to implement judicial decisions. Often these policies included such activities as state-level strategic planning, establishment of magnet schools, and funding formula revisions.

The 1980s: The Educational Reform Movement

If the primary educational policy concern of the 1960s and 1970s was equity, all that changed in 1983 with the publication of *A Nation at Risk*. This report, and the attendant publicity it received, contributed to a rising preoccupation with the quality of education received by students in the nation's schools and led to unprecedented policy activity in the states. In the two to three years following the report, most states convened their own task forces or commissions on education and developed special legislation designed to address the perceived shortcomings of the schools. The characteristics of the legislative activity were remarkably similar across the states as news spread about the types of policy initiatives being enacted. This policy activity, especially the legislative packages enacted in the states, is referred to as the *school reform movement*.

The policies enacted during the school reform movement focused almost exclusively on the attempt to improve educational quality through tighter educational standards. A school reform package typically entailed increased graduation requirements (often including a test), teacher competency testing, and a reduction in electives. The reform packages were usually accompanied by additional state financial support for education, frequently targeted specifically to increases in teacher salaries and class-size reductions.

State and federal policies toward higher education also shifted during the 1980s to issues of educational quality, mirroring the concerns of the school reform movement. These policies shifts were often reflected at the state level by a tightening of educational standards for students, both for admission to college and occasionally for advancement to degree status. States also enacted funding initiatives targeted to the improvement of program quality. At the federal level, the changing emphasis was reflected in a softening of commitment to the reduction or elimination of economic barriers to college attendance, as traditionally addressed through financial aid programs, and a reduction in the attention paid to equity issues by the federal court system. These changes were accompanied by an alarming decrease in both minority enrollments and graduation rates over the decade (American Council on Education, 1991).

The jury is still out on the effect of the school reform movement on minority education, but few would argue that the relative condition of minority students improved during the 1980s. The reduction of state and federal commitment to equity in the educational system was never expressly stated, but in fact there are indications that the progress of minority students was halted or reversed during the decade. Between 1986 and 1988, the percentage of whites enrolled in college increased by 4 percent, while that of Hispanics increased by only 1.5 percent. The rate of participation by blacks actually decreased by 1.6 percent in that period. Put another way, between 1976 and 1985, the percentage of black high school graduates entering college declined by 26 percent (Stewart, 1988). The change is even more significant over the ten-period from 1975 to 1985. Over this period, the rates of attendance for blacks and Hispanics declined, while the rate for whites increased (American Council on Education, 1991). The inability to reconcile higher standards of educational quality as traditionally defined and improved equity for minority students is a legacy of the educational reform movement.

The 1990s: The Rise of Economic Concerns

In the late 1980s, the policy environment for education began to shift away from the concerns that had led to the school reform movement. The change was caused by an increasing awareness in the states of the effects of two parallel trends: the fundamental demographic shifts occurring in the United States and concerns about economic competitiveness (Education Commission of the States, 1990; Jennings, 1990; Newman, 1985). The result has been a dawning realization that a much larger percentage of the workforce of the future will be members of minority groups (Hodgkinson, 1985; Wilson, 1990). At the same time, the workplace will be demanding ever-higher levels of skills and educational preparation (Anderson, 1990; Anderson and Meyerson, 1990). This emerging policy perspective was heralded in 1985 by Frank Newman in *Higher Education and the American Resurgence:* "If one considers the forces with which this country must contend over the next decade, it is clear that all segments of society must be drawn into the fullest possible participation" (p. 89).

Policy makers have begun to focus on the fact that minorities are increasing substantially as a proportion of the pool of students for the educational system. The number of blacks in the total population will increase from 26.5 million in 1985 to 44 million in 2020. The number of Hispanics will increase over the same period from 14.7 million to 47 million. As the total population grows from 238 million to over 260 million by 2020, most of the increase will be accounted for by increases in minority populations. The states with the greatest population growth will be those with the greatest ethnic diversity (Hodgkinson, 1985).

As the size of the youth cohort moves from sixty-four million in 1990 to sixty-five million in 2000, the percent of the cohort that is nonwhite will increase from 30 to 38 percent. At the same time that this change is occurring, it is now estimated that fully one-third of all schoolchildren are at risk because of demographic and social trends, such as increasing numbers of poor, single-parent households (Hodgkinson 1991). Since a large proportion of these at-risk youth are minorities, and because their numbers are growing, the challenge for education is obvious.

More state policy makers are concluding that these demands of the educational environment will need to be met by simultaneously increasing the rates of minority student success as measured by high school graduation and college degree attainment (the prerequisite for which is increasing the levels of school and college participation by minorities) while maintaining, or even improving, levels of program quality (Callan, 1988; Education Commission of the States, 1990).

Evolution of Minority Education Policy: Current Issues

As mentioned above, state policy toward public education in the 1980s was dominated by an increased emphasis on educational standards to address a perceived lack of instructional quality.

This emphasis, incorporated in the school reform movement, shifted the attention of states away from issues of educational equity. While some voices were raised that school reform was ignoring large numbers of students (most notably, state and national initiatives related to at-risk youth), school reform generally pushed equity issues off of state policy agendas.

Minority Education and the School Restructuring Agenda

In the aftermath of the school reform movement of the 1980s, state and federal educational policy has shifted toward more fundamental structural change in the educational system. This shift in policy is the result of a general dissatisfaction with the results of school reform (Finn and Rebarber, 1992). In spite of the unprecedented attention paid to educational issues during the 1980s, especially by the states, the most common indicators of educational performance (such as SAT and ACT scores and high school graduation rates) were unchanged or continued their downward slide (Educational Testing Service, 1990).

The emerging educational policy environment views the schools as suffering from an outmoded organizational structure that prevents improvement, avoids accountability, and promotes inefficiency. For the first time, policy makers are less concerned with grafting new programs, mandates, and requirements onto the schools and more concerned with the underlying structure of the schools.

This change in state policy toward elementary and secondary education has been called school restructuring to distinguish it from the earlier school reform movement. School restructuring tends to emphasize the outcomes of the educational system, particularly outcomes related to student learning. Proponents of school restructuring suggest that basing educational policy and practice on their effects on student outcomes will result in fundamental changes in the organizational structure of schools (Peterson, 1992). Restructured schools are characterized by site-based management, teacher empowerment, and a greater emphasis on "higher-order" skills such as abstract reasoning, problem solving, and the ability to function effectively as a member of a group (Murphy, 1992).

One effect of the school restructuring movement has been to increase the attention paid to issues of minority student success in elementary and secondary education. There are several reasons for this shift in attention. Because school restructuring makes much greater use of student outcome data, the persistent high rates of minority high school dropouts and lower-than-expected performance by minority students on measures of student learning have received more attention. Likewise, school restructuring's emphasis on individual student success is coupled with the increased concern of state policy makers about the educational performance of all students rather than merely a stratum of high performers.

As a result of the school restructuring movement, concern about minority education issues has increased. However, progress on minority education issues is increasingly seen as being dependent on changes in the overall system of public education. The perceived need by states to improve the level of success gained by minority students has become one of the primary drivers for change in the entire educational system.

State Initiatives and Minority Higher Education

Because of continuing concerns over issues of equity and growing concerns about economic competitiveness, the success of minority students in higher education is a major policy issue in most states (Callan and Jonsen, 1987; Callan and Finney, 1988; Mingle, 1987; State Higher Education Executive Officers, 1987). For example, many states have raised the issue of minority student success through the appointment of blue-ribbon commissions by governors or state higher education boards (Johnson and Marcus, 1986). This attention has resulted in a variety of initiatives, most of which have been sponsored by state higher education boards. These state initiatives related to minority student success can be classified into four categories: planning, coordination and collaboration (including both K–12 education and community colleges), finance (including funding strategies and tuition and financial aid), and assessment.

Planning. The importance to the states of the issue of minority student success has resulted in an increased emphasis on statewide planning activities by state higher education boards. Planning is a traditional way for state higher education boards, particularly coordinating boards, to develop a consensus of policy makers and institutions to take action (Greer, 1986). Planning has been particularly important in the area of minority student success because of the need to bring together the full range of actors in higher education to take concerted action (Sheheen, 1988). Minority education concerns have been included in overall statewide higher education plans as well as special plans developed specifically to deal with the issue (Callan and Finney, 1988).

Coordination and Collaboration. One of the first state policy initiatives to improve higher education for minority students has been to better coordinate state-level higher education and elementary and secondary school policies (Hines, 1988; Layzell and Lyddon, 1990; Marcus, 1990). These policies depend on a collaboration between the state higher education board and the state board of education for public schools. These state-level policies support such school-college collaboration as the coordination of curricula between high school and college, statewide student recruitment programs, and outreach programs to motivate more public school students to become prepared for college (Justiz, Bjork, and Wilson, 1988). As these forms of collaboration mature, one author has urged them to become "academic alliances" involving higher education faculty and elementary and secondary school teachers in an equal relationship (Stickney, 1990). At the policy level, this recommendation follows the trend of state policy makers to see educational issues as cutting across the traditional boundaries of elementary, secondary, and higher education. Finding solutions to the educational problems of minority students requires policy makers to see education, in Hodgkinson's (1985) phrase, as "all one system."

State policies to promote coordination are also evident in initiatives to promote collaboration between community colleges and universities (Justiz, Bjork, and Wilson, 1988). Since community colleges in some states enroll a disproportionate share of minority students, policies designed to promote transfer from community colleges to universities have a significant effect on minority educational attainment. These policies may include common academic calendars and course articulation agreements to facilitate the transfer of academic credit (Lang and Ford, 1990).

Finance. States have also examined their policies for financing the higher education system to determine their relationship to support for improved educational outcomes for minority students (Millett, 1986). The need to review funding policies results in part from the realization that states are facing increased demands for funding from the higher education system, which must compete with other priorities for scarce state revenues (Chambers, 1987). As a result of the need to do more with less, states are increasingly seeing their budgets as tools for the implementation of public policy priorities. One result of these concerns has been policies to use revenues as an incentive to encourage activities that support state policy goals, including efforts to improve outcomes for minority students.

An example of the emerging view of the state higher education budget as a policy document is the development of categorical competitive grant programs to address the state's policy goals (Kemmerer, 1986). This approach has often been used to encourage institutions to develop programs targeted to improved education for minority students (Marcus, 1990). New Jersey has established a competitive grant program, which has been credited with significant success in encouraging institutions to place a higher priority on improved higher education for minority students (Jaschik, 1986). However, the long-term effectiveness of this approach is unknown. There is a danger that the desire for quick results could limit the time span allowed for overcoming difficult problems and thereby undermine effective action (Layzell and Lyddon, 1990).

Categorical funding is not the only way that funds have been targeted to state policies to improve educational outcomes for minority students. Some states have also tied their base funding for higher education to incentives to accomplish state goals (Cage, 1990). This approach attempts to provide institutions with an incentive to improve education for minority students by including such efforts in the funding base through the regular funding formula. Tennessee is an example of a state that has followed this approach (Marcus, 1990).

As states increasingly consider the effect of funding policies on minority student success, policies regarding tuition and financial aid have been reviewed. States have traditionally funded need-based financial aid programs as a way to support the college attendance of economically disadvantaged students. Many states, particularly those with a history of large public higher education systems, have also traditionally seen the maintenance of low tuition rates as a way to promote access (Fischer, 1990). These policies are now under review in many states as the difficulty of raising revenue for higher education places increased pressure on tuition. Some have suggested that the traditional emphasis on low tuition has acted more as a form of subsidy for middle- and upper-class students than as a support for access by low-income students (Fischer, 1990). The resolution of this issue will have a significant impact on the status of minority students in higher education, but will be very complex. As Ostar (1987, p. 149) has stated, "The issues of equity and opportunity raised in discussing tuition and student financial aid policies relate to broad social policies, not just to higher education finance."

The effect of state higher education finance policies on the educational success of minority students may also come under scrutiny from the court system (McKeown, 1986). Texas has recently faced court action related to the fairness of its funding of the higher education system. More such action could occur as an outgrowth of court reviews of public school funding approaches.

Assessment. Policy makers' perception of the increased importance of higher education in the society and economy has resulted in growing pressures for accountability. The difficulty faced by most states in finding adequate revenues to finance higher education is increasing those pressures (Anderson, 1990). At least partly in response to these pressures, several states have developed policies to promote the assessment of educational outcomes (Astin, 1991). In part, these policies are based on the desire of policy makers for greater accountability from the higher education system (Birnbaum, 1988). These policies differ from past state initiatives that used assessment as a means of screening the suitability of individual students for higher education—a practice found to have a negative effect on minority student success in some states (Richardson, 1991). The emerging policies view assessment as a way to measure institutional effectiveness in meeting the educational needs of students. These policies include the assessment of the educational outcomes of minority students (Justiz, Bjork, and Wilson, 1988). By documenting and quantifying the educational problems of minority students, and by making the success of minority students an issue of institutional effectiveness, these policies have the potential to create significant institutional action to improve their educational effectiveness with minority students (Morante, 1990).

The State Policy Environment for Minority Education

This cursory review of state policy influences on education for minority students makes it clear that separating the issue of improvement of education for minority students from the issue of overall change in the educational system is impossible. Everything that happens in the schools and colleges affects minority students, and anything that undermines the effectiveness of educational institutions disproportionately harms minority students.

However, it is also obvious that targeted initiatives have been successful in improving education for minority students in both the K–12 system and higher education. State policy for the improvement of education for minority students must take into account both special initiatives and the influence of the overall system on minority students. The balance of this chapter describes an approach for understanding the respective roles of special, targeted initiatives and overall system change in promoting the improvement of education for minority students. The approach is based on the description of four phases of policies for minority education. The phases were identified by the author in a recent study of the influence of state policy on higher education institutions (Matthews, 1992). While the study was limited to state policies related to minority students in higher education, the findings may be useful in understanding state policy toward elementary and secondary education as well.

Data on state policy and higher education institutional practice related to minority student participation, retention, and graduation were collected from state higher education boards and four-year degree-granting institutions in ten states. To obtain a representative balance of size, geographic region, governance structures, and student enrollments, the participating states were California, Florida, Illinois, Massachusetts, New Jersey, New Mexico, Ohio, South Carolina, Tennessee, and Texas. A multiple-case study of the ten states examined the relationship between state policy and institutional practices affecting minority students. The case studies show that institutions vary significantly by state, and sometimes dramatically, in their emphasis on particular strategies. Often, these differences are the effect of state policy influences. The analysis led to the identification of four phases of state policy influences on institutional practice affecting minority students: priority setting, program initiation, strategic planning, and consistency of policy. The next sections will describe each of the four state policy phases and their effects on higher education institutions, using examples drawn from the state case studies.

Priority Setting

Several of the state case studies describe how the issue of minority student participation first became significant to state policy. In South Carolina, minority student participation became an important state policy issue because of federal and state mandates to desegregate the higher education system. In New Jersey, the governor and state higher education coordinating board have been active in speaking out on the need for improved higher education outcomes for minority students. In New Mexico, the history of the state and its large proportion of minority residents—reflected in its political structures—have resulted in a long-term concern with minority issues.

State priorities for issues other than improved higher education for minority students can also have significant effects on institutional practices. Florida's state-level emphasis on traditional measures of academic quality has significantly affected the state's higher education system, including outcomes for minority students.

A state priority for improved minority student outcomes can be established in many ways. Public statements from such policy makers as the governor and legislators, policy papers by state coordinating and governing boards, and legislative or court mandates all communicate to higher education institutions that improving higher education for minority students has become a priority of the state.

Establishing a state priority will stimulate an immediate response from institutions but will not, unless followed up by other approaches, result in long-term institutional change. New Mexico, and perhaps Texas, are examples of states where an initial state priority has not resulted in the widespread implementation of effective institutional strategies for minority students. More substantive institutional change requires the presence of other state policy factors.

Program Initiation

After the initial impact of establishing a state priority, the next phase in the development of state policy is usually the implementation of special programs for minority students. The first such programs initiated by states are usually targeted toward increasing the participation of minority students in higher education by reducing barriers to college attendance. An example of program initiation is the extensive student financial aid programs enacted in Ohio. States may also mandate the creation of special admissions categories from the state level or fund remedial and developmental education programs.

Massachusetts is an example of a state that has seen significant state-level initiation of special programs in the areas of minority student outreach and transition. State-level outreach and transition programs have also been created and funded in California.

The initiation of programs from the state level can result in a significant change in the practices of higher education institutions toward minority students. The evidence from several states indicates that the availability of targeted state funding is a powerful inducement to develop programs. However, special programs initiated with targeted funding will not become part of the institutional mainstream and will often suffer when funding becomes tight. The experience of Massachusetts indicates that programs can be jeopardized even after many years of state funding. The phase of program initiation appears, therefore, to be an interim step before ways are found to more fundamentally change higher education institutions.

Strategic Planning

According to the evidence of the state case studies, the next step in the development of state policy for higher education is for states to attempt to change the practices of higher education in more long-term and fundamental ways. This stage in the development of state policy mirrors the stage in the process of institutional adaptation where institutions realize that producing substantive, long-term change in higher education outcomes for minority students requires planned institutional change. Producing a climate at the state level that encourages and allows institutional change requires a state commitment to strategic planning.

Strategic planning activities have been initiated in several of the study states, such as New Mexico and Illinois. It is still too early to tell what the long-term effect of the planning efforts in those states may be. However, in at least two of the study states, strategic planning has been a significant activity at the state level for many years. In those states, the effect of planning on institutional practices can be clearly seen.

The classic example of state planning in higher education is California. The California case study shows that strategic planning has been institutionalized at the state, system, and institutional level and affects all aspects of higher education. California higher education institutions show more evidence of data collection and analysis than other institutions and show a greater emphasis on articulation with community colleges. Both of these practices are related to state-level strategic planning activities.

New Jersey is the best example of a state that has targeted strategic planning directly to the issues of higher education for minority students. The first state plan for minority higher education was developed in 1981 and has been followed by several others. New Jersey's case study indicates that these activities have had a significant effect on higher education institutions.

Consistency of Policy

The last phase of the state policy environment for minority higher education seems to be the one that separates states that have been able to produce long-term institutional changes from those that have not. The conclusion is inescapable from the state case studies that consistency in the state policy environment is necessary for fundamental change to occur.

Policy consistency has two dimensions: consistency across policy actors and consistency across time. The first dimension means that the governor, legislature, and state coordinating and governing boards all act consistently on the issue of minority student outcomes. Consistency is particularly evident when the governor and legislature demonstrate long-term support for coordinating and governing board initiatives to change institutional practices in order to improve higher education outcomes for minority students. The case of New Jersey indicates how effective this consistency across policy actors can be. On the other hand, the case of Texas shows how the lack of engagement by one set of policy actors may undermine otherwise effective state initiatives.

The second dimension of policy consistency is time. Unfortunately, there seems to be no substitute for time in establishing a state policy environment that creates fundamental institutional change. California and New Jersey both show that state-level commitment to a set of policy objectives over a period of years can produce remarkable levels of institutional change. Several state case studies show more recent evidence of the establishment of state-level commitment to improved higher education outcomes for minority students. The ability of these states to convert this state-level policy concern into institutional change will depend on the state sustaining its commitment to a set of policies. The case studies show that consistency in the state policy environment produces results.

Conclusion

It is one thing for states to decide to improve education for minority students; it is quite another thing to actually accomplish it. The actual implementation of state policies determines whether the desired effects will occur. Unfortunately, successful implementation cannot be taken for granted. As McLaughlin (1987, p. 172) summarized: "Perhaps the overarching, obvious conclusion running through empirical research on policy implementation is that it is incredibly hard to make something happen, most especially across layers of government and institutions."

Unfortunately, state educational policy almost always must be implemented "across layers of government and institutions." As a result, finding effective ways to meet the educational needs of minority students is only half the challenge. Finding ways to successfully implement change in schools and colleges is equally important.

The policy phases described above suggest that both targeted initiatives for minority education and broader system change are necessary to improve education for minority students. Unfortunately, the phases suggest that targeted initiatives, in the form of priority setting by policy makers and program initiation, will not cause the more fundamental change in schools and colleges that is ultimately necessary for minority students to succeed at the same rate as other students. Establishing a state or federal policy to improve education for minority students is not enough. The policy must also be implemented by educational institutions, and that depends on more fundamental change.

Effective state policy must promote institutional change that will foster the attainment of desired educational outcomes for minority students (Education Commission of the States, 1990; Richardson, 1991). To do so will require an understanding of two things: the type of institutional change that will foster improved educational outcomes for minority students and the nature of the process through which state policies will actually be implemented by schools and colleges. Strategic planning and policy consistency are examples of how policy makers can begin to create the climate for more fundamental change to occur.

The policy phases outlined in this chapter imply a connection between specific types of state policy and the range of educational strategies related to minority students. The phases suggest that state education policies can be analyzed in terms of the "fit" of state policy to the conditions of schools and colleges in the state and the type of student outcomes desired. Further refinement of the phases could allow for future analysis of the influence of particular policies on specific educational practices to determine the "goodness of fit" of state policy to a particular educational environment.

The full participation and success of minority students in the educational system will depend on fundamental change in the way schools and colleges affect minority students (Richardson, 1991). Effective state and federal policy must promote the type of institutional change that will foster these changes.

References

American Council on Education. *Minorities on Campus: A Handbook for Enhancing Diversity.* Washington, D.C.: American Council on Education, 1991.

Anderson, R. E. "The Economy and Higher Education." In R. E. Anderson and J. W. Meyerson (eds.), *Financing Higher Education in a Global Economy* (pp. 13–40). New York: American Council on Education and Macmillan, 1990.

Anderson, R. E., and Meyerson, J. W. (eds.). *Financing Higher Education in a Global Economy.* New York: American Council on Education/Macmillan, 1990.

Astin, A. W. *Assessment for Excellence: The Philosophy and Practice of Assessment and Evaluation in Higher Education.* New York: American Council on Education/Macmillan, 1991.

Birnbaum, R. "Administrative Commitments and Minority Enrollments: College Presidents' Goals for Quality and Access." *Review of Higher Education,* 1988, *11*(4), 435–457.

Cage, M. C. "Government Officials Urged to Create Incentives for Colleges to Increase Minority Enrollment." *Chronicle of Higher Education,* Dec. 12, 1990, p. 17.

Callan, P. M. "Minority Degree Achievement and the State Policy Environment." *Review of Higher Education,* 1988, *11*(4), 335–364.

Callan, P. M., and Finney, J. E. "State Policy and Minority Achievement in Higher Education." *Peabody Journal of Education,* 1988, *66,* 6–19.

Callan, P. M., and Jonsen, R. W. "Trends in Statewide Planning and Coordination." In L. E. Goodall (ed.), *When Colleges Lobby States: The Higher Education/State Government Connection* (pp. 185–193). Washington, D.C.: American Association of State Colleges and Universities, 1987.

Chambers, M. M. "Long-Term Expectations for Financing Higher Education." In L. E. Goodall (ed.), *When Colleges Lobby States: The Higher Education/State Government Connection* (pp. 123–132). Washington, D.C.: American Association of State Colleges and Universities, 1987.

Education Commission of the States. *Achieving Campus Diversity: Policies for Change.* Report of the National Task Force for Minority Achievement in Higher Education. Denver, Colo.: Education Commission of the States, 1990.

Educational Testing Service. *The Education Reform Decade.* Princeton: Educational Testing Service, 1990.

Finn, C. E., Jr., and Rebarber, T. "The Changing Politics of Education Reform." In C. E. Finn, Jr., and T. Rebarber (eds.), *Education Reform in the '90s* (pp. 175–194). New York: Macmillan, 1992.

Fischer, F. J. "State Financing of Higher Education: A New Look at an Old Problem." *Change,* 1990, *22,* 42–56.

Greer, D. G. "Politics and Higher Education: The Strategy of State-Level Coordination and Policy Implementation." In S. K. Gove and T. M. Stauffer (eds.), *Policy Controversies in Higher Education* (pp. 27–49). New York: Greenwood Press, 1986.

Hines, E. R. *Higher Education and State Governments: Renewed Partnership, Cooperation, or Competition?* Washington, D.C.: Association for the Study of Higher Education, 1988.

Hodgkinson, H. L. "The Changing Face of Tomorrow's Student." *Change,* 1985, *17*(3), 38–39.

Hodgkinson, H. L. "Reform Versus Reality." *Phi Delta Kappan,* 1991, *73*(1), 8–16.

Jaschik, S. "New Jersey Board Will Base Colleges' Budgets Partly on Efforts for Minority Students." *Chronicle of Higher Education,* Apr. 9, 1986, p. 18.

Jennings, J. F. "Economic Competitiveness: The Sputnik of the Eighties." In L. R. Marcus and B. D. Stickney (eds.), *Politics and Policy in the Age of Education* (pp. 4–16). Springfield, Ill.: Thomas, 1990.

Johnson, J. R.-C., and Marcus, L. R. *Blue Ribbon Commissions and Higher Education: Changing Academe from the Outside.* Washington, D.C.: Association for the Study of Higher Education, 1986.

Justiz, M. J., Bjork, L. G., and Wilson, R. "Minority Faculty Opportunities in Higher Education." In M. J. Justiz and L. G. Bjork (eds.), *Higher Education Research and Public Policy* (pp. 109–145). New York: American Council on Education and Macmillan, 1988.

Kemmerer, F. "Higher Education Reform: Recommendations for Research and Practice." In M. P. McKeown and K. Alexander (eds.), *Values in Conflict: Funding Priorities in Higher Education* (pp. 261–282). New York: Ballinger, 1986.

Lang, M. A., and Ford, C. "From Access to Retention: Minority Students in Higher Education." In L. R. Marcus and B. D. Stickney (eds.), *Politics and Policy in the Age of Education* (pp. 111–124). Springfield, Ill.: Thomas, 1990.

Layzell, D. T., and Lyddon, J. W. *Budgeting for Higher Education at the State Level: Enigma, Paradox, and Ritual.* ASHE-ERIC Higher Education Report No. 4. Washington, D.C.: School of Education and Human Development, George Washington University, 1990.

McKeown, M. P. "Funding Formulas." In M. P. McKeown and K. Alexander (eds.), *Values in Conflict: Funding Priorities in Higher Education* (pp. 63–90). New York: Ballinger, 1986.

McLaughlin, M. W. "Learning from Experience: Lessons from Policy Implementation." *Educational Evaluation and Policy Analysis,* 1987, *9*, 171–178.

Marcus, L. R. "Far from the Banks of the Potomac: Educational Politics and Policy in the Reagan Years." In L. R. Marcus and B. D. Stickney (eds.), *Politics and Policy in the Age of Education* (pp. 32–55). Springfield, Ill.: Thomas, 1990.

Matthews, D. "State Policy Influences on Institutions of Higher Education: Promoting Improved Outcomes for Minority Students." Unpublished doctoral dissertation, Arizona State University, 1992.

Millett, J. D. "Trends and Emerging Issues in Funding Priorities for Higher Education." In M. P. McKeown and K. Alexander (eds.), *Values in Conflict: Funding Priorities in Higher Education* (pp. 283–308). New York: Ballinger, 1986.

Mingle, J. *Focus on Minorities: Trends in Higher Education Participation and Success.* Denver, Colo.: Education Commission of the States and State Higher Education Executive Officers, 1987.

Morante, E. A. "Assessing Collegiate Outcomes." In L. R. Marcus and B. D. Stickney (eds.), *Politics and Policy in the Age of Education* (pp. 125–147). Springfield, Ill.: Thomas, 1990.

Murphy, J. "Restructuring America's Schools: An Overview." In C. E. Finn, Jr., and T. Rebarber (eds.), *Education Reform in the '90s* (pp. 3–22). New York: Macmillan, 1992.

National Commission on Excellence in Education. *A Nation at Risk.* Washington, D.C.: National Commission on Excellence in Education, 1983.

Newman, F. *Higher Education and the American Resurgence.* Princeton, N.J.: Carnegie Foundation for the Advancement of Teaching, 1985.

Ostar, A. W. "State Tuition Policies and Public Higher Education." In L. E. Goodall (ed.), *When Colleges Lobby States: The Higher Education/State Government Connection* (pp. 133–149). Washington, D.C.: American Association of State Colleges and Universities, 1987.

Peterson, T. K. "Designing Accountability to Help Reform." In C. E. Finn, Jr., and T. Rebarber (eds.), *Education Reform in the '90s* (pp. 109–132). New York: Macmillan, 1992.

Quality Education for Minorities Project. *Education That Works: An Action Plan for the Education of Minorities.* Cambridge: Massachusetts Institute of Technology, 1990.

Richardson, R. C., Jr. *Promoting Fair College Outcomes: Learning from the Experiences of the Past Decade.* Denver, Colo.: Education Commission of the States, 1991.

Richardson, R. C., Jr., and Skinner, E. F. *Achieving Quality and Diversity: Universities in a Multicultural Society.* New York: American Council on Education and Macmillan, 1991.

Sheheen, F. R. "The Role of State Boards of Higher Education in Influencing Access and Retention of Minorities in Higher Education." *Peabody Journal of Education,* 1988, *66,* 20–31.

State Higher Education Executive Officers. *A Question of Degrees: State Initiatives to Improve Minority Student Achievement.* Denver, Colo.: State Higher Education Executive Officers, 1987.

Stewart, D. M. "Overcoming Barriers to Successful Participation by Minorities." *Review of Higher Education,* 1988, *11*(4), 329–336.

Stickney, B. D. "Empowering Education Through Partnerships." In L. R. Marcus and B. D. Stickney (eds.), *Politics and Policy in the Age of Education* (pp. 149–176). Springfield, Ill.: Thomas, 1990.

Wilson, R. "Democracy and Demography: The Impact of Demographic Change on Educational Policy." In L. R. Marcus and B. D. Stickney (ed.), *Politics and Policy in the Age of Education* (pp. 17–31). Springfield, Ill.: Thomas, 1990.

Restructuring Schools to Foster Minority Student Success

In Part One, we presented an overview of the major issues and challenges confronting schools and colleges, as well as insight into the role of state legislatures and the federal government in providing leadership for the education of poor and minority students. The inextricable link between education and the economy was reviewed as a means of providing an economic imperative to reform schools and colleges. Throughout this book we stress that truly effective reform can only come about when issues are addressed systematically, so that change occurs at each stage of the educational pathway.

Part Two focuses on the first stage of reform: the K–12 system. In Chapter Six, Ruth S. Johnson reviews the institutional conditions that contribute to impoverished academic cultures in schools and argues that new, bold steps should be taken to create the fundamental changes needed to make the K–12 system truly effective for all students.

Next, in Chapter Seven, Vinetta C. Jones and Rochelle Clemson focus on some of the most critical issues that schools need to address: the shortage of minority teachers, creating systemic change, developing effective strategies to help students learn, infusing the curriculum with multicultural perspectives, and determining how to create change.

In Chapter Eight, Jeannie Oakes and Martin Lipton explain the detrimental effects of tracking and testing on both minority and majority children. The authors propose alternatives to create a culture of detracking and enhanced student learning.

Given that minorities are most underrepresented in mathematics and the sciences and that one of the nation's foremost educational goals is to have American students be first in the world in these areas, Beverly J. Anderson explains the need to view mathematics as a "pump" rather than a "filter." Educators often speak of mathematics as critical to minorities. In Chapter Nine, the author outlines the barriers that preclude minority success in math and outlines the important role of schools, professional organizations, the media, government, business and industry, and foundations in promoting mathematics education for minority students.

The school reform literature has asserted the importance of parental involvement, and in Chapter Ten Estrella M. Triana and Shirley M. Malcom outline the need to empower parents and describe the role that existing community organizations can play in assisting parents to become more active in their children's education. The authors also review model programs that highlight parental involvement and strategies to increase parent participation in schools. Among the most neglected cohorts of native-born minorities are American Indians and Alaska Natives.

In the concluding chapter, William G. Demmert, Jr., discusses historical, structural, economic, and social factors that have placed Native children at risk. He underscores the need to address these barriers, in light of the fact that Native children are in danger of losing their distinctive identities. This chapter is essential in view of the unique case of Native peoples, whose education has been even more neglected than that of other American minorities.

Chapter 6

Understanding the Need for Restructuring

Ruth S. Johnson

As a nation, we have never invested systematically in the development of our young people, especially the increasing number who are growing up in poverty. Indeed, even though worldwide economic changes portend the need for higher educational requirements, we have been content with an educational system that systematically underestimates and undereducates vast numbers of poor, African American, Latino, and American Indian children (and many others as well). This results in terrible consequences for these young people and the nation as a whole.

A report from the Mathematical Sciences Education Board (1990, p. 4), describes future challenges: "Jobs requiring mathematical skill are growing at nearly double the rate of overall employment. In the past such jobs have been filled by white males. But by the year 2000 there will not be enough white males trained in mathematics to satisfy workforce demands. Women and minorities must fill these workforce gaps, or the

I would like to thank Kati Haycock, Jessica Levin, and Linda Winfield for their thoughtful comments on the contents of this chapter.

United States will be unable to compete with technologically advanced countries in global markets."

In spite of the reform efforts of the 1980s, a wide achievement gap still exists between white middle-income students and those who are poor, African American, Latino, and American Indian (National Center for Education Statistics, U.S. Department of Education, 1993). Orfield (1988, p. 47) suggests that the reformers of the 1980s operated under faulty assumptions: "They much too simply assumed that whatever would be good for the suburban students would also help their central-city and poor rural counterparts. Too often they ignored the fact that, in a society profoundly fragmented by race and income, policies that work for one type of school may often misfire in or even do harm to other schools. Schools differing in fundamental ways will almost certainly be affected differently by the same policy."

There is good reason for concern about whether current efforts to "restructure" American schools will produce the results we need among the emerging majority of this country, most of whom are being undereducated in our nation's schools. In this chapter I address some major concerns about typical approaches to restructuring, focusing on why they rarely create fundamental changes in student achievement for poor, racially and ethnically different children. I then propose some alternative notions about restructuring that call for profound systemic change, with deliberate attention to six key elements of schools and schooling.

I pay particular attention to the need to assist urban schools in moving away from the current programmatic approach, with its series of discrete stacked-on activities and events, to a coherent systemic approach focused on teaching all students to high levels of achievement. The latter approach requires fundamental changes in institutional policies, practices, and values—changes that can markedly increase the capacity of both the *students* and the *adults* in schools to learn at high levels (Johnson, 1994).

Based on my work and that of others with inner-city schools, I offer alternative ways of thinking about change in the urban environment. Much of the work has been done through the California-based Achievement Council. Founded in 1984 by a cross section of citizen leaders and educators concerned about the dismal educational outcomes of African American, Latino, and poor students in public schools, the council's goal is to achieve long-term systemic change in the school environment in order to dramatically improve learning outcomes for these students. The council's role is one of providing technical assistance to schools, facilitating the change process, serving as a resource connector, and monitoring progress toward the achievement of the designated educational outcomes.

Current Approaches to Restructuring

Many current approaches to restructuring focus on symbolic rather than fundamental changes in underlying assumptions about children's capacity to learn. Some of the normal demands we hear are for:

1. More "authority" to the school building level
2. Greater community governance
3. Special-focus curricula
4. Program rather than educational outcomes

The approaches usually reflect:

1. Limited focus on the district context
2. Limited focus on student achievement
3. No recognition that all students have the capacity to learn
4. Little understanding of and attention to the skills needed to initiate, implement, and institutionalize high-level learning in schools with diverse student populations

Those dissatisfied with current school outcomes seek quick fixes and superficial approaches to change. Single-focus proposals such as choice, charter schools, and single school efforts fall short of uprooting school and district current policy and practices. Johnson (1994, p. 19) argues that the issue is not whether a particular program or project is good or bad. The concern is about the prevalence of a one-dimensional approach to restructuring that acts as gatekeeper to "1) an intensive analy-

sis of institutional policies and practices related to student outcomes and 2) the development and implementation of a set of
coherent strategies and assessment processes throughout the system to make high student achievement a reality."

What Needs to Change: A Profile
of an Urban Elementary School

The following description of an urban elementary school highlights the deep impact of the district's and school's institutional
culture on student achievement outcomes.

School X is located in an inner-city neighborhood. Outside its walls a community exists where most of the residents
are poor. At one time it was a thriving community with many
wage earners. Because of a decline in jobs and some middle-
income residents moving out, the nature of the community has
changed.

Most community members rent their homes or apartments.
Homes range from those that are well maintained (many inhab-
ited by older homeowners who have chosen to remain) to others
that are dilapidated from lack of repair. There are also buildings
that have been abandoned. The teachers and administrators who
work in School X do not live in the neighborhood near the
school, although many of the paraprofessionals do.

On the way to school, the children walk by three liquor
stores and two mom-and-pop grocery stores where residents
buy high-priced groceries because there is no major supermar-
ket. The children see a variety of representations on buildings
walls. Some have colorful images of the community painted by
local artists. Others are covered with gang graffiti. They also
walk by churches; some are storefront, others have more traditional edifices.

Along the route to school, the children notice groups of
the unemployed and the homeless. The children may be greet-
ed as "little man" or "homeboy" by gang members displaying the
latest clothes fashions, gold jewelry, and an expensive car. Mothers escorting their children to school hold their hands tightly
and walk quickly.

As we watch these future adults of the twenty-first century

in this inner-city school, we see a rich ethnic mixture of Africans Americans, Asians, Latinos, American Indians, and Pacific Islanders. We hear a variety of languages. These children will spend the weekends and summers in their community with virtually no organized activities for them to do. There are no recreational facilities for young people. However, some community-based organizations are attempting to address this and other needs in the community, but they have limited funding.

As the children approach their school, security aides are at the gates with walkie-talkies. The school building that they enter is fairly well maintained. Most of the children are neatly dressed and well behaved, although there has been some conversation among teachers in the past few years about the children who are drug babies and out of control.

Teachers in this school talk a lot about how to discipline and control the children, and they have had staff development on classroom management. In the lunchroom, teachers typically talk about the poor working conditions, the lack of parental involvement, the children's poor attitude toward learning, and their lack of motivation to learn. Little if any time is spent talking about ways to fundamentally improve teaching and learning. About 50 percent of the staff have had less than five years teaching experience. Even the principal has been at this school for less than two years. The school has had four different principals in the past seven years. The last principal was beginning to get the staff to focus on student achievement, but the district office felt she was needed at another school that "needed to be cleaned up."

The standardized test results reveal that most children in School X achieve at very low levels, particularly the African American, Latino, and American Indian students. The school receives extra dollars because of the low test scores and the low income of the neighborhood. Funding is provided to help children whose primary language is other than English. There are more than fifteen special programs and projects to address different needs, but it is hard to find evidence on which, if any, is making a big difference in how the students achieve. There is no rigorous analysis of the impact of these efforts on student outcomes over the short or long term.

As we walk through the school, we see children moving in and out of classrooms to attend special programs. Our observations indicate that there are inconsistent approaches in how the teachers teach from program to program and from grade level to grade level. Children may be exposed to several different approaches to reading during their school careers. Students with learning problems in reading and math are often taught by paraprofessionals.

On the whole, the staff believe that the income levels and the children's families are the cause of these low achievement results. The staff think they are doing the best they can. What else can be expected under such circumstances? They have tried many different programs, but the children just have not learned.

A few staff members, however, feel that things could be better. But they do not have an inkling as to where to begin, and they are fearful of talking to others lest they be derided. Some feel it is useless to even try because they have been rebuffed in the past, both by their colleagues and by administrators. They are isolated in the school and in their classrooms.

The district mandates most of the staff development topics for the school year. During the last two years the staff have had three two-hour sessions on classroom management, a half-day workshop on stress management, and two hour-long sessions on cooperative learning. The district inservices are mandatory for all schools. The school can schedule its own staff development, but there is little funding to initiate or sustain it.

The principal does not allow any deviation from district mandates and does not question the rationality of these decisions at routine principals' meetings. The district culture does not encourage critical thinking and problem solving. Principals are supposed to know how to solve school-site problems. Asking for help is a sign of weakness. Risk taking is not encouraged.

For the most part, no one demands that things really change for the children. Low achievement has become an acceptable and unquestioned norm. The systemic pattern of low expectations and poor instructional strategies are set in motion beginning in kindergarten. This will follow the students into the upper grades. Most of the other schools in the system operate in the same way. The children are not viewed as high-status learners or "college material."

The "educational pipeline" for students from School X ruptures at several locations. Some of the students make it through, but all too many of the new majority students spill out of the educational system into lives that provide few choices for a high-quality life. In spite of these dismal outcomes, the staff at School X continue to do "business as usual."

Why Most Approaches Don't Work

Although it is widely recognized that major factors outside of school affect the quality of children's lives, fundamental changes in the levels of student achievement cannot wait until all of these factors are ameliorated or eliminated. To wait would be to ignore the schools' and districts' contribution to the low levels of learning. When we step back from School X, it is clear that there are institutional conditions independent of external factors that contribute to its impoverished academic culture. These conditions include a highly bureaucratic school and district culture, fragmentation of efforts, abdication of responsibility for student learning, low expectations, low-level curriculum and instructional practices, and inadequate professional development.

Bureaucratic Culture

Bureaucracies are characterized as impenetrable and extremely difficult to change. Urban schools have crafted these bureaucratic systems to a fine art. The final product displays a set of largely impersonal, isolated, hierarchichal routines and events that are unresponsive to the adults who implement them and the children and the families they ostensibly serve. Educational issues about teaching and learning take a backseat to record keeping, compliance, and daily routine tasks (Haberman, 1991; Sarason, 1990). Darling-Hammond (1990, p. 294) suggest that "the system might work if students were car doors to be assembled."

Fragmentation of Efforts

Another factor contributing to institutional inertia is fragmentation of efforts. School X and many urban schools have myriad categorical and other special programs for students, ranging from programs for those whose first language is not English to programs for others with learning disabilities to programs addressing broad societal issues such as human and race relations. Many separate administrative structures exist to regulate these programs. The administrative infrastructures often create practices and polices that weaken their effect on student learning. Winfield, Johnson, and Manning (1993, p. 118) describe the impact of all of these separate programs on student learning:

> Over time, formal regulations and informal practices have built invisible walls around each program. These perceived walls inhibit collaboration at both the program and school level. The absence of communication, coordination, and a common instructional philosophy have resulted in fragmentation and a lower quality instructional program. Oddly, these programs may assist in perpetuating and exacerbating the very achievement patterns they were intended to eliminate. In many instances these program structures create rigid remedial tracks and groupings which lock students into low level learning for their entire school career.

My experiences lead me to believe that unless these kinds of ingrained practices are dismantled, new restructuring efforts will be implemented as add-on programs rather than as fundamental systemic changes.

Abdication of Responsibility for Student Learning
With this fragmentation of efforts, the responsibility and accountability for the child's education becomes elusive. Little coordination of instructional efforts occurs, and the student's opportunity to learn high levels of knowledge is limited or totally eliminated. The deficits of the core educational program are rarely recognized or analyzed (Winfield, 1986). Regular classroom teachers may abdicate their responsibility to teach the child, particularly when children are in pull-out programs for their major academic subjects. Many of these programs, which are rooted in a "fix-the-child" mentality, encourage low expecta-

tions and flawed belief systems about what students are capable of achieving. A "What more can you expect? We are doing all we can" attitude is expressed through behaviors or words and permeates the K–12 pipeline.

Low-Level Curriculum and Instructional Practices

In schools where routines and practices are rarely questioned, profound thinking about the implications of practice for student life outcomes is nonexistent. Teachers in School X do not analyze practice. The pervasive systemic practices of tracking that result in low expectations for achievement rest not only on how learning opportunities are structured, but, more important, on the daily level and content of the curriculum and the teachers' instructional skills. Low expectations, low-level work, low-level responses, and inconsistencies from grade to grade and group to group communicate negative messages to children about how and what they are expected to achieve (Braddock, 1990; Oakes, 1985, 1992).

Urban schools' learning environments are characterized by what Haberman (1991) describes as the "pedagogy of poverty." This pedagogy results in a classroom focused on a series of acts oriented toward low-level skills, rather than a pedagogy that will result in high-level thinking. Teachers, parents, and students become acclimated to this pedagogy, and it becomes an unquestioned practice.

The vast majority of public schools in this country reflect "mainstream" American cultural values. These values are usually implicit—a part of the school's hidden curriculum—and are deeply embedded in the school's culture. These values exert a powerful influence in defining "intelligence" and acceptable learning behaviors in the classroom.

Students whose cognitive patterns fit this mainstream model do well academically. Teachers are familiar and comfortable with these learning styles, because they grew up with this model in school and in college. Therefore, they reward students who follow the same path. But if educators work in ethnically diverse communities in which their students reflect a broad range of learning styles and intelligences, these heretofore accepted norms may not be broad enough to incorporate the performance of students who are culturally different (Sleeter and Grant, 1991). Without an awareness of these norms and the organizational structures that reinforce them, it is not surprising that so many of these students fall through the cracks and fail. Even less surprising is the lack of consensus about how to address the current educational inequities or how to identify the outcomes to measure success (Winfield and Woodard, 1994).

The perceived academic ability of some children is linked to their economic status and their culture. These perceptions are rooted in faulty assumptions about their capacity to learn high level curricula. Hilliard (1991, p. 34) describes how these faulty assumptions play themselves out in schools:

> We have maintained historical commitment to the same paradigm that we had when public school education began in the U.S., ascribing genius to a select few. We have embraced a related prediction paradigm that tells us that the major task of assessment professionals is to forecast future performance, not to assist with problem solving in teaching and learning. We have continued to embrace the tracking paradigm. Even when children have been untracked organizationally, in our minds they remain "gifted," "average," and "retarded." Otherwise our national achievement results would leave us with a greater sense of urgency than we now manifest.

How teachers are assigned to different groups and/or tracks is another practice that affects which students will be exposed to high-quality curricula. Teachers who are newer and those with less academic qualifications are given the lower-track classes or assigned to remedial programs. These teachers become tracked and are isolated from knowledge about the higher-level curricula and effective instructional strategies. Some schools assign paraprofessionals to teach remedial students. In secondary schools, high status is attached to those who teach the higher-track courses. These teachers are ostensibly the "best" teachers because they teach the so-called "best students" (Oakes, 1992; Winfield, Johnson, and Manning, 1993).

Inadequate Professional Development

Policies and practices relating to adult learning often use the wrong paradigm. Typical staff development models provide inadequate levels of knowledge and/or continuous feedback and practice while teachers are learning new content and instructional skills. As a result, curriculum delivery and expectations for teachers and students are negatively affected.

Cohen (1990) observed that teachers' lack of knowledge about the complexities of changing practices affects their understanding about their need to grow. Without knowledge and guidance, teachers may feel that they have revolutionized practices when they have simply introduced new materials or a new methodology. Cohen (1990, p. 45) states: "If Mrs. O's past affected the changes in her practice, it also affected how she saw them. I asked where her math teaching stood. She thought that her revolution was over. Her teaching had changed definitively. She had arrived at the other shore. In response to further queries, Mrs. O evinced no sense that there were areas in her math teaching that needed improvement. Nor did she seem to want guidance about how well she was doing or how far she had come."

Teachers are often uncomfortable about taking risks and trying new ways, when they do acquire new knowledge. This fear emanates from a lack of genuine encouragement and support (Goodlad, 1990; Lortie, 1975; Rosenholtz, 1989).

The overall effect of the above conditions—bureaucratic cultures, fragmentation of efforts, abdication of responsibility for the students' learning, low level curriculum and instructional practices, and inadequate professional development—are powerful, pervasive contributors to inhibiting fundamental change in the academic culture of schools—particularly urban schools with majority populations of minority and poor students. Knowing this, then, what are the implications for change?

Alternative Notions on Restructuring

If the real goal for the twenty-first century is high educational attainment for all children, schools and districts must take bold steps to create fundamental changes. These must be changes that systemically create institutional cultures fostering high expectations that result in high levels of learning for both adults and children.

Currently, slogans such as "All children can learn" are echoed by many educators. Unfortunately, if we probed further, many of these educators would likely have differential belief systems related to the possible levels of achievement and the race or ethnicity and gender of the child. Hilliard (1991, p. 36) argues that: "To restructure we must first look deeply at the goals that we set for our children and the beliefs that we have about them. Once we are on the right track there, then we must turn our attention to delivery systems, as we have begun to do. Untracking is right. Mainstreaming is right. Decentralization is right. Cooperative learning is right. Technology access for all is right. Multiculturalism is right. But none of these approaches or strategies will mean anything if the fundamental belief system does not fit the new structures that are being created."

Educators must have clarity of purpose. Schools and school districts must focus on educational practices that give *all students* an opportunity to compete at high levels in a global society. This requires leaders of change to abandon the quick-fix mentality and to gain the conceptual and practical knowledge needed to change their institutional cultures. It is essential for leaders of change to understand the complexities, time demands, frustrations, and hard work needed to change. They also must believe that the rewards are worth it.

To achieve systemic, fundamental changes, I propose that the basic character of schools and districts must be changed by transforming knowledge and practices, reconceptualizing how professionals work, reforming curriculum and instruction, reconceptualizing the support needs of students, revising how changes are implemented, and monitoring change and redefining the reward system. I do not offer an add-on program, but what I consider the essential elements needed for fundamental restructuring. These six elements should not be viewed as separate and linear, but as interactive and dynamic.

Transforming Knowledge and Practices
To build a community of adult learners who believe that racial

and ethnic minorities can achieve at the highest levels, professional educators need critically important knowledge that enables them to analyze school practices and their own behaviors, assess how those practices and behaviors contribute to patterns of high and low underachievement, and discover that old practices can be replaced with new practices that work for both educators and students.

When school communities work from rich knowledge bases, understandings evolve about why expectations for teaching and learning must be raised, why systemic practices such as ability grouping and tracking that perpetuate and exacerbate underachievement must be dismantled, why roles and relationships need to be altered, and why the nature of curriculum and instruction must change. Hilliard (1991, p. 35) argues:

> The restructuring that educators need to do, then, is much more a matter of theory, philosophy, perception, conception, assumptions, and models than it is a matter of rearranging the technical and logistical chairs on the educational *Titanic*. . . . Deep restructuring is a matter of drawing up an appropriate vision of human potential, of the design of human institutions, of the creation of a professional work environment, of the linkage of school activities and community directions, of creating human bonds in the operation of appropriate socialization activities, and of aiming for the stars for the children and for ourselves academically and socially.

In our work in California, we have learned that merely telling teachers and other educators that all kids are capable results in little fundamental changes in schools and classrooms. Since teachers have been socialized and educated to operate from a different set of beliefs and values, they must be provided with compelling evidence and experiences that uproot faulty beliefs and assumptions. They also need the opportunity to practice new strategies. We also learned that to dispel myths about who can learn, teachers and other professionals must learn much more about learning and intelligence. These experiences, for example, should include: (1) the implications for teaching and learning based on research about the similarities of intellectual capabilities across cultures, (2) current knowledge about multiple intelligences and the implications for teaching and learning (Gardner, 1983), (3) information and interactions with other professionals—administrators and teachers—who have successfully shattered the status quo by dramatically raising the academic achievement patterns of racial and ethnic minority students (Comer, 1987; Haycock and Navarro, 1988; Mathews, 1988), (4) the historical and societal context from which many debilitating policies and practices emanated (Hilliard, 1991; Howard, 1991; Oakes, 1985), and (5) what it takes to change schools (Fullan, 1992; Sarason, 1982, 1990).

Professionalism must reach new heights and be anchored in knowledge from a variety of sources—professional literature, practitioners in the field, and experts, including educators and others at the school sites who are engaged in the change process. Along with this rich content, professionals will need ongoing structures (discussed in the next section) to engage in discussions about how to use this knowledge to create the needed changes.

Reconceptualizing How Professionals Work

High levels of achievement are more likely to occur in healthy learning environments. Altering power bases and roles and changing interaction patterns creates the potential for changing the organizational culture. In my work with schools, this involves addressing at least the following dimensions: adult interaction patterns, opportunity structures for rich dialogue, and changes in the decision-making process.

Adult Interaction Patterns. Sarason (1982, 1990) argues that the behavioral regularities or norms and practices must be altered for meaningful changes to be implemented and institutionalized. For example, roles and responsibilities and changes in the locus of control must be addressed. This requires, in many instances, painful but necessary changes (Sizer, 1991). Teachers and administrators who have been working in isolation or at odds must come together around a common focus—student learning. Walls of isolation built up over time by the creation of departmental and administrative program structures must be dismantled. Teachers must assume leadership roles in making decisions about conditions that affect teaching and learning. Networking about teaching and learning must become a common practice.

As principals and other administrators change roles, they will need support and guidance in how to implement fundamental changes. One inner-city school principal has described the impact of support:

> I never would have thought to meet with a group of teachers to plan change in my school. Nothing in my training prepared me to do that. Principals' meetings are gripe sessions, or we talk about operations. The focus on student achievement and the assistance of an outside person helped bring me back to the purpose of why I came into the profession. Now there is a focus on instruction. I didn't know how I was going to change the school. In my first year I was going from one day to the next. [The assistance] helped me to develop ways to look outside of the paradigm and free up ways to develop teachers.

Central offices also need to change their norms and practices. There is a need to transform the rigid, hierarchical mentality to one that supports, inspires, and guides the restructuring process. More than likely, central office administrators' power bases will be shaken or dismantled. These professionals will need professional development to prepare them for new roles and responsibilities such as opportunities for in depth dialogue and changes in the decision-making process. These areas have been largely ignored in the restructuring literature.

Opportunity Structures for Rich Dialogue. If the staff are to view student achievement and school functioning as its responsibility, consistent regularly scheduled opportunities that allow for in-depth dialogue must be provided. The content of the discussions must center on sharing knowledge and problem-solving techniques so that rich teaching and learning can be implemented for all youngsters.

Our experience in urban schools supports Hilliard's (1991) observations that when given quality opportunities, the untapped genius of teachers is awakened and they are able to create substantially higher-level learning. This occurs because they are involved in more qualitative types of growth experiences and expectations. Their capacity to learn and grow is high. The majority of these experiences are designed and led by teachers. It seems hypocritical to ask teachers to implement fundamentally different learning environments when they work in climates that cripple their capacity to change in meaningful ways. Hilliard (1991, p. 36) aptly describes what is needed:

> Teachers need their own intellectual and emotional hunger to be fed. They need to experience the joy of collaborative discussion, dialogue, critique, and research. An enriched academic foundation is definitely a prerequisite for an enriched pedagogical foundation, and together the two provide a level of comfort for the teacher who supports professional dialogue as well as teacher student dialogue. The primary roles that the teacher ought to play in service to children are enhanced by the development of the teacher's intellectual power and professional socialization.

Time is an essential resource that must be provided to accomplish this rich dialogue (National Education Commission on Time and Learning, 1994). This factor will be discussed further in the implementation section of this chapter.

Changes in the Decision-Making Process. Schlechty (1990) suggests that we look carefully at the nature of the decision-making process. He cautions that involvement may make teachers happier but may not result in better outcomes for students if the involvement is not focused on learning outcomes. Professional contributions to decision making should be based on substantive information about ways to improve practice and assess school and classroom outcomes. Decision makers will have to constantly assess whether the process is promoting fundamental change or just creating another bureaucratic structure. New skills in how to facilitate decision making are required. Some of the skills needed are in the areas of problem solving, conflict resolution, and conducting meetings.

Reforming Curriculum and Instruction

Restructured schools should have (1) a well-articulated curriculum with (2) high standards and (3) an emphasis on the learner.

Well-Articulated Curriculum. In a school with a rich and well-defined curriculum, the teachers within and across grade levels and subjects must know and understand what they are expected to teach and how it relates to the broader educational outcomes of the school. Lessons must be aligned with the curriculum. It is systemically articulated that students are expected to learn a high-level problem-solving curriculum. Rich, integrated knowledge, where students make connections, is an educational outcome from a well-articulated curriculum.

High Standards. All children need to have the opportunity to learn high-level knowledge and skills that will enable them to compete in the twenty-first century. Remedial curricula should be eliminated (Levin and Hopfenberg, 1991). The curricula need to reflect the national and state content standards defining what children should know and be able to do.

The curriculum must be multicultural. This requires a fundamental change in the ways the school views itself and a curriculum that is restructured rather than added on. This is accomplished when students are empowered to view concepts, themes, and problems from several ethnic perspectives. Available instructional resources maximize the fit between programs and student learning regardless of race, ethnic group, or gender (Winfield, Johnson, and Manning, 1993; Sleeter, 1991).

Emphasis on the Learner. By emphasizing the learner, lesson plans are developed in response to how to best teach children. Expectations for success are evident. Students are taught at and above grade level using a variety of approaches to accommodate their learning differences. Students are pushed toward higher-order thinking. Instructional strategies such as cooperative learning are responsive to cultural learning styles and are powerful influences on learning the curriculum (Sapon-Shevin and Schniedewind, 1991). Teachers must focus on key educational outcomes and refine their lessons using a variety of approaches to meet diverse student needs.

Reconceptualizing the Support Needs of Students

Reconceptualizing support needs of students involves shifting from fragmented, isolated activities to coherently integrated support systems that engage schools, parents, neighborhoods, the religious and business communities, and higher education.

Support services inside and outside the school community must be personalized around real instructional and affective needs of students. Reformers must dismantle inadequate programs that creat "second systems" for students not succeeding in mainstream educational environments (Wang, Reynolds, and Walberg, 1988). Students should be assisted in becoming successful regardless of their backgrounds.

Within schools, support systems must be oriented toward student learning. This involves support to learn high levels of knowledge rather than "watered-down" versions usually offered in pull-out programs or tracks. A reconceptualization involves the reallocation of resources—including money, time, and people—to (1) reteach teachers, counselors, and other support staff to be more effective with all students, regardless of their background; (2) provide students with sustained additional time on tasks, either at school or in the community; and (3) concentrate efforts and resources at the early childhood level and/or at entry grades at each school level, such as the ninth grade in a four-year high school.

Some districts and schools are exploring the integration of social services to address the other needs, such as health needs, that affect the well-being of children (Comer, 1987). Students also must be supported by their parents and or other significant adults. Meaningful engagement of parents as full partners requires fundamental shifts in thinking, interaction patterns, and role changes as well as heightened expectations by school personnel and parents (Comer, 1987; Epstein, 1990). We must eliminate practices that simply tack parents and community members onto existing committee structures dominated by an "educators-only" agenda. Collaborative efforts must embody the notion that all have equal status in defining the problems, designing the strategies, and evaluating the results.

The success of support systems for students must be measured by how well they produce enhanced learning opportunities and outcomes. Educational results rather than compliance should be measured.

Revising How Changes Are Implemented

In a school with a 100 percent African American and Latino student body, teachers are meeting during their planning time to discuss the implementation of the new math curriculum. The school is involved in schoolwide improvement. Teachers are worried about how to find time to implement the new strategies they have just learned about in a recent after-school inservice. Their plates are too full. They cannot make sense of all the new information and are not sure how to incorporate this new knowledge into an already full day. They are feeling frustrated and unsuccessful and are searching for answers. Some of the comments the teachers make:

I feel that the activities are too disjointed.

I have not had time to learn the new skills.

I want a framework; I'm not sure where and when new curriculum fits into thematic units.

I want more hands-on.

I want to see, talk about, and share ideas, with other teachers.

There is the pervasive concern and fear about the student test and accountability. "How do these new strategies fit with the test?" "What if the test scores go down?"

These remarks reflect the frustrations and doubts that teachers experience when they are expected to instantly implement new strategies for which they feel unprepared. Implementing deep-level changes necessitates an understanding of the change process, time, leadership, and at times external assistance.

Change. Fullan and Stiegelbauer (1991, p. xiv) aptly states, "It isn't that people resist change as much as they don't know how to cope with it." The best-intended efforts to implement fundamental changes in the academic culture, if made without understanding resistance, authority, and control issues as well as the complexity of skills and hard work needed over time, are doomed (Elmore, 1987; Fullan, 1992; Sarason, 1982, 1990). Change agents need knowledge of organizational change and of the unique issues related to changing the behavior of professionals in schools and districts. Powerful norms and practices that have built up over time cannot be eliminated by mandates and two-hour inservices.

The staff will need to be guided skillfully in assessing the academic culture and identifying which practices are perpetuating low achievement. New ideas will need to be tried out, monitored, revised. The environment will need to be free of fear so that teachers and administrators can try new practices.

Changing institutional priorities may require integration or the possible elimination of some programs. An analysis of existing improvement efforts may reveal practices that focus on allocating positions in order to maintain the adult status quo. There may be no link to improved student outcomes.

Time. The National Education Commission on Time and Learning (1994, p. 10) suggests that "both learners and teachers need more time—not to do more of the same, but to use all time in new, different, and better ways." Professionals need uninterrupted time to analyze and reflect on conditions affecting both adult and student achievement. Providing time to create deep-level change will probably require reorganization and possibly extension of the school day and/or year to provide teachers with collaborative planning time on an ongoing basis. It may also be necessary to reallocate the current use of time in faculty meetings, to release teachers during the school day, and to provide staff retreats for intensive work on change. For instance, the nature of faculty meetings should change from discussing administrative trivia to having teachers experience the power and synergy of learning in cooperative groups about teaching and learning and engaging in rich dialogue about the results of new practices. Previously mundane meetings can become forums to empower teachers in change.

Leadership. Since 1985, my work and that of others with the California Achievement Council has focused on the development of leadership teams to design strategies for schoolwide changes in student achievement. This is a critical element in a comprehensive strategy that moves professionals away from isolation to collaboration around common issues. The principal and other key members of the school community intensively engage in a "bottom-up" process of change. The process begins with the team spending several days in a retreat setting. Within this framework, the emphasis is on "ownership" of the restructured learning environment by its key stakeholders. The school teams help in the initiation, implementation, and institutionalization of changes that affect student achievement. Maeroff (1993, p. 514) suggests that "if elementary and secondary education are to improve, the school community has to learn how to look at itself, make judgements, and figure out how to get the educational train running on the right set of track. Seldom are teachers or principals equipped to take these steps without an intervention of some sort. Team building and all that it represents can be that intervention."

Leadership team(s) can be instrumental in establishing the validity of the process and moving the focus from "fixing" the student to looking at institutional changes, forging a consistent schoolwide philosophy, and helping in the implementation and monitoring of the change. Many schools have developed teams that focus on both schoolwide issues of practice and on classroom issues of practice. Teacher-leader clusters focus on improving classroom curriculum and instruction. Leadership becomes collective throughout the school.

Some words of caution, however, are needed. We have found that leadership teams must make a special effort not to become elitist or to be viewed as an extension of the principal. Leadership teams must function to help make fundamental changes a reality—they should not be self-serving entities for the individuals involved. The role of the team should be clearly defined and monitored by the team and the larger school community. Membership must not be static.

Outside Assistance. To build capacity for fundamental systemic changes, schools and districts may benefit from the assistance of external change agents such as the California Achievement Council. These change agents can act as coaches to assist in developing the skills needed for long-term systemic change of the school culture, monitoring the change process, providing ongoing feedback to keep the institutions focused on student outcomes, and identifying and harnessing resources for change.

Monitoring Change and Redefining the Reward System

While schools and districts are being urged or mandated to engage in deep restructuring, the major criterion for improvement continues to be the standardized basic skills and competency tests. This type of reward structure works against implementing practices that require time for schools to reflect on and engage in changing institutional cultures of underachievement (Fullan, 1992; Hilliard, 1991; Johnson, 1994; Winfield and Woodard, 1994). Rewards systems need to be expanded and linked to efforts that change practice.

Current tests gear the curricula of schools to rote types of teaching and do not encourage higher-level learning (Madaus and others, 1992). Darling-Hammond (1990, pp. 291–292) describes the power of testing and its stronghold on schools:

> The power of testing is in large part the result of the increasing use of test scores as arbiters of administrative decisions in American schools. To avoid having to struggle with more complex and valid assessments of student, teacher, or school performance, policy makers and administrators have begun to use standardized test scores to determine student promotion and graduation, to decide class or track placement, to evaluate teacher competence and school quality, and to allocate reward and sanctions. Evidence from many studies demonstrates that, when such high stakes are attached to scores, tests can be expected to exert a strong influence on "What is taught, how it is taught, what pupils study, how they study, and what they learn."

The reauthorization of the Elementary and Secondary Act

(formerly known as Chapter 1) as the Improving America's Schools Act of 1994 (IASA) offers new hope for changes in assessment practices. The intent is to link performance-based assessment and accountability to content and performance standards. In spite of this encouraging news, we cannot be so naive to believe that this is the only step needed to change deeply rooted practices. Winfield and Woodard (1994) offer some compelling challenges to the notion that changes in types assessment will address issues of equity:

> The last three decades of testing have not led to dramatic improvements in the education system, particularly for students in financially strapped urban districts. Newer types of assessments are promising as measures of how student learn; however, the use of such tests as a policy tool carries certain risks. . . . Changes in national standards and assessments are not the necessary conditions for improving student and school achievement. Policies and practices that directly address conditions of current inequities in opportunities to learn at the school, district, and state levels have a great probability of improving school learning and achievement. . . . Only when policymakers consider the opportunity to learn standards as important as implementing national standards and assessment will we ensure that those students and individuals historically disenfranchised will share in the American dream of opportunity for educational achievement and economic success [p. 22].

District personnel must play a major role in providing support and encouragement. When principals and teachers are initiating new practices, test scores may fluctuate. Central administrators can be key in assisting in developing and designing alternative measures.

To develop indicators of change in addition to test scores, school professionals must learn how to use the rich sources of qualitative and quantitative data at their disposal. They are in the habit of gathering and reporting data for use by central administration or outside sources. Limited or no use is made of data to monitor ongoing improvements and to make midcourse corrections. I propose that, in addition to test scores, schools and districts develop process indicators of change. Porter (1991, p. 13) gives three motivations for creating process indicators:

> One is purely descriptive. Schools provide educational opportunity; they do not directly produce student learning. It is important to know, therefore, about the nature of educational opportunity as a direct policy output of schools. . . . A second motivation is to have indicators of school processes that serve as an evaluation instrument in monitoring school reform. Indicators of school processes can serve as an evaluation instrument in monitoring school reform. . . . A third motivation for indicators of school processes is to provide explanatory information when student output goals are not reached. School process indicators may point to possible causes and, thus, to possible solutions for inadequacies in school outputs.

He argues that "the descriptive questions of interest concern issues of amount, quality, and distribution of education. Do children from poor families have the same opportunity in school to learn high order thinking and problem solving as do children from affluent families?" (p. 14).

It is essential to measure progress in the six areas I have addressed in this chapter. Measuring the degree of these changes over time will indicate how well the academic culture of the school is changing. The development of these indicators will require defining the condition that needs to change, the desired educational outcome indicators, processes that will be used to change the condition (which may include structural and behavioral changes), and types of measurements to be used (for example, this may include interviews, observations, videotaping of before-and-after lessons, and taping of collegial meetings to assess depth and breadth of implementation).

These indicators should be a major tool for schools to assess the depth and breadth of their restructuring efforts over time. School professionals will need to develop new skills to measure changes and may initially require professional development and assistance.

Both qualitative and quantitative data on student outcomes are needed. Data should be tied to aspirations and expectations and to actual outcomes. Do teacher, student, and parent expectations about achievement and life opportunities change as a result of restructuring? Data on course enrollments, grades, shifts in test-score quartiles, attendance, suspensions, dropout rates, course failures, and retention are needed to get a comprehensive view of what is occurring over time.

At the school level, reassignments need to be viewed as incentives for change rather than as punishments. The best teachers should teach all levels of students and get incentives for doing so rather than only being assigned to the top-achieving students. Teachers will need to clearly understand the payoffs for changing and know the types of supports available.

In the end, of course, student achievement is what is important. We always try to focus, regardless of leadership, on student outcomes. But to achieve the high-level learning outcomes we aspire to for all students requires fundamental changes in policies and practices—changes that require multiyear efforts. To sustain that kind of effort over time, schools and school districts must identify and reward changes that can transform institutional conditions that inhibit student achievement.

Conclusion

Over the long haul, everyone will benefit when all children—rich and poor, students of all ethnic backgrounds—are well educated. As Hodgkinson (1991, p. 12) succinctly states, "What do we call 'minorities' when they constitute a majority? It behooves us all to make sure that every child in America has a good education and access to a good job. We cannot, as a nation, afford to throw any child away; we need them all to become successful adults if the economy, the community, the work force, the military—indeed, the nation—are to thrive."

References

Braddock, J. H. II. "Tracking the Middle Grades: National Patterns of Grouping for Instruction." *Phi Delta Kappan,* 1990, *71*(6), 445–449.

Cohen, D. "Revolution in One Classroom: The Case of Mrs. Oublier." *American Educator,* 1990, pp. 16–48.

Comer, J. P. "Academic and Affective Gains for the School Development Program: A Model for Improvement," 1987. (ED 274 750)

Darling-Hammond, L. "Achieving Our Goals: Superficial and Structural Reform." *Phi Delta Kappan,* 1990, *72*(4), 286–296.

Elmore, Richard F. "Reform and the Culture of Authority in Schools." *Educational Administration Quarterly,* 1987, *23*(4), 60–78.

Epstein, J. L. "School and Family Connections: Theory, Research, and Implications for Integrating Sociologies of Education and Family." In D. G. Unger and M. B. Sussman, *Families in Community Settings: Interdisciplinary Perspectives.* New York: Haworth Press, 1990.

Fullan, M. G. "Visions That Blind." *Educational Leadership,* 1992, *49*(5), 19–22.

Gardner, H. *Frames of Mind: The Theory of Multiple Intelligences.* New York: Basic Books, 1983.

Goodlad, J. I. *Teachers for Our Nation's Schools.* San Francisco: Jossey-Bass, 1990.

Haberman, M. "The Pedagogy of Poverty Versus Good Teaching." *Phi Delta Kappan,* 1991, *73*(4), 290–294.

Haycock, K., and Navarro, M. S. *Unfinished Business: Fulfilling Our Children's Promise, Report from the Achievement Council.* Emeryville, Calif.: Achievement Council, 1988.

Hilliard, A. III. "Do We Have the Will to Educate All Students?" *Educational Leadership,* 1991, *47*(1), 31–36.

Hodgkinson, H. "Reform Versus Reality." *Phi Delta Kappan,* 1991, *73*(1), 8–16.

Howard, J. *Getting Smart: The Social Construction of Intelligence.* Lexington, Mass.: Efficacy Institute, 1991.

Johnson, R. "Exploring Systemic Change: Goals for the Future." *Alliance,* 1994, *1*(2), 18–22.

Levin, H. M., and Hopfenberg, W. S. "Don't Remediate: Accelerate." *Principal,* 1991, pp. 11–14.

Lortie, J. *School-Teacher: A Sociological Study.* Chicago: University of Chicago Press, 1975.

Madaus, G. F., and others. *The Influence of Testing on Teaching Math and Science in Grades 4–12.* Report of a Study Funded by the National Science Foundation (SPA 8954759) and conducted by the Center for the Study of Testing, Evaluation, and Educational Policy, Boston College, 1992.

Maeroff, G. I. "Building Teams to Rebuild Schools." *Phi Delta Kappan,* 1993, *74*(7), 512–517.

Mathematical Sciences Education Board. *Making Mathematics Work for Minorities: Framework for a National Action Plan 1990–2000.* Report of a convocation. Washington, D.C.: Mathematical Sciences Education Board, 1990.

Mathews, J. *Escalante: The Best Teacher in America.* Troy, Mo.: Holt, Rinehart & Winston, 1988.

National Center for Education Statistics, U.S. Department of Education. *The Condition of Education 1993.* Washington, D.C.: U. S. Government Printing Office, 1993.

National Education Commission on Time and Learning. *Prisoners of Time.* Washington, D.C.: U.S. Government Printing Office, 1994.

Oakes, J. *Keeping Track: How Schools Structure Inequality.* New Haven, Conn.: Yale University Press, 1985.

Oakes, J. "Can Tracking Research Inform Practice? Technical, Normative, and Political Considerations." *Educational Researcher,* 1992, *21*(4), 12–22.

Orfield, G. "Race, Income, and Educational Inequality." In Council of Chief State School Officers, *School Success for Students at Risk.* Orlando, Fla.: Harcourt Brace Jovanovich, 1988.

Porter, A. "Creating a System of School Process Indicators." *Educational Evaluation and Policy Analysis,* 1991, *13*(1), 13–29.

Rosenholtz, S. J. *Teacher's Workplace: The Social Organization of Schools.* White Plains, N.Y.: Longman, 1989.

Sapon-Shevin, M., and Schniedewind, B. "Cooperative Learning as Empowering Pedagogy." In C. E. Sleeter (ed.), *Empowerment Through Multicultural Education.* Albany: State University of New York Press, 1991.

Sarason, S. B. *The Culture of the School and the Problem of Change.* (Rev. ed.) Needham Heights, Mass.: Allyn & Bacon, 1982.

Sarason, S. B. *The Predictable Failure of Educational Reform: Can We*

Change Course Before It's Too Late? San Francisco: Jossey-Bass, 1990.

Schlechty, P. C. *Schools for the 21st Century: Leadership Imperatives for Educational Reform.* San Francisco: Jossey-Bass, 1990.

Sizer, T. R. "No Pain, No Gain." *Educational Leadership,* 1991, *48*(8), 32–34.

Sleeter, C. E. "Introduction." In C. E. Sleeter (ed.), *Empowerment Through Multicultural Education.* Albany: State University of New York Press, 1991.

Sleeter, C. E., and Grant, C. A. "Mapping Terrains of Power: Student Cultural Knowledge Versus Classroom Knowledge." In C. E. Sleeter (ed.), *Empowerment Through Multicultural Education.* Albany: State University of New York Press, 1991.

Wang, M. C., Reynolds, M. C., and Walberg, H. J. "Integrating the Children of the Second System." *Phi Delta Kappan,* 1988, *70*(3), 248–251.

Winfield, L. F. "Teacher Beliefs Toward Academically At-Risk Students in Inner Urban Schools." *Urban Review,* 1986, *18*(4), 253–268.

Winfield, L. F., Johnson, R., and Manning, J. "Managing Instructional Diversity." In P. B. Forsyth and M. Tallerico (eds.), *City Schools: Leading the Way.* Newbury Park, Calif.: Corwin Press, 1993.

Winfield, L. F., and Woodard, M. D. "Assessment, Equity, and Diversity in Reforming America's Schools." *Educational Policy,* 1994, *8*(1), 3–27.

Chapter 7

Promoting Effective Teaching for Diversity

Vinetta C. Jones, Rochelle Clemson

Imagine for a moment a scenario with two African American sisters, one ten years old and the other six. The ten-year-old is patiently advising the six-year-old not to pursue a variety of professions because they are not open or receptive to people of color. Is this a scene from 1955 or 1995?

Who Will Teach the Children?

There has been much talk in recent years about the importance of ensuring that government agencies, corporate boardrooms,

For more information on EQUITY 2000, contact the College Board, 45 Columbus Avenue, New York, NY 10023. The nine consultants who made contributions to this report are Ursula Casanova, Arizona State University; Lisa Delpit, Georgia State University; Lily Wong Fillmore, University of California, Berkeley; Michelle Foster, University of North Carolina, Chapel Hill; Asa Hilliard, Georgia State University; Jacqueline Irvine, Emory University; Gerald Mohatt, University of Arizona; Sharon Nelson-Barber, Stanford University; and José Vasquez, Hunter College (CUNY). Each of the contributors nominated relevant literature to be reviewed and critiqued the report before its publication. They also provided examples of successful instances of culturally responsive pedagogy.

and the media "look like America." That is, those organizations should be comprised of people from a wide range of ethnic and cultural backgrounds, not simply as a matter of justice but because the rich diversity in backgrounds, experiences, and cultures that individuals from different ethnic groups contribute to the dialogue is likely to increase the effectiveness of any projects or activities. It is equally important to have a teaching force that "looks like America"—one that includes teachers of African American, Hispanic American, and American Indian heritage who share the ethnicity, culture, and backgrounds of the nation's increasingly diverse student population. As the number of students of color comprising the student population in our nation's public schools increases—particularly in urban school districts—there is a sense of urgency in training a teaching force that reflects the diversity of that student population. Regrettably, few policy or program reforms have been effective in addressing this issue.

This chapter examines the implications of an increasingly diverse student population from two perspectives: (1) the importance of increasing the number of minority teachers in the college pipeline, particularly through programs that increase the number of minority students who enroll in college, so that the teaching force is reflective of the student population; and (2) ensuring that all teachers, regardless of their ethnicity, are prepared to teach effectively in multicultural classrooms and therefore are culturally responsive and sensitive to the ethnic backgrounds of their students.

Minority Teacher Recruitment

During the 1980s, it became commonplace to hear about the critical shortage of "minority" teachers. Numerous reports have cited minority teacher recruitment as an educational priority for the decade. Patricia Graham (1987), in her now famous prediction, warned that only 5 percent of the teaching force in the year 2000 will be composed of individuals of ethnic minority groups. Reports such as *New Strategies for Producing Minority Teachers* (Education Commission of the States, 1990) and *Recruiting Minority Teachers: A Practical Guide* (American Association of Colleges for

Teacher Education, 1989) echoed the grim prediction. State and national reports on teacher supply and demand (for example, Maryland Department of Education, 1978, 1990) provided a rich array of data supporting the dwindling number of African American, Hispanic, and Asian teachers. In Maryland, for example, minority teacher candidates represented almost 9 percent of the pool in 1987 and dropped to less than 6 percent in 1990 (Maryland Department of Education, 1978, 1990).

As a result of dire projections of the disappearance of minority teachers in an era of proliferating minority public school students, many groups and individuals sought to address the problem. Groups such as the American Association of Colleges for Teacher Education (AACTE), the Association of Teacher Educators (ATE), the Education Commission of the States (ECS), the National Education Association (NEA), and state and regional affiliates established commissions, task forces, and standing committees to explore solutions to the "minority recruitment problem." Foundations and other agencies dedicated to funding educational programs targeted grants to colleges, universities, school systems, and/or state agencies that committed themselves to developing plans for minority teacher recruitment. Many of the projects initiated during this period were well intentioned but shortsighted. They emphasized a narrowly construed set of incentives that addressed only part of the problem. Scholarships, fellowships, and recruitment "prizes" such as low-cost car loans and a free month's rent served to whet the appetites of a few minority teacher candidates, but they did not significantly increase the overall pool of ethnic minority students entering teacher education.

When school systems in places such as Pittsburgh, Pennsylvania, and Prince Georges County, Maryland, offered incentives to minority teachers to accept teaching contracts, they simply siphoned away the talent from other school systems. They did not, however, increase the number of African American, Hispanic, and Asian American high school students that went to college, nor did they increase the number of minority college students pursuing teaching as a career. Even "grow-your-own" programs, in which school systems promise scholarships and future teaching jobs to minority students in their schools, have had limited success. The popularity of these programs, however, has not diminished in the 1990s, since school systems such as those of New York City and Washington, D.C., have created magnet schools with "future teachers" as their theme. Coolidge High School in Washington, D.C., is an example of one such "magnet." Its program emphasizes academic preparation for college and a set of motivational, experiential activities, such as tutoring and field trips related to the profession of teaching.

Barriers and Solutions

Although there is a consensus that fewer minority teachers are entering and remaining in the profession, there is no general agreement on the reasons for this phenomenon and therefore no agreement on strategies for addressing it. Among the many solutions proposed are (1) future teachers' groups that target minority students; (2) monetary incentives, such as scholarships, fellowships, and recruitment "prizes"; (3) grow-your-own-programs with promises of guaranteed future jobs; (4) postbaccalaureate teacher training programs geared to minority career changers, retirees, and non–education majors in colleges; (5) alternative certification (that is, fast-track teacher training) programs with targeted recruitment of nonwhite candidates; (6) advertisements featuring minority role models aimed at improving the image of teaching as a career; (7) development of mentor programs for beginning teachers who are ethnic minorities; and (8) data collection and dissemination to make the public aware of the "crisis."

These and many other strategies have been tried in recent years, but the problem persists. According to G. Pritchy Smith (1992), this is a result of a lack of will on the part of the educational community and a lack of commitment to the goal. Smith claims that the existence of policies such as teacher certification testing, despite the knowledge of the adverse impact of these tests on minority populations, is proof of the unwillingness and inability of educators to address the real structural and policy solutions to the gradual obsolescence of the minority teacher. Smith's data show that nationally approximately 20,000 black teachers and teacher candidates have been eliminated as a result of competency tests. For example, in a state with almost one-third minority student enrollment, 80 percent of the black test takers did not meet the qualifying scores necessary to be admitted to teacher education programs.

In a provocative discussion of minority recruitment, Martin Haberman (1988) describes "promising practices and attractive detours." The major criteria for the Haberman detours are: they divert our attention away from the immediate need to recruit minority teachers; they require radical, comprehensive (and therefore long-range) change; and they are indirect solutions to the problem and have major resource implications. They are "attractive" precisely because they address some of the underlying problems associated with the shortage of minority teachers, but focusing on them may actually prevent or delay development of a solution. The following list reflects the full set of detours: (1) increase teacher salaries—Haberman applauds this idea but claims that it should not be a prerequisite for minority recruitment because it is a goal that will undoubtedly take a long time to achieve; (2) empower and raise the status of teachers—this is also a problem that has proven resistant to the abundant efforts of researchers, unions, politicians, and others; linking minority recruitment objectives to this goal is likely to retard the progress of the former because of the complexity and change resistance of the latter; (3) modify university teacher education programs—a noble goal but one that will not be readily accomplished because of the conservative and unresponsive nature of these programs.

Instead of these idealistic approaches to minority teacher recruitment, Haberman proposes four that are more "realistic." Each of the four is actually a collection of strategies. The list includes the following: (1) designing strategies for recruiting more minorities into teaching (for example, instituting scholarship programs, modifying teacher testing policies, adapting admission and exit requirements for teacher education); (2) cultivating partnerships between two- and four-year institutions for the purpose of recruiting and training minority teachers (nearly half of all minority college students are enrolled in two-year schools); (3) creating new forms of postbaccalaureate teacher training programs aimed specifically at minorities (for example, teacher corps and master of arts in teaching programs); and (4) developing new forms of teacher training not controlled by colleges and universities (such as alternative certification programs).

Haberman provides a great deal of demographic and statistical data to buttress his case for the four "promising practices." Although some of his proposals, such as alternative certification, are controversial among professional educators, his prediction that university-based teacher training will not attract a more ethnically diverse cohort of teacher candidates has proven correct in states such as New Jersey, California, Texas, and Maryland.

The Quality Education for Minorities (QEM) Network has identified many of the problems that underlie the shortage of minority teachers. This project and others like it are predicated on the assumption that enhancing the education of minority children and youth ultimately will resolve the issues related to minority teacher recruitment. The argument they present is that minority children are at an unfair disadvantage because many of them lack the rigorous academic preparation (especially in mathematics and science) that would allow them to succeed in college preparatory courses in high school and in undergraduate programs at most colleges and universities. Therefore, the number of minority college students is not increasing quickly enough to produce a critical mass of teacher candidates to replace teachers of color who are retiring and changing careers.

The solution advocated by QEM, as well as by projects such as Academic Champions of Excellence (ACE) in Maryland and the College Board's national initiative, EQUITY 2000, is early intervention: the infusion of massive resources into urban school systems to ensure that minority students pursue academically challenging courses that prepare them for college. EQUITY 2000 offers one approach to improving the academic preparation and increasing the college-going rate of minority students, which will ultimately enhance minority teacher recruitment.

College Board's EQUITY 2000

EQUITY 2000 is a comprehensive districtwide reform model that seeks to create systemic change in school systems (K–12) across the nation in order to eliminate academic tracking and to promote academic excellence and equity for all students. The goal of EQUITY 2000 is to close the gap in the college-going and success rate between minority and majority students, and between advantaged and disadvantaged students by the year 2000. The reform was stimulated by research (using the High School and Beyond data) commissioned by the College Board and published in *Changing the Odds* (Pelavin and Kane, 1990), which found mathematics and expectations to be the critical variables in closing the achievement and college-going gap. In fact, the study found that when you hold constant students taking algebra and geometry and aspiring to go to college, the gap nearly disappears. And yet Pelavin and Kane found that only 19 percent of African American students and 17 percent of Hispanic students ever take both algebra and geometry at any grade level. Thus, the vast majority of students of color leave high school inadequately prepared to succeed in college.

These findings led to the development of the EQUITY 2000 districtwide reform model, which focuses on eliminating tracking and setting high expectations for all students. Using mathematics as leverage, the program is aimed at reaching minority and disadvantaged students who traditionally have been tracked into watered-down dead-end courses. The model encompasses six components:

- Policy changes to end tracking and raise standards, beginning with the requirement that all students complete algebra by the ninth grade and geometry by the tenth grade
- Ongoing professional development for teachers, counselors, and principals
- "Safety net" programs such as Summer Scholars Programs and Saturday Academies
- Empowering parents to become advocates for their children's education
- School-community partnerships that include links with colleges and universities
- Use of student enrollment and achievement data broken down by ethnic group and gender to monitor the reform progress

The principles and components of EQUITY 2000 provide a vehicle for raising standards and expectations for all students, with the aim of preparing every student for college and/or work—that is, of keeping the option of college open to all students.

The ultimate aim of EQUITY 2000 is systemic change in entire school districts. This includes the elimination of tracking—a policy that leads students to an academic dead end—and also includes rethinking the way teachers and counselors interact with students.

The underlying premise that guides all of EQUITY 2000's activities is that all students can learn at high levels, given an encouraging environment, high expectations, and academic support. At each EQUITY 2000 site, all students are to be enrolled in mathematics courses that place them on the college-bound path. These students receive the academic enrichment and support needed to excel in those college-prep courses. Guidance counselors and mathematics teachers work jointly to increase their expectations of student performance and to develop strategies for raising students' expectations of themselves. Mathematics teachers attend intense summer institutes that strengthen their mathematics instruction skills and enhance their awareness of educational equity. Guidance counselors also attend intense summer institutes that increase their college and career-planning knowledge. These institutes can help them develop strategies for increasing student aspirations for a college degree by providing early information on college and career choices and on issues such as available financial aid that will enable students to pursue college degrees.

EQUITY 2000 is being implemented in entire school systems at the following urban sites, all with significant minority and disadvantaged student populations: Fort Worth, Texas; Providence, Rhode Island; Nashville, Tennessee; Prince Georges County, Maryland; Milwaukee, Wisconsin; and San Jose, California (a consortium of nine school districts). More than 700 schools in the fourteen school districts are formal participants in the program; the student population (K–12) in these districts exceeds 450,000.

For the past four years the College Board has carefully

monitored the progress of the districts and students at the six EQUITY 2000 sites. While this effort is still a "work in progress," there have already been significant increases in the number of students taking and passing higher-level mathematics courses, and important changes have also been seen in attitudes among teachers and guidance counselors about what they believe all young people can achieve. For example, during the 1993–94 academic year, enrollment among ninth graders in Algebra 1 or higher began to approach 100 percent at the EQUITY 2000 sites. The estimated breakdown for the fall 1993 semester is shown in Table 7.1.

Of equal significance is the fact that the "passing rates" for Algebra 1 have remained relatively constant since the inception of EQUITY 2000, even with substantial increases in student enrollment in that course. The result is that thousands of students who likely would not have enrolled in and completed Algebra 1 without EQUITY 2000 are now doing so at the six sites—a significant step toward the enrollment of all students in college-prep courses across subject areas at all grade levels. Because algebra and geometry are often the "gatekeepers" to the college-prep curriculum, it is important that students enroll and succeed in those courses in order to open up the college-prep path of study.

EQUITY 2000 is among the most promising of the many proposed reforms aimed at addressing the crisis in minority recruitment and retention because of its focus on early intervention and its emphasis on setting high standards for minority students. Such efforts must be at the core of any national commitment to increasing minority student enrollment in college—the first step in increasing the number of minorities in the teacher preparation pipeline.

Awareness of Cultural Diversity

In the videotape *Who's Missing from the Classroom . . .* , produced by AACTE, many experts propose strategies for attracting and retaining a culturally diverse teaching force. According to Lisa Delpit of Georgia State University, it is incumbent on educators

Table 7.1. Enrollment in Algebra 1 Among Ninth Graders, 1993–1994.

Location	Enrollment
Fort Worth	90%
Milwaukee	94
Nashville	60
Prince Georges County	87
Providence	100
San Jose Unified	90

Source: College Board, 1994.

to understand the culture of minority students in order to educate them. Only then, claims Delpit, can we begin to direct their futures toward careers in education. "If there is someone who doesn't understand what I'm teaching, I try to understand who they are," says Delpit. This is the first step to creating effective, culturally responsive pedagogy (Villegas, 1992). Others, such as Asa Hilliard, have emphasized the importance of understanding one's own culture and the culture of one's students. Hilliard cites "power pedagogues" who have been unpredictably successful with underserved populations. Jaime Escalante and Marva Collins, two folk hero examples of power pedagogy, have stirred their students' minds and hearts and created environments of high expectations challenging students to achieve at levels far beyond those they or their peers had reached.

In Hilliard's words, quality education for minorities requires educators to create "visions of success" instead of "rationales and autopsies of failure." Only these visions will help to eliminate minority youth imprisonment in low-status school "tracks" that create vicious cycles of low expectations and student failures. The QEM Project report, *Education That Works: An Action Plan for Educating Minorities* (1990), lays out several myths that impede the improvement of educational services for minority children. Included among these myths are the following: (1) learning is due to innate abilities; minorities are less capable; (2) the situation is hopeless; the problems of minorities are insoluble; (3) quality education is a luxury; (4) education is an expense, not an investment; (5) excellence and equity are in conflict; (6) minorities do not care about education; (7) the problem will go away; (8) education is an individual responsibility; and (9) in America, anyone can make it.

In considering the area of minority recruitment of teachers, some theorists have highlighted the problem of recruiting and retaining teachers for urban schools. Haberman (1988) identifies the problems of urban teacher recruiters in several categories: expanded career opportunities for women, which divert them from careers in teaching; conditions of practice, such as large class size, clerical duties, lack of supplies and equipment, and poor safety conditions; irrelevance of teacher education programs; institutional racism at colleges and universities, which restricts minority teacher candidates and steers the best teachers away from urban schools; fear of the urban setting; lack of urban teaching experience among teacher educators.

Haberman's analysis is relevant to the minority recruitment problem in several ways. First of all, a large percentage of children of color reside in urban areas. They are the majority population (75 percent) in twenty-three of the nation's twenty-five largest school districts (Baratz, 1986). Often, these children receive relatively little from their schools that reflects their culture. The curriculum is often Eurocentric, and the teachers are of European descent. Thus, African American, Asian American, Hispanic, and American Indian children—the new "majority" in our public schools—still do not "see themselves" in their studies or their classroom environments. Given statistics by Harold L. Hodgkinson (1986) that indicate that urban children and youth are experiencing difficult home conditions, the responsibility of urban schools to provide students with a powerfully effective educational experience is vital. The schools can help to close the gaps that exist in many urban students' lives. Hodgkinson indicates that every day, forty teenagers give birth to their third child. In addition, since 1983, 60 percent of the children born in this country will have lived in one-parent households by the age of eighteen. Also, 45 percent of black children, 36 percent of Hispanic children, and 25 percent of all children live in poverty.

Teenage homicides and delinquency are increasing, while teenage unemployment rises every year. Equally dramatic is that the dropout rate is more than 50 percent in many large cities.

The recruitment of minority teachers who understand from their own direct experience the lives of minority youth is one part of a multifaceted approach to effective practice in urban schools. Minority teachers bring with them a wealth of personal experiences and an understanding of their culture that uniquely equip them to educate minority students. This argument does not preclude the recruitment of nonminority teachers and their assignment to schools with high minority enrollment. It simply makes the case for vigorous efforts to recruit minority teachers, especially for urban schools. In the following discussion, we represent a model for teacher training that prepares teachers to be culturally responsive. This training model can be used to sensitize both minority and nonminority teachers to the cultural diversity they will increasingly encounter in the schools. Considering the fact that most teacher candidates are not members of ethnic minority groups and that it is unlikely that this condition will change in the near future, it is critical to prepare teachers to be effective multicultural educators, despite their personal backgrounds and experiences.

The broader problem of educating minority students is related to the narrower problem of minority teacher recruitment in the following ways: (1) minority children need a critical mass of minority role models in high-status positions within schools and school systems; (2) inferior education of minority students leads to fewer minorities entering professions, especially teaching; and (3) minority teachers possess a direct knowledge of the culture of minority youth, a prerequisite for success in teaching them. They also have a high level of empathy with the problems of minority students because they have experienced them in their own lives.

Some observers claim that despite our best efforts to attract a larger population of minority teachers for our nation's public schools, it will still be necessary, at least in the short run, to train teachers of the majority culture to effectively educate minority children. Therefore, it is important to understand the concepts of *culturally responsive pedagogy* and *multicultural educa-*

tion. Both terms refer to teaching methods and approaches that honor and respect the contributions of diverse cultures in a pluralistic society.

Culturally Responsive Pedagogy

Many eloquent voices speak to the need to infuse culture into the public school curriculum. The myth that the American public school curriculum is culture-free (and therefore bias-free) has recently been debunked by scholars such as Lisa Delpit, Asa Hilliard, and Ana María Villegas. These voices and others (such as James Banks, Christine Bennett, and Carl Grant) have advanced substantive suggestions for multiculturalizing the curriculum.

If, as we are now learning, children need a curriculum that allows them to understand the influences of culture on them and the contributions of members of their cultural/racial/ethnic group to society, then there must be significant changes in the way public schools educate students. The curriculum, environment, and policies of the schools currently convey the majority culture's values, norms, and characteristics. In a pluralistic society, curriculum, environment, and policies should reflect diverse cultures.

In a study supported by the Educational Testing Service (ETS), Villegas (1992) addresses the need for culturally responsive pedagogy by providing examples of explanations of the differential achievement of minority and majority students and describing three culturally responsive educational initiatives. Villegas concludes her analysis with a set of implications for beginning teacher assessment.

Included among the "explanations" of differential minority/majority student achievement are: (1) deficit theories, based on fallacious assumptions about the genetic and/or cultural inferiority of minority students; (2) low teacher expectations for minority students, creating a self-fulfilling prophecy of failure; and (3) disjunctures between the "home culture" and "school culture," resulting in difficulties with cross-cultural communication. Villegas repudiates the cultural deficit explanation, validates the low-expectations theory, and provides a discussion of home-school cultural disjunctures.

The three educational initiatives highlighted by Villegas are the Kamehameha Early Education Project, geared to Polynesian children in Hawaii; the San Diego Project, aimed at bilingual Hispanic youth in California; and the "Marva Collins Way," an initiative involving African American students in Chicago. The common threads in all these successful efforts are clear goals, high expectations for students, and recognition and celebration of culture. Each of these projects, according to Villegas, utilizes "culturally sensitive" strategies.

The generalizations drawn from Villegas's review of the research may be summarized as follows: (1) teachers should know about and respect their students' cultures; (2) teachers must believe their students are capable of learning academically challenging material; (3) teachers should view themselves as capable of making a difference in the lives of their students (that is, they should have a sense of efficacy); (4) effective teachers plan, implement, and adapt enriched curriculum that links students' cultural experiences with instruction; and (5) teachers must manage their classrooms and evaluate students in culturally sensitive ways.

Multicultural Education

Although Villegas and others provide an intriguing analysis of teacher behaviors and attitudes and their influence on culturally diverse students, this analysis must be supplemented by the vast array of diagnostic and prescriptive models that are referred to as approaches to multicultural education. These approaches range from checklists and "tips" for multiculturalizing a classroom environment, the curriculum, or instructional strategies, to collections of materials deemed effective in culturally diverse settings.

Many theorists believe that the challenge of educating the new majority is best met by adopting instructional approaches and curricular material that serve three purposes: inclusion, access, and support. In Prince Georges County, Maryland, inclusion, access, and support are the major components of the multicultural education initiative. "Inclusion" refers to the development in students and staff of an understanding, appreciation, and awareness of the contributions and historical development of the major cultural groups in Prince Georges County, the United States and the world (Prince Georges County Public Schools, 1991). Suggested strategies for accomplishing the goals of inclusion are: (1) curriculum transformation to reflect information about diverse groups' histories, cultures, and contributions; (2) identification and development of instructional materials that present a multicultural perspective; and (3) staff development to promote human relations skills, develop an instructional repertoire for diverse groups' learning styles and preferences, and provide information about the contributions of many cultures.

This conceptual approach to multicultural education is similar to that of Christine Bennett and her associates, whose model includes knowledge, understanding, attitudes, and skills. The Bennett model provides an outline of multicultural competence, including the areas of historical perspective, reduction of racism, prejudice, and discrimination, and teaching strategies.

The other components of multicultural education relate to the opportunities and resources available to diverse populations of students, especially ethnic minorities. Among the many suggestions for enhancing minority access and support in the classroom are the establishment of uniformly high expectations for all students, the creation of a positive school climate, and the utilization of state-of-the-art instructional techniques, such as cooperative learning, computer technology, and approaches to developing higher-order thinking. In the multicultural initiative of Prince Georges County Public Schools, the elements of access and support are given as much attention as inclusion. Therefore, programs such as Teacher Expectations Student Achievement (TESA) are part of the staff development program for teachers and administrators. TESA's purpose is threefold: to improve the interactions in the classroom by providing equity in response opportunities, equity in appropriate feedback, and equity in expressions of personal regard. More specifically, teachers are taught to recognize and change their patterns of calling on students so that all students have a chance of participating, and to provide as much individual help to minority students as majority students. Teachers are encouraged to stimulate higher-level questioning among minority as well as majority students, and to delve and probe persistently with all students when engaged in classroom discussions.

In addition to providing equity, teachers are advised to be affirmative, good listeners, and accepting of the feelings of all students. They are instructed to demonstrate proximity (that is, physical closeness), courtesy, and personal interest to students on an equitable basis. TESA's three strands: response opportunities, feedback, and personal regard seem to relate directly to the goals of access and support for minority students. Its national success as a staff development program is probably attributable to its solid grounding in principles of educational psychology, which emphasize the primacy of teacher expectations. Many research projects have validated the theory that students tend to "live up to" or "live down to" the expectations of their teachers. These expectations are reflected in the quantity and quality of attention teachers give to various groups of students. Too frequently, African American and Hispanic students are labeled as low achievers, and this sets up a vicious cycle of labeling, low expectations, and failure. African American males are particularly vulnerable to this treatment.

In addition to setting high expectations, teachers must have a high sense of efficacy to deal effectively with multicultural populations. "Efficacy" refers to the extent to which teachers believe they have the capacity to affect student performance (Ashton, Webb, and Doda, 1983). It includes the following two components: (1) teaching efficacy—a teacher's belief that her or his ability to effect change in a student is limited by factors external to the teacher (for example, students' heredity, background, home environment) and (2) personal efficacy—a teacher's belief that he or she has the skill and abilities to bring about student learning. Recent research has indicated that levels of efficacy are often low in white teachers who work in schools with predominantly black students (Gray, 1992).

To increase teachers' sense of efficacy with minority students, they must develop the knowledge base that will allow them to be effective multicultural educators. This knowledge base should include information about the students' cultures and daily lives as well as instructional techniques that do not violate cultural norms. Some theorists support group approaches such as cooperative learning because of their success in Israel and Europe with diverse populations of learners. The basic premise underlying most forms of cooperative learning is that students and teachers working together toward a common goal will enhance positive attitudes and decrease bias, prejudice, and stereotyping. Robert Slavin of Johns Hopkins University touts cooperative learning as an excellent antidote to intergroup conflict.

Conclusion

It is apparent, then, that three issues are key in determining this nation's success in educating the new majority. The first is increasing the number of minority students in the college pipeline from which to develop and nurture the next generation of minority teachers. The second is ensuring that all teachers—regardless of their own ethnic background—are culturally sensitive and responsive to the culture and ethnicity of all their students, especially minority students. The third is the need for stronger leadership from schools of education in addressing the preparation of a new breed of teachers for the classrooms of the twenty-first century. Programs that hold the greatest potential for increasing the pool of minority teachers are those that focus on increasing the college-going rate of minority students through early intervention, including national models such as the College Board's EQUITY 2000. Such programs already in place and highly successful or showing great promise in the case of EQUITY 2000 are ripe for broad replication in schools and school systems throughout the nation. The second issue—multicultural learning—holds great promise for increasing minority student aspirations to excel in school and to pursue a college degree. Multicultural learning models represent student-centered approaches to learning and include practices that raise student consciousness about their history and culture and encourage teachers to exercise sensitive teaching practices that produce equity in the classroom.

The questions are no longer "What can we do?" or "What might work?" when it comes to providing minority students with equal access to a quality education, or when it comes to increasing minority student enrollment in college. We know what works. The question now is, do educators, taxpayers, and elected officials have the resolve and commitment to implement what works? Some do, as evidenced by programs such as the College Board's EQUITY 2000 and Prince Georges County Public Schools TESA staff development program. The next step is urging societal and education leaders at every level to look beyond the traditional approaches and broaden their program agendas so that minority and majority students will be fully empowered throughout the educational system.

References

American Association of Colleges for Teacher Education. *Recruiting Minority Teachers: A Practical Guide.* Washington, D.C.: American Association of Colleges for Teacher Education, 1989.

Ashton, P., Webb, R., and Doda, N. *A Study of Teachers' Sense of Efficacy.* Gainesville: University of Florida, 1983. (ED 231 835)

Baratz, J. C. "Black Participation in the Teacher Pool." Paper prepared for the Carnegie Forum's Task Force on Teaching as a Profession. Princeton, N.J.: Educational Testing Service, 1986.

College Board. *Creating a National Equity Agenda: First Lessons from EQUITY 2000.* New York: College Board, 1994.

Education Commission of the States. *New Strategies for Producing Minority Teachers.* Denver, Colo.: Education Commission of the States, 1990.

Graham, P. "Black Teachers: A Drastically Scarce Resource." *Phi Delta Kappan,* 1987, *68,* 598–605.

Gray, J. "A Comparative Study of the Sense of Efficacy Between Novice African-American Teachers Who Graduate from Historically Black Colleges and Universities and Traditionally White Colleges Who Teach in Urban School Systems." Unpublished doctoral dissertation, Department of Curriculum and Instruction, University of Maryland, 1992.

Haberman, M. "Proposals for Recruiting Minority Teachers:

Promising Practices and Attractive Detours." *Journal of Teacher Education,* 1988, *33,* 38–44.

Hodgkinson, H. L. "Here They Come Ready or Not." *Education Week,* 1986, *6,* 13–37.

Maryland Department of Education. *Teacher Supply and Demand in Maryland.* Baltimore: Maryland Department of Education, 1987.

Maryland Department of Education. *Teacher Supply and Demand in Maryland.* Baltimore: Maryland Department of Education, 1990.

Pelavin, S., and Kane, M. *Changing the Odds: Factors Increasing Access to College.* New York: College Board, 1990.

Prince Georges County Public Schools. *Successful Learning for All Students: Multicultural Education in Prince Georges County Public Schools.* Upper Marlboro, Md.: Prince Georges County Public Schools, 1991.

Pritchy Smith, G. *Recruiting Minority Teachers.* Paper presented at the 44th annual convention of the American Association of Colleges for Teacher Education, San Antonio, Tex., February 1992.

Quality Education for Minorities Project. *Education That Works: An Action Plan for the Education of Minorities.* Cambridge: Massachusetts Institute of Technology, 1990.

Villegas, A. M. *Culturally Responsive Pedagogy for the 1990's and Beyond.* Princeton, N.J.: Educational Testing Service, 1992.

Chapter 8

Developing Alternatives to Tracking and Grading

Jeannie Oakes, Martin Lipton

Tracking includes a whole range of ability-related grouping practices in elementary and secondary schools. Though specific practices differ widely, they all organize schools so that students who appear to be similar in their educational needs and potential can be taught together, and taught separately from other students. Tracking is closely connected with testing, since many tests were created during the early part of the century precisely to sort students into different tracks. Even now, tracking is, in part, both the result of and the reason for much of the testing that takes place in schools. There is no question that tracking, the assessment practices that support it, and the differences in educational opportunity that result from it limit many minority students' schooling opportunities and life chances. Schools relying heavily on test results to form and legitimate their judgments about students' intellectual capacities determine that African American and Latino students, far more than others, have learning deficits and limited potential. Not surprisingly, then, schools place these students disproportionately in low-track, remedial programs that provide them with restricted educational opportunity.

But just as testing and tracking are inextricably linked to each other, so are they linked to all of the other dimensions of schooling that affect students' opportunities and achievement. Tracking and testing are two problematic school structures that support and are supported by much else that is wrong with schools—low expectations for many students; thin, skills-based curricula; and passive, teacher-dominated instructional strategies, to name just a few. It follows, then, that any effective solution to tracking requires attention to these other conditions. Regrouping students into heterogeneous classrooms is necessary but not sufficient to solve these problems. What is needed is a comprehensive set of mutually supportive changes that include new ways of thinking as well as new practices. Such changes are not only solutions in the sense of a technical "fix" for the tracking problem; these are promising directions for reinventing schools generally—schools where tracking would not make sense. Effecting such far-reaching change is no easy matter. Testing and tracking are well entrenched, not only as educational practices intended to help schools to identify and address differences in how quickly and easily students learn, but also as a societal mechanism for sorting students and preparing them for future schooling (if they are thought to be suited for it) and for the adult occupations they will assume. Both functions have legitimacy in and outside of schools. Thus, changing tracking and the tests that support it must include a strategy that engages schools and communities in rethinking basic school purposes. Simply concentrating on how to make schools more technically "effective" misses the point if schools' purposes are misguided. Schools already are effective at much of what they attempt: sorting, limiting the best opportunities to a few, and so on. A successful strategy to examine school practices and purposes must be slow, incremental, inclusive, and artfully orchestrated. In the following sections, we elaborate a cultural view of tracking and testing problems and examine some promising strategies for making schools places where the status quo of testing and tracking no longer make sense.

The Problem

From their earliest school years, African American and Latino students are consistently overrepresented in low-track, remedial, and special education programs. Educators justify these placements by pointing out that children from these groups typically perform less well on commonly accepted assessments of ability and achievement. Moreover, conventional school wisdom holds that low track, remedial, and special education classes help these students, since they permit teachers to target instruction to the particular learning deficiencies of low-ability students. However, research about human capacity and learning suggests that conventional placement tests measure only a very narrow range of students' abilities; in particular they provide little information about students' higher order cognitive abilities, such as how well they generate ideas or solve problems, or about how well they can accomplish real-world tasks. Furthermore, students do not profit from enrollment in low-track classes: they do not learn better, and they have less access than other students to knowledge, engaging learning experiences, and resources (see Oakes, Gamoran, and Page, 1991, for a review).

Testing and Tracking: "As the Twig Is Bent . . ."

Testing and tracking often begin prior to kindergarten. Over the past decade, a growing number of local school systems have begun to administer "readiness" tests to select some five-year-olds for the academic demands of kindergarten, others for a less academic prekindergarten class, and still others to stay home and wait another year. Many systems use such tests to guide placement decisions about first graders. Because children's prior academic learning opportunities have considerable influence on their scores, it is not surprising that children with academically rich preschool and school-like home environments do better on such tests and are more likely to be judged as developmentally "ready" for "regular" kindergartens and suited for high-ability first-grade classrooms. Thus, these tests place low- income children—a group in which most minority children fit—at a clear disadvantage, since most of them have less educationally advantaged preschool opportunities, and, on average, minority children score less well than whites (Ellwein and Eads, 1990; Ellwein, 1991). Thus, it is no surprise that we find disproportionate numbers of young minority children in special "transitional" classes, in separate programs for "at-risk" children, and in other types of low-ability primary classrooms. Even more troublesome, these "readiness" tests are not sufficiently accurate to be used as a basis for placement decisions. They were not designed to predict whether or not children will succeed in a particular placement, and they do not do it well (Meisels, 1989; Shepard, 1992).

In spite of good intentions, elementary schools do not increase achievement when they divide students into whole classes by ability levels. And, while some limited and flexible regrouping schemes do often yield positive effects on *average* achievement (particularly plans that increase student mobility between "levels" with a multigrade structure), they also usually increase the *inequality of achievement.* That is, children in high groups often benefit the most, and those in low groups the least. Over time, then, the achievement gap between high- and low-group students widens. We have no evidence that the slight positive effect on average achievement is sustained over years of schooling.

Tracking propels children through the system at different speeds—even though the slower groups have as their goal "catching up." Low groups spend relatively more time on decoding activities, whereas high groups move on to consider the meanings of stories and progress farther in the curriculum. High-group students do more silent reading and, when reading aloud, are less often interrupted than low-group students. The high-group advantage presumably accumulates as the years pass, and students with a history of membership in high-ability groups are more likely to have covered considerably more material by the end of elementary school.

In this way, tracking in the elementary grades determines much of what happens later. Differences in *pace* through a sequenced curriculum (particularly in mathematics and reading) lead to differences in coverage. Coverage differences result in kids falling further and further behind and in receiving increasingly different curricula. These differences further stabilize students' track placements. Before long, students in slower groups lack the prerequisite curricular experiences needed to qualify (score well on tests) for faster groups or to succeed in faster or higher groups. Moreover, they are likely to have internalized the judgment that they are less able and less likely to succeed, and, as a consequence, are no longer eager to put forth the hard work it might take to do well in a higher-ability class (Rosenholtz and Simpson, 1984).

Secondary School Tracking: ". . . So Grows the Tree"

Early in the middle-school years, there begins an intentional shift away from the goal of propelling kids through the same curriculum at different speeds (with the illogical intention that these students will "catch up"). Instead, middle schools—still relying on slow, special, and remedial classes—change their *intentions* for students. Now, not only is the speed different, so is the direction. Rather than being propelled through the *same* curriculum at different speeds—albeit with much missed by those in slower groups and classes—students are pulled intentionally through different curricula toward different "end points": different high schools, different posthigh school expectations. Increasingly, these different destinations influence judgments about appropriate placements and coursetaking. They confront different courses with different names—sometimes prefixed with "basic," "regular," "pre-," "honors," or "gifted"—and clearly different in content and rigor (for example, slower-track students taking a "crafts" elective instead of foreign language). The differentiated curriculum conforms to a larger social purpose— preparing students for different futures—and creates even greater curricular differences than would be expected from differences in pace and consequent losses in coverage.

As students proceed through middle and high schools, increasingly disproportionate percentages of African American and Latino middle-grade and high school students enroll in low-ability tracks (Braddock, 1989; Braddock and Dawkins, 1993; Oakes, 1990; Oakes, Gamoran, and Page, 1991). For example, Oakes (1990) found that all-minority secondary schools enroll far greater percentages of their students in low-track classes compared to all-white schools, and that in racially mixed schools the concentration of minority students in low-track classes is dramatic. For example, 66 percent of the science and mathematics classes with disproportionately large minority enrollments (compared to their representation in the student body as a whole) were low track, compared with only 5 percent of the disproportionately white classes. In contrast, only 9 percent of the disproportionately minority classes were high track, compared to 57 percent of the disproportionately white classes. These findings were echoed in an Educational Testing Service study of the effects of middle school tracking in six minority, urban districts, which found that minority students were overrepresented in low-track math classes (23 percent compared to only 8 percent of the white students) and underrepresented in high-track classes (36 percent of the minorities compared to 56 percent of whites) (Villegas and Watts, 1991).

In part, these disproportionate placements stem from real differences in minority and white students' opportunities and achievements in elementary school—differences that are often a consequence of earlier tracking. These differences—and disproportionate placements—are exacerbated by schools' reliance on standardized tests in making tracking decisions. Even though such tests underestimate minority students' capabilities, they typically carry more weight than information about students' past classroom performance or teachers' recommendations, particularly when students move into new schools where counselors may have little or no contact with students' former teachers (Oakes, Selvin, Karoly, and Guiton, 1992; Villegas and Watts, 1991).

However, even when white and minority students are comparable in their scores on achievement tests, minorities are more likely than their white peers to be placed in lower tracks. Oakes (1995) documents school-by-school and districtwide placements in two school systems—Rockford, Illinois, and San Jose, California—whose ability grouping and tracking systems were subject to scrutiny in 1993 in conjunction with school desegregation court cases. The data showed that in both school systems, tracking created racially unbalanced classes in elementary, middle, and senior high schools. This imbalance took two forms: (1) white (and Asian, in San Jose) students were consistently overrepresented, and African American and Latino students were consistently underrepresented, in high-ability classes in all subjects; and (2) in contrast, African American or Latino students were consistently overrepresented, while white and Asian students were consistently underrepresented, in low-ability tracks in all subjects.

In both San Jose and Rockford, placement practices skewed enrollments in favor of whites over and above that which can be explained by measured achievement. As a group, African American and Latino students scored lower on achievement tests than whites and Asians in both school systems. However, African American and Latino students were much less likely than comparably scoring white or Asian students to be placed in accelerated courses. For example, in San Jose, Latino eighth graders with "average" scores in mathematics were three times less likely than similarly scoring whites to be placed in an "Accelerated" math course. Among ninth graders, the results were similar. Those Latinos scoring between 40 and 49, 50 and 59, and 60 and 69 Normal Curve Equivalents (NCEs) were less than half as likely as their white and Asian counterparts to be placed in accelerated tracks. The discrimination was even more striking among the highest-scoring students. While only 56 percent of Latinos scoring between 90 and 99 NCEs were placed in accelerated classes, 93 percent of whites and 97 percent of Asians gained admission to these classes.

In Rockford, white students whose scores fell within a range that would qualify them for participation in either a higher or lower track (that is, their scores were the same as those of students in the lower track) were far more likely to be placed in high-track classes than were African American students whose scores fell within that same range. Additionally, in a number of schools, Rockford's high-track classes included exceptionally low-scoring students; rarely were these students African American. In contrast, quite high-scoring African Americans were often found in low-track classes; this was seldom the case for high-scoring whites. Among several striking examples of skewed placements in Rockford's junior highs was one school where the range of reading comprehension scores among eighth graders enrolled in Basic (low-track) English classes was from the 1st to the 72nd National Percentile. Of these, ten students scored above the national average of 50 NP. Six of these high-scoring students were African American, including the highest-achieving student in the class. A seventh was Latino.

Interestingly, both school districts defended their skewed placements as fair, given the proportionately higher mean scores for whites than for African Americans and Latinos. However, these averages simply masked the systematic discrimination against individual minority students in the placement process.

At least two additional and related factors play a role in creating the skewed pattern of track placements. One is the pervasive stereotypical expectations that society and schools hold for students of different racial and ethnic groups that can negatively influence the placement of minority students with marginal test scores (for example, "Latino parents don't care much about their children's school achievement and are unlikely to help their children at home"). A second is "politicking" by savvy parents who want their children placed in the best classes. Although such parents are not exclusively white, in most schools white parents, especially middle-class white parents, better understand the inequalities in the school structure and feel more confident that the school will respond positively to their pressure (Oakes and Guiton, 1995; Useem, 1992a, 1992b). Students from different backgrounds sometimes receive different information, advice, and attention from counselors and teachers. While many secondary schools claim that students "choose" their tracks, low-track, minority students most often report that others made decisions for them (Villegas and Watt, 1991).

Low-track courses consistently offer less demanding topics and skills, while high-track classes typically include more complex material. Teachers of low-track classes give less emphasis than teachers of other classes to such matters as basic science concepts, students' interest in math and science, their development of inquiry and problem-solving skills, and preparation of students for further study in math and science (Oakes, 1990). It is important to note that these goals need not depend on students' prior knowledge or skills. On the contrary, math and science educators increasingly see these goals as essential for all students—regardless of their current skill levels. High-track teachers in all subjects often stress having students become competent and autonomous thinkers. In contrast, low-track teachers place greater emphasis on conformity to rules and expectations (Oakes, 1985, 1990, 1995).

Teaching strategies differ in ways consistent with this pattern of curricular disadvantage. Teachers allocate less time to instruction (as opposed to routines, discipline, and socializing) in low tracks, and learning activities more often consist of drill and practice with trivial bits of information, seatwork, and worksheet activities. When technology is introduced in low tracks, it is often in conjunction with low-level tasks, such as computation. Computer activities, for example, often mimic texts and worksheets (Oakes, Gamoran, and Page, 1991). Low-track teachers tend to tightly control students' opportunities, activities, and interactions. Furthermore, while these disadvantages affect all the students in the class, low-track minority students may be especially disadvantaged, because teachers may treat them less favorably. For instance, Villegas and Watts (1991) found that in racially mixed, low-track classes, teachers focused their interactions with minority students on behavioral rather than educational concerns (six times more often than with whites), both telling students what to do (three times more often for minorities than for whites) and criticizing them (five times more often).

Since many schools track their teachers as well as their students, low-track students have less exposure to well-qualified teachers. While some schools rotate the teaching of low- and high-ability classes, it is more typical for teachers to jockey among themselves for high-track assignments, or for principals to use class assignments as rewards and sanctions. Such political processes work to the detriment of low-track students, since the least well-prepared teachers are usually assigned to low-track students. For example, teachers of secondary low-ability science and mathematics classes are typically less experienced, less likely to be certified in math or science, hold fewer degrees in these subjects, have less training in the use of computers, and less often report themselves to be "master teachers" than their colleagues in upper-track classes. These differences are particularly troublesome for students in schools with large minority and low-income populations because these schools have fewer well-qualified teachers to begin with. In such schools, for instance, low-track students are frequently taught math and science by teachers who are not certified to teach those subjects, if they are certified at all (Oakes, 1990).

These track-related differences have pernicious consequences stemming from conceptions and judgments about human capacity and individual differences that connect with students' race and social class. The differences are not educationally appropriate adaptations to variation in students' learning aptitude, speed, or style. Not surprisingly, the combination of separating students into different groups and providing different knowledge and learning conditions to these groups affects students' aspirations, further schooling opportunities, and achievement. For example, Sanford Dornbush (1994) documents a striking impact of tracking on minority students' ability to realize their post–high school aspirations. Dornbush looked separately at the group of students who met three criteria: (1) wished to graduate from a four-year college, (2) expected to graduate, and (3) believed they were in a college-prep program that would prepare them for entrance to four-year colleges. He found that nearly half the disadvantaged minorities in that group were actually not taking the right courses in math and science, compared to only about 20 percent of non-Hispanic whites and Asians. In mathematics, for example, 50 percent of the African Americans and 52 percent of the Latinos in the sample had these track misperceptions. The percentages were far lower for non-Hispanic whites and Asians (29 and 18 percent, respectively), but they were still considerable. With the analysis limited to those student who had scored above the 50th percentile nationally in mathematics on their ninth-grade test, the percentages remained significant. In this latter group, 32 percent of minority students compared with 12 percent of whites and Asians held a mistaken view of where their high school courses would lead them.

Moreover, Braddock and Dawkins (1993) show that track

assignments impact students' future learning opportunities in their analyses of the National Educational Longitudinal Study of U.S. students who were eighth graders in 1988 (NELS:88). As tenth graders, those students who were in high-ability groups as eighth graders were the most likely to enroll in college-prep courses, and those who had been in low-ability eighth-grade classes the least likely, independent of such factors as grades, test scores, aspirations, and social background factors. Interestingly, too, students in eighth-grade mixed-ability classes were more likely than comparable peers in low tracks to enter college-prep classes. However, those enrolled in high-ability groups as eighth graders were more likely than their counterparts in mixed-ability classes to do so. Similarly, Dornbush (1994) found that the initial high school track placements of students who scored in the middle ranges of achievement in the eighth grade influenced the courses students took throughout their high school years. For example, students scoring in the fifth decile on eighth-grade tests and who were placed in biology as ninth graders had a 71 percent change of taking physics or chemistry later. In stark contrast, similarly scoring students who were placed in low-level science in grade nine had only a 7 percent chance of enrolling in these advanced courses. In fact, at every level of the eighth-grade achievement hierarchy, students placed in college-track classes far outpaced their peers in later advanced science coursetaking. Overall, Dornbush and his colleagues found that 85 percent of high school students end up in the same science and math tracks in which they began. Additionally, as much other work has suggested, with levels of achievement controlled, low-track students feel less challenged, try less hard, do less homework, and say that teachers are less likely to ask them to demonstrate their understanding.

With regard to achievement outcomes, Gamoran (1990) found in a longitudinal study of tracking and the transition between middle school and senior high that about 25 percent of the variance in track-related learning differences was attributable to differences in curriculum and instruction. Additionally, longitudinal analyses of the NELS:88 students show that when students with similar achievement levels in the eighth grade are placed in different tracks, their subsequent achievement diverges. Those placed in higher tracks benefited; those in the lower track suffered negative effects on learning. Similarly, Oakes's (1994) study of San Jose and Rockford schools found a differential effect of tracking; high placement led to achievement gains, and low-track participation had a negative effect on students' learning outcomes. In San Jose, for example, students who were placed in lower-level courses consistently demonstrated lesser gains in achievement over time than their comparably scoring peers placed in high-level courses. These results were consistent across achievement levels: whether students began with relatively high or relatively low achievement, those placed in lower-level courses showed lesser gains over time than similarly situated students placed in higher-level courses. In both systems, achievement differences accrued in the context of the opportunity differences noted earlier.

In short, low-track students—disproportionately African American and Latino—get less and learn less than their high-track peers.

Promising Alternatives

Regrouping students into heterogeneous classrooms is necessary but not sufficient to solve the problems of current sorting practices. Rather, what is needed is a comprehensive set of mutually supportive changes that lead to new ways of thinking as well as new practices. The following are some brief descriptions of promising alternatives that both challenge prevailing school norms and incorporate new organizational structures, curriculum, teaching strategies, and other necessary accompaniments to detracking.

New Norms
Schools wrestling with detracking do not adopt an exclusively practical focus on alternatives. They also challenge the philosophies, values, and beliefs that underlie tracking practices and that make detracking such a difficult technical and political

matter. Developing new norms concerning intelligence and learning are particularly important.

Current sorting practices are grounded in faulty conceptions that intelligence is global (for example, a single entity that can be measured by IQ) and fixed quite early—either before birth or soon thereafter—and that learning is primarily the accumulation of a linear sequence of knowledge and skills. Also important are historically rooted beliefs about individual and group differences in intelligence and learning.

As long as the *capacity to learn* is understood, for all practical purposes, as unalterable, and the range in capacity among schoolchildren is perceived as great, tracking will seem sensible. Schools will continue to accommodate differences by separating students by ability and adapting curriculum and instruction accordingly. The fact that learning capacity seems to be unevenly distributed among groups—with disadvantaged minorities exhibiting less—appears to schools to be beyond their control. Thus, schools typically conclude that the disproportionate assignment of low-income and minority students to low-track classes is an appropriate, if regrettable, response.

Alternatives to tracking only make sense when schools seriously entertain new conceptions of intelligence and learning. For example, work by Howard Gardner (1983; see also Gardner and Hatch, 1989) and Robert Sternberg (1984, 1986; Sternberg, Okagaki, and Jackson, 1990) argues compellingly that intelligence is multifaceted and developmental and that learning is a complex process of constructing meaning. Serious consideration of such work enables schools to give new credibility to popular notions such as "all children can learn," rather than clinging to the limiting interpretation that all children can achieve their very different "potentials." Importantly, because this new knowledge largely discredits the types of tests schools use to assess students' "ability"—that is, their "potential"—this work also helps many educators shake the lingering suspicion that minority students are not as intelligent as whites because they tend to score less well. To accompany new practices, then, detracking requires a critical and unsettling rethinking of fundamental and widely accepted educational norms.

New Practices That Embody New Norms

While some successful alternatives to traditional practices may emerge in schools that simply place students in mixed-ability classes and leave everything else the same, there is little to recommend this sink-or-swim approach. For example, altered norms about individual and group differences in learning capacity are unlikely to be sustained if teachers and students lack the working conditions and learning conditions to support them. Successful tracking alternatives do not gloss over the fact that children are different and that they need opportunities to learn differently within heterogeneous schools and classrooms. Meeting these diverse needs may required schools to participate in a full agenda of school reform. (For a more detailed accounting of how several current national reform efforts have embodied this agenda, see Oakes and Quartz, 1995.)

Initial steps to achieve successful heterogeneity may be seen as a way to blend previously distinct reforms in curriculum, teaching practices, parent involvement, school organization, and so on. Seen in this much larger context, first steps may be modest. Schools may reconsider the time—the grade or year—in students' careers that introducing particular types of experiences is appropriate. In some schools, for example, learning that was thought to be prerequisite to the successful completion of a particular grade (for example, mastery of a common set of basic reading skills in grade one) may give way to longer-term learning goals in ungraded classes (for instance, individual development of literacy between ages five and eight). Practices such as group work, once reserved for elementary school, may become valued in high school. Rigorous conceptual knowledge previously "saved" for high school may reach children much earlier (Oakes and Lipton, 1990).

Students Working Together

The research on and development of cooperative small-group learning strategies, which has roughly paralleled the recent interest in detracking, have produced a body of theory and practice that demonstrates that it is not only possible for students previously in lower tracks to meet high-track standards, it is possible for students previously in the middle and high tracks to meet new, more rigorous standards for intellectual development than what schools have been aspiring to achieve. Furthermore, a consistent finding in cooperative learning research has been that in heterogeneous groups students, whether highly skilled or struggling with the subject, can make gains in achievement and social skills that exceed the gains they would have made in homogeneous groups or classrooms.

Cooperative learning, then, occupies a central spot in many if not most schools' efforts to detrack students. However, even within the cooperative learning research and development "communities" there may be a tendency to oversell the method and neglect the need for dramatically reconceptualized curricula and lessons. Current curricula undermine the power of cooperative learning to make a difference. While an otherwise ordinary lesson may be enhanced by slight modifications that allow children to work together, some teachers and schools are at work to *combine* with cooperative learning strategies long-range, complex, multidimensional lessons that stretch the learning challenges for all students while allowing all students to succeed.

Moreover, we have empirical evidence suggesting that African American and Latino children may achieve better when they work with others (Slavin, 1990; Cohen, 1994), particularly when they are working on tasks that focus on whole concepts or real situations rather than fragmented skills or abstractions. (Of course, there is also considerable evidence that these approaches help nonminority students learn as well.) One of the most striking examples of a fully developed cooperative learning strategy is Edward DeAvila's and Elizabeth Cohen's conceptually rich, experience-based bilingual science curriculum that has achieved remarkable success with heterogeneous groups of young Latino and Anglo children (Cohen, 1994; Cohen, Kepner, and Swanson, 1995). In their *Finding Out/Descubrimiento* program, groups of students rotate among classroom "centers" at which they work together solving complex science problems. The tasks they engage in also require acquisition of fundamental math knowledge and skills; the interactive process they use promotes the literacy development of both English- and Spanish-speaking children.

Rich, Complex Curriculum

Combining cooperative groups with a thematic or problem-solving orientation can provide a rich intellectual, yet concrete, context to help students organize knowledge, construct meanings, and sustain interest. It also acknowledges and attends specifically to the social construction of knowledge—that much learning takes place in a "community of learners" (Shoenfeld, 1988)—and to the necessity of highly developed social skills to accomplish most productive work.

Henderson, Landesman, and Marshall (1992) describe an example of a thematic approach to mathematics instruction for Latino students in detracked classes. They demonstrate how even subject areas thought to be highly sequential and skills based are amenable to a richer and more complex treatment.

> The first project taken up in the mathematics classes as part of the Careers theme involved designing and building bridges. Within each of the Theme classes, students were divided randomly into groups of five. These groups then formed construction companies, giving their enterprises names such as The Pajareo Builders, Albert Einstein Co., The Mexican Corporation, Trust Us Co., Inc. Within each company, different career-related roles were assigned by the group to its members. These roles were those of Manager, Engineer, Transportation Officer, Architect, and Accountant. The duties of each career group were explained at meetings of all students assigned to a particular role. All goods needed for construction were purchased from a warehouse. Materials included cardboard (representing land), glue, toothpicks, and so on.
>
> Each company was allotted 1.5 million dollars for its project. Calculating amounts, writing checks, and keeping records of accounts brought arithmetic operations into play. Determining the amount of material needed to construct the bridges involved estimation. Before constructing the bridge, students had to develop their plans on graph paper, drawing figures to scale. This involved measurement. At the next stage students dealt with lengths, perimeters, and

areas, to assure the bridge would fit where they wanted it. Next came geometric visualization and discussions of similarity and congruence of figures. Finally, stress tests on the bridge and a discussion of optimal design involved some basic concepts of physics. The finished products were subjected to stress testing, using weights. . . .

The key mathematical topics (each with myriad subtopics) included in the scope and sequence were 1) addition, subtraction, multiplication and division of whole numbers; 2) decimals; 3) fractions; 4) numbers and number theory; 5) problem solving; 6) estimation; 7) geometry; 8) measurement; 9) ratio, proportion, percent; 10) statistics and probability; 11) pre-algebra; and 12) technology [p. 24].

It appears that this large-concept, thematic unit not only allowed for but invited teachers to include additional abstract topics that might not have been written into a traditional grade-level scope and sequence, including: "the solving of simple linear algebraic equations with one unknown (e.g., $50x - 600 = 0$). Geometry topics . . . included material on angles, measurement in degrees, the use of a protractor, and the classification of different types of angles . . . equilateral and isosceles triangles and their properties . . . rays, parallel lines, perpendicular lines, intersecting lines, transversals, regular polygons, congruent figures, symmetry, and reflections" (pp. 25–26).

Clearly, the rich and complex lesson partly described above will raise concerns regarding teacher training, curricular coverage, planning time, class size, acceptance of interactive, noisy classes, and much more. Even so, the payoff in terms of students' deep and lasting understanding warrants the concerns and costs. Importantly, because this curriculum frames learning tasks as complex problems, provides contexts that give facts meaning, takes students' informal knowledge seriously, allows for multiple "right" answers, and promotes socially constructed knowledge, it promises to be much more accommodating of groups of students diverse in prior knowledge and skills. More practically, it provides learning opportunities where it is less likely that some students will have to be left behind or that some will be bored because the lessons have been watered down.

Broadening Assessment

The team that developed this thematic approach to mathematics is confident that their observations are consistent with Roland Tharp's (1989) findings that hands-on activities combined with complex problem solving are more effective in promoting the learning of low-achieving Latino students than a conventional mathematics curriculum. But how does one assess the learning that results from such rich and complex mathematics lessons? This learning is filled, to be sure, with facts and algorithms but also abounds in sophisticated processes, enhanced intuition, social skills (including leadership), and knowledge of all sorts that could not have been anticipated prior to or even during the lesson. Exclusive reliance on typical terminal testing—that is, paper-and-pencil exams at the end of "units" with numbers and a few contrived "word problems"—could kill much of the value of such a lesson. Typical assessments do not encourage returning to the lesson and clarifying misconceptions experienced earlier, and rarely do they provide feedback at a point in the learning process where the student can or is willing to make use of it. They serve to falsely identify what is "really" important in the lesson (successfully solving numerical problems, getting a good grade, and little else). Because they are expressed as a single score or grade, they result in easy public comparisons and reinforce a classroom status hierarchy that can eventually sabotage successful mixed-ability groups (Cohen, 1994; Cohen, Kepner, and Swanson, 1995). This last is a particularly telling point in light of the consistently lower scores achieved by African American and Latino students.

Grant Wiggins (1991, p. 10) observes that "learning is authentic and effective when the assessments are authentic." We would propose this blend of authentic learning and assessment: both learning and assessment have occurred when the entire class completes the learning task—when there is no distinction between ending the lesson and successfully completing the lesson.

Going beyond typical assessments toward a blend of

authentic learning and assessment may be one of the toughest challenges schools face. The new norms, skills, and professional teaching conditions required for sophisticated new instruction are exactly those needed to assess the complex learning that results. Just as a rich, complex, well-planned lesson allows teachers and students alike to "cover" the curriculum by seizing unanticipated learning opportunities and capitalizing on prior knowledge, that same sensitivity must be employed in student assessment. While there is much interest in process evaluations (watching students work at each step of a problem-solving process), product evaluations that include the results of projects or portfolios, structured observations of students' problem solving, and more, it is difficult to imagine how these technologies (arts?) can overcome the habits, politics, and tradition that hold conventional testing, grades, and comparisons in place. Perhaps, for the short range, the most we can hope for is a dual system of assessment where educators and policy makers affirm their commitment and obligation to *protect* students from the effects of traditional assessments while they *educate* them with promising authentic evaluations.

Extra Time and Extra Help

Even when schools adopt norms reflecting confidence in all students' capabilities, schools are still confronted with the reality that some students need more time and instructional support than others. If detracking schools are not to water down the rigorous curriculum they have in place for high-achieving students, the logical alternative is for them to find ways for students formerly in the lower tracks to meet the rigorous expectations now found only in the high track. Thus, they face the challenge of reconfiguring schedules, course offerings, and staffing patterns to enable all students to get the time and help they need without being removed from heterogeneous classrooms. Most schools find that, once the *idea* makes sense—once norms change—devising strategies for providing extra time and help is quite easy.

For example, some schools schedule students' time with special education or Chapter 1 resource teachers after school.

Others team regular teachers and teachers assigned to categorical programs so that specialized help can be incorporated into the regular classroom. This latter strategy is quite consistent with the intent of the new Chapter 1 legislation. Other schools employ peer or cross-age tutoring programs for after-school help. Still other schools make available tape-recorded reading assignments so less accomplished readers can participate. Increasingly popular and successful (and effective) are tutorial or "booster" classes that provide a "double dose" of rigorous academic curriculum to help them keep up in their heterogeneous classes (MacIver, 1991). Some schools add extra class periods to their schedules so that students have time to take these courses; others ask students to give up an elective course to free up time for their booster classes.

For example, Parkway South High School, a suburban Missouri school that draws 80 percent of its students from surrounding middle- and upper-middle-class neighborhoods and 20 percent from central-city St. Louis (by virtue of the school's participation in the voluntary metropolitan desegregation plan) has experimented with providing students who are having difficulty in regular English class with an additional "tutorial" class. This tutorial both replaces the low-track "basic" class and prepares students for success in the regular English class—a supremely logical program that provides extra help instead of a watered-down substitute. It also prevents the resegregation of the African American "transfer" students into remedial tracks. In addition, Parkway South has eliminated its ninth- and tenth-grade social studies honors classes and replaced them with "blended" social studies classes in which students many contract to earn a weighted honors grade. This program reflects the social studies faculty's desire to have a heterogeneous class (in both race and ability level) discuss social issues.

Promising Programs

A few increasingly visible programs demonstrate how new norms and practices can support a culture that provides both access and success for minority students who might otherwise be locked into low-track classrooms. These programs defy tidy categorization as alternatives to tracking. These are programs that have either used their detracking experiences to create school cultures hospitable to a wide range of new practices or that have found that their adoption of alternative practices invites detracking.

AVID is such a program. Conceived by a high school English teacher in 1980 and now widely adopted in San Diego city and county schools, AVID succeeds by providing to underachieving students—especially those from ethnic and linguistic minority backgrounds—massive amounts of social support, including study skills, intensive practice in writing literary, social science, and scientific essays, and intensive tutorials in their coursework. They receive campus tours and hear firsthand from college students and professors what college life is like. To build confidence and self-esteem they work in cooperative learning groups. In short, program developers claim that AVID provides students explicit instruction in the hidden curriculum of the school (Mehan, Hubbard, and Villanueva, 1992; Swanson, Mehan, and Hubbard, 1995).

AVID seems to be of sufficient scope and magnitude to sustain itself as a locus for curriculum and organizational changes; it includes subject matter cadres, has incorporated mentor teacher resources, oversees extensive teacher training, and works cooperatively with university researchers who participate in training, program analysis, and evaluation. But it must be noted that AVID is not an isolated program that has been given the responsibility to "take care of" a problem while the rest of the educational enterprise is business as usual. The development of AVID over the years has paralleled a broader commitment by San Diego City Schools' district administration to increase the access of all students to high-quality curriculum and instruction through the reduction of tracking.

Another large-scale reform effort that promises to reduce the ill effects of tracking on minority students is the Accelerated Schools Project, headquartered at Stanford University. Accelerated Schools for at-risk elementary and middle school students represent an attempt to "create schools that 'speed-up' the learning of such students to bring them into the educational mainstream by the end of elementary school" (Levin, 1991, p. 2). Now expanding to include middle schools, the Accelerated Schools use an enrichment strategy, rather than remediation, to enable students to succeed in mainstream classrooms. This approach is characterized both by the development of new norms of equity (for example, high expectations for at-risk students that are reinforced by deadlines for making all children in the school academically able) and the development of new curricula and practice (such as curricula that build on students' personal and cultural strengths, instruction based on problem-solving and interesting applications, and creative school organization).

Like AVID schools, Accelerated Schools do not see themselves primarily as "track busters." However, they do consider heterogeneous classes as the most appropriate way to educate all children when sufficient supports are in place both in and out of those classes so all students can succeed.

Like the Accelerated Schools program, the Success for All program, developed by researchers at Johns Hopkins University for Baltimore Public Schools, sees ensuring children's early competence, especially in reading, as a way to narrow the divergence in students' skills by the end of the third grade, thus making heterogeneous classes less daunting to students and teachers alike. "Success is defined as performance in reading, writing, language arts, and mathematics at or near grade level by the third grade, maintenance of this status through the end of the elementary grades, and avoidance of retention or special education" (Madden and others, 1993, p. 1; Slavin and Madden, 1995). Cooperative groups as well as tutoring (often on an as-needed, rotating basis) combined with frequent assessments assure that students do not "fall through the cracks."

AVID, Accelerated Schools, and Success for All are examples of relatively formal, external support systems that provide initial and ongoing help and protection for individual schools' to depart from convention and serve at-risk students. But sometimes individual schools are themselves the cornerstones of dramatic change. Sure, they receive help and support, particularly from their central administration and university researchers, but they march to their own drummers and it is outsiders who stand

amazed at their achievements. Pioneer Valley Regional Middle
School in Northfield, Massachusetts, is such a school:

> Eight years ago, a small cadre of teachers at Pioneer Valley
> Regional School decided it could do more for students by
> ending tracking. . . . An ad hoc committee pushing for het-
> erogeneous grouping found a strong ally in the chairman
> of the school committee, who told them, "I'm a product of
> that school. I was a 5, 'the lowest track.' It took me years to
> get over it, it hurt so bad."
>
> In its next step, the school held teacher workshops,
> and faculty from the University of Massachusetts at Am-
> herst taught a course on teaching styles and strategies to
> prepare the faculty for implementing the changes. . . .
>
> [The] chairman of the English Department was ada-
> mantly opposed to the change in the beginning . . . [but]
> decided to give heterogeneous grouping a try after read-
> ing the research that showed it furthered things he be-
> lieved in as a teacher. When he was working with a mixed
> group of students, he found that neither teaching as he
> always had nor watering down the curriculum worked with
> a mixed group of students. The English department de-
> cided to "get rid of the concept that the classroom is where
> you go to be evaluated" and develop a new curriculum
> around themes. . . . "The first year it bombed." . . . "We did
> not know what to do. We had always been the center of the
> class, made the decisions, told the kids how to look at mate-
> rial and judge its quality. . . . The secret . . . was to create a
> situation where everyone learned together, and no one
> dominated."
>
> They created new structures within the classroom. . . .
> Students are paired; an absentee calls his partner to get
> assignments and the day's work. Small groups are formed
> according to skills. A terrific writer is told his or her job is
> to help everyone in the group succeed in writing.
>
> [The principal] reports a noticeable change in the
> school climate since tracking ended. "There are fewer dis-
> cipline problems, and more kids are engaged in learning.

The teachers are doing more exciting things because they can't lecture." The faculty has become so confident about the value of heterogeneous grouping that, backed by a variety of educational groups and corporate sponsors, the school recently sponsored a conference on "Derailing the Tracked School" that drew some 200 participants. . . .

[The principal's] caveat to those attending was that derailing tracking "was not a painless process" and is still continuing [Caldwell, 1990, p. 61].

The example of Pioneer Valley shows what can be accomplished within a school community with unity of purpose, emphasizing that this unity and its results have been nine years in their development. However, countless other schools in all stages of change are making similar efforts with partial but encouraging success (see, for example, Wheelock, 1992).

While full-blown projects like those described above provide helpful examples for other schools, they should not be regarded as models to be copied, but as purveyors of a more general lesson. This lesson, we argue, is that creating a culture of detracking is more important than any particular alternatives or implementation strategies a school might attempt. The particulars of detracking vary considerably among schools. (Even the AVID and Accelerated Schools projects observe that the nature and pace of school changes vary enormously.) However, we can also detect commonalties in the cultures of successfully detracking schools. Two such commonalties are readily apparent from the previous discussion:

- *Recognition that tracking is supported by powerful norms that must be acknowledged and addressed as alternatives are created*
- *Willingness to broaden the reform agenda, so that changes in the tracking structure become part of a comprehensive set of changes in school practice*

While it is convenient to organize this look at detracking into the categories of (1) norms and (2) practices embedded in the larger school reform agenda, each category must be seen as inclusive of the other. Some changes in programs and practices are driven by the adoption of new norms. At the same time, sometimes experimentation with new programs and practices can alter old norms. For example, when skeptical parents or teachers discover many benefits and few disadvantages to heterogeneous classes in pilot or experimental programs, they may change their beliefs about individual and group differences in ability to learn. That, in turn, generates enthusiasm for new technologies of curriculum, instruction, and organization consistent with the new beliefs.

Change Strategies: Moving from Problems to Promise

Going a step further, successful detracking also depends on change strategies that are never distant from norms and practice. The *medium* (strategy) for bringing forth change can never run counter to the *message* (norms and technology) of change. Schools' and communities' democratic and inclusive purposes for attending to neglected and ill-served poor and minority youth must be mirrored in democratic and inclusive processes of change.

Again, the Accelerated Schools project provides a useful example of how new norms and practices combine to help move school from problem-creating practices, like traditional assessment and tracking, toward more promising approaches for minority students. While expecting and finding rapid gains in student achievement, the project attends to both norms and technical change strategies grounded in educational research and democratic principles. The project recognizes explicitly that improved opportunities for at-risk children must take place in a *culture* that welcomes departures from usual school practice. Toward this end, normative changes in the schools include participation, communication, community, reflection, experimentation, risk taking, and trust. These latter drive what the project calls its "capacity-building" elements. These include creating a vision that permeates all school activities; locating decision making about crucial educational matters at the school site; developing an accountability system that monitors process as well as outcomes; providing tangible incentives; providing access to information about options that includes access to data bases, collaboration with university-based facilitators, school and other agencies, and so on; building processes for open inquiry, discourse, reflection, and deliberation on difficult-to-recognize problems; ensuring central office support; and devising creative and idiosyncratic ways to provide teachers with time for all of the above (for example, one Accelerated School principal teaches a daily aerobics class to students to free up time for teachers to meet) (Levin, 1991).

A closer look at these and other capacity-building elements helps to identify three other characteristics of many other schools that are successfully detracking.

- *Engagement in a process of inquiry and experimentation that is idiosyncratic, opportunistic, democratic, and politically sensitive*

Schools finding some measure of success engage in difficult but fascinating inquiry into their own schools. They experiment with small-scale tracking alternatives of their own design—moving and changing where they can, when they can, and with those who are eager to go along. This process is not merely politically well advised; even in the unlikely event that everyone favored detracking, schools could not simply replace tracking with the "correct" alternative.

Detracking requires opening up the dialogue about tracking—both inside and outside the school. Some districts and schools convene school-community task forces that read research on tracking, assess local practices, and explore alternatives (a recent example is Boston Public Schools). Other school systems collect data about their own grouping structures and course placements and analyze these by race, socioeconomic background, language, gender, and special education status (see, for example, San Diego City's five-year data collection effort). Such strategies promote serious consideration of a number of important questions: What are our school's grouping goals, and are they being met by our use of grouping? What is the procedure for placing students into ability groups? Are there ample opportunities for interaction among students from different ability groups? What successful practices are employed within high-ability classes that can be replicated schoolwide?

Such inquiry-based approaches allow schools to *make sense* out of their own experiences, to bring competing interests and opinions into the open, and in the process, generate ideas for pilot projects and, eventually, new policies and practice.

- *Alterations in teachers' roles and responsibilities, including changes in the way the adults in the school work together*

Serious detracking—just like any significant school reform—needs hands-on, practical-minded, experimenting administrators, and it requires philosophical, inquiring teachers. Where changes are occurring, site and district administrators take the time to become immersed in new practices and become familiar with the new roles teachers are being asked to assume. When they do, administrators sense firsthand the full range of schoolwide alterations needed to support new classroom practice, they can better explain and defend new practices to their communities, and they can more completely assess the effectiveness of the practices. Teachers, on the other hand, must help create new practices and structures—not just implement them. If their roles are reduced to following new sets of teaching protocols or learning new classroom scripts, they are unlikely to be effective—if they adopt the new practices at all.

Moreover, the comprehensive changes that detracking requires almost always triggers significant changes in the way teachers work together. In nearly every school we have encountered, teachers report that it is neither technically nor emotionally possible to undertake the shift to heterogeneous grouping in isolation. Teaming is the most common solution, although that does not necessarily mean that teachers actually teach together. Sometimes teaming means that teachers at a particular grade level or of a particular subject pool their resources to create new lessons for heterogeneous classes, try them out individually, then collectively assess and revise them for future use. In other cases, teachers form cross-disciplinary teams that share responsibility for a group of students for one or more years. This approach seems particularly useful among middle school teachers, who then are able to make decisions together about their students' academic and social needs. Of course, productive working together imposes some demands on the school schedule; it requires additional time—some of which must be provided during the school day.

- *Persistence over the long haul that is sustained by risk-taking leaders who are clearly focused on scholarship and democratic values*

Tracking is entrenched; sensible alternatives are complex, sometimes counterintuitive, usually controversial. In the final analysis, even when alternatives emerge from an inclusive, democratic process of inquiry and experimentation, steering the detracking process through inevitably troubled waters calls for strong leaders who unequivocally and unambiguously—if gently—assert the research and theory and democratic values that support detracking.

At schools we have watched struggle over tracking, we have heard leaders clearly identify specific ways that student success is thwarted by traditions that hold tracking in place. They have openly, often courageously, acknowledged that curricular, administrative, teaching, and other traditions are more powerful than the profession's best knowledge of how children actually learn, and that sometimes these traditions are contrary to deeply held democratic values.

Conclusion

Clearly, new ways of organizing schools and the new instructional practices that must accompany them can improve education for low-income and minority students. In searching for examples of better, more equitable organization and instruction (and the norms that underlie them), we have found many schools serving low-income and minority youth that are making progress, though it should surprise no one that "best practice" in this regard (as in most others) is often found in schools that serve advantaged, white students. On the other hand, it may surprise many that advantaged schools are as ripe for testing and tracking reforms as are schools whose disadvantaged students make the problems more serious because they combine faulty notions of *race* with discredited conceptions of *ability*. Even so, advantaged schools have as many different tracks as disadvantaged schools (although they do have better qualified teachers and proportionately fewer students in the lowest tracks). The very tests schools use to reify the "low ability" of low-income and minority children are also used to make subtle but powerful distinctions among white youth in advantaged schools. These schools, too, send strong messages via labels and lowered expectations that *most* of their students are not-honors, not-gifted, not-the-very-best. Finally, these schools offer low-track instruction dominated by the same kind of low-level curriculum, drill and practice, and lowered expectations that plague less privileged schools.

Why should an advocate for low-income and minority youth be concerned about exposing these practices in schools that are relatively superior? The answer is complex—encompassing both narrow self-interest and broad social concerns. We would like to believe that no other reason is necessary for removing the barriers that testing and tracking create for minority children's educational opportunities and attainments than the fact that it is possible to do so. Unfortunately, the nation has a rather poor record of making broad institutional changes on behalf of disadvantaged children. We only have to look to the history of desegregation and Head Start programs to know that such efforts engender, in the worse cases, violent resistance and in the best cases, grudging and stingy compliance. Detracking, carrying with it as it does the specter of within-school desegregation, is unlikely to be well received if it is argued exclusively as a reform on behalf of minority children.

As important, however, is that tracking and the testing that supports it is *not* an exclusively minority issue, even if minority children are disproportionately harmed by it. These are broad institutional norms and practices that affect all children. As noted above, most of the children stigmatized and disadvantaged by "low-ability" judgments and low-track placements are neither minority nor poor. Advocates for low-income and minority students will most effectively serve their constituents *and* the rest of society if they place their demands for changes in testing and tracking in the context of seeking better schools for all children.

References

Braddock, J. H. *Tracking of Black, Hispanic, Asian, Native American, and White Students: National Patterns and Trends.* Baltimore, Md.: Center for Research on Effective Schooling for Disadvantaged Students, Johns Hopkins University, 1989.

Braddock, J. H., and Dawkins, M. P. "Ability Grouping, Aspirations, and Attainments: Evidence from the National Educational Longitudinal Study of 1988." *Journal of Negro Education,* 1993, *62*(3), 1–13.

Caldwell, J. "A School on Track Without 'Tracking.'" *Boston Globe,* Aug. 5, 1990, pp. 60–61.

Cohen, E. G. *Designing Groupwork: Strategies for the Heterogeneous Classroom.* New York: Teachers College Press, 1994.

Cohen, E. G., Kepner, D., and Swanson, P. "Dismantling Status Hierarchies in Heterogeneous Classrooms." In J. Oakes and K. H. Quartz (eds.), *Creating New Educational Communities: 94th Yearbook of the National Society for the Study of Education.* Chicago: University of Chicago Press, 1995.

Dornbush, S. "Off the Track." Paper presented as the Presidential Address to the Society for Research on Adolescence, San Diego, Calif., 1994.

Ellwein, M. C. "Using Readiness Tests to Route Kindergarten Students: The Snarled Intersection of Psychometrics, Policy, and Practice." *Educational Evaluation and Policy Analysis,* 1991, *13,* 159–175.

Ellwein, M. C., and Eads, G. M. "How Well Do Readiness Tests Predict Future School Performance?" Paper presented at the annual meeting of the American Educational Research Association, Boston, Apr. 1990.

Gamoran, A. "The Consequences of Track-Related Instructional Differences for Student Achievement." Paper presented at the annual meeting of the American Educational Research Association, Boston, Apr. 1990.

Gardner, H. *Frames of Mind: The Theory of Multiple Intelligences.* New York: Basic Books, 1983.

Gardner, H., and Hatch, T. "Multiple Intelligences Go to School: Educational Implications of the Theory of Multiple Intelligences." *Educational Researcher,* 1989, *18*(8), 4–9.

Henderson, R. W., Landesman, E. M., and Marshall, M. *Mathematics and Middle School Students of Mexican Descent: The Effects of Thematically Integrated Instruction.* Research Report No. 5. Santa Cruz: National Center for Research on Cultural Diversity and Second Language Learning, University of California, 1992.

Levin, H. *Building School Capacity for Effective Teacher Empowerment: Applications to Elementary Schools with At-Risk Students.* New Brunswick, N.J.: Rutgers University Consortium for Policy Research in Education, 1991.

MacIver, D. J. *Helping Students Who Fall Behind: Remedial Activities in the Middle Grades.* Paper presented at the annual meeting of the American Educational Research Association, Chicago, Apr. 1991.

Madden, N., and others. "Success for All: Longitudinal Effects of a Restructuring Program for Inner-City Elementary Schools." *American Educational Research Journal,* 1993, *30,* 123–148.

Mehan, H., Hubbard, L., and Villanueva, I. *Untracking and College Enrollment.* Santa Cruz: National Center for Research on Cultural Diversity and Second Language Learning, University of California, 1992.

Meisels, S. J. "High-Stakes Testing in Kindergarten." *Educational Leadership,* 1989, *46,* 16–22.

Oakes, J. *Keeping Track: How Schools Structure Inequality.* New Haven, Conn.: Yale University Press, 1985.

Oakes, J. *Multiplying Inequalities: The Effects of Race, Social Class, and Tracking on Opportunities to Learn Mathematics and Science.* Santa Monica, Calif.: RAND Corporation, 1990.

Oakes, J. "Two Cities: Tracking and Within-School Segregation."

In L. Miller (ed.), *Brown Plus Forty: The Promise.* New York: Teachers College Press, 1995.

Oakes, J., Gamoran, A., and Page, R. N. "Curriculum Differentiation: Opportunities, Outcomes, and Meanings." In P. W. Jackson (ed.), *Handbook of Research on Curriculum.* New York: Macmillan, 1991.

Oakes, J., and Guiton, G. "Matchmaking: Tracking Decisions in Comprehensive High Schools." *American Educational Research Journal,* 1995, *32.*

Oakes, J., and Lipton, M. *Making the Best of Schools: A Handbook for Parents, Teachers, and Policymakers.* New Haven, Conn.: Yale University Press, 1990.

Oakes, J., and Quartz, K. H. (eds.). *Creating New Educational Communities: 94th Yearbook of the National Society for the Study of Education.* Chicago: University of Chicago Press, 1995.

Oakes, J., Selvin, M., Karoly, L., and Guiton, G. *Educational Matchmaking: Curriculum and Tracking Decisions in Comprehensive High Schools.* Santa Monica, Calif.: RAND Corporation, 1992.

Rosenholtz, S. J., and Simpson, C. "The Formation of Ability Conceptions: Developmental Trend or Social Construction?" *Review of Educational Research,* 1984, *54,* 31–63.

Shepard, L. A. "Psychometric Properties of the Gesell Developmental Assessment: A Critique." *Early Childhood Research Quarterly,* 1992, *7,* 47–52.

Shoenfeld, A. "On Mathematics as Sensemaking: An Informal Attack on the Unfortunate Divorce of Formal and Informal Mathematics." In J. F. Voss, D. N. Perkins, and J. Segal (eds.), *Informal Reasoning and Instruction.* Hillsdale, N.J.: Erlbaum, 1988.

Slavin, R. *Cooperative Learning.* Englewood Cliffs, N.J.: Prentice Hall, 1990.

Slavin, R. E., and Madden, N. A. "Success for All: Creating Schools and Classrooms in Which All Children Can Read." In J. Oakes and K. H. Quartz (eds.), *Creating New Educational Communities: 94th Yearbook of the National Society for the Study of Education.* Chicago: University of Chicago Press, 1995.

Sternberg, R. J. *Beyond I.Q.: A Triarchic Theory of Human Intelligence.* New York: Cambridge University Press, 1984.

Sternberg, R. J. *Applied Intelligence.* Orlando, Fla.: Harcourt Brace Jovanovich, 1986.

Sternberg, R. J., Okagaki, L., and Jackson, A. "Practical Intelligence for Success in School." *Educational Leadership,* 1990, *48*(1), 35–39.

Swanson, M. C., Mehan, H., and Hubbard, L. "The AVID Classroom: A System of Academic and Social Supports for Low-Achieving Students." In J. Oakes and K. H. Quartz (eds.), *Creating New Educational Communities: 94th Yearbook of the National Society for the Study of Education.* Chicago: University of Chicago Press, 1995.

Tharp, R. G. "Psychocultural Variables and Constants: Effects on Teaching and Learning." *American Psychologist,* 1989, *44*(2), 1–11.

Useem, E. L. "Getting on the Fast Track in Mathematics: School Organizational Influences on Math Track Assignment." *American Journal of Education,* 1992a, 325–353.

Useem, E. L. "Middle Schools and Math Groups: Parents' Involvement in Children's Placements." *Sociology of Education,* 1992b, *65,* 263–279.

Villegas, A. M., and Watts, S. M. "Life in the Classroom: The Influence of Class Placement and Student Race/Ethnicity." Paper presented at the annual meeting of the American Educational Research Association, Chicago, Apr. 1991.

Wheelock, A. *Crossing the Tracks: Alternatives to Tracking and Ability Grouping in the Middle Grades.* Boston: New Press, 1992.

Wiggins, G. "Authentic Work: Implications for Assessment and School Structures." *Newsletter of the National Center on Effective Secondary Schools,* 1991, *5,* 9–12.

Chapter 9

Strengthening Mathematics Education: Critical Skills for the New Majority

Beverly J. Anderson

Today, the United States is faced with an extraordinary challenge: a growing population of minorities who have been historically disenfranchised in mathematics, and a country striving for its students to be all that they can be by the year 2000, "first in the world in science and mathematics achievement." This goal was set in 1990 at the historic Charlottesville Education Summit with the president of the United States and the state governors.

The goal of having American students be first in the world in mathematics achievement is an ambitious one worth striving for, since mathematics is the hub of the sciences. But, at the least, the United States must address the problems that preclude minority success in mathematics—problems of educational equity and ineffective schools, of intellectual perception, and of motivation. Simply stated, the United States must foster an atmosphere that will make it possible for minorities to become better educated in mathematics so that this population will help the country maintain its place as a world leader in science and mathematics, as well as in industry and technology. The need to reach out to this growing population of underachieving minorities, especially blacks, Hispanics, and American Indians, and the need to assist these students in achieving on a much higher level, is a great challenge facing America—one that has to be met for America to be all that it can and should be.

This chapter brings a challenge and a vision for American education regarding the education of underachieving minorities in mathematics. The major challenge proffered is for this country to think of equity and excellence in mathematics as conjoining terms that naturally go together, and for all students, without regard to race, gender, economic status, ethnicity, creed, and so on, to be given an opportunity for equity and excellence in mathematics in an affirmative atmosphere. The vision makes provisions for actions that can and should be taken to reverse trends of underachievement and underrepresentation in mathematics for specific groups of minorities.

This vision of equity in mathematics, developed over a twenty-five-year period of teaching and research in mathematics education, calls for all of America to work in concert to improve educational opportunities for all students. The chapter acknowledges that minorities are underrepresented in fields other than mathematics and that there is a need to stress other skills such as communications, reading, writing, and computer literacy. It will not be enough to prepare only some students in the area of mathematics; it will be crucially important to prepare all students for productivity and citizenship in the multiethnic, global, and technologically driven society of the twenty-first century. However, it is the field of mathematics that raises most concern about the gross underrepresentation of minority students, for students who forgo a mathematics education are essentially eliminated from a broad range of careers that require some form of math preparation. This chapter will make it clear that it is no longer a matter of goodwill to allow for the emergence of talent from minorities in mathematics; rather it is in the best interests of the United States.

The Challenge

Plato and other philosophers acknowledged centuries ago that mathematics is the foundation of the sciences. During the 1980s, the mathematics community spoke endlessly of the research by Lucy Seels that showed mathematics to be the invisible filter. Students who do not acquire a sufficient background in mathematics prior to college are virtually eliminated from careers in the physical sciences and engineering, as well as from many in the social sciences and psychology (Seels, 1980). Since 1989, several major reports on reform in mathematics education have viewed mathematics as a pump, rather than a filter—students who acquire skills and knowledge of mathematics are pumped through the education pipeline and become prepared for productive citizenship in today's society (Mathematical Sciences Education Board, 1989, 1990, 1991; National Council of Teachers of Mathematics, 1990, 1991).

Jobs requiring skills in mathematics are growing at nearly double the rate of overall employment, and jobs requiring advanced skills in mathematics are held by relatively few blacks, Hispanics, and American Indians. In 1991, blacks and Hispanics made up approximately 17.6 percent of the workforce but only 7 percent of the employed scientists and engineers in America (Bureau of Labor Statistics, U.S. Department of Labor, 1992). In the past, young people without skills in mathematics could expect to enter the workforce as unskilled, low-paid workers. However, even this minimal kind of employment opportunity is becoming less and less prevalent.

In 1992 while visiting one of the pedagogical institutes in Russia, I heard a shocking pronouncement from a Russian professor. He said, "America understands that it is easier to buy a mathematician or scientist than to grow one." These words troubled me. His words to the mathematics education delegation with the Citizens' Ambassador Program were deliberate. I realized during my two-week stay there that his belief was shared by many of his fellow citizens as they anticipate a "brain drain" of Russian mathematics and science professors and scientists to fill job needs in the United States. Russia had painstakingly developed these professionals, but some of them have been and would continue to be lured to the United States mainly because of improved economic conditions for them in America. No longer would Russian professors have to earn wages of 3,000 rubles (about \$30) per month to teach; they could come to America, teach in our most prestigious schools, and earn at least a hundred times that amount. However, some strong nationalist professors, even those who have mastered the English language, would refuse the offer to teach in America. This Russian professor and several other professors like him appeared to take visible pleasure in investing their energy in the future of their country by educating their own citizenry.

After digesting his surprising assertion, I thought of how expensive it is for America not to develop its own citizens to make a living in today's world, and how much more expensive it will be in years to come. I thought about the expense of having nearly one-third of America's black males ages eighteen to thirty involved in the penal system; about how expensive it is to finance the current welfare system and indigent health care; about how expensive it is to finance violence in America. Clearly, the expense of the violence is passed on to Americans through insurance premiums and hospital care. It is more expensive for a large group of citizens to be supported by American social systems than for them to be prepared to contribute in a meaningful way to American society. America must not and cannot be perceived as a rich country with an insufficient supply of human resources. That suggests a threat to our national security. America must come to see that it is, and will continue to be, considerably more expensive to buy rather than to grow its own mathematicians and scientists.

Restructuring and Revitalizing Schools

Between 1989 and 1991, several major reports appeared in planned sequence calling for fundamental changes in both school (elementary and secondary) and college mathematics curricula and instruction. These reports include *Everybody Counts: A Report to the Nation on the Future of Mathematics Education* (Mathematical Sciences Education Board, 1989); *Making Mathematics Work for Minorities: A Framework for a National Action Plan* (Mathematical Sciences Education Board, 1990); *Curriculum and Evaluation Standards for School Mathematics* (National Council of

Teachers of Mathematics, 1990); *Professional Standards for Teaching Mathematics* (National Council of Teachers of Mathematics, 1991); and *Moving Beyond Myths: Revitalizing Undergraduate Mathematics* (Mathematical Sciences Education Board, 1991). The reports are having a profound impact on mathematics education by inspiring and motivating schools and colleges around the nation to reexamine their mathematics programs and to work toward full compliance with the recommendations. They challenge teachers to create classroom environments in which more students can thrive. They also challenge teachers to use relevant and meaningful materials in the mathematics classroom and to freely use technological tools, such as computers and calculators, to enhance student learning. It is now widely recognized that providing conditions in which all students can reach a higher level of achievement in mathematics is an extraordinary challenge to U.S. education, and one with critical implications for the future well-being of the country.

The report on reform in mathematics receiving the most attention is the *Curriculum and Evaluation Standards for School Mathematics* by the National Council of Teachers of Mathematics (NCTM) (1990). This report recommends standards for the mathematics curriculum in grades K–12 and for evaluating the quality of both student achievement and curriculum. The *Standards* emphasize the language of mathematics, problem solving, reasoning, patterns and functions, algebra, geometry, trigonometry, probability and statistics, discrete mathematics, conceptual underpinnings of calculus, and mathematical structures. Mathematics educators realize that some of the mathematics content in the *Standards* required for all students throughout the curriculum in grades K–12—such as probability and statistics—has not been included in the curriculum in teacher preparation programs. Clearly, preservice teachers of mathematics must be prepared in areas that they are expected to teach in, and inservice teachers of mathematics must be given opportunities to broaden their knowledge in those areas.

At the same time that these reports are calling for fundamental changes in school mathematics, schools are faced with a growing population of minorities that have generally not achieved at high levels in mathematics. Likewise, the schools are also faced with increased societal problems, exacerbated by drugs and violence, and are experiencing a diminishing supply of teachers of mathematics, especially minority teachers. Today, minority students make up nearly one-third of the school population, and twenty-two of the twenty-five largest city school districts in the nation are predominantly minority (Quality Education for Minorities Project, 1990). Many of these minorities come from poverty-stricken homes and communities where healthful meals are scarce and where the environment may not be conducive to school learning. Approximately 44 percent of all black children, 38 percent of all Hispanic children, and 15 percent of all white children live in poverty (Bureau of the Census, Economics and Statistics Administration, U.S. Department of Commerce, 1991). In 1991, Sam Husk, executive director of the Council of Great City Schools, reported that approximately 60 percent of the children in urban schools live in poverty. Moreover, nearly half of all poor children (47 percent) score in the bottom quarter on achievement tests, more than twice the rate of nonpoor children (19 percent) (National Center for Education Statistics, U.S. Department of Education, 1990). Low achievers are five times more likely than other students to become dependent on welfare (National Center for Education Statistics, 1991). Thus, the cycle repeats itself.

Research on effective schooling indicates, however, that some urban schools have been effective in dramatically improving the performance of their students. High-performing urban schools have been compared with schools that were demographically similar but had inferior student outcomes. These investigations led several researchers to identify and list school and classroom factors that seemed to make the difference between effective and ineffective schools. They found that effective schools are characterized by strong administrative leadership focused on basic skills acquisition for all students, high expectations for students, teachers who take responsibility for their students' learning and adapt instruction to make sure that learning is taking place, safe and orderly school environments, the provision of incentives and rewards for student performance, and regular monitoring of student progress (Edmonds, 1979; Brookover and Lezotte, 1981; Sizemore, 1985). We should note that this research finding attributed differences in children's performance to the schools themselves, rather than to family income, ethnic status, and education of parents. Some of the "effective" schools have breakfast and lunch programs, and some "effective" schools have after-school programs to provide academic assistance for students who need such support. The challenge, then, is to use the major reports on reform in mathematics education, the research findings on effective schools, and the knowledge of societal factors so that we can become more inclusive in whom we educate. Bearing in mind the community problems of the students served, it is imperative to determine how to better educate underachieving minorities in mathematics, while setting higher goals and expectations.

Teachers for the Twenty-First Century

Although blacks, Hispanics, and American Indians make up about 22 percent of the total U.S. population (12.1 percent blacks, 9 percent Hispanics, and 0.8 percent American Indian) and about one-third of the public school population, these groups make up about 11 percent of the teacher population, and only 6 percent of the high school teachers of mathematics, in grades ten to twelve (Council of Chief State School Officers, 1990). The minority population is growing much faster than the majority population. From 1980 to 1990, the white population grew 6 percent, the black population grew 13.2 percent, the American Indian population grew 37.9 percent, and the Hispanic population grew 53 percent (Bureau of the Census, Economics and Statistics Administration, U.S. Department of Commerce, 1991). By the year 2000, when roughly one-third of the nation will be minority, population trends suggest that the school-age population will approach a majority of minorities. At that time, projections also show that well over 50 percent of today's schoolteachers will have reached retirement age. However, the pipeline in teacher education programs suggests that there will be an insufficient pool to replace the aging faculty, and the proportion of minority elementary and secondary school students is far greater than that of the future teaching force. In 1989, for every 439 students enrolled in teacher education programs nationally, there were 28 (6.4 percent) blacks, 11 (2.5 percent) Hispanics, and 2 (0.4 percent) American Indians.

Hence, it is crucial to explore what has been done and what more must be done to increase high-quality teachers, especially minority teachers of mathematics. The need to increase the pool of minority teachers is crucial today in view of the wide disparity between the supply of minority teachers of mathematics and the proportion of minority students in virtually every state in the United States. Not only is it important to ensure that minority students have an opportunity to be taught mathematics by minority teachers, specifically black, Hispanic, and American Indian teachers, but it is equally important for majority students to be taught by minority teachers from these ethnic groups to eliminate some of the stereotypes associated with "who can do mathematics." According to the American Association of Colleges for Teacher Education (1990), a quality education requires that all students be exposed to nationally representative cultural perspectives. Such exposure can be accomplished through a multiethnic teaching force in which racial and ethnic groups are included at a level of parity with their numbers in the population.

As more and more professionals have become aware of the dearth of underrepresented minority secondary school teachers of mathematics and of the possible reasons for it, programs have been developed to increase the pool. Programmatic activities aimed at producing minority teachers target various groups of potential teacher candidates. These activities include magnet school and intervention programs at the precollege level, articulation programs between two- and four-year colleges, special focused baccalaureate degree programs, and programs for retirees and/or career changers. The goals of these programs generally are the following: (1) to stimulate the interest of minorities in the teaching profession, particularly in teaching mathematics; (2) to provide incentives (including financial aid) for promising minority students to become teachers of mathematics; (3) to prepare minorities to teach mathematics in urban school districts; and (4) to provide a supportive environment to make it possible for minorities to be successful in undergraduate programs in mathematics education. These programs have been developed by schools, colleges and universities, private and public agencies, and professional organizations concerned about increasing the supply of minority secondary school teachers of mathematics.

Although there has been a serious attempt to increase the minority teaching force in America, the programs are few in number and are somewhat fragmented. Another challenge, then, is to increase the number of these programs and students served by them, and to maintain successful programs to increase the minority teaching force over the long run, realizing that there is no quick fix to reversing current trends. There is also a need to create a network of successful programs—a network that could be accessed across the country.

While minority teachers of mathematics are sorely needed in schools around the country, there is also a need to strengthen the current teaching force in mathematics, and to strengthen teachers' ability to teach mathematics to all students. Also, teacher preparation programs should be modified to ensure that the "new" teachers will be prepared to teach the mathematics content specified in the NCTM *Standards*. Current teachers of mathematics must become keenly aware of these *Standards* and must also be provided opportunities to expand their content base, as well as being given strategies to use in teaching relevant and meaningful material. There is an urgent need for education in the history of mathematics for all preservice and inservice teachers to include contributions to the field of mathematics by individuals from various ethnic and racial groups, so that this information could be passed on to their students. Ultimately, this well-educated mathematics teaching force will be the critical change agents in the schools for reform in mathematics education. It is important to note here that many white teachers of mathematics have been and will continue to be effective in developing minority students in mathematics. These teachers, like their minority counterparts, have been successful because they have taught under the assumption that all students can and must learn mathematics and have sought ways to support this perspective.

The Importance of Vision

Those who should share the vision for broadening access to minorities in mathematics include the U.S. government, parents, schools, opinion leaders, and other stakeholders advocating stronger school programs in mathematics and stronger teachers of mathematics for all children to prepare them for productive citizenship in today's and tomorrow's society. Associated with productive citizenship are rights, responsibilities, and privileges— the right to job opportunities, the responsibility to reach back to others in the community and to protect the quality of their education, and the privilege of assuming a leadership role to ensure educational opportunities for the next generation.

This vision asserts that "effective schools" will appear in more urban districts across the country and in suburban schools committed to developing minority students in mathematics. School programs in mathematics developed using the NCTM *Standards* and relying on effective school research findings will need to be created. All segments of the population supporting schools and colleges to increase minority participation in mathematics, mathematics education, and science will have to work together. Teachers of mathematics in schools will need to demonstrate that they believe that all students can and must learn mathematics, and they must foster environments in schools to make it possible for all students to learn this powerful subject matter. Teachers must enthusiastically get involved in inservice education on many topics, including the following: using technology in the mathematics classroom; preparing lessons in meaningful subject areas, such as probability and statistics, for students at all levels; preparing meaningful graphic and tabular data for students at all levels; infusing multiculturalism in mathematics; and encouraging minority students to view themselves as "can-doers" of mathematics. Parents will need to be empowered to support strong mathematics programs in the schools, and they should volunteer services to enhance those programs.

Parents have to be taught to believe that their children can and must perform well in mathematics and to encourage their children to do so. Parents must also learn to be involved in school programs to help them become better parents for the "new majority" in the schools. Communities across the country must learn to use their resources to strengthen the education of their children, especially in mathematics, and these communities must embrace and foster the idea that minority students can be successful in mathematics.

In tomorrow's schools, teachers of mathematics at all levels must be prepared to confidently analyze, discuss, and use quantitative data, understanding the connections between mathematics and other disciplines and using technological tools such as the computer and calculator to enhance instruction. Hence, more minority students should have an opportunity to be competitive at the national and international levels, and more students and teachers should be exposed to a learning environment that will make it possible for them to become prepared to contribute in a meaningful way to the society of the twenty-first century.

A vision for the future involves teachers setting high expectations for all students and the elimination of low-end tracking in mathematics classes. Programs like the one developed by the famous mathematics teacher Jaime Escalante, formerly at Garfield High School in Los Angeles, must spring up all over the country. Escalante believed that Hispanic students could learn calculus while in high school and set out to prove this to his peers at Garfield High School. He was successful despite the apparent skepticism of some mathematics faculty in the school and some parents in the community. Escalante and a team of teachers set high expectations for these students and provided quality instruction and challenging materials in mathematics. The result was that the students lived up to the expectations, and year after year an unusually high number of these students passed the Advanced Placement calculus examination administered by the College Board.

A new vision involves all students, especially minority students, being required to take mathematics every year while in high school, and some of them working after school and on weekends with teachers. Students will need to have access to study groups and/or work with community volunteers to improve their skills and understanding of mathematics. Schools will need to expect these students to take the challenging courses in mathematics on the academic track, and to have qualified teachers assigned to teach these courses. Minority students should be actively engaged in mathematics clubs and problem-solving teams. New programs will be needed, patterned after the Arlington, Virginia, model featuring all-day kindergarten, parent education, support services, after-school enrichment, and multicultural education infused in the entire curriculum. Multicultural education should also be infused in the parent education component. In addition, opportunities must exist for promising students to participate in summer and after-school academic intervention programs at local universities. School will need to address testing discrepancies in a sensitive manner, while not separating minority students and educating them differently.

Conclusion

In the future, more school programs will be designed to increase the minority teaching force in mathematics. The magnet school program at Calvin Coolidge High School in Washington, D.C., is one of approximately twelve national college preparatory programs designed for students interested in the educational profession. This four-year school program includes specially designed education courses for students in grades nine to twelve, emphasizing pedagogy, teaching methodology, and practice. Approximately 30 to 40 percent of the students (almost all black) have developed an interest in becoming secondary school teachers of mathematics. Christine Easterling, the program director, recruits high-achieving students for the Coolidge program and encourages them to pursue mathematics and science teaching.

Two-year colleges have a critical role to play in developing articulation programs with four-year institutions to increase the minority teaching force in America. More programs must be developed like the Urban Teacher Program (UTP), which provides a community college articulation model at Wayne

County Community College, Eastern Michigan University, and Wayne State University. These higher education institutions sponsor the program along with the state department of education and three urban school districts. The UTP allows students to earn an associate's degree at Wayne County Community College, then to complete their bachelor's degree requirements as students at Eastern Michigan University or Wayne State University. The program places emphasis on field work and mentor relationships with outstanding teachers identified by school principals. To participate in the program through all four years, students must follow a mathematics, science, or bilingual education track. If they choose another area or specialty, they must apply to the upper division institution independently. This requirement was initiated to ensure that teachers were being trained in fields with the most critical shortages.

Intervention programs patterned after the Clark Atlanta University program for high school students interested in the teaching profession will also be needed. Betty Clark has created the Summer Camp Opportunity for Potential Educators (SCOPE) program at Clark Atlanta University, explicitly designed to stimulate student interest in the teaching of secondary school mathematics and science.

Colleges and universities, especially majority institutions, have an imperative to create college intervention programs in an affirmative atmosphere for minority students. Support programs to strengthen, and thus retain, underrepresented minority students can help minority students create for themselves a community of academic friends with whom to study. One such program is the well-structured, well-documented Mathematics Workshop at the University of California at Berkeley. Black students engaged in the Mathematics Workshop, developed by Uri Treisman, outperformed the white students in Calculus I on the final departmental examination in at least one semester. Of importance is not so much that they outperformed the white students at Berkeley, but that they could demonstrate on a written measure that they learned Calculus I as well. Their performance level in Calculus I has remained relatively high throughout the course of the project. Workshop students were given challenging material and were led to believe that they could be successful in their calculus class. They were not given remediation support services. Also, this program was supported by the entire university, sending a message to the academic communities across the country that minority student success efforts cannot be invested in only one person or one office.

Another set of academic intervention programs designed to increase minority participation in the mathematical sciences are the long-standing programs at the University of the District of Columbia (UDC) and the University of Texas at San Antonio (UTSA). These programs for junior and senior high school students—A Summer Program in Mathematics and Computer Science at UDC and TexPrep at UTSA—provide challenging subject matter presented by highly qualified and interested faculty, a career awareness component, and field trips to see the mathematical scientists at work in society. Also, these programs stress the importance of hard work and commitment to excellence as the keys to success. The Mathematical Association of America (1992) received a grant from the Carnegie Corporation of New York to encourage the creation of college-based academic intervention programs of this type for underrepresented minority school students. Between 1990 and 1992, the Mathematical Association of America provided planning grants to nearly fifty colleges and universities for such programs.

Departments of mathematics across the country can foster a different perception of mathematics and the mathematics major. Clarence Stephens, the creator of a successful undergraduate mathematics program at the State University of New York (SUNY)-Potsdam, where approximately 24 percent of the bachelor's degrees were in mathematics, stated: "We focus on the human factor, to change students' perception that mathematics is an almost impossible subject for students to learn and that only the most gifted can be expected to achieve any degree of success." Stevens asserts that students want to learn mathematics because of the supportive environment at SUNY-Potsdam.

To recruit more minorities into mathematics, institutions of higher education will need to develop successful comprehensive college programs that include special admissions programs, adequate financial aid, sensitive academic and personal counseling, prefreshman summer programs, tutoring and support of instruction (when necessary), and an affirmative atmosphere. Comprehensive programs are commonly seen at minority institutions where minority students have been unusually successful in majors based on mathematics.

More private philanthropic organizations will need to get involved, investing large sums of money to address the problem of underrepresentation of minorities in the mathematical sciences. The William Penn Foundation's Minorities in Higher Education Initiative, which focuses on increasing the number of black and Hispanic students who graduate with degrees in mathematics, science, and engineering and which encourages more of these students to prepare for university faculty positions, is exemplary in reversing trends of underrepresentation in the mathematical sciences.

Finally, government agencies must invest significant resources to increase minority representation in the mathematical sciences. Precollege programs, teacher preparation and enhancement programs, and innovative undergraduate and graduate programs to prepare minority mathematical sciences majors and prospective teachers of science and mathematics are sorely needed. The National Science Foundation should be applauded for its initiatives in this area, and its commitment to this goal is clearly seen by the recent substantive increase in programs designed for the underrepresented groups, as evidenced in the Urban Systemic Initiative.

Over the next few years, every stakeholder must take significant steps to keep minorities in school and focused on the appropriate academic areas so that they will meet the workforce demands in the United States. Hence, minority education in mathematics and the mathematical sciences is no longer just an educational issue but rather a serious economic issue as we begin to prepare more of our citizens to solve the problems in this country and to contribute to fundamental U.S. systems such as social security.

The teachers and professors of mathematics are critical to the solution of the problem because their investment in students will indeed be an investment in America, and will determine the extent to which this country will be self-sufficient in the years to come. No longer can we allow the growing minority population in the United States to be ill equipped to handle many of the jobs needed in a technological society. No longer can we discourage minorities from pursuing mathematics, which Galileo called the "alphabet with which God has written the earth." No longer can we allow anyone to say that America chooses to buy its scientists and mathematicians rather than to grow its own. Ultimately, the beneficiary of America's commitment to quality education for minorities and for all of its citizens will indeed be America.

References

American Association of Colleges for Teacher Education. *Teacher Education Pipeline: Schools, Colleges, and Departments of Education Enrollments by Race and Ethnicity.* Washington, D.C.: American Association of Colleges for Teacher Education, 1990.

Brookover, W. B., and Lezotte, L. W. *Effective Secondary Schools.* Philadelphia: Research for Better Schools, 1981.

Bureau of the Census, Economics and Statistics Administration, U.S. Department of Commerce. *1990 Census Profile.* Washington, D.C.: U.S. Government Printing Office, 1991.

Bureau of Labor Statistics, U.S. Department of Labor. *Projections 2000.* Bulletin No. 2302. Washington, D.C.: U.S. Government Printing Office, 1992.

Council of Chief State School Officers. *State Indicators of Science and Mathematics Education: Course Enrollment and Teachers.* Washington, D.C.: Council of Chief State School Officers, 1990.

Edmonds, R. R. "Effective Schools for the Urban Poor." *Educational Leadership,* 1979, *37,* 15–27.

Mathematical Association of America. *Statistical Abstract of Undergraduate Programs in the Mathematical Sciences and Computer Science: The 1990–1991 CBMS Survey.* (D. J. Albers, D. O. Lottsgarden, D. Rung, and A. Watkins, eds.) Washington, D.C.: Mathematical Association of America, 1992.

Mathematical Sciences Education Board. *Everybody Counts: A Report to the Nation on the Future of Mathematics Education.* Washington, D.C.: National Academy Press, 1989.

Mathematical Sciences Education Board. *Making Mathematics Work for Minorities: A Framework for a National Action Plan.* Washington, D.C.: National Academy Press, 1990.

Mathematical Sciences Education Board. *Moving Beyond Myths: Revitalizing Undergraduate Mathematics.* Washington, D.C.: National Academy Press, 1991.

National Center for Education Statistics, U.S. Department of Education. *Digest of Education Statistics.* Washington, D.C.: U.S. Government Printing Office, 1990.

National Council of Teachers of Mathematics. *Curriculum and Evaluation Standards for School Mathematics.* Reston, Va.: National Council of Teachers of Mathematics, 1990.

National Council of Teachers of Mathematics. *Professional Standards for Teaching Mathematics.* Reston, Va.: National Council of Teachers of Mathematics, 1991.

Quality Education for Minorities Project. *Education That Works: An Action Plan for the Education of Minorities.* Cambridge: Massachusetts Institute of Technology, 1990.

Seels, L. *The Invisible Filter. Engineering Review,* 1980.

Sizemore, B. A. "Pitfalls and Promises of Effective Schools Research." *Journal of Negro Education,* 1985, *54*(3), 269–288.

Task Force on Women, Minorities, and the Handicapped in Science and Technology. *Changing America: The New Face of Science and Engineering.* Washington, D.C.: Task Force on Women, Minorities, and the Handicapped in Science and Technology, 1989.

U.S. Department of Education. *America 2000.* Washington, D.C.: U.S. Government Printing Office, 1991.

Chapter 10

Involving Parents and Communities in School Reform

Estrella M. Triana, Shirley M. Malcom

The significant role parents and community members play in the education of children has been a prime issue in school reform movements. Yet many parents, especially minority parents, are often unaware of what makes up and what ought to make up their child's education, and consequently, they are frequently uncertain about the role they should play in the educational process. A number of community organizations, such as the National Urban League and the National Council of La Raza, have facilitated parental involvement in schools. However, their value in this process has been largely unexplored.

While meaningful school reform is not possible without a significant degree of parental involvement, parents cannot be part of school restructuring efforts if they are unaware of their potential role in the educational process or in educational reform. The former assistant secretary for research of the U.S. Department of Education, Christopher Cross, has asserted that parents need to understand they can make a difference and that teachers and the principals have to understand the importance of parental involvement (Bacon, 1990). In this chapter, we will explore the vital roles parents can take in the educational process and the role existing community organizations can and do play in assisting parents. Additionally, we will explore strategies and resources that can increase minority parental involvement and highlight models that have employed these strategies to engage parents in education.

Parental Role in Education

"Parents are the child's first teachers." This often-repeated slogan is true. However, it fails to capture the notion that parents must prepare themselves and their children to engage with formal systems of education and that they must become advocates for their children, negotiating their interaction with the school system. To successfully engage minority parents is to successfully move them through more sophisticated levels of commitment and empowerment. The primary level focuses on parental involvement in the education of their children. Central to achieving success at this level is providing clear and adequate information for parents to understand their roles, keeping in mind barriers such as lack of education and time. It is essential to communicate the critical nature of that role as well as specific information as to how and what parents should do. Similarly, it is crucial to address myths and fears that parents may have about their involvement, particularly inadequacies in content areas. In many cases, workshops designed to engage parents in activities—for example, hands-on science and mathematics—will allow them to experience success, and in the process, demonstrate what parents can do at home to help their children.

The succeeding level of involvement highlights the empowerment of parents. At this level, parents need to understand how they can take part in the decision-making aspects of their children's education. Information regarding their children's course scheduling, graduation requirements, and achievement testing enables parents to take a more active role in assisting their children to make decisions and in monitoring their children's progress through the educational system.

At the highest level, empowered parents can be education

advocates to improve education for all children. At this level, the
emphasis is on providing information on how the curriculum is
put together, how it can include appropriate references to culture, and how the processes and procedures of schools can promote sharing responsibility for children's education. It is equally
important to provide parents with a "voice" and opportunities
to express and address their concerns.

The common element of these direct and "political" levels is in providing adequate information to engage parents—especially minority parents—in the education of their children.
Yet, despite some understanding and concern among educators
about increasing parental involvement, Coleman (1991) argues
that educators often cling to policies that keep activist parents
and community groups at arm's length. The authors point out
that parents, for the most part, lack the information and support necessary to get involved in their children's education. Consequently, to communicate to parents the necessity for monitoring their children's homework assignments is to assume that
parents know how much homework their child is to do, how
much time their child is supposed to allow for homework assignments, and what to do to assist their child in getting their homework completed.

Parental lack of information and communication with
schools is substantiated in a nationwide survey conducted in the
spring of 1988. The National Educational Longitudinal Survey
(NELS: 1988), conducted for the U.S. Department of Education
(1990), shows that nearly two-thirds of the parents of 25,000
eighth graders surveyed had had no communication with school
officials about their child's academic program. Other findings
further illustrate parent lack of interaction with schools. Only
half had attended school meetings or had communicated with
schools about their child's academic performance. Furthermore,
only a third of all parents reported membership in a parent-
teacher organization. Membership rates for Hispanic and American Indian parents were even lower. From these data it would
be easy to conclude that the parents do not care. Alternatively,
one could argue that appropriate routes to getting parents
involved have not been fully explored, especially those that ad-

dress socioeconomic and structural attributes that tend to be predictors of minority parental involvement in school activities (Zill and Nord, 1994). Our experience suggests that the latter hypothesis deserves more attention.

Community Organization Programs

Community organizations that target minority populations provide a wide variety of services. Their success is due to their accessibility and attentiveness to the particular needs of their constituents. Their success is due as well to their use of incentives and to the efforts of dedicated, charismatic individuals who coordinate these programs.

One such program, the National Urban League (NUL) Preschool Science Collaborative, highlights parental involvement. The program focuses on improving science education for African American preschool children. The program objective is twofold in that it includes both a preschool science curriculum, developed for NUL centers, and a parent component, additionally developed to reinforce the centers' work. A manual of activities produced for NUL centers includes activities to educate parents in their role. An initial three-site pilot program has expanded to more than twenty NUL sites around the country. While developed using League preschools as models, the program's "parent-shared" curriculum model has clear general application to child-centered early childhood programs.

AVANCE, serving low-income Mexican American families, is another program focused on parent education. AVANCE offers parents basic parenting and social skills. During the nine-month program, parents meet monthly for two-and-a-half-hour sessions, which cover toy making, child development, and resources in the community. To ensure parent participation, the program offers transportation, home visits, day care, special trips and outings, employment training, family planning, community resource skills, and driver education. The comprehensive program is already demonstrating success and is observing parents more involved in school and in the community.

Another program with a parent component is the National

Council of La Raza's Excellence in Community Educational Leadership (Project EXCEL). Working with the Hispanic community, the "Parents as Partners" component of the program concentrates on providing information and instruction to parents on home activities and strategies that will assist their children in the elementary grades. Resource materials and workshops are provided in English and Spanish. Although child care and other incentives are provided at many of the affiliate sites that are implementing this model, continued parent participation depends on establishing productive relationships with individual program coordinators, and to some degree with other parents.

Community organizations in many cases rely on linking with a variety of groups to establish their programs and improve their materials. One such collaborative effort is Partners for Reform in Science and Math (Project PRISM). Working with the National Council of La Raza, Thirteen/WNET, and the National Center for Improving Science Education, the National Urban League will involve parents as spokespersons in activities designed to increase awareness and involvement in mathematics and science education reform nationwide. Since the program's origin in 1992, print materials have been developed, in English and Spanish, that emphasize ways parents can get involved in math and science reform.

While community partnerships help program objectives, numerous existing resource materials also provide assistance to program activities. These include materials such as *Get into the Equation,* a publication produced by the College Board (1987) in cooperation with the American Association for the Advancement of Science (AAAS), that have been developed to provide information to minority parents. The pamphlet just mentioned highlights information about coursework and assessment testing in school, while also detailing how parents can take part in their child's education. Although the publication is designed for parents' at-home reading, a number of organizations have adopted *Get into the Equation* as a format in their workshops for parents. These workshops explore, in greater depth, the main points of the publication and provide parents with the opportunity to engage in hands-on science and mathematics activities they can do with their child. The Spanish translation of this publication, *Contamos con ustedes* (American Association for the Advancement of Science, 1989), and a complementing videotape, *Compañeros en la educación,* were produced by AAAS in conjunction with the College Board. The publication and videotape are intended to reach Hispanic parents who may be limited in their English knowledge or who may be illiterate in both Spanish and English and who especially need to understand the educational process.

Family Math (Stenmark, Thompson, and Cossey, 1986) and the Spanish translation *Matemática para la familia*—publications from the Lawrence Hall of Science at the University of California—are written for parents of children in kindergarten through grade eight, to work and learn math by doing hands-on activities at home with their children. The English and Spanish books are directed to parents with activity presentations and directions for parents to understand and easily follow. A secondary audience for the publication includes community leaders, educators, and others who are interested in conducting *Family Math* workshops for parents. Numerous community organizations, such as National Council of La Raza affiliates, conduct *Family Math* workshops that provide hands-on activities and information for parents about their children's math programs and about how mathematics concepts relate to each other.

Math Power, a series of books published by AAAS and directed to parents, schools, and community organizations working with children in middle/junior high grades, provide math problem-solving activities. While *Math Power at Home* (Kulm, 1990) contains activities similarly presented in *Math Power in School* and *Math Power in the Community,* the objective is to provide enrichment to the child's school assignments. The successful effort in developing these materials is attributed to writing teams in these city locations: Baltimore, Chicago, and Los Angeles. Writing teams consisted of parents, mathematics teachers, college mathematics professors, and community educators who contributed activities drawn from a number of sources to produce the final publications.

Las matemáticas cuentan, the Spanish translation of *Math Matters,* is a National Parent-Teacher Association (NPTA) (1990) effort to outreach to Hispanic parents who often are not members of parent-teacher associations. Consequently, unlike the English kit distributed to 50,000 PTAs around the country, distribution of the kit in Spanish was primarily directed to organizations that work with Hispanic parents. The translated kit, like the English counterpart, provides activities for parents to do with elementary school children at home, or almost anywhere. The kit will be deemed a success if it contributes to the creation of a positive attitude about mathematics for both students and parents.

The *Count on Me* program, led by television station KCET in Los Angeles and partnering with AAAS, is a nationwide effort to disseminate information and involve parents in the mathematics education of their children. The effort highlights the production of the *Count on Me* public broadcast program using well-known actors to present information about mathematics through a story line, and at the same time the program presents activities emphasizing important basic mathematical concepts. To complement the program and continue disseminating information to parents, KCET, with AAAS assistance, produced a folder for parents that included an informational booklet outlining ways parents can get involved in their child's mathematics education, and provided specific instructions on eight mathematics activities parents can do with their children. In addition, AAAS conducted a series of *Count on Me* workshops in six cities around the country to involve minority parents in the program's efforts. The workshops engaged African American and Hispanic parents in the activities outlined in the *Count on Me* folder, and also provided parents with a kit of materials to continue the activities with their children.

Model Programs

Model programs have incorporated nontraditional approaches and utilized resources in the community to actively enlist parental involvement. Programs such as the Stay in School Program in New York, developed by Fordham University and funded by the state, target kindergarten through third grade at three inner-city public schools with high Hispanic enrollment and with poor parent-school relationships. The program provides children with tutoring and materials, while the parents receive modest monetary incentives to attend parent workshops at their children's schools. Parent workshops at these schools concentrate on teaching parenting skills. Social workers are available to assist with family problems. The program is showing positive results for both children and parents. Standardized test scores have significantly improved, and absences have been reduced by half. In addition, parent participation has increased in the nonpaid informal component of the program.

Another model project—AAAS Proyecto Futuro—demonstrates a comprehensive program involving parents. Originally developed and implemented in Chicago in 1991, the project works with schools that have a high Hispanic enrollment and with those schools' parents to improve science and mathematics teaching and learning. The parent component of the project features workshops, coordinated by local community organizations, that highlight the role of parents. Additionally, the workshops address parents' science and mathematics fears by engaging them in "fun" hands-on science and math activities. To reinforce the concept of parents working at home with their children, parents are given science and mathematics kits to take home. The kits contain instructions and information in English and Spanish and sufficient materials to do the kit activities at home. Incentives are provided for parents to participate in the workshops and to participate in evaluation of the kits. The project is being implemented in Albuquerque, New Mexico; Barceloneta, Puerto Rico; Los Angeles; and New York. Over 400 parents have participated in project activities and have received kit materials.

A foundation for Proyecto Futuro is AAAS's Linkages Project. Linkages is a nationwide effort to connect community organizations with scientists and engineers to work toward improving science education for female and minority students and students with disabilities. A major component of Linkages is to empower parents. Providing information and training to parents, schools, and community organizations with parent programs, Linkages reached more than 30,000 parents.

A fourth model program, the Math, Engineering, and Science Achievement Program (MESA), similarly stresses a comprehensive approach by highlighting partnerships between schools, universities, industry, and parents. The program offers tutoring and counseling and provides role models from industry to encourage students to maintain good grades. Parents are provided information and participate in workshops to learn how they can support their children throughout their education. The partnership works with about 4,000 students yearly in California alone and demonstrates the success of the partnership with startling results. Ninety percent of these students enter a college or university, and 66 percent major in science or engineering.

Strategies for Success

Model programs, whether based in school or out of school, have similar approaches that make them successful in reaching and engaging parents in their programs. While information is provided in all programs, various approaches are used in their dissemination. Nonetheless, a combination of the strategies proposed in this section have all been implemented in various areas of the country and have been well received in that they provide solutions reflecting an understanding of parents and promote the concept that parental involvement is a partnership of parents, school, and community members. Examined separately, the strategies incorporated in these programs provide a basis for eliciting parental involvement.

Fostering Communication

Schools, as well as community organizations that recognize and address working parents, especially the increasing single heads of households in the workforce, have seen a change in parental participation. Although a number of corporations and businesses have started to give parents flexibility in their work schedules to attend parent conferences and other school functions, many still do not have this flexibility. Scheduling meetings and parent-teacher conferences at various times in the day, including times in the evening or on weekends, has proven most effective in encouraging parent participation.

While setting up a flexible time for parents to participate is imperative, of equal importance is making schools a comfortable, nonthreatening place for them. A fine example of this is provided by James Comer and his colleagues at the Yale Child Study Center, in working with the New Haven inner-city elementary schools located in low socioeconomic neighborhoods with a high African American enrollment. Comer's group observed that schools and parents needed to learn to communicate with each other. As a result, the group created an intervention team in the schools that consisted of school staff, parents, and specialists (for example, a social worker and a psychologist). Through these teams, work relations with parents improved, as did the schools' ability to change (Hamburg, 1992).

The message that needs to be conveyed to parents is that they are needed and wanted throughout the educational process. Parents are more likely to be encouraged to get involved at the primary grades than at the middle and upper grades. As a result, the NELS:1988 survey points out that communication is perilously close to nonexistent at these levels. Schools can address this in several ways. First, they can provide regular communication via newsletters and can encourage parent-teacher conferences and telephone communication to discuss their child's progress. Second, schools can make sure written communication with Hispanic parents is provided in English and Spanish and that translators are available during conferences and meetings. Finally, schools should recognize that parents may not be able to arrange for child care to attend parent meetings and conferences. By providing on-site child care during such times, schools would be assisting parents with this responsibility and, at the same time, making school an inviting place for families to attend with children of all ages.

Another approach in expanding communication efforts focuses on using technology. While telephones cannot always be readily accessed by teachers during instructional times, fax and message machines, electronic mail, and other telecommunications techniques are beginning to be part of more and more schools. For some parents and teachers, utilizing this approach would be convenient for receiving and sending messages. As example, a school in Baltimore, Maryland, with a history of poor parental attendance at parent meetings nonetheless attracted hundreds of calls each week to its hotline, which recorded messages from parents who needed information to monitor homework assignments.

Utilizing Community Organizations

Schools need to recognize that community organizations are a common ground where many minority parents and schools can meet to forge a positive parent-school relationship. First, linking with community organizations that conduct educational programs and workshops for parents would be beneficial in fostering communication between schools and parents. Second, educating and assisting parents in how to get involved in the educational process would at the same time assist schools and educators in their communications about children's program and academic progress. Finally, community organizations that work with special populations can be utilized as a resource for materials developed and/or compiled from a variety of sources to provide the parents they serve with relevant materials and information in cultural- and language-sensitive forms. These specifically developed materials could give schools the tools they need in fostering greater communication, learning, and understanding in their work with parents.

Designating a Liaison

To increase parental participation, establishing a liaison in the school would both assist with building communication between parents and educators and make school more accessible for parents. Ideally a liaison working with a minority population would need to be sensitive to different values and cultures, and, in many instances, be bilingual. The liaison would be more in contact with the community to answer questions and consequently could be perceived as a catalyst for forging school-parent relationships. In a similar capacity, the school liaison could work with community organizations to assist with questions about educational processes and school procedures, while returning to the school with strategies and approaches for increasing parental involvement.

Incorporating Parents in the Classroom

If the community is seen as a resource and incorporated into the school, then parents and children will benefit. Observing that a number of parents in the community worked in construction, a teacher invited parents to speak to her class about what they did and how they used mathematics in their work. The teachers then had the students build simple structures applying mathematical concepts discussed. The responses from parents and students alike were positive. The success in part was due to the parents perceiving themselves as contributors and students seeing their parents as active contributors in their education. Consequently, by actively involving parents as resources in the classroom, parent attitudes and perceptions about themselves changed, and as a result, their involvement increased.

Conclusion

Involving parents, especially minority parents, in school reform efforts is imperative if these efforts are to impact the education of all children. While involvement can be at many different levels, at all levels parents need to have information in order to initially engage with schools. Yet information cannot be disseminated in only one form. Successful efforts to involve parents provide information in a number of ways to ensure that parents understand and are aware of the different roles they can play. A hands-on approach combined with specifically developed materials, implemented by community organizations and model programs, has demonstrated success with minority parents. Moreover, the strategies utilized by these programs have increased and promoted parental involvement. While one strategy may be easier to implement than others, a combination of these strategies will likely be most effective in engaging parents in their child's education. We cannot expect minority parents to play significant and comfortable roles in proposed public choice programs or to fully take advantage of the opportunity to reshape schooling available through service on school councils as exists in some communities unless they are informed, engaged, and empowered. Ultimately, these strategies will facilitate a parent-school-community partnership that will engage all parents equally in the restructuring of our schools to enable all children to achieve their potential.

References

American Association for the Advancement of Science. *Contamos con ustedes.* Washington, D.C.: American Association for the Advancement of Science, 1989.

Bacon, K. H. "Many Educators View Involved Parents as Critical to Children's Success." *Wall Street Journal,* July 31, 1990, p. B1.

Coleman, J. S. (ed.). *Parental Involvement in Education.* Washington, D.C.: U.S. Department of Education, 1991.

College Board. *Get into the Equation.* New York: College Board, 1987.

Hamburg, D. A. *Today's Children: Creating a Future for a Generation in Crisis.* New York: Random House, 1992.

Kulm, G. *Math Power at Home.* Washington, D.C.: American Association for the Advancement of Science, 1990.

National Parent-Teacher Association. *Las matemáticas cuentan: El futuro de nuestros niños depende de Usted.* Washington, D.C.: National Parent-Teacher Association, 1990.

Stenmark, J. K., Thompson, V., and Cossey, R. *Family Math.* Berkeley: Lawrence Hall of Science, University of California, 1986.

U.S. Department of Education. *A Profile of the American Eighth Grader.* Washington, D.C.: U.S. Government Printing Office, 1990.

Zill, N., and Nord, C. W. *Running in Place: How American Families Are Fairing in a Changing Economy and Individualist Society.* Washington, D.C.: Child Tends, 1994.

Chapter 11

Indian Nations at Risk:
An Educational Strategy for Action

William G. Demmert, Jr.

American Natives (American Indian and Alaska Native) are in a unique position as citizens of the United States. As individuals they hold the same rights and responsibilities of all citizens. As American Indians and Alaska Natives they have a special fiduciary relationship with the United States. The federal government maintains a trust responsibility as guardian of Native lands and resources, and federal officials must follow strict codes of conduct in their dealings with Indians, including Native Alaskans (Strickland, 1982).

The *Indian Nations at Risk: An Educational Strategy for Action* report (Bell and Demmert, 1991, p. xi) describes federal responsibility for Native education:

> The Constitution of the United States provides for a special political relationship between American Indians and the U.S. Congress. This relationship includes broad federal authority and special trust obligations. Congressional authority over Indian affairs is generally recognized as emanating from the Indian Commerce Clause and treaty-making responsibility.

Although treaty obligations are still in force, the trust responsibility and commitment to provide services depend on Congressional action. This responsibility, recognized as legal and moral, is one that Congress has extended to both tribes and individuals over time, by setting aside special funding for Indians in programs for a variety of education, health, social service, economic development, and other programs. This practice has also expanded authority for providing services for Indians from the Department of the Interior to other federal agencies.

Over 400,000 American Natives attend the public schools of this nation. Within this total, in the 1994–95 school year there were approximately 45,000 American Indian students in ninety-two federal schools operated by the Bureau of Indian Affairs or in ninety-three "contract schools" operated by Indian tribes or organizations. With one of the highest dropout rates in the nation among all school-age children, and a record of poor academic performance, few American Natives enter the colleges and universities of this country. Native students represent about 1 percent of the public school population in the United States but make up at least 9 percent of the school enrollments in Alaska, Oklahoma, and New Mexico.

With these demographics in mind, the U.S. Department of Education decided to undertake a special effort to address the problems of Native students in the nation's elementary and secondary schools. On March 8, 1990, it chartered the Indian Nations at Risk Task Force at the historic Shawnee Methodist Mission in Kansas. This task force was charged with the responsibility of investigating the status of Native education in the United States and with issuing a report that recommended ways to improve schools and schooling for Native American children. Terrell H. Bell, former U.S. Secretary of Education, and William G. Demmert, Jr., Commissioner of Education for the state of Alaska at that time, were appointed co-chairs of the task force, which later issued the report just quoted from (Bell and Demmert, 1991).

The purpose of this chapter is to review the issues and recommendations presented in the report and to elaborate on what has happened subsequently and what still needs to happen. To put the issues in context, a historical overview will first be presented.

Historical Overview

The challenge of developing an effective system for passing on the knowledge and skills of an ever-changing culture to American Indian and Alaska Native youth actually predates the educational systems created with the founding of the United States as a nation. Teaching the young has always been a tribal and clan priority of Native people. The traditional systems developed did not allow failure on the part of the mentors. Unfortunately, because of the changes that have taken place in American Indian and Native Alaska tribal sovereignty, ownership of aboriginal resources in the Americas, and the social structures of tribes, the education of Native youth has become a federal and state responsibility where certain percentages are expected to fail.

The formal education of Native children and young adults, in whatever form it is practiced today, is commonly referred to as *Indian Education.* The term currently includes the schooling of Native youth by church groups, tribes under contract with the federal government, other private schools, Bureau of Indian Affairs schools, and public schools at the elementary, secondary, and postsecondary levels.

Whether the schools Native children attend have succeeded or failed in their mission to educate depends on one's perspective and what the ultimate goals are seen as. The early churches wanted to "Christianize"; the government wanted to "civilize" or assimilate; tribes have wanted to develop skills and knowledge about new ways; parents have wanted their children to fit in and not endure the racism they have encountered; others have wanted to retain some of the old ways, including the language, the arts, certain customs—in other words, a Native linguistic and cultural identity.

Many reports have been produced over the years on whether schools have succeeded or failed in meeting their responsibilities to the Indian communities and why. The various reports have tended to criticize and emphasize the failures. The most influential—the Meriam Report of 1928, the Kennedy Report of 1969, and the Havighurst Report of 1970—were no exceptions. They reinforced each other, though each provided additional insights and a new focus following their release.

The Meriam Report (Meriam and others, 1928) emphasized the poor quality of services available to Indians, including education and the lack of opportunity to manage their own affairs. The report identified Native languages and cultures as important to the educational process and recognized parents as key in the education of young children. It recommended strengthening the Indian family and social structure. This recommendation caused the Bureau of Indian Affairs to reconsider its past policies of removing young children from their homes early in life and of discouraging Native language use in the school. In 1933, under President Franklin Roosevelt, a series of new approaches were initiated in education that included bilingual education, adult basic education, training of Indian teachers, reinforcement of Indian culture, and inservice teacher training. Closure of boarding schools also became a priority (U.S. Senate Special Subcommittee on Indian Education of the Committee on Labor and Public Welfare, 1969).

According to *Indian Education: A National Tragedy, A National Challenge,* commonly referred to as the Kennedy Report, these innovative programs ended after World War II (U.S. Senate Special Subcommittee on Indian Education of the Committee on Labor and Public Welfare, 1969). A new Congressional attitude of "de-Indianizing the Indian" emerged. Efforts were made to move Indians into the mainstream of American life through termination (removal of Indian tribes from federal services), moving Indian students to public schools, and where public schools were not available, to boarding schools far from home. The Kennedy Report noted the physical and mental health problems, low achievement rates, poor graduation rates, and lack of local control of their own schools as major concerns. The schools were criticized for not meeting the educational needs of Indian students and communities. The report recommended sweeping changes that resulted in the Indian Education Act of 1972 (now called Title IX of the Improving America's Schools Act of 1994). This act, comprehensive in nature, provides direct financial support to Bureau of Indian Affairs schools, public schools, Indian contract schools, and Indian tribes and organizations. The monies can be used for the operation of education programs serving preschool, elementary, secondary, and postsecondary Indian students and adults.

The Havighurst Report (Havighurst, 1970), like earlier reports, emphasized greater Indian control of schools, encouraged parents to become more involved with schools, and suggested that more attention be given to Native language and culture. The report recommended increasing the number of Indian teachers and school administrators and suggested that historians give a more accurate description of Indian history. Havighurst noted that the great majority of Indian young people were fairly well adjusted—they thought well of themselves. Havighurst also pointed out that Indian students did not do as well as average white students on written achievement tests as a result of the socioeconomic positions of Native families but that they did very well on nonverbal tests. The national study of Indian education conducted by Havighurst was not the usual series of hearings and papers that have been the norm in studies of Indian education. It was a carefully designed study based on questionnaires and analysis of socioeconomic demographics. But in the final analysis the Havighurst recommendations were similar to those of both the Meriam and Kennedy reports.

The Indian Nations at Risk Task Force, created by the U.S. Department of Education in 1990, found many of the same conditions described in these earlier reports. The conditions and problems facing many families and individuals still center around social problems like alcohol abuse, suicide, family violence, and poverty. The educational setting still includes teachers that are not prepared to work with Native children and a curriculum that has never been exciting or challenging and that is still presented as if all citizens were descendants of Europeans. The task force found that schools had not yet learned to create a multicultural institution for the various citizen groups they served. It did find that significant progress had been made in a variety of areas. Parental involvement, early childhood education programs, greater interest in higher education, and a curriculum more sensitive to Native perspectives were in evidence. The report produced by the task force expanded its recommendations to include more than just the federal government. It included recommendations for parents, schools, and states, as well as for colleges and universities.

At its initial meeting, the Indian Nations at Risk Task Force agreed on a set of principles to guide their work. The principles were:

- The United States has a responsibility to help tribal governments and communities strengthen and protect their original languages and cultures—languages and cultures unique to the Americas and found in no other part of the world.
- The educational strategies and reforms that will be needed to achieve Native educational goals must guide improvement in all schools that serve American Indian and Alaska Native students.
- Schools must provide enriching curricula and assistance that encourage students' personal best in academic, physical, social, cultural, psychological, and spiritual development.
- Parents, elders, and community leaders must become involved in their children's education, in partnership with school officials and educators. They must participate in setting high expectations for students, influencing the curriculum, monitoring student progress, and evaluating programs.
- A genuine commitment to real change will be required not only on the part of school systems, but also from federal, state, and local governments, educational organizations, business, labor, and community organizations, as well as Native groups [Bell and Demmert, 1991, p. 2].

The report explains that Native peoples are at risk and describes the current situation and background. It summarizes recent progress in resolving problems and identifies proven practices for improving schools. It proposes a set of priorities and purposes and a strategic framework for improving schools.

And finally, it presents a list of recommendations that apply to all partners important in the process of education, including parents of Native children, tribal leaders, schools and teachers, Native communities, state governments, the federal government, and colleges and universities.

The report explains that issues facing Native communities and Native education in the United States are similar to issues facing indigenous peoples worldwide. In effectively responding to educational issues in the United States, the task force believed models could be offered for solutions to problems in a nation and a world becoming increasingly more culturally diverse yet interdependent.

Why Native Peoples Are at Risk

American Indians and Alaska Natives are at risk because:

- Our schools have failed to nurture the intellectual development and academic performance of many Native children, as is evident from their high dropout rates and negative attitude toward school.
- Our schools have discouraged the use of Native languages in the classroom, thereby contributing to a weakening of the Natives' resolve to retain and continue the development of their original languages and cultures.
- Indian lands and resources are constantly besieged by outside forces interested in further reducing their original holdings.
- Political relationships between the tribes and the federal government fluctuate with the will of the U.S. Congress and decisions by the courts [Bell and Demmert, 1991, p. 1].

The report points out that the task challenging Native communities is to retain their distinct cultural identities while preparing members for successful participation in a world of rapidly changing technology and cultural diversity. The task force felt strongly that Indian communities must select educational and cultural priorities for their children and future generations.

American Indian and Alaska Native parents and leaders must clearly determine the school's role in promoting Native languages and cultures as well as the school's educational priorities. The Native community must make a strong statement about what they expect of their youth, or the schools will probably continue to fail.

The Changing Context of Native Education

The report points out that the American Native political and economic structures, educational needs, and cultural and social practices are constantly being challenged and reshaped. There is a great contrast between rural and urban life among members of the same tribe, as well as between tribes. The report refers to the Inuit in the circumpolar north as dependent on the sea mammals, caribou, waterfowl, and other animals for their daily food and clothing. The people of the north also depend on ancient traditional skills, as well as on modern technology and equipment such as rifles and snowmobiles. City-dwelling Inuit and other Native people buy their food, clothing, and other items from modern shopping malls and live in modern well-built, comfortably furnished homes. American Indians and Alaska Natives in every walk of life have members of their extended families that exist between these two extremes.

The task force believed that where Native people lose the opportunity and therefore the ability to practice traditional subsistence activities and where they do not develop other skills that will enable them to participate fully in the daily activities of the world around them, they develop a different perspective on life. When the workplace demands new skills and these are compounded by rapid social, cultural, and political changes, it is apparent that attitudinal and social changes occur. The report points out that there are significant increases in individual apathy, excessive use of alcohol, suicide, and loss of purpose and pride among too many individuals and groups. The task force members felt that greater attention must be paid to how schools, and society in general, should adjust to meet these challenges. They were concerned about schools not providing a curriculum and social environment that will strengthen the physical, mental, and spiritual health of Natives.

The report notes that Native peoples are increasingly concerned about the mounting social problems they face and about the loss of their original cultural and language base. Many American Native educators believe that language and culture are inseparable, that one supports the other. The report states that the ability to speak and learn from their elders, the music and art forms, the historical and practical knowledge, and the traditional social and cultural practices are being lost to tribes and the nation as a whole. A growing number of Native people believe schools must enable children and adults to adapt and flourish in the modern environment while maintaining ties to their traditional cultures.

Many children in primary and secondary school are not adequately prepared to take advantage of postsecondary opportunities. First, as many as 35 percent of the Native students in high school leave early, and in some schools 40 to 60 percent of American Indian and Alaska Native students drop out. Native students are reported to have the highest high school dropout rate in the nation. Second, tragically, not all Native students developing their basic language and academic skills have the opportunity to go to college because of the high costs. The tribal and federal dollars provided for student postsecondary support are not sufficient to meet the demand.

Educational Barriers

The report identifies a number of barriers that Native children must overcome if they are to succeed in school. These include:

- Limited opportunities to enrich their language and developmental skills during their preschool years.
- An unfriendly school climate that fails to promote appropriate academic, social, cultural, and spiritual development among many Native students.
- Curriculum presented from a purely Western (European) perspective, ignoring all that the historical perspective of American Indian and Alaska Natives has to contribute.
- A loss of Native language ability and the wisdom of the older generations.

- Extremely high dropout rates, especially in urban schools, where Natives are in the minority and where the school climate does not support Native students.
- Teachers with inadequate skills and training to teach Native children effectively.
- Limited library and learning resources to meet the academic and cultural needs of the community.
- A lack of Native educators as role models.
- Economic and social problems in families and communities, including poverty, single-parent homes, family violence, suicide, substance abuse, and physical and psychological problems. These problems act as direct barriers to the education of Native children.
- A shift away from spiritual values critical to the well-being of individuals and society as a whole.
- A lack of opportunity for parents and communities to develop a real sense of participation.
- Overt and subtle racism in the schools Native children attend, combined with a lack of a multicultural focus in the schools.
- Limited access to colleges and universities because of insufficient funding.
- Unequal and unpredictable funding for preschool and many elementary, secondary, and postsecondary programs and for tribal colleges. For example, the seventy-five approved but unfunded public school construction applications, dating back to 1973, amount to a backlog of $193.7 million, of which two projects per year are funded.
- Limited use of computers and other technological tools, principles, and research important in a modern society [Bell and Demmert, 1991, pp. 7–10].

Recent Progress and Proven Practices

Regardless of the problems and barriers that still exist, many successful schools and programs emerged in the two decades between *Indian Education: A National Tragedy, A National Challenge* (U.S. Senate Special Subcommittee on Indian Education of the Committee on Labor and Public Welfare, 1969) and the release of *Indian Nations at Risk: An Educational Strategy for Action* (Bell and Demmert, 1991). These effective schools and programs clearly demonstrate that Native students can succeed in achieving their goals, especially when provided with parental and community support, adequate funding, and other resources.

Specifically, the Indian Nations at Risk Task Force reviewed the progress of Indian education over the past twenty years and found that many programs funded under the Indian Education Act of 1972 (as amended) have made a difference. First, Native parents have developed a forum for influencing programs affecting their children. They have begun to develop a sense of ownership in these school programs because of that influence. Second, state and local education agencies have recognized that Native students were not being served well by schools and that they have a responsibility to do something about students' problems. Third, parent-based early childhood programs have had an impact on students' academic performance, and academic as well as social behavior has shown improvement. Fourth, larger numbers of Native teachers and school administrators have found jobs in schools. In addition, greater numbers of university professors are represented in the nation's colleges and universities, along with larger numbers of Native students entering those colleges and universities. Fifth, language and cultural programs are gaining acceptance in both the Native community and in the school community. Sixth, Native educators are beginning to change the nature of the curriculum materials offered to Native students. The materials use Native perspectives, as well as incorporating Native music, the visual arts, and legends. Seventh, the self-image of Native students has been strengthened, and they have developed more positive attitudes about being Native. Eighth, tribally controlled schools and colleges have emerged as a viable alternative and filled a void not met by the nation's colleges and universities. Tribal schools have been very successful in graduating their students.

In addition, the report suggests that Native educators have gained some important understandings over this quarter of a century. From a tribal perspective we have learned that our elders were wise—that the information and knowledge base they developed over thousands of years is valuable. We have learned that many of the ways used to pass on knowledge to the generations that followed are recognized by researchers as effective and still appropriate today.

We know that establishing a learning base early in one's life is important to academic and intellectual development. Learning begins with parents and other family members in the home and significantly influences a young person's academic future.

We have learned that we must strengthen language use. We know that language is the base for intellectual development and for transmitting that knowledge. We know that language is strongly influenced or significantly set by age three.

We have been told that the environment and culture of the school can have a significant impact on a student's attitude toward schooling and on success. We recognize that having a visionary or leader, an academically challenging curriculum, a safe and comfortable setting, well-trained sensitive teachers, and an honest curriculum all contribute to success.

We also realize the importance of partnerships between schools and parents, social service agencies, and business and industry. We understand the role parents can play in providing the support students need to enable them to concentrate on schooling. We have been sensitized about students having to contend with emotional or physical health problems on their own and about the need to provide support to help youngsters work through the complex set of relationships that are a part of schooling and the real world.

Finally, we know that schools must be held accountable for the effects of their policies on student performance. Curriculum and assessment strategies should be driven by parental and community goals set for the schools. Results must be used to guide curricular and instructional changes designed to improve student achievement.

Task Force Priorities, a Strategic Framework, and Recommendations

We turn now to the specific recommendations of the Indian Nations at Risk Task Force.

Task Force Priorities

How to improve schools and schooling for improved academic performance became the major focus of the task force. Early childhood education and parenting were recognized as among the most important priorities. The development of a youngster's language base (including other intelligences) early in life was recognized as key to developing academic skills necessary to intellectual development. Native language and cultural programs in schools were seen as critical, not only for identity purposes, but because of the influences they could have on academic performance and social/cultural development.

School administrators and teachers were recognized as having a prime responsibility for improving the quality of education for Native students. The cultural climate of the school, teacher expectations, and the teachers' skills are all realized as tied to student success.

Self-sufficiency of Native communities was introduced as necessary to healthy economies and social and cultural well being. Without Native professionals (such as schoolteachers and school administrators, doctors, university faculty, scientists, and librarians), Native communities will have problems creating healthy, self-sufficient communities, and the independence they enjoyed in earlier times will be severely limited.

The task force emphasized the direct relationship between understanding and appreciating one's culture on the one hand and success in the modern world on the other. The responsibility of parents and communities for the education of their children was recognized. Positive political relationships between tribes and state and federal governments are important to self-image and to the acceptance of the schools by Native students. Task force members noted that school reform will not occur with fragmented activity. The improvement of schools and schooling must be comprehensive, and reform efforts must address all aspects of a youngster's learning environment from birth to adulthood. The effective schooling research on communitywide commitment to change, performance-based goals, incentives and accountability for performance, better ways of assessing results, and the importance of adequate resources all influenced the thinking of the task force. Task force members recognized that teacher respect and appreciation of cultures and communities served are also necessary ingredients in school reform.

A Strategic Framework

What then is the strategic framework that Native education must incorporate to improve schools and schooling? The Indian Nations at Risk Task Force recommended five major strategies. These included developing a set of comprehensive educational plans that bring together federal, state, local, and tribal resources to achieve a set of Native educational goals. These plans should draw on the most promising research and effective practices identified over the past twenty years. Developing partnerships among schools and parents, tribes, universities, business and industry, and health and social service agencies was deemed important. These partners must play an active role in developing local programs. Four national priorities that would significantly improve academic performance and promote self-sufficiency among American Indians and Alaska Natives were identified. These priorities included: (1) establishing parent-based early childhood education programs that are developmentally appropriate and linguistically and culturally attuned to the community served; (2) including a student's tribal language and cultural priorities as a responsibility of the schools; (3) training larger numbers of professionals—for example, enhancing the teaching skills of Native educators; and (4) strengthening tribal and Bureau of Indian Affairs colleges as a way of supporting community development as well as preparing students for higher levels of success as they move on to the nation's four-year colleges and universities.

In addition, the strategic framework included the importance of creating mechanisms to hold local tribal, state, and national officials accountable for carrying out their educational responsibilities to the Native communities. Finally, the task force noted the necessity of fostering a better understanding of the relationships between tribes and all levels of government.

Within the strategic framework, the task force made a series of recommendations for each of the specific partners responsible for the education of Native children and adults. In summary, these recommendations were targeted at the following:

Parents of Native Children. In general, parents must develop their parenting skills and take responsibility for becoming their children's first and most important mentor, especially in the development of language skills. They must become active in the process of schooling to ensure that schools meet their educational expectations and should show support for schools as an important and expected activity. To ensure proper attention for schools and schooling, parents must work closely with local, tribal, state, and national officials. Schools and educators must be held accountable for educational outcomes.

School Officials and Educators. The task force emphasized that educators must hold high expectations for all students. Schools must prepare all students for competition in the modern world with appropriate vocational, technical, business, and other professional skills. The school curriculum must become academically challenging, with an integrated Native perspective on history and other subject areas. The culture of the school must take on a multicultural focus as a way to help eliminate racism and promote understanding among all races. A code of conduct for students, teachers, and administrators must be established and enforced. Schools must become comfortable and safe places for students; they must be kept free of alcohol and drugs. Top-quality teachers and administrators must be recruited, trained, and hired. They must be properly rewarded for their efforts. Teachers from the Native community must be found in greater numbers in the school setting for students to model. Student progress must be monitored with appropriate evaluation and assessment information to improve instruction. Results must be shared with parents. Parents, tribal leaders, and other members of the community must be welcomed as partners and must be encouraged to become involved in their children's education. Students must be helped to explore the connection between what they learn in school and what they need to know to experience productive and satisfying lives. They must be encouraged to find jobs, seek advanced training, or go on to a university. Health and social service organizations must be organized to help reduce the difficulties facing many Native children. Partnerships with local colleges, business and industry, and other community organizations must be formed as a way to expand the human and financial resources of the schools.

Tribal Governments and Native Communities. The task force recommended that tribal governments and communities take responsibility and accountability for the education of their Native students and support the intellectual, cultural, social, spiritual, and physical development of member children and adults as priorities of the tribe. Activities must be carried out that would establish their own educational plans that define the purposes of education and outline the goals and strategies necessary to carry out those purposes. Financial and other kinds of support necessary to train the professionals who can play a role in creating self-sufficient communities must be provided. Students seeking education in vocational and technical fields must be encouraged and supported. Tribal leaders with the skills and interest in working directly with local and state agencies to promote the tribe's education goals and to ensure the representation of these goals in local educational plans and initiatives must be promoted. Job opportunities in local communities and on reservations must be created to encourage students to continue their education. Finally, partnerships with government, philanthropic organizations, and business and industry must be encouraged to create educational endowments (with tax adjustments) to help meet the costs of operating tribal schools and colleges.

Local Governments and Schools. The task force urged that social and political barriers that prevent Natives from being elected to school boards in their communities be removed. Governments must ensure that schools address the multicultural educational needs of the students they serve and that budgets support those efforts. Opportunities must be provided in order for parents from the multicultural communities to develop partnerships with schools serving their communities. Principals must be given direct authority and responsibility for building partnerships and improving schools. Textbooks and other library and learning resources that provide contemporary and historical information on American Natives from a variety of perspectives must be included in the school setting.

State Governments. Suggestions were made to build comprehensive educational plans in partnership with schools and tribal governments as a way to initiate school reform and improve the academic achievement and other needs of Native students. State departments of education should be required to allocate funding and technical assistance to local schools to encourage the incorporation of early childhood education principles in the primary grades. The development of curricula that are culturally and linguistically appropriate for all grades and inservice training for teachers of Natives must be incorporated. Specific funding must be allocated for schools serving Native children in order to develop and incorporate linguistically, culturally, and developmentally appropriate curricula. Legislation for implementing Title I of P.L. 101-477, the Native American Languages Act of October 30, 1990, in public schools must be developed. Legislation must be enacted that allows tribal language, culture, and vocational experts to attain certification as classroom teachers. State departments of education must be expected to report annually on the progress schools are making toward improving academic performance. They must also report on how well schools are meeting the national American Indian and Alaska Native Education Goals. Alternative education options such as model schools, magnet schools, and other schools designed to meet the unique language and culturally related educational needs of Native students must be encouraged.

Federal Government. Recommendations for the federal government (the primary partner in the education of Native students under the Bureau of Indian Affairs) included recommendations for systemic reform, priorities for additional funding, and priorities for research, statistics, and evaluation.

Recommendations for systemic education reform included

issuing a statement that declared the improvement of schools
Native children attend and improved academic performance of
Native children as the nation's highest priority for services to
American Indians and Alaska Natives. Established educational
priorities must be coordinated across federal agencies, along with
an annual review of funding for the education of Native children
and adults. Opportunities must be encouraged for schools and
universities to develop comprehensive plans to meet the educational needs of Native students by waiving rules and regulations
of individual programs that incorporate the Indian Student Bill
of Rights and the national American Indian and Alaska Native
Education Goals. Legislation must be developed to support public and Bureau of Indian Affairs school efforts to incorporate the
participation of tribes, Native communities, and parents of Native
children in the development, implementation, and evaluation of
local, state, and federal comprehensive educational plans. Tribal
government approval for local and state educational plans must
be sought as a condition of approval by the U.S. Department of
Education for reducing rules, regulations, and requirements of
federal educational programs serving Native children and adults.
An assistant secretary for Indian Education in the U.S. Department of Education must be created to provide national direction
and coordination for all Department of Education programs
serving Native students. Legislation to amend the Bilingual Education Act to allow for the retention and continued development of Native languages in accordance with Title I of P.L. 101-
477, the Native American Languages Act of October 30, 1990,
must be introduced.

Priorities for additional funding incorporated recommendations for a number of select priorities. These included
funding to support early childhood education programs that are
linguistically, culturally, and developmentally appropriate, prenatal care, and parental training programs. Legislation was recommended to require federal programs providing social services
to young children to join forces with schools and tribal groups.
Prenatal care, parental training, and early childhood education
as well as health care for expectant mothers and young children
were recommended as top priorities. A national research and

school improvement center for Native education was recommended. The center would be expected to serve as a resource for schools educating Native children, tribes, state departments of education, and universities. It would serve as a source of funding support for research designed to improve schools and schooling of Native students. Legislation was recommended to provide long-term discretionary funding designed to improve schools and academic performance through model projects and outreach activities for Native parents and students as part of the Indian Education Act of 1972, as amended. A recommendation to amend the Higher Education Act of 1965, as amended, was suggested to establish a set-aside for Natives in the Special Programs for Disadvantaged Students (Title IV of the Higher Education Act) programs to ensure increased access to and completion of higher education, and for an Indian College set-aside in Title III of the Act.

The priorities for research, statistics, and evaluation included suggestions to create a national information center to collect and distribute information on programs that use educational technology as a way to improve schools and learning. A system of independent evaluation and dissemination of programs and projects shown to be effective for Native children was recommended. The extent of adult illiteracy in Native communities was recommended for review. A review of the adequacy of current funding and programs and the development of plans to eliminate illiteracy among Natives were also suggested. An assessment of the unmet higher education financial and academic needs of Native students was proposed. The coordination and development of specific plans, programs, and budgets to increase the number of Native students attending and graduating from our nation's colleges and universities was also recommended. The funding priority for training Native educators for elementary, secondary, and university teaching and for training other professionals was reinforced. A recommendation to expand Indian self-determination in Bureau of Indian Affairs schools was made. Legislation to ensure equity in funding for schools and facilities was made as a way to improve effectiveness of Bureau of Indian Affairs and Impact Aid schools serving

Native students. Parity in funding for federal Indian colleges at levels that match the average national per-pupil expenditures in public community colleges was recommended.

Colleges and Universities. Institutions of higher education were encouraged to institutionalize funding for Native faculty, programs, and students. The need to improve teacher training efforts by preparing teachers of Native students to work in multicultural settings was stressed. A priority for recruiting, hiring, and retaining American Indian and Alaska Native faculty was suggested. Scholarly work on curricula and textbook development that incorporates Native perspectives in partnerships with school districts to improve elementary and secondary education programs for Native students was proposed. Finally, the development of partnerships with Native communities to provide technical assistance, train professionals, and address research questions important to those communities was recommended.

Conclusions of the Report

The conclusions of the report are presented as written. The task force reported that:

> American Indians and Alaska Natives, with languages and cultures found in no other place in the world, are in danger of losing their distinctive identities. Many members of the younger generation know little or nothing about their Native languages, cultures, rich histories, fine arts, and other unique features of their cultural identities. The knowledgeable Elders, once important teachers in transmitting the historical, cultural, and practical knowledge to the young, are no longer a part of the educational systems. In addition, the intellectual leaders—the historians, the spiritualists, the medical experts, the philosophers—are no longer trained through a formal tribal process of education.
>
> If Native cultures remain important today, as many Native political and educational leaders believe they do, they must again become a part of the educational process.

Tribal groups must develop educational structures built on their cultural priorities and foster continued development and growth. Schools must do their part in supporting this movement.

Partnerships between schools and Native communities and tribes must become one of the schools' highest priorities. Schools must encourage positive political relationships, recognize the value of a people's language and culture, and support broad community participation in the schools. The American Indian and Alaska Native children of this nation must not be overlooked as the United States begins building a stronger educational system. Native students have a legitimate right to participate in this effort and can expect no less as indigenous peoples and citizens of this great nation. The motivation, spiritual well-being, physical health, and intellectual development of the American Indian and Alaska Native students require it; their leaders are demanding it; and their survival as a people depends upon it.

The recommendations in this report reaffirm the value of Native languages and cultures. They call for an educational system that will equip all tribal members with the skills and knowledge necessary to participate fully in today's society. They set the stage for Natives to build strong self-sufficient communities.

The responsibility for improvement is shared by all those involved in the education of Native students—public, tribal, and federal school personnel and government officials; parents and students; and community members. The Task Force calls for all involved to take the necessary action to implement the recommendations of this report.

American Indians and Alaska Natives have demonstrated that they are a resourceful and resilient people. Despite many challenges they have faced over the past 500 years of contact with European, Asian, African, and other Old World nations, they have survived as distinct peoples. This nation owes a great debt for all that Natives have contributed to help it become the great nation it is today.

Natives must and will continue their participation in the national effort to strengthen America economically and culturally.

The most important responsibility of any society is to ensure the health, protection, and education of its young children. The Indian Nations at Risk Task Force believes that the American people will ensure that all children in the United States have equal opportunity to receive these benefits, including all American Indian and Alaska Native children.

A Strategy for Action Revisited

What has happened since the Indian Nations at Risk Task Force report was released in October 1991? The White House Conference on Indian Education (authorized under P.L. 100-297) was held in Washington, D.C., on January 22–24, 1992. The conference was designed to promote solutions to problems that Native communities were having with schools and educational programs serving Native students. In addition, conference participants looked at the federal responsibilities for Native education, specifically funding responsibilities for federal schools and programs, school construction needs, and legislative priorities important to improved schools and schooling. The national goals established under the auspices of the Indian Nations at Risk Task Force were used as the guide for organizing the White House conference.

The conference was valuable for several reasons. These include the following: (1) The conference brought together 234 delegates from thirty state, tribal, and regional groups (and reports made from these groups) for a discourse on issues of Indian (Native) education; (2) most, if not all, of the recommendations included in the Indian Nations at Risk Task Force report were reinforced in the White House Conference report; and (3) specific sets of recommendations were repeated. One of the most important was the focus on Native languages and cultures as being a necessary part of schools serving Native students (*Final Report of the White House Conference on Indian Education*, 1992).

A second major event that supported recommendations from the *Indian Nations at Risk: An Educational Strategy for Action* report was the creation of what came to be called the Stanford Working Group. This group, chaired by Kenji Hakuta of Stanford University, brought together a mix of professionals interested in federal programs for limited-English-proficient students. The focus of the group was a review of the literature on language and language development (especially English as a second language); the relationship between that research and what Title I and Title VII of the Elementary and Secondary Education Act authorized for language-minority children; and what changes could be made in the legislation for serving language-minority children more effectively. The Working Group's report, *A Blueprint for the Second Generation,* developed a set of recommendations for the newly proposed Improving America's Schools Act. Included in the recommendations was a provision for promoting Native language learning. Native languages were recognized as a national resource found in no other part of the world and in danger of being permanently lost. The final result of the work of some of the Working Group members, and others, was an amendment to Title VII of the Improving America's Schools Act of 1994. This amendment authorizes the eligibility of American Native languages for funding under Title VII (as long as English is one of the objectives of the program).

A third major event pertaining to the education of Native students was the planning and implementation of a series of seminars on Native languages and culture. The National Indian Policy Center brought together a mix of Native leaders, practitioners, and university faculty interested in strengthening Native languages and cultures in the schools and in Native communities. This series has focused more and more attention on the pending loss of Native languages. In addition, the Office of Bilingual Education funded a seminar at Northern Arizona University that brought experts on Native languages together to discuss ways to reverse the loss of these languages among Indians in the Southwest.

Fourth, I am personally interested in creating a discourse on Native education that will focus on improving schools and schooling. The most pressing issues include the loss of language, cultural priorities, and the role of schools in saving what can be salvaged. As a part of that interest, I have proposed a coalition of select Native educators, school and program people, and national policy and program representatives that could serve as a nucleus for establishing a national discourse and promote new innovations for improving educational opportunities for Native students. A national discourse on the kinds of things that must be done to improve schools and schooling for Native students can be used as a forum for creating local and regional activity for school improvement priorities. A proposed coalition of this type should consider six necessary and fundamental questions:

1. Could a national coalition of Native educators, schools and programs serving Native students, and policy and program representatives provide a forum for creating a national Native dialogue on school improvement?
2. Are there components essential to improving schools and schooling for Native students (for example, language development, quality of teachers, nature of the curriculum, early childhood education and parenting, and community involvement—specifically of elders and parents)?
3. If there are important components necessary to improve schools and increase academic performance of Native students, how can national policy and program people be influenced to adjust the national agenda to focus on the essential components for improving schools and schooling for Native students?
4. What important strategies should coalition members consider in order to strengthen their own programs? Also, what specific activities could members undertake to disseminate information on their efforts to improve schools and schooling for Native students?
5. What monitoring and evaluation strategies should be used to provide feedback on successes and for updating and improving programs focusing on school improvement?
6. Is there a need to establish a research agenda, and if so, what should that include?

A meeting to finalize the language and culture series as part of the national Indian policy center agenda, as well as to discuss the formation of a coalition of Native educational leaders and tribal and national policy and program people, was convened at Western Washington University on January 11–13, 1995.

The group decided that the focus of such a coalition should be language and culture, and that a focus on the issues of school reform and improved academic performance of Native students could evolve naturally out of a language and culture priority. The group generally agreed to the formation of a coalition and suggested a follow-up meeting.

In discussing ideas for a coalition and the issues of language and culture, participants proposed the following position on language and culture as a principle for the group to adopt: "Language and culture are the central organizing themes of Native education and must be the foundation of any school reform movement."

In addition, reasons for a focus on language and culture were discussed. Possible considerations included: (1) identity as Indian and Native Alaskan; (2) social and cultural activity; (3) a national resource that needs to be preserved; and (4) improved academic performance, intellectual development, spiritual and physical well-being, and citizenship.

National Indian and Native education leaders, National Indian education organizations, and the presidentially appointed National Advisory Council for Indian Education were part of a White House Summit meeting on the issues of Native education in March 1995. Areas discussed included budget considerations, sovereignty issues, Goals 2000 requirements, federal policy on education, and language and culture issues.

The historical perspective tells us that before the advent of the early Europeans and permanent visitors from other continents to the Americas, individual American Native (American Indian and Native Alaskan) families and their respective clans, bands, and tribes were responsible for the education of their youth. As the original thirteen colonies, and later the United States, gained more and more control over Indian lands, natural resources, and political activity, responsibility for educating Native American students increasingly fell to the federal government. This responsibility, defined as both legal and moral, developed as the result of events that included treaty obligations for some tribes, federal legislation designed specifically for Indians (and later other Native Americans), and the emergence of state responsibilities for the education of all their citizens, including Native Americans.

There are currently 350,000–400,000 elementary and secondary Native American (American Indian and Native Alaskan) students in the nation's schools out of a total population of about 1.9 million people. Approximately 45,000 of these students are in the federal system (Bell and Demmert, 1991). The federal government funds ninety-two schools operated by the Bureau of Indian Affairs, with another ninety-three contract schools operated by Indian tribes or organizations (schools funded through the Bureau of Indian Affairs under P.L. 93-638, the Indian Self-Determination Act of 1973). In addition, three postsecondary federal institutions and twenty-four Indian community colleges receive their basic operational support from the federal government through the Indian Community Colleges Education Act of 1990 or through the Developing Institutions Act. The U.S. Department of Education provided additive support through Impact Aid (P.L. 874), Title I (ESEA), Title VII (Bilingual Education), Title IX (Indian Education Act of 1972, as amended), Individuals with Disabilities Act (P.L. 101-476), and other programs that support public education generally.

Challenges Ahead

The current systems (federal, tribal, public, and church schools) serving the many Native American communities have had differing levels of success in preparing Native students for their adult roles in society. While many students (between 40 and 60 percent) have done well academically by completing high school, graduating from college, or developing their vocational and technical skills, an unacceptably high number have not done well. In addition, and equally important from the Native American perspective, the Native language and cultural base has been severely compromised. This erosion has occurred as part of a historical design by the Bureau of Indian Affairs schools originally, because of the absence of Native language and cultural opportunities in public schools, and because of the resulting decrease in cultural and social use of tribal languages in Native communities. The absence of support for continued development of Native languages and cultures has had a devastating effect on the physical and mental health of many Native Americans, as evidenced by years of high dropout rates, high levels of alcoholism, high suicide rates, unemployment, and negative changes in cultural values. The challenge facing Native educators, policy makers, tribal leaders, and ultimately parents is one of creating an educational system that meets their needs as Native people and citizens of the United States.

One of the first priorities has to be for parents to articulate what they want their children to become. As a parent, my priorities have included providing my children with the best education possible, while creating opportunities to understand and appreciate their responsibilities as Tlingit (and ultimately as Native Americans). As a parent as well as a grandparent, I have a concern that my children and grandchildren have not had a real opportunity to learn the Tlingit language as well as English (their first language). The youngest also have not had ample exposure to their uncles, granduncles, aunts, and grandaunts as mentors and examples to follow and learn from. Not all members of my extended family have had the same opportunities my children have had. Other children have lacked those opportunities as well, and it seems that any educational reform movement to improve schools and schooling for Native America must meet certain critical standards.

From my position as parent, grandparent, educator, and citizen, such a reform movement must reflect the following principles:

1. An early childhood environment that encourages the development of children's language skills in a setting culturally and developmentally consistent with their identity as Native Americans and citizens is critical to the academic and social future of those individuals.

2. A safe school environment where the teachers are intellec-
    tually prepared to motivate and challenge students to
    become academically competent, socially conscious, physi-
    cally and spiritually sound, and culturally secure is a neces-
    sary ingredient for improving schools and schooling
    serving Native children.
3. A school-community partnership that values the develop-
    ment of one's intellect as one of the most important
    human qualities, and that develops a sense of ownership
    and joint responsibility for the quality of schools and
    schooling, must be part of any school reform effort.

School improvement strategies for Native students must
include an opportunity for individual Native communities and
tribes to develop a statement outlining the academic and cultural priorities important to them and necessary for schools to
incorporate into the curriculum. The process for accomplishing this can be carried out as part of the Goals 2000 activity now
being implemented as part of federal school reform policy (this
legislative effort currently includes the development of state
education and Bureau of Indian Affairs systemwide education
plans that require community involvement). The U.S. Department of Education must encourage and help develop a variety
of forums for the different Native community and tribal groups
to present the statements outlining their academic and cultural
priorities to local schools and state departments of education.
These priorities must be reflected in the different local school
improvement strategies and curricula of the various schools that
serve Native communities and tribes and must be represented
in the larger state plans.

Monitoring and evaluation systems must be established
for assessing the extent to which the Native community and
tribal priorities are being met and the consequences of meeting
those priorities for relationships between Native American communities and schools.

Another level of discussion is important to the education
of Native students. This discussion deals with the specific characteristics of school reform essential to improving schools and

schooling opportunities for Native students. Many of them are important enough to be included in school improvement plans; these plans should incorporate the following:

- *Identification of an educational leader.* Identify and provide training for an educational leader (principal or master teacher) in each school site to serve as the contact person and to play a leadership role in the school improvement priority.
- *Establishment of school-community partnerships.* Build partnerships between each school and the community it serves through the development of a local education plant incorporating local language, culture, and educational priorities along with a challenging academic curriculum design to enable students to reach national standards in all subject areas while building each student's sense of identity as Indian and as citizen.
- *Expansion or development of early childhood education.* Expand existing parent- and community-based early childhood education programs that are linguistically, culturally, and developmentally appropriate to the age of the children (building new ones where they do not exist); establish partnerships with social service agencies where they do not exist and strengthen them where they do exist; build community-based parenting programs that combine important tribal practices of the communities with the best early childhood practices identified by research.
- *Improvement of primary grades.* Expand the best practices of early childhood education programs to the primary grades (kindergarten through grade four), focusing on language development, social and cultural development, and the creation of an environment where all children will succeed in the classroom, on the playground, and at home.
- *Creation of partnerships with colleges and universities.* Build partnerships with tribal colleges and local universities for identifying and preparing Native teachers for the classroom and for inservice training of all Bureau of Indian Affairs school administrators and teachers. Incorporate

strategies for curriculum and teacher training that build on the most recent information available on improving teaching and managing classrooms.

- *Early identification of promising students.* Identify college-bound students early and provide programs that begin preparing them for the college environment and for the academic rigors of college and ensure adequate student financial support for covering the costs of a college education.
- *Restructuring.* Review the administrative and funding structures of the Bureau of Indian Affairs and public educational systems to access the strengths and weaknesses of the systems as they exist, and to determine whether structural and funding changes must be made for the school improvement priority to succeed.
- *Accountability and assessment.* Develop an accountability program to evaluate school progress. A student assessment program should also be created that is linguistically, culturally, and developmentally appropriate to the community served and that assesses students' progress in meeting both community education priorities and national standard achievement goals.

Funding Priorities

If parents and Native communities are going to improve opportunities for their children to reach their full academic potential, if young children are going to develop physically, socially, and spiritually, and if youngsters are going to develop a social consciousness, I believe several funding priorities must be established.

First and foremost, additional resources must be provided for the expansion and development of parent- and community-based early childhood education programs. These programs must incorporate the best there is in program environment and child development activity in a cultural atmosphere that supports community goals.

Second, resources must be allocated for preparing Native teachers for early childhood programs as well as for elementary and secondary schools. These teachers must be competent in their content areas, able to transfer their pedagogical knowledge into practice, and able to use modern technological devices as tools for innovative teaching.

Third, the physical environments for schools must be significantly improved. School buildings, teaching equipment, and materials must be provided that offer safe, environmentally sound, and challenging school climates. Children must have an opportunity to feel safe and have fun in an intellectually stimulating environment if they are to be motivated.

Any effort to reform and improve schools and schooling for Native students must look to intellectual development, improved academic performance, and citizenship in the context of the Native community's language and cultural base and the relationship of that culture and language to the larger American society. Native languages, traditional Native values, and identity as Indian or Native Alaskan are all important aspects of the school climate if students are to succeed academically.

Conclusion

A new educational agenda is being forged from the national discourse taking place in Native America. The final results of the many discussions on education are not known. What we do know, as educators of Native students, is that we still have much to learn about challenging intellectual development and improving academic performance. In efforts to establish a national Native agenda for improving schools and schooling for Native students, and in placing Native language and culture in the schools and Native communities as a priority, we must concentrate on training teachers, developing curricula (with the aid of technology), and creating partnerships with local communities. We must also continue the national discourse to monitor what we are doing and to stimulate new and innovative ideas for things that work.

References

Bell, T. H., and Demmert, W., Co-chairs. *Indian Nations at Risk: An Educational Strategy for Action.* Final report of the Indian

Nations at Risk Task Force, U.S. Department of Education. Washington, D.C.: U.S. Government Printing Office, 1991.

Conklin, N. F., and others. *Language Development: A Base for Educational Policy Planning.* Portland, Oreg.: Northwest Educational Regional Laboratory, 1990.

Final Report of the White House Conference on Indian Education. 2 vols. Washington, D.C.: U.S. Government Printing Office, 1992.

Havighurst, R. J. *The National Study of American Indian Education: The Education of Indian Children and Youth Summary Report and Recommendations.* USCE, OE0-0-8-080147-2805, series IV, no. 6. Chicago: University of Chicago, 1970.

Meriam, L., and others. *The Problems of Indian Administration.* Baltimore, Md.: Johns Hopkins Press, 1928.

Northwest Regional Education Laboratory. *Effective Schooling Practices: A Research Synthesis, 1990 Update.* Portland, Oreg.: Northwest Regional Education Laboratory, 1990.

Strickland, R. (ed.). *Felix S. Cohen's Handbook of American Indian Law.* Charlottesville, Va.: Michie Bobbs-Merrill Law Publishers, 1982.

U.S. Senate Special Subcommittee on Indian Education of the Committee on Labor and Public Welfare. *Indian Education: A National Tragedy, A National Challenge.* Senate Report No. 91501, Washington, D.C.: U.S. Government Printing Office, 1969.

PART THREE

Reforming Higher Education

Because the nation's educational systems may be viewed as a linked pathway, the academic progress of students of color cannot be assessed simply by examining K–12 schools. Consequently, Part Three focuses on the next stage of the educational pathway: higher education.

In Chapter Twelve, Mildred García and Daryl G. Smith discuss the importance of the college curriculum, including the debate over what is to be taught, who is to teach it, and how it is to be taught. The authors present a rationale for transforming the college curriculum in the context of the role and purpose of education, the continuing need to create new knowledge, and the dimensions of curricular change.

Given that nearly half of all minorities enrolled in higher education are found in community colleges, in Chapter Thirteen Laura I. Rendón and Héctor Garza focus on the role of these colleges in expanding access. The authors note, however, that despite promises of equal opportunity, the colleges have largely tolerated high attrition rates and low transfer rates to senior institutions. They then outline a vision for restructuring community colleges.

In Chapter Fourteen, Lionel A. Maldonado and Charles V. Willie describe the shortage of minorities in graduate school and elaborate on a model to increase the numbers of minority faculty developed by the American Sociological Association.

In recent years, the increasingly hostile climate on predominantly white college campuses has fueled the need to make campus environments more hospitable for minority students. In Chapter Fifteen, Shanette M. Harris and Michael T. Nettles assert that a national commitment to diversity requires that institutions create environments conducive to the academic and psychosocial well-being of students. To this end, they present recommendations to increase cultural and ethnic diversity. They also elaborate on the need to employ assessment techniques to clarify and identify factors relevant to minority participation and achievement.

Foundations can play and have played a critical role in fostering access for low-income and minority students. In Chapter Sixteen, Steven Zwerling outlines the historical forces that have influenced access in both positive and negative ways. Zwerling presents a case study of how the Ford Foundation has supported and influenced access to baccalaureate opportunities for at-risk students.

We conclude Part Three with Chapter Seventeen, in which Richard O. Hope discusses the historical origins of minority institutions, including historically black colleges and universities, the Hispanic Association of Colleges and Universities, and tribally controlled colleges. The author outlines the critical role of and contributions made by these institutions and presents arguments that support the survival of minority institutions.

Chapter 12

Reflecting Inclusiveness in the College Curriculum

Mildred García, Daryl G. Smith

The issues related to curriculum, teaching, and learning in higher education today present us with unparalleled opportunities for educational transformation and success. The process of transformation, particularly as we think about educating the new majority, goes beyond adding books to course syllabi and beyond making broad generalizations about new students and their distinctive learning styles. The process goes to the heart of the educational enterprise in terms of what is to be taught, who is to teach it, and how it is to be taught. More fundamentally, as this process develops, we believe that we will continue to see important developments in scholarship and in teaching that have the potential to improve the education of all students. While this chapter will focus on the curriculum of higher education, these changes will have an impact beyond the academy, for higher education educates those who will become teachers and administrators at all levels of education and influences policy and standards that impact the society. Indeed, without the scholarship on multiculturalism, race, gender, sexuality, and class that has been developed over the last three decades, much of the curriculum revision that has already taken place in the K–12 system would not have been possible.

As is evident on many campuses and in the larger society, the changes emerging, and the discussion of change, are fraught with tension and difficulty. As a result, it is important to be clear about the rationale for curricular and pedagogical changes, particularly as they relate to shifting demographics. This chapter will place in context the discussions about changes that are occurring and will attempt to develop a framework for understanding and undertaking this very important process.

Curriculum Transformation: The Rationale

Much of the literature on curriculum and diversity appears to reflect the assumption that the curriculum ought to mirror the background of the learners. While it may seem obvious that students' background should have a relationship to what is taught, this has not been a prevailing assumption of curricular development in higher education. More often, the curriculum has been developed based on the definitions of knowledge in specific disciplines or areas. This content focus to the curriculum has been largely independent of the learner. Thus, in higher education, focusing the rationale for curriculum transformation on changing demographics is not sufficient. It is important to explore the reasons for curricular transformation more completely.

Curriculum and Learning

The characteristics of students relate to what is taught in three important ways. First, from a learning point of view, learning is best done when a connection between the learner and the curriculum exists. The more the content is disconnected from the experience students bring, the greater burden for the teacher who has to make the connection. For example, current discussions among mathematicians reflect the concern that the importance of mathematics to ethnic/racial minorities is not being introduced in the curriculum and pedagogy of traditional approaches to mathematics (Massey, 1989; Widnall, 1988). On the one hand, students who see their curriculum—the literature they read, the history they learn—closely connected to their own background surely find themselves more connected, more involved in the learning. On the other hand, students who find no one like themselves reflected struggle with a sense of alienation, either from an educational system that does not recognize the worth of their background or from subject matter that suggests that their background holds no interest.

Second, to the degree that the curriculum is centered around the white, male, middle-class experience in America or in the world, we convey the idea that this perspective is the primary one and that other perspectives have little or no value.

Third, and perhaps more centrally, as the demographics among students and faculty shift, more questions are appropriately raised by those whose experience and perspective might be different. In studying psychological theories developed with reference to white men, for example, students of color or white women may wonder why the theory does not seem to fit. A traditional view of the American colonial period would leave students familiar with the experiences of American Indians wondering why that perspective is not being introduced. In other words, the generalizability and, in some cases, the validity of what is taught is questioned because those who introduce new perspectives not only see things differently but may also have knowledge that counters what is taught.

Indeed, while the prevailing view of the curriculum has been that it contains "the truth" arrived at scientifically or objectively, it has become clear that the curriculum development is a profoundly human process. The content of disciplines has included bias, omission, and stereotypes. For higher education to play a significant role in both the generation of new knowledge and the transmission of the "cultural heritage" requires rethinking whose cultural heritage is being taught, how it gets defined, and by whom (Darder, 1991; Fausto-Sterling, 1992; Hull, Scott, and Smith, 1982; McIntosh, 1989).

The presence of diversity on campus, then, challenges assumptions about content and also raises important issues about how effective the teaching and learning process will be as students perceive themselves to be left out or alienated by what is taught.

The Role and Purpose of Education

A second rationale for curriculum transformation relates to the question of institutional mission. As faculties revisit the question of curriculum, inevitably the question "What are we educating students for?" must be addressed. When computer technology was being developed, campuses across the country made explicit a goal of educating students to live in a technologically sophisticated world. From that purpose came the development of new curricula, the introduction of sophisticated technology, even at the freshman level, and wholesale efforts and funds to introduce faculty to the technology.

In the same way, we are facing a similar challenge today as campuses recognize that educating students to live in a demographically diverse society and in a complex world is an important goal. Campuses are asking about the kind of curriculum that will support that goal and are also recognizing that the campus community itself becomes a micro setting in which issues about democratic pluralism come in to play. If our campuses cannot embrace this challenge, how will a large and even more diverse society engage it? Moreover, where will the leaders be developed who are capable of harnessing the resources of diversity for the future? Campuses that are diverse have an important educational resource that more homogeneous campuses lack.

Given our perspective today, multiculturalism and diversity are central to almost everyone's vision of preparing students for the future. Is the curriculum educating for diversity as it once articulated a goal of educating for technology? Indeed, we might ask—what would our institutions, our classrooms, our curriculum look like if we were truly prepared to educate a diverse student body for a pluralistic world?

The excitement and the fear of such change come, in part, because few of us have been educated for diversity. Even those who enjoy the benefit of a bicultural experience rarely have had experiences with the multiplicity of cultures that make up the United States today. Most Americans live in segregated and homogeneous environments. Those who have truly had multicultural experiences are rare, indeed. And even those who have had bicultural or multicultural experiences have often found that these experiences were not supported by educational or scholarly resources. Nevertheless, to educate for and about diversity is to fundamentally change the curriculum in virtually every field (Duster, 1993; Smith, 1989).

There are, however, two important issues that can be lost in the more generic discussions about educating for diversity. The first relates to important questions concerning culture and power, and the second relates to the distinction between non-Western studies and American studies.

Part of the important impetus for curriculum transformation comes from the recognition of such injustices as racism, sexism, and homophobia in our society. For some, this alone is a sufficient rationale for educating students more fully about one another. For others, this moral argument raises concerns that the curriculum will be vulnerable to a variety of social agendas and thus will become "politicized." While it is clear that exclusion of such issues is political, it is also true that a fully developed approach to studying societies and the particular experiences of cultural groups and their histories must necessarily include issues of domination and subordination and discrimination if students are to fully engage the intellectual context for their study (Reyes and Halcon, 1988; Hooks, 1990; Katz, 1991; Zita, 1988).

A second important issue relates to a differentiation between studying non-Western cultures and American cultures. The recognition of the increased globalization of our society and interdependence among countries has renewed interest in the study of non-Western cultures and foreign languages. Those who oppose that approach often express concern about students needing to study "their own history and culture" before embarking on the study of other cultures. For some, this means that students should study the history and cultures of the West. Interestingly, those who offer this argument often do not interpret the history and cultures of the West as including the study of diversity within American culture. Campuses often find it easier to encourage and even require the study of foreign cultures and languages than to encourage and require the study of the many perspectives involved in American cultures and histories.

Whether the decision is to embrace global studies and/or the study of American cultures, a diversity of perspectives—including those of non-Western cultures—is often relevant. These two emphases are quite different, but also deeply related.

The Continuing Need to Create New Knowledge
The primary responsibilities of the academic community include not only the transmission of knowledge but also the creation of new knowledge. A third challenge of curriculum transformation is to make sure the curriculum at all levels reflects the best and most current thinking in all knowledge domains.

Two decades ago or more, a series of developments related to ethnic studies and women's studies began to provide important scholarship that has pushed virtually every discipline to rethink the questions it asks, the methods it uses, and the standards by which excellence is judged. Feminist scholarship in psychology has not only prompted a fundamental rethinking of important theoretical claims, it has also prompted questions about the presumed neutrality and objectivity of the scientific process used in psychology. In history, renewed interest and enthusiasm occurred as social history, the history of ideas, and the history of education became more central. With each of these new developments, important understandings and questions have emerged that cannot be ignored (Butler and Walter, 1991; Fiol-Matta and Chamberlain, 1994; Giddings, 1984; Harding, 1986; Kelly, 1984; Minnich, 1990; Wilkerson, 1992).

At the same time, other new perspectives are being introduced in virtually every discipline. The canon of major texts is not the only facet being reevaluated. In fields as diverse as physics, philosophy, and literature, a fundamental review of the underlying assumptions, epistemologies, areas of interest, and methodologies is occurring (Gleick, 1987; Keller, 1985; Lincoln, 1985).

Numerous authors have suggested that what these changes represent is nothing less than a paradigm shift in our views of knowledge. Interestingly, tremendous consistency is being identified in the shifts regardless of field or motive for the change. One of the more helpful descriptions of these changes has been developed by Yvonna Lincoln (1985), who describes the emerging shifts in a wide variety of disciplines as reflecting movement from the simple to the complex, from the mechanical to the holographic, from linear causality to mutual causality, from the possibility of objectivity to the probability of perspectivity, and from assumptions about a rational universe to a more unpredictable, "chaotic" universe (Gleick, 1987). She indicates how basic epistemological shifts are occurring in numerous disciplines. Certainly the developments related to multiple perspectives in the curriculum reflect these changes as well.

Curriculum Transformation: The Process

A number of writers have described a process of transformation that is heuristically useful in seeing the changes occurring in the curriculum as an ongoing developmental process. Peggy McIntosh (1989) originally developed a model that attempted to describe the process by which women began to be included in the curriculum. Numerous writers have modified and supplemented her theory and oriented it toward issues of race, class, gender, science and diversity in general (Fausto-Sterling, 1992; Schuster and Van Dyne, 1985).

The model is often described in stages as if there is a linear progression of change. We suggest that the model be seen as containing a number of dimensions that can reflect curricular change. It is important to note that the history of the development of knowledge and ideas has been ever changing. Understandings about human behavior, technology, science, and human experience continue to evolve. Even those most steeped in the current efforts at curriculum transformation would probably not presume to have a vision about what we will come to know. Indeed, the curriculum transformation process is at the heart of the creation of new and hopefully more adequate knowledge—closer to our understandings about truths and about good scholarship.

Five Phases of Curricular Change

There are five phases that underscore curricular transformation, as discussed in the following subsections.

Phase 1. Much of the curriculum in higher education continues to be shaped by the prevailing perspective of academic scholarship, which emerged out of the Eurocentric, white, male experience. In this phase, the absence of diversity is not viewed in terms of the exclusion of others, but rather from the standpoint that the prevailing perspectives represent an objective approach to some subject matter. For example, the description of Columbus's "discovery" of America would be seen as historical fact, not as reflecting a European colonial perspective.

Phase 2. The second phase involves efforts to diversify the curriculum by trying to focus on those who might reasonably be added. This is where "notable exceptions" or notable examples are added to the picture. Here one finds white women, or persons of color, who have, indeed, had a place in history or psychology or science. For example, American Indian chiefs who assisted Columbus might be discussed. Martin Luther King's legacy is introduced. Alice Walker's *The Color Purple* is included on a reading list of great American contemporary authors. The challenge of this approach is that in many disciplines and subject areas, there is a certain stretch one makes to find these notable exceptions. The result is that the approach to the subject matter has not fundamentally changed, and one often feels a certain dissatisfaction in including, for example, a Joan of Arc as a warrior to demonstrate that there have been women warriors. Nevertheless, in these efforts, students are more likely to "see themselves," and many heretofore ignored scholars and works have been uncovered.

Phase 3. In the third phase, people begin to ask why the absent groups have been absent. In this phase, the group as "problem" or "anomaly" is the focus. In the early years of feminist scholarship, there was a lot of work on women and depression or on women and the absence of assertiveness. The classical research paradigm in many of the social science disciplines framed questions about the lack of "success" of groups of color in terms of the characteristics and values of the group itself. Researchers investigated issues of intelligence, attitudes toward education, matriarchal family structures, and so on. These approaches, however, have taken a deficit approach to scholarship or have tended to blame the victim (Jaramillo, 1988; Lorde, 1990). While phases 2 and 3 attempt to broaden through greater inclusiveness, the first three phases leave unchanged the core of the traditional curriculum and disciplinary work, the subject matter, the standards, and the methods of the core curriculum.

Phase 4. The next phase of curriculum development begins to ask questions from other perspectives. Women's studies and ethnic studies over the years have sought to focus not just on why this or that group was outside the mainstream, but rather to study the particular group in its own right. Using the example of Columbus's "discovery" of America, we see that looking at that period from the American Indian perspective clearly indicates the problem with the concept of discovery or with the view that this voyage was one of the most positive and important developments in history. More critically, however, serious scholarship that has taken the lives of indigenous people seriously has resulted in important information about sophisticated civilizations that predated European cultural centers, and important ways in which indigenous populations were central to the survival of colonial populations of America. It is clear that scholarship focusing on otherwise marginalized groups has created new knowledge, which if taken seriously, critically informs traditional views (Anzaldúa, 1990). These efforts have resulted in an appreciation of the role of race, class, and gender in almost all aspects of American scholarship and society. Issues relating to dominance and subordination and center and margin have emerged as important theoretical components of the new approaches to diversity and knowledge (Dill and Zinn, 1990; Hooks, 1984).

The more theoretical literature on curriculum transformation often describes this approach as one of decentering the curriculum (West, 1990). The notion of decentering the curriculum has been useful in attempting to create multiple perspectives in the creation of knowledge. The focus of study is on a particular cultural perspective, not one that is "deficient" from the standpoint of a dominant culture. Taking a variety of perspectives on fields like history, literature, art, psychology, and so on sometimes requires rethinking the question of what is excellence, and who defines it, as well as the question of the methods by which our scholarship is generated. Scholars studying African American history, or women's history, have had to rely on diaries or oral traditions to access information. Having been published by a large press can no longer be the requirement for excellence, since research that addresses these questions using alternative methods has been systematically excluded from such venues. In many areas of the social sciences, the prominence of quantitative methodologies has come into serious question, as has the effort to develop macro theories of human behavior based on information about limited segments of a population (Martin, 1985).

Phase 5. The developments in many areas of scholarship over the last three decades have provided higher education with a rich source of information through which transformation of the curriculum itself is occurring. Phase 5, understood to be the transformation of education, reflects the rethinking of disciplines, of areas of study, of methodologies, and of pedagogies that has resulted from the ferment just described. If the goal of the curriculum is, in part, the transmission of knowledge, students of all backgrounds will be better served by a curriculum informed by the new knowledge being generated. Such a curriculum will also encourage complex thinking, the capacity to see multiple perspectives, and the ability to solve problems in a far more complex environment.

A word about science here is probably appropriate. In an article on race, gender, and science, Anne Fausto-Sterling (1992, p. 6) asks, "Doesn't science, after all, offer us objective accounts of the physical world?" She goes on to describe how language has affected the working of science (by describing the development of a female embryo as the absence of male development). Recent developments in ecology, which take on the perspectives of indigenous populations and feminist approaches, reflect transformations of these fields. Sandra Harding (1986) argues that physics and chemistry have always been the result of human and historical social projects. To recognize this is to prompt the kind of questioning that facilitates understanding of science, its development, its methodologies, and its truth claims.

Indeed, the kind of curriculum transformation we are now a part of is far more exciting and far reaching than simply adding and stirring a few new voices to the standard fare.

Emerging Pedagogical Shifts

While the view of the curriculum as the content of a body of knowledge would appear to be separate from the notion of teaching and learning, much of the new scholarship has reinforced the notion that teaching and learning are deeply connected to the content of the curriculum. Indeed, as scholars continue to investigate questions that might be placed in phase 3, it has become clear that the effect of our educational system, in general, and higher education, in particular, has been to alienate the vast majority of students from education and often from themselves (Smith, 1989).

In studying a variety of cultural groups that have been underrepresented in higher education, numerous authors have pointed to some of the prevailing values in higher education, and to the ways that our institutions discourage learning through ineffective pedagogies and through classroom and institutional climates described as "chilly" (Moses, 1989; Sandler, 1987).

Moreover, as a result of beginning to see how positions of power dictate choices about what knowledge is to be explored, and in reflecting on the importance of education in creating democratic pluralism, many scholars have pointed to the importance of encouraging students to find their own voices. Student involvement and participation in the educational process, then, begins to transform some of the approaches and roles of academic life. The lecture format, the teacher as all knowing, the subject matter as True and Objective, all have come under great scrutiny by a wide variety of scholars from a wide variety of backgrounds and disciplines (Bruffee, 1993; Darder, 1991; Freire, 1970).

Courses that specifically address such topics as racism,

sexism, and other forms of discrimination inevitably require careful attention to the environment of the class and to the ways dialogue among students can be facilitated (Cannon, 1990; Higginbotham, 1988; Osajima, 1991; Tatum, 1994). In general, an increasing amount of work is being done to explore the question of how to create classrooms in which differences in perspective, opinion, and knowledge can be safely explored so that the goal of educating students to live in a pluralistic society and world can be accomplished. Part of the challenge and part of the excitement of a multicultural classroom is to develop approaches that enhance "the ability to navigate within various cultures" (Zita, 1988, p. 67). Most of this literature acknowledges the difficulty of having true dialogues in institutional contexts where issues of racism and harassment and feelings of dominance and subordination are present.

If a summary were to be made reflecting the common elements of the literature related to the implications for teaching, there would be a focus on the value of cooperation (not competition), description (not just argumentation), collaboration (not just individualized learning), and participation (not just passive learning). These approaches not only emerge from research with specific groups of student learners, they emerge from the literature on instruction and learning, and they emerge from the literature that emphasizes variety in student learning styles (Astin, 1989; Bruffee, 1993; Claxton and Murrell, 1987; Palmer, 1987).

Exemplars of Change

Curriculum change, then, is not only about what we teach but how we teach, the questions we ask, the methods used, and the ability of students to shift perspectives. Colleges across the country are, therefore, reexamining their curriculum, seeking different ways of viewing truth and seeking educational equity.

Different approaches have been taken in order to include voices that have been silent in our canon. Yet what each approach has in common is that as educators we have recognized that our curriculum needs to change so as to incorporate other cultures and other voices. As Schmitz (1991, p. 20) states, "We are calling into question . . . the very nature of learning, the meaning of knowledge, basic assumptions of the discipline, and the substance and organization of the curriculum" in order to truly achieve educational excellence.

For these reasons, colleges have instituted diversity course requirements, created ethnic studies programs or departments, or have begun entire curriculum transformation projects. What follows is a description of a few of the many programs developed across the country. The patterns and approaches usually reflect the context of the institution, and most represent the beginnings of change.

Diversity Course Requirements

Colleges and universities are instituting diversity course requirements because they recognize that all students need to know more about other cultures. These course requirements can have two separate goals. Some institutions emphasize a global perspective. Others focus on the diversity within American culture and the study of the diverse cultures in our country. Many try to cover both goals within the same requirements to introduce students to global diversity and American diversity and, increasingly, to reflect the overlap between those areas.

Marymount College has a three-semester humanities sequence where students learn about both non-Western and Western cultures throughout history. Marymount's mission in requiring these courses is to make students aware that they are a part of a global society. The faculty who teach these courses are afforded the opportunity of participating in three-hour seminars every other week throughout the academic year. The seminars cover non-Western cultures, such as Asia and Africa, and cover literature, language, and social and political perspectives (Edwards, 1973, pp. 29–30).

Western New England College requires all its undergraduates to fulfill the cross-cultural studies requirements by taking a course titled "Cultures Past and Present." This course requires that students analyze two cultures and compare them from five different perspectives: physical environment, historical context, aesthetic expression, social organization, and economic/political structure. The course is team taught by three faculty members. The team teaches one culture in the first five weeks, a second culture in the next five weeks, and compares the two at the end of the semester. The faculty attend a summer workshop where they choose the cultures to be studied and prepare the syllabi and reading material (Edwards, 1973, pp. 32–33).

Indiana State University united the faculty through four faculty open forums to discuss the ways to incorporate change in the general education program. This process resulted in a requirement that all undergraduates need to take at least five semester hours of coursework designed to broaden their perspectives. Courses included in this category are, for example, African American Studies, foreign languages, women's studies, anthropology, and so on.

While at the University of California at Berkeley only one course—"American Cultures"—is required, Hunter College of the City University of New York has proposed a diversity requirement of nine credits. The three courses would include a course on women, a course on American minorities, and a course on non-Western civilizations. In the same university system, Queens College requires a three-credit course in preindustrial or non-Western civilizations of all its arts and science students, and City College requires all students to take two semesters of world civilization and two of world literature. In these courses, students are exposed to women, minorities, and non-Western cultures (Berger, 1991).

The State University of New York and its campuses have also imposed diversity requirements on their students. Stony Brook, for example, has an American pluralism requirement that can be met by a wide range of courses (Berger, 1991). Pennsylvania State University has also implemented a six-credit diversity requirement for all its students. Similarly, in the College of Liberal Arts at the University of Minnesota, after two years of analysis and debate, a cultural pluralism requirement was adopted for all students. All undergraduates must complete two courses that have a primary focus on African American, American Indian, and/or Chicano cultures (Zita, 1988).

Each of these efforts might be critiqued. However, each represents an attempt to articulate a relationship between the curriculum and the goal of educating students in a diverse society. Moreover, many can be seen as starting points for change in the curriculum (Disch, 1993).

Ethnic Studies

Ethnic studies has been an essential interdisciplinary resource that highlights the fourth phase of transformation, focusing on the study of groups in their own right. There are over 700 programs and departments, which range from African American Studies, Asian American Studies, Native American Studies, Puerto Rican, Chicano, or Latino Studies, to a few programs and departments in comparative ethnic studies (Butler, 1991). These comparative programs go to the very core of questioning the parameters of the traditional canon, give students alternative perspectives on various cultures, and develop alternative ways of looking at a number of backgrounds.

A bachelor's degree in Comparative American Cultures with a concentration in Asian American, Black, Chicano, and Native American Studies is offered at Washington State University through its Comparative American Cultures Department. Similarly, at the University of California at Berkeley, a B.A. and Ph.D. are offered through the Ethnic Studies Department. Each of the cultures represented has a separate major in addition to a comparative major.

At the University of California at San Diego, an interdisciplinary major and minor in Ethnic Studies focusing on people of color in the United States and, ultimately, having an international focus are offered. The University of California at Irvine offers a major in its Comparative American Cultures Department. A Ph.D. is also offered in Comparative American Cultures.

In addition, Bowling Green State University offers a B.A. through its Ethnic Studies Department in three areas: General Ethnic Studies, African American Studies, and Latino Studies (Butler, 1991).

Curriculum Transformation

As described earlier, McIntosh characterizes curriculum transformation as phase 5 in her developmental model. It is "history redefined and reconstructed to include us all." It is the process by which the contributions of women and people of color are infused into every course on our campuses. In this phase there is no dominant culture in our disciplines, and all voices are studied and examined. Students are exposed to different ways of viewing the same discipline. Although as McIntosh states, this process will take a very long time for completion, many campuses have taken this path toward inclusion. A major Ford Foundation project to mainstream women's studies and to integrate women's studies and ethnic studies has resulted in a book called *Women of Color and the Multicultural Curriculum,* which includes syllabi and suggestions for projects (Fiol-Matta and Chamberlain, 1994).

At Plattsburgh State College (SUNY), a curriculum-inclusion program was embarked on once the faculty senate recognized the need for such a program: "The faculty senate mandated that almost all courses offered for general education credit must demonstrate inclusion of scholarship on women and minorities in their syllabi and teaching materials" (Pryse, 1992, p. 67). It then created a committee to approve such courses. This action led to the appointment of a visiting professor in charge of curriculum inclusion for the institution. The task was to implement an ongoing structure for the campus in order to transform the entire curriculum. An environment was therefore created whereby there was ongoing dialogue, opportunity for participation, visibility of the project, and individual faculty support for the revision and adaptation of their curriculum. At the end of the first year, the project had met its objectives, and the program continues among the faculty at Plattsburgh.

The Department of Higher Education in New Jersey began the first statewide curriculum transformation project and funded the New Jersey Project. The goal of the New Jersey Project is to encourage and support all higher education institutions of the state to integrate race/ethnicity, class, and gender and sexuality into the curriculum. Each summer, a residential institute is held to bring together faculty and scholars in the area. Furthermore, a journal is published; conferences, workshops, and regional meetings are scheduled throughout the academic year; and scholarships are given to students for excellence in multiculturalism in their undergraduate studies (Pryse, 1992). As a result of these efforts, each of the following serves as an example of individual campus progress.

Ramapo State College in New Jersey revamped its collegewide mission. Multiculturalism and internationalism became the institution's focus. The goal has been to transform the entire curriculum, and all academic programs are included. Its mission states that both multiculturalism and internationalism need to be incorporated because students must understand the composition and diversity of the United States, as well as appreciating the diversity in the world. Not only are faculty members required to review their syllabi to reflect this collegewide priority, but they are encouraged to embrace this priority in their research and community service (Scott, 1987).

Ramapo's transformation project includes professional and staff development, curriculum development, skill development of students, experiential learning opportunities for both faculty and students, and outreach efforts so as to recruit and retain students, faculty, and staff of color. The college has also developed liaison relationships with the United Kingdom, Canada, Puerto Rico, France, Jamaica, Mexico, Italy, and Japan.

Bloomfield College, a private institution in New Jersey, has instituted diversity across the curriculum and highlights the Nursing Department as one of the disciplines in order to demonstrate that even the health sciences can embrace this transformation (Wiley, 1989, p. 10).

Following the lead of the New Jersey Project, Bergen Community College embraced the integration of the new scholarship and established a mechanism to begin the transformation. Through lecture series, seminars, co-mentoring, strong leadership from a faculty team, and administrative support, the project at Bergen has reached over one-third of the faculty in two years. On their campus, a faculty-directed and faculty-oriented approach has been the most successful (Kievitt, Silverberg, and Anderson, 1990).

An innovative approach by Wesleyan University in Connecticut has been to use the arts to explore other cultures. All the departments in the arts provide opportunities for majors to

experience traditions unfamiliar to them. The dance department, for example, requires beginning dance students to "look
at films about dance in different cultures and write papers on
the symbolic function of the dance, or the ways in which dance
fits into the society" (Edwards, 1973, p. 32).

Mt. St. Mary's College in California has received national
recognition for its success in serving students of color and for
its work in curriculum transformation over the last twelve years.
The college has published a series of monographs, *Celebrating
Cultural Diversity in Higher Education* (Mt. St. Mary's, 1993).

Recommendations

As they read all that is happening across the country in colleges
and universities regarding curriculum and teaching transformation, colleagues ask, "How do we begin?"

Of critical importance is that senior-level administrators
and especially the president and senior academic officer must
support the initiative for change. Not only should they express
their support verbally, but they should also reconfirm their commitment in written statements to the campus community. A
strong message is sent when this type of involvement from senior
administrators communicates to the campus that curriculum
transformation is high on the institution's list of priorities.

Faculty development is a common link that ties the programs that have been implemented together. The beginning
point must be intellectual integrity. The faculty need to be encouraged and supported to incorporate new perspectives in the curriculum and to consider both the process of teaching and the
climate of the classroom. Provisions for attendance at summer
institutes, workshops, and conferences, released time, research
stipends, and grants for new course development all need to be
explored to inspire the faculty to pursue these new initiatives.

Institutional policies can also be reviewed to lend support
to this venture. Are faculty efforts to transform the curriculum
seen as important enough to be considered in the tenure, promotion, reappointment, and merit pay deliberations? Are the
policies for these actions supportive of the change being em-

barked on by the faculty? How important is effective teaching? Are departments that are particularly successful in learning and retention rewarded? (Green, 1989; Pearson, Shavlik, and Touchton, 1989; Smith, 1989).

Furthermore, we need to remember that changes of this type usually do not begin on a large scale. What is important is that an ambience conducive to discussing the issues involved in transformation be present. Many of the projects that have been discussed were begun by several faculty colleagues talking about the curricula in their departments (Disch, 1993; Duster, 1993). Small work groups—for example, involving colleagues working together in department meetings or on task forces—are necessary starting points for discussing the issues of curriculum change. Curriculum transformation and multicultural transformation must evolve out of the same groups that are going to implement change and teach the new curriculum. Control of the discussion, involvement, and implementation must belong to the faculty.

Conclusion

Building an inclusive curriculum is the first step toward educating the new majority and the new minority. The traditional classroom is challenged, different perspectives and paradigms are explored, and alternative pedagogies are used. In short, a transformed curriculum incorporates new ways of teaching and learning. The new ways of knowing connect teachers to new ways of transmitting knowledge. They become empowered social agents for change. Students are encouraged to question and challenge, to actively participate in learning, and to be active in their acquisition of knowledge. Instead of detaching students from their cultures and their everyday lives, the new approaches connect them to knowledge, so that through this connection they are encouraged to learn about others. Learning, therefore, becomes a critical process of discovery and empowerment for both teachers and students. Emerging studies of the impact of multiculturalism on the curriculum suggest, indeed, that there are benefits for all students and for the learning process itself (Astin, 1993).

Additional Resources

Below are additional resources that readers may turn to as they address issues of curriculum transformation.

Journals

Change Magazine, the American Association for Higher Education.
Initiatives, National Association of Women Deans, Administrators and Counselors.
Liberal Education, American Association of Colleges and Universities.
Transformations, the New Jersey Project.

Research Centers and Projects

Association of American Colleges and Universities Project on American Pluralism, American Commitments; Washington, DC 20009, ph. (202) 387-3760.
Center for Research on Women, Memphis State University, 339 Clement Hall, Memphis, TN 38152, ph. (908) 678-2770.
Center for Research on Women, Wellesley College, Wellesley, MA 02181, ph. (901) 678-2770.
Mt. St. Mary's College, 12001 Chalon Rd., Los Angeles, CA 90049, ph. (310) 476-2237.
National Institute for Women of Color, 1301 20th Street, N.W., Suite 702, Washington, DC 20036.
New Jersey Multicultural Studies Project Office, Jersey City State College, 2039 Kennedy Blvd., Jersey City, NJ 07305, ph. (201) 200-2072.
New Jersey Project, White Hall 315, William Paterson College, Wayne, NJ 07470, ph. (201) 595-2296.
Women's Studies Research Center, University of Wisconsin, Madison, WI 53706, ph. (608) 263-4703.

References

Anzaldúa, G. *Making Face, Making Soul: Haciendo Caras.* San Francisco: Aunt Lute Foundation, 1990.
Astin, A. "Competition or Cooperation." *Change,* 1989, *19*(5), 12–19.

Astin, A. "Diversity and Multiculturalism on the Campus: How Are Students Affected?" *Change,* 1993, *25*(2), 44–50.

Berger, J. "Hunter Debates What to Teach About Diversity." *New York Times,* 1991, pp. B1–B2.

Bruffee, K. A. *Collaborative Learnings: Higher Education, Interdependence, and the Authority of Knowledge.* Baltimore, Md.: Johns Hopkins University Press, 1993.

Butler, J. E. "Ethnic Studies: A Matrix Model for the Major." *Liberal Education,* 1991, *77*(2), 26–32.

Butler, J. E., and Walter, J. C. *Transforming the Curriculum.* Albany: State University of New York Press, 1991.

Cannon, L. W. "Fostering Positive Race, Class, and Gender Dynamics in the Classroom." *Women's Studies Quarterly,* 1990, *1, 2,* 126–133.

Claxton, S. C., and Murrell, P. H. *Learning Styles: Implications for Improving Educational Practice.* ASHE-ERIC Report No. 4, Washington, D.C.: George Washington University Press, 1987.

Darder, A. *Culture and Power in the Classroom.* New York: Bergin and Garvey, 1991.

Dill, B. T., and Zinn, B. (eds.). *Race and Gender: Re-Visioning Social Relations.* Memphis, Tenn.: Center for Research on Women, Memphis State University, 1990.

Disch, E. "The Politics of Curricular Change: Establishing a Diversity Requirement at the University of Massachusetts at Boston." In B. W. Thompson and S. Tyagi (eds.), *Beyond a Dream Deferred: Multicultural Education and the Politics of Excellence* (pp. 195–213). Minneapolis: University of Minnesota Press, 1993.

Duster, T. "The Diversity of California at Berkeley: An Emerging Reformulation of 'Competence' in an Increasingly Multicultural World." In B. W. Thompson and S. Tyagi (eds.), *Beyond a Dream Deferred: Multicutural Education and the Politics of Excellence* (pp. 231–256). Minneapolis: University of Minnesota Press, 1993.

Edwards, J. "Rhetoric and Pragmatism in International Education." *Liberal Education,* 1973, *73*(4), 22–33.

Fausto-Sterling, A. "Race, Gender, and Science." *Transformations,* 1992, *2*(2), 4–12.

Fiol-Matta, L., and Chamberlain, M. (eds.). *Women of Color and the Multicultural Curriculum.* New York: Feminist Press, 1994.

Freire, P. *The Pedagogy of the Oppressed.* New York: Seaburg Press, 1970.

Giddings, P. *When and Where I Enter: The Impact of Black Women on Race and Sex in America.* New York: Long Haul Press, 1984.

Gleick, J. *Chaos: Making a New Science.* New York: Viking, 1987.

Green, M. *Minorities on Campus.* Washington, D.C.: American Council on Education, 1989.

Harding, S. *The Science Question in Feminism.* Ithaca, N.Y.: Cornell University Press, 1986.

Higginbotham, E. *Integrating All Women into the Curriculum.* Memphis, Tenn.: Center for Research on Women, 1988.

Hooks, B. *Feminist Theory: From Margin to Center.* Boston: South End Press, 1984.

Hooks, B. *Yearning: Race, Gender, and Cultural Politics.* Boston: South End Press, 1990.

Hull, G. T., Scott, B., and Smith, B. (eds.). *All the Women Are White, All the Blacks Are Men, But Some of Us Are Brave: Black Women's Studies.* New York: Feminist Press, 1982.

Jaramillo, M. L. "Institutional Responsibility in the Provision of Educational Experiences to the Hispanic American Female Student." In T. McKenna and F. I. Ortiz (eds.), *The Broken Web.* Encino, Calif.: Floricanto Press, 1988.

Katz, J. "White Faculty Struggling with the Effects of Racism." In P. Altbach and K. Lomotey (eds.), *The Racial Crisis in American Higher Education.* Albany: State University of New York Press, 1991.

Keller, E. F. *Reflections on Gender and Science.* New Haven, Conn.: Yale University Press, 1985.

Kelly, J. *Women, History, and Theory.* Chicago: University of Chicago Press, 1984.

Kievitt, D., Silverberg, S., and Anderson, M. (eds.). "The Integration Project: A Program of Faculty Development and Curriculum at Bergen Community College." *Transformations,* 1990, *1*(1), 17–24.

Lincoln, Y. *Organizational Theory and Inquiry: The Paradigm Revolution.* Newbury Park, Calif.: Sage, 1985.

Lorde, A. "Age, Race, Class, and Sex: Women Redefining Difference." In R. Ferguson and others (eds.), *Out There: Marginalization and Contemporary Cultures* (pp. 281–287). Cambridge, Mass.: MIT Press, 1990.

McIntosh, P. "Curricular Revisions: The New Knowledge for a New Age." In C. Pearson, D. Shavlik, and J. G. Touchton (eds.), *Educating the Majority* (pp. 400–412). New York: Macmillan, 1989.

Martin, J. R. "Becoming Educated: A Journey of Alienation or Integration." *Journal of Education*, 1985, *167*(3), 71–84.

Massey, W. "Science Education in the U.S.: What the Scientific Community 'Can do'." *Science*, 1989, 915–921.

Minnich, E. *Transforming Knowledge*. Philadelphia: Temple University Press, 1990.

Moses, Y. *Black Women in Academe: Issues and Strategies*. Washington, D.C.: Association of American Colleges, 1989.

Mt. St. Mary's, *Celebrating Cultural Diversity in Higher Education*. Los Angeles: Prism, 1993.

Osajima, K. "Challenges to Teaching About Racism: Breaking the Silence." *Teaching Education*, 1991, *4*(1), 145–152.

Palmer, P. "Community Conduct and Ways of Knowing." *Change*, 1987, *19*(5), 20–25.

Pearson, C., Shavlik, D., and Touchton, J. (eds.). *Educating the Majority*. Washington, D.C.: American Council on Education, 1989.

Pryse, M. "A Developmental Approach to Curriculum Transformation." *Transformations*, 1992, *2*(2), 66–76.

Reyes, M. de la Luz, and Halcon, J. J. (eds.). "Racism in Academia: The Old Wolf Revisited." *Harvard Educational Review*, 1988, *58*(3), 69–83.

Sandler, B. "The Classroom Climate: Still a Chilly One for Women." In C. Lasser (ed.), *Educating Men and Women Together: Co-Education in a Changing World*. Illinois: University of Illinois Press, 1987.

Schmitz, B. "Diversity and Collegiality in the Academy." *Liberal Education*, 1991, *77*(4), 19–25.

Schuster, M. R., and Van Dyne, S. R. *Women's Place in the Academy: Transforming the Liberal Arts Curriculum*. Totowa, N.J.: Rowan and Littlefield, 1985.

Scott, R. A. *Developing an Institutional Strategy for International Education: Principles, Objectives, and Programs.* Paper presented at the Higher Educational International Leadership Summit, Florida, January 23, 1987. (ED 288 445)

Smith, D. *The Challenge of Diversity: Involvement or Alienation in the Academy.* ASHE-ERIC Report No. 5. Washington, D.C.: George Washington University Press, 1989.

Tatum, B. D. "Teaching White Students About Racism." Paper presented at the 75th annual meeting of the American Educational Research Association, New Orleans, La., Apr. 5, 1994.

West, C. "The New Cultural Politics of Difference." In R. Ferguson and others (eds.), *Out There: Marginalization and Contemporary Cultures* (pp. 286–287). Cambridge, Mass.: MIT Press, 1990.

Widnall, S. "AAAS Presidential Address." *Science,* 1988, *241,* 1740–1745.

Wiley, E. III. "Scholars Push for Cultural Diversity in Curriculum." *Black Issues in Higher Education,* 1989, *6*(15), 1, 10.

Wilkerson, M. "Beyond the Graveyard: Engaging Faculty Involvement." *Change,* 1992, *24*(1), 59–63.

Zita, J. "From Orthodoxy to Pluralism: A Postsecondary Curricular Reform." *Journal of Education,* 1988, *170*(2), 1–16.

Chapter 13

Closing the Gap Between Two- and Four-Year Institutions

Laura I. Rendón, Héctor Garza

Nearly half (46.6 percent) of all minorities in higher education attend community colleges (Carter and Wilson, 1995). The pivotal role the community college plays in educating minority students is well known. They (1) are less expensive than four-year institutions; (2) are for the most part open-door colleges, admitting students who are academically unprepared to enroll in four-year colleges and universities; (3) offer an alternate route to initiating college-level studies for homebound students, as well as for those who must be employed while studying; and (4) are a means to an end for students who wish to prepare to find a job, adapt to life, learn English, and get the most for their money in a relatively short time period. The fact that minority students, especially Hispanics and American Indians, are clustered in two-year colleges is not incidental. For these students, the colleges are not merely a matter of choice, they are a matter of necessity.

This chapter reviews the literature on ethnic and racial minority enrollments in the two-year college sector and the factors that influence retention and transfer. Given the underrepresentation of minorities in the share of baccalaureate degrees

earned and the fact that earning bachelor's degrees is to a large
extent contingent on minorities successfully transferring from
two- to four-year institutions, this chapter will give special emphasis to the transfer function. While community colleges have
sought to find their niche in postsecondary education by concentrating on career-based education to prepare students to enter the job market, many educators are concerned that higher expectations should be set for students of color, particularly since
minorities occupy few privileged positions in society in which
undergraduate and graduate degrees are necessary. Finally, the
chapter outlines a forward-looking vision of the restructuring
principles that could shape the community college of the twenty-
first century.

Community College Enrollments

According to Carter and Wilson (1994) much of the progress of
students of color is occurring at two- rather than four-year institutions. From 1988 to 1992, students of color posted a 35.5 percent increase in two-year colleges, as opposed to a 28.7 percent
increase in four-year institutions. The general profile of these
minority students is that they are nontraditional (that is, first
generation, part-timers, employed while attending college, low
socioeconomic backgrounds, and poor high school achievement
records). On the other hand, some minorities are honors students, come from middle-class backgrounds, and fit the "traditional" student profile.

In fall 1993, 56.3 percent of Hispanic students enrolled
in public colleges and universities were attending two-year institutions. The comparable enrollment for American Indians was
51.6 percent; for blacks, 42.4 percent; and for Asians 40.7 percent. Conversely, only 37.3 percent of white students were attending public two-year colleges (Carter and Wilson, 1995).
States with large minority populations tend to have large numbers of minority students enrolled in community colleges. For
example, in Alabama and Texas 47 percent of all minority students enrolled in higher education institutions are in the two-
year college sector. States with more than 50 percent minority

enrollments in two-year colleges include: Alaska, 62 percent; Arizona, 70 percent; California, 65 percent; Colorado, 52 percent; Florida, 54 percent; Illinois, 63 percent; Nevada, 59 percent; North Dakota, 52 percent; Washington, 58 percent; and Wyoming, 71 percent ("State Proportion . . . ," 1989).

Major urban centers such as Chicago, New York, Los Angeles, and Detroit now have community colleges that enroll "minority majorities." These include colleges with large black student concentrations such as the City Colleges of Chicago, including Harold Washington College, Olive-Harvey College, and Kennedy-King College, as well as La Guardia Community College and Monroe College in New York and Wayne County Community College in Detroit. American Indian students tend to enroll in tribally controlled or predominantly Native American colleges in states like Montana (Salish Kootenai Community College), Arizona (Navajo Community College), North Dakota (Standing Rock Community College), and Kansas (Haskell Indian Junior College). Hispanic students are the majority student population in community colleges that are largely concentrated in the U.S.-Mexico border region, including Texas (Laredo Junior College, Texas Southmost College, El Paso Community College, and Palo Alto Community College), California (East Los Angeles Community College), and New Mexico (Northern New Mexico Community College and Santa Fe Community College). Multicultural two-year colleges such as Miami-Dade Community College serve Cuban, Dominican, and Haitian students, among others. Colleges such as those in Los Angeles and San Diego are also multicultural, enrolling Asian, Hispanic, and African American students.

While the colleges mentioned above include only a sampling of "majority minority" community colleges, it is important to note that regions of the country with large minority communities are likely to include sizable proportions of students of color in two-year colleges. These are the very students that society expects to cross class boundaries, and a college-based education—in particular the bachelor's degree—is widely recognized as the ticket to the top of the career and social mobility ladder.

The next section examines retention and transfer issues, since these two dimensions are critical to preserving access and opportunity for students of color.

Retention

With regard to minority students, concern has been raised about the possibility that attending a community college reduces the chances of staying in college or transferring to earn a baccalaureate. Attrition is highest during the critical first semester of college. According to Tinto (1987), the estimated rate of freshman attrition in 1992 was 67.7 percent in two-year colleges and 53.3 percent in four-year institutions. In 1989 Grubb conducted a longitudinal study that focused on the attrition of community college students. Using National Longitudinal Study (NLS) *High School and Beyond* survey data of the class of 1980, Grubb (1989) found that 42 percent of the 1980 class that had entered a community college had left prior to completing any credential. He reported that the dropout rate within community colleges was similar for both vocational (43.9 percent) and academic-transfer (38.8 percent) students. The study further reported that only 19.1 percent completed an associate degree or certificate, 25.1 percent had transferred to a four-year institution, and 13.8 percent were still in school. In contrast, among those entering four-year institutions, only 19.3 percent dropped out within their first four years.

Other studies document that surviving the first two years of college in the community college is difficult. Attrition is highest for nonwhite students, as well as for those from low social-class origins and those with modest academic aptitudes (Rendón and Nora, 1989; Astin, 1985; Olivas, 1979).

Recent research indicates that making the transition to college is an important phase in terms of its impact on retention, although more research is needed to verify this relationship. For example, Terenzini and others (1994) found that many nontraditional students who were the first in their family to attend college found the transition to college to be a disjuncture in their life trajectory, given that college-going was not a part of their family's traditions or expectations. On the other hand, traditional students considered college attendance to be rational and expected. Those students who break their family traditions often find that they have to come to terms with difficult issues such as changing their identity, being perceived as different, leaving old friends behind, separating from their families, and breaking family codes of unity and loyalty (Rodriguez, 1975; Rendón, 1992; London, 1989; Weis, 1985). A student who finds that going to college is tantamount to living between two worlds and retaining two separate sets of identities, mannerisms, and peer associations may find surviving college to be quite difficult.

Another important phase related to retention appears to be making connections in college. Numerous studies (Pascarella and Terenzini, 1983; Anderson, 1984) have documented that student retention is affected by academic integration (grades, attendance, contact with faculty and students, as well as intellectual development) and social integration (participation in extracurricular activities, clubs, and organizations). Similarly, Astin (1985) developed a theory of involvement indicating that the more students devoted physical and psychological energy to involvement in the academic and social culture of the college, the greater the potential for student success. However, at least one retention study of Hispanic community college students did not find these factors as having a significant effect. A major finding from a study conducted by Nora (1990) was that the strongest effect on Hispanic student retention in community colleges was through commitment to the institution and to attaining educational goals. The study suggested that academic and social integration may be secondary to having a commitment to clear, concrete, and realistic goals at an early point in college enrollment. Students with diffuse goals appeared to have a disadvantage over those with clear commitments to their educational goals and to attending their institution of choice.

Rendón and Jalomo (1993) conducted a qualitative study of first-year majority and minority community college students that was part of the research program of the National Center for Postsecondary Teaching, Learning and Assessment. The study attempted to determine the in- and out-of-class influences that made a difference for students during the first semester in college. Validating experiences, such as when in- and out-of-class agents reached out to students to help them believe in their innate capacity to learn, as well as helping them believe that they could be successful college students, were found to be having a significant impact during early stages in the students' academic careers. The researchers noted that many students came to the community college "wounded," having experienced one or more unconfirming experiences that cast doubt over their academic abilities. What had helped these students survive the first year of college were numerous instances of validating experiences encountered in and out of the community college. Nurturing faculty who worked one on one with students, as well as faculty who gave students their home phone numbers or drove to their homes to take homework assignments, were able to generate in students the feeling that their teachers were supportive to the extent that they would not allow them to fail or to drop out. Faculty who structured academic experiences that allowed students to experience themselves as powerful knowers instilled motivation and the drive to succeed. Counselors and faculty who recognized students by name made many students feel special.

Out-of-class validation came from family and friends who served as significant others such as role models and encouragement agents. Rendón's (1994) findings on validation suggested that something other than getting involved in institutional life was the key to college success. Involvement theory implies that students take the responsibility for getting integrated into the academic and social fabric of the college. However, students who are unaccustomed to asking questions or taking advantage of opportunities are unlikely to get involved on their own. It appears that many minority and first-generation students need what Rendón describes as validation—active intervention from an in- or out-of-class agent who lends a helping hand or who initiates an action that affirms students as being capable of learning.

Retention may be influenced by both student- and institution-related factors. Student-related factors include poverty, unemployment, inadequate preparation in high school, weak study habits, and lack of clarity in defining academic goals, as well as psychological factors such as self-doubt, low self esteem, anxiety, and cultural separation (Nora, 1987; Voorhees, 1985a, 1985b; Rendón and Nora, 1990; Aguirre and Martinez, 1993; Valadez, 1993; Rendón, Justiz, and Resta, 1988; London, 1989; Weis, 1985). Institution-related factors are distinguished by their academic or student services nature. Academic factors include limited class offerings, few minority faculty, a curriculum that ignores multicultural perspectives, antiquated teaching styles, a passive learning environment, lax dropping-in and dropping-out policies, and encouragement of part-time attendance (Cohen and Brawer, 1982; Rendón, 1994). Student service factors include rising tuition and registration fees, diminishing financial aid opportunities, improper counseling and advising, cutbacks in various student service programs, and an overreliance on student-initiated involvement in campus academic and social activities (Terenzini and others, 1994; Rendón, 1994; Carter and Wilson, 1994; Cohen and Brawer, 1982).

Transfer

The case for advocating the need to improve the transfer rates of minority students from two- to four-year institutions is simple: if minority students do not transfer, they are not likely to earn undergraduate and graduate degrees. Given the acute under-representation of minorities in the share of college degrees earned, the imperative to increase transfer rates of minority students is a national concern. It is important to note that minority students do have transfer aspirations. In a national study of urban community colleges with large black and Hispanic enrollments, more than 74 percent of students expressed a desire to obtain a B.A. or higher at some time in their lives (Bensimon and Riley, 1984). Similarly, Rendón, Justiz, and Resta (1988) studied six community colleges with large Hispanic enrollments and found that 87 percent of Hispanics and 94 percent of white students had plans to transfer to one or more four-year institutions. In another study, Richardson and Bender (1987) surveyed urban community college students. They estimated that 40 to 50 percent of entering students had transfer aspirations.

Having transfer aspirations does not necessarily translate to reality. Alba and Lavin (1981) found that community college entrants to the City University of New York (CUNY) were 11 percent less likely than four-year college entrants to earn a bachelor's degree after five years, even after controlling for initial background characteristics. Similarly, Astin's (1982) review of the Higher Education Research Institute's survey of fall 1971 entering freshmen found baccalaureate completion rates two to three times lower for community college entrants than for four-year institutions.

Despite the fact that some states—such as Arizona, California, Kansas, and Maryland—have reported increases in transfer activity, the transfer rate for minorities continues to fall below whites across the nation. According to Grubb (1991), of the 1980 high school graduates entering two- and four-year institutions, approximately 22 percent of whites transferred to four-year colleges within four years compared to only 16 percent of Hispanics and 10 percent of blacks. Among California full-time community college students, minorities and whites expressed similar intentions to transfer, yet only 28 percent of the 1983 transfers to the University of California and California State University system were minority, even though they comprised 39 percent of the 1981 full-time enrollment (Board of Governors, California Community Colleges, 1984). Although the number of minority transfers to the University of California and California State University System was beginning to increase, the transfer rate for blacks was about half that of whites. Among full-time freshmen in California community colleges, blacks represented approximately 10 percent of the student population but only 7 percent of the students transferring two years later. Hispanics represented 17 percent of the freshmen and only 9 percent of the transfers (Office of the Chancellor, California Community Colleges, 1989). Of course, there are problems calculating transfer rates, and students have been known to "swirl" back and forth from two- to four-year institutions. But the fact remains that to increase the numbers of minority students earning undergraduate and graduate degrees, many more will have to successfully complete the transition from a two- to a four-year institution.

A controversial study conducted by Orfield and Paul (1992) suggested that states with the heaviest reliance on community college systems tended to have the lowest proportion of high school graduates continuing their education. According to the authors, higher postsecondary enrollment was found with less use of community colleges, or a tendency to avoid them altogether. Further, the authors found that "the states with the least reliance on community colleges had higher freshman baccalaureate enrollment and higher bachelor's degree attainment" (p. 88). The fact that these patterns held particularly true for minorities seriously challenged the notion that community colleges offered these students a viable route toward the baccalaureate.

How well students perform after transferring is of equal concern. Studies document that many transfer students experience a "transfer shock" the first year of enrollment in a four-year college. Many students do recover from the initial drop in grade-point average and from feelings of anxiety associated with attending larger classes and taking a rigorous academic workload. Nonetheless, four-year college faculty often believe that transfer students are not up to par with native students. A 1990–91 *Minority Student Progress Report* of three Arizona state universities indicated that less than half of new full-time lower division transfers (that is, transfer students classified as freshmen or sophomores at entry) graduated within four years and just over half of upper division transfers (transfer students classified as juniors or seniors at entry) graduated within three years. These rates are significantly lower for minority students. These findings point to the need to improve not only the rate of transfer but also the educational experience of minority students once they have completed the transfer process at four-year colleges and universities.

Several studies have examined factors impacting transfer rates of minority students. For example, Rendón, Justiz, and Resta (1988, pp. 157–158) suggested that while student characteristics and institutional factors affect both nonminority and minority students, "their effect on minorities may weigh more heavily because socialization has not prepared them well to either recognize or take advantage of transfer opportunities."

These researchers asserted that "minorities often exhibit a na-
iveté about the costs and benefits of the higher education system; they are unaccustomed to peer networking or penetrating
the resources and information networks, and they may find that
they are committing themselves to goals that they don't fully understand" (p. 158). They also found that minority students generally do not take advantage of the available academic and student support services that facilitate student retention and
transfer. Moreover, because many minority students enroll on a
part-time basis, they are less likely to become academically and
socially integrated into the college environment and are therefore more likely to drop out from college.

A qualitative study by Rendón and Valadez (1993) noted
that family influence, economic factors, knowledge of the system, the absence of cultural knowledge on the part of some faculty, and poor relationships with feeder schools contribute to low
transfer rates. The researchers cautioned that unless parents are
advised to do otherwise, many could actually steer students away
from transfer programs and instead guide them toward pursuing vocational courses of study. Further, the researchers emphasized that faculty who insist that minority students conform to
traditional teaching and learning models and faculty who hold
belief systems that perpetuate negative stereotypes of minorities
might create an organizational culture hostile to minorities.

Pincus and DeCamp (1989) explored the institutional impact on minority student transfer and degree attainment and
found that social integrative experiences had a significant positive impact on transfer and degree attainment. The social integrative experiences that were found to be important for minority students included being a member of student government
and/or minority organizations; receiving encouragement from
college faculty, staff, and classmates; being employed on campus; and having a positive perception of the college environment. Noting a difference in the level of social integration between successful and unsuccessful minority transfer students,
Pincus and DeCamp asserted that "community colleges must do
more to promote a lively campus culture" (p. 24).

A study examining Maricopa Community College District

transfers to Arizona State University conducted by Gebel (1993) sought to identify the factors that characterized successful minority and nonminority transfer students in terms of baccalaureate degree completion. Gebel found that the profile of successful minority transfer students included having a greater percentage of credits accepted, remaining in good standing at the senior institution, enrolling full time, and maintaining continuous enrollment. The profile of successful nonminority transfers was similar. Gebel also found that experiencing a decline in grade-point average after transfer, transferring with low hours, returning to the community college after transfer, and failing to change majors at the senior institution decreased the likelihood of graduating for nonminorities.

The literature on student enrollment, retention, and transfer points to the need for community colleges to come to terms with the changing profile of students to facilitate academic progress. Community colleges are the vital link that connects students to the full range of higher education opportunities. To realize those opportunities requires a forward-looking vision on the part of the community colleges of the twenty-first century.

Restructuring Community Colleges

Improving retention and transfer requires more than developing interventions that focus on these two areas. As community colleges, particularly those in urban centers, move toward educating "majority minority" students, it will become necessary to rethink and refashion the educational model with which many have been operating. The Wingspread Group on Higher Education report titled *An American Imperative: Higher Expectations for Higher Education* (1993) stated that educators in higher education have taken failure for granted and called for a restructuring of colleges and universities. Community colleges would do well to heed this challenge and direct their attention to a holistic reform of the institution, including the curriculum, faculty composition, student assessment, and organizational structure. An emerging body of research supports rethinking and restructuring higher education to accommodate diversity

(Belenkey, Clinchy, Goldberger, and Tarule, 1986; Lincoln, 1991; Rendón, 1994; Tierney, 1993). For example, like four-year institutions, most two-year colleges operate with a faculty-driven Eurocentric curriculum, a predominantly white faculty and staff, an instructional delivery system that is competitive as opposed to collaborative, and an institutional culture that is reflective of middle-class values. This model may have been appropriate for students in the past, but as many more immigrants and students of color enter the colleges, a new model responsive to these new student populations is needed to impact a larger segment of students.

The effective community college of the twenty-first century will need to create an institutional culture where success for *all* students becomes possible—one where learning is the main focus, where high, attainable standards are set, where mediocrity is not tolerated, and where the curriculum is diverse and of high quality. To build a new model of the community college—one that educates for diversity—will require restructuring the entire college, not just developing special add-on programs that impact only a few students or involve only a few faculty and administrators. Restructuring means designing new models of governance, teaching and learning, admissions, graduation, and assessment that promote the academic success of culturally diverse student populations, including majority and minority students.

Essential Restructuring Principles
At the core of restructuring in community college are guiding principles that administrators, faculty, counselors, and staff will need to keep in mind as they rethink and refashion a new model that impacts more than just a few students.

Keep the Culturally Diverse Learner at the Center of Restructuring. Everything that the community college engages in must reflect student diversity. This means that admissions, financial aid, assessment, student services, and instructional delivery systems should be examined to see if they truly reflect the full diversity of the student population.

Create Conditions for Optimal Learning. A strong teaching and learning program is key to the success of the culturally diverse student. To facilitate optimal learning, faculty should focus on:

- Active learning
- A curriculum that includes multicultural perspectives
- Early validation of students as capable of learning
- Close student-faculty interactions, especially those in which faculty are engaged in validating students
- Diverse teaching strategies such as collaborative learning, learning communities, field trips, demonstrations, debates, and simulations
- Multiple means of assessment that provide diverse sets of information about student learning and growth
- The use of technology as a teaching tool
- Identification of what students need to learn—for example, communication skills, learning how to learn, computer skills, and higher-order thinking skills
- Setting clear academic expectations, including probation/dismissal standards, basic skill requirements, course prerequisites, standards for academic progress, and disciplinary standards
- Faculty development programs related to understanding, appreciating, and working with culturally diverse students

At the heart of improving student learning is an all-out effort on the part of the college staff to break belief systems that have stifled learning, such as viewing minority students as capable of limited learning. What is needed is to challenge students at higher levels, beyond the limits they think they have. This will require getting closer to students, including valuing their past experiences, helping them negotiate the transition to college, and liberating them from invalidating beliefs they may hold.

Build a Sense of Community. The power and governance structure should give everyone an opportunity to participate, taking the power of diversity and incorporating it as a strength to build what Tierney (1993) calls "communities of difference." Rather than building a model based on norms and similarities, Tierney (1993) proposes that a collective identity can come about by understanding differences and using those differences to forge alliances to create a new organizational culture.

Diversify Faculty and Staff. A community college's Statement of Faculty Excellence should include a commitment to identifying, recruiting, and selecting faculty and staff that are representative of the community it serves.

Designate Transfer Education as a High Institutional Priority. There is no more important source of potential minority baccalaureates than minority students now enrolled in two-year colleges. Tracking minorities into vocational-technical fields is unlikely to generate potential baccalaureate degree recipients, although some minorities may benefit from less than a bachelor's degree. Every effort must be made to facilitate transfer, including the following measures:

- Provide financial aid packages for transfers
- Develop a common core curriculum in major fields of study
- Arrange for dual admissions
- Provide summer experiences for students on four-year campuses
- Set numerical goals for minority student transfer and bachelor's degree recipients
- Clarify and strengthen articulation agreements with four-year colleges
- Conduct research on the progress of transfer students
- Identify and resolve institutional barriers to student transfer
- Develop interinstitutional and interdepartmental connections and collaboratives between two- and four-year college faculty
- Provide faculty development programs that offer incentives for faculty to become more involved with transfer education
- Initiate faculty exchange programs with four-year colleges
- Involve two- and four-year college faculty in collaborative research projects on transfer students

- Provide released time for faculty to conduct research on transfer students
- Develop a credit-bearing course on "The Transfer Year Experience" that provides potential transfer students with complete information about becoming a successful students in two- and four-year colleges
- Develop and implement intersegmentally staffed transfer centers
- Provide students with exposure to collegiate life at a senior institution
- Establish an intersegmental board to provide leadership and coordination
- Encourage more African American, Latino, Asian, and American Indian/Alaska Native students to transfer

Strengthen Student Assessment. A comprehensive student needs assessment model should be developed to determine academic competencies and clarify the educational goals of each community college entrant. Assessment instruments should be culturally and linguistically appropriate for testing diverse students. The assessment model should include:

- Quantitative and qualitative measures of student growth
- Assessment of educational goals, including degree and career aspirations
- Exploration of individual student characteristics, including family background
- Ongoing academic advising
- An early academic warning/alert system

Foster Involvement and Validation. The new profile of entering students suggests that many more first-generation immigrant and students from poverty backgrounds will be entering two-year colleges. Unlike traditional students who come from families where the precedent of going to college is well established, these new-wave students experience college-going not as a normal rite of passage, but as a traumatic separation from family and friends that results in a redefinition of identity. These students need early and sustained intervention that fosters involvement and connection to college. More important, they need early validation—to experience themselves as capable of learning, to realize that they can be successful college students. Rather than merely providing opportunities for involvement, faculty and staff can engage in validating students such as:

- Working one on one with students
- Designing learning activities early in the semester that allow students to experience success
- Providing consistent feedback to students
- Engaging in mentoring
- Meeting with students outside of class
- Learning students' names
- Praising students when they have done good work

Conclusion

The community college of the twenty-first century must learn to function better with diversity. Now is the time for a forward-looking approach to rethinking and redesigning a new community college. The sense of hope that students of color, immigrants, and students from poverty backgrounds have in community colleges as a means of attaining economic mobility must be sustained. Community colleges are the vital link to the fulfillment of complete access to higher education for a new student majority. Breaking the barriers toward full access, including improving retention and transfer rates, can ensure that greater numbers of students will fulfill their academic potential—a resource we can no longer afford to lose.

References

Aguirre, A., and Martínez, R. *Chicanos in Higher Education: Issues and Dilemmas for the 21st Century.* ASHE-ERIC Higher Education Report No. 3. Washington, D.C.: School of Education and Human Development, George Washington University, 1993.

Alba, R. D., and Lavin, D. E. "Community Colleges and Tracking in Higher Education." *Sociology of Education,* 1981, *54*(4), 223–237.

Anderson, K. *Institutional Differences in College Effects.* Boca Raton, Fla.: Florida Atlantic University, 1984. (ED 256 742)

Astin, A. W. *Minorities in American Higher Education: Recent Trends, Current Prospects, and Recommendations.* San Francisco: Jossey-Bass, 1982.

Astin, A. W. *Achieving Educational Excellence: A Critical Assessment of Priorities and Practices in Higher Education.* San Francisco: Jossey-Bass, 1985.

Belenkey, M., Clinchy, B., Goldberger, N., and Tarule, J. *Women's Ways of Knowing.* New York: Basic Books, 1986.

Bensimon, E. M., and Riley, M. J. *Student Predisposition to Transfer: A Report of Preliminary Findings.* Los Angeles: Center for the Study of Community Colleges, 1984.

Board of Governors, California Community Colleges. *Student Matriculation: A Plan for Implementation in the California Community Colleges.* Sacramento: Board of Governors, California Community Colleges, 1984. (ED 261 738)

Carter, D. J., and Wilson, R. *Minorities in Higher Education.* Washington, D.C.: American Council on Education, 1994.

Cohen, A. M., and Brawer, F. B. "Transfer and Attrition Points of View: The Persistent Issues." *Community/Junior College Journal,* 1982, *52*(4), 17–21.

Gebel, M. A. "Impacts on Baccalaureate Degree Completion: A Longitudinal Analysis of Community College Transfer Students." Unpublished doctoral dissertation, Arizona State University, Tempe, 1993.

Grubb, W. N. "The Effects of Differentiation on Educational Attainment: The Case of Community Colleges" *Review of Higher Education,* 1989, *12*(4), 349–374.

Grubb, W. N. "The Decline of Community College Transfer Rates: Evidence from National Longitudinal Surveys." *Journal of Higher Education,* 1991, *62*(2), 194–222.

Lincoln, Y. "Advancing a Critical Agenda." In W. Tierney (ed.), *Culture and Ideology in Higher Education: Advancing a Critical Agenda.* New York: Praeger, 1991.

London, H. "Breaking Away: A Study of First Generation College Students and Their Families." *American Journal of Education,* 1989, *97,* 144–170.

Nora, A. "Determinants of Retention Among Chicano College Students: A Structural Model." *Research in Higher Education,* 1987, *26*(1), 31–59.

Nora, A. "Campus Based Aid Programs as Determinants of Retention Among Hispanic Community College Students." *Journal of Higher Education,* 1990, *61*(3), 312–331.

Office of the Chancellor, California Community Colleges. *Community College Transfer Performance.* Sacramento: Office of the Chancellor, California Community College, 1989. (ED 314 110)

Olivas, M. A. *The Dilemma of Access.* Washington, D.C.: Howard University Press, 1979.

Orfield, G., and Paul, F. G. *State Higher Education Systems and College Completion.* Final report to the Ford Foundation. New York: Ford Foundation, 1992.

Pascarella, E., and Terenzini, P. "Predicting Voluntary Freshman Year Persistence/Withdrawal Behavior in a Residential University: A Path Analysis Validation of Tinto's Model." *Journal of Educational Psychology,* 1983, *75,* 215–226.

Pincus, F. L., and DeCamp, S. "Minority Community College Students Who Transfer to Four-Year Colleges: A Study of a Matched Sample of B.A. Recipients and Nonrecipients." *Community/Junior College,* 1989, *13*(3–4), 191–219.

Rendón, L. I. "From the Barrio to the Academy: Revelations of a Mexican American Scholarship Girl." In L. S. Zwerling and H. B. London (eds.), *First Generation Students: Confronting the Cultural Issues.* New Directions for Community Colleges, no. 80. San Francisco: Jossey-Bass, 1992.

Rendón, L. I. "Eyes on the Prize: Students of Color and the Bachelor's Degree." *Community College Review,* 1993, *21*(2), 3–13.

Rendón, L. I. "Validating Culturally Diverse Students: Toward a New Model of Learning and Student Development." *Innovative Higher Education,* 1994, *19*(1), 23–32.

Rendón, L. I., and Jalomo, R. "Validating Students." Paper presented at the annual conference of the American Association of Higher Education, Washington, D.C., Mar. 1993.

Rendón, L. I., Justiz, J., and Resta, P. "The Transfer Function in Southwest Border Community Colleges. Columbia: University of South Carolina, 1988. (ED 296 748)

Rendón, L. I., and Nora, A. "A Synthesis and Application of Research on Hispanic Students in Community Colleges." *Community College Review,* 1989, *17*(1), 17–24.

Rendón, L. I., and Valadez, J. R. "Qualitative Indicators of Hispanic Student Transfer." *Community College Review,* 1993, *20*(4), 27–37.

Richardson, R. C., Jr., and Bender, L. W. *Fostering Minority Access and Achievement in Higher Education: The Role of Urban Community Colleges and Universities.* San Francisco: Jossey-Bass, 1987.

Rodríguez, E. "A Review of the SHEEO/Ford Foundation Minority Achievement in Higher Education Project." In *Proceedings of the Invitational Conference on Developing Jointly Registered Teacher Education Programs to Increase Minority Baccalaureate Achievement.* Albany: New York State Education Department, 1990.

Rodríguez, R. "Coming Home Again: The New American Scholarship Boy." *American Scholar,* 1975, *44*(1), 15–28.

"State Proportion of Enrollment Made Up of Minority Students." *Chronicle of Higher Education Almanac,* Sept. 6, 1989.

Terenzini, P., and others. "The Transition to College: Diverse Students, Diverse Stories." *Research in Higher Education,* 1994, *35*(1), 57–73.

Tierney, W. "Culture and Alienation: Discovering Voice, Discovering Identity." Paper presented at the conference of the American Educational Research Association, Atlanta, Ga., Apr. 1993.

Tinto, V. *Leaving College: Rethinking the Causes and Cures of Student Departure.* Chicago: University of Chicago Press, 1987.

Valadez, J. "Cultural Capital and Its Impact on the Aspirations of Nontraditional Community College Students." *Community College Review,* 1993, *21*(3), 30–43.

Voorhess, R. A. "Financial Aid and Persistence: Do the Federal Campus-Based Aid Programs Make a Difference?" *Journal of Student Financial Aid,* 1985a, *15*(1), 21–30.

Voorhess, R. A. "Student Finances and Campus-Based Financial Aid: A Structural Model Analysis of the Persistence of Higher

Need Freshmen." *Research in Higher Education,* 1985b, *22*(1), 65–91.

Weis, L. *Between Two Worlds: Black Students in an Urban Community College.* Boston: Routledge, 1985.

Wingspread Group on Higher Education. *An American Imperative: Higher Expectations for Higher Education.* Racine, Wisc.: Johnson Foundation, 1993.

Chapter 14

Developing a "Pipeline" Recruitment Program for Minority Faculty

Lionel A. Maldonado, Charles V. Willie

The American Sociological Association (ASA) has designed a program to encourage and enhance the career attainments of minorities in sociology. The ultimate goal is to increase the number of minorities with the credentials necessary for faculty appointments. The success of this program makes it a viable model for adoption by other disciplines concerned about achieving diversity among their members. The ASA's program enlarges the talent pool of people of color with Ph.D.'s from which faculty usually are recruited. The program also has proven to be an effective means of transmitting the culture and canons of the discipline and offers excellent potential for institutional change.

Begun initially as a graduate fellowship program in the mid 1970s, it has evolved into a cooperative longitudinal program that draws on the resources of the ASA, college and university undergraduate and graduate programs in sociology, regional and sister associations, foundations, and the federal government. The program identifies talented minorities early in their academic careers, recruits them to the discipline, and enhances the development of their careers.

To achieve these objectives, the program provides a supportive environment for young scholars that socializes them into the field of sociology. The program also has a strong mentoring component and has developed a network of scholars who offer support over the course of participants' professional career. The ASA's Minority Affairs Program may be characterized as highly interactive. It seeks to bond together various components of the higher education community. In addition, the program has cultivated a network of constituent groups. Through this network, a wide array of educational and funding resources can be mobilized to help students with special needs.

Minorities in Graduate School

This chapter begins with a general discussion of the status of minorities in graduate school. With the exception of Asians, all minority groups are underrepresented in their proportion of students in graduate school, compared to their percentage in the population at large. Like whites, Asians are overrepresented (National Center for Education Statistics, U.S. Department of Education, 1992).

In 1990, colleges and universities conferred 37,980 doctoral degrees. Ninety-one percent of these degrees were awarded to white or nonresident aliens. Only 9 percent were received by Asians, African Americans, Latinos, and Native Americans; these groups received 3.4 percent, 3.0 percent, 2.1 percent, and 0.3 percent of the terminal degrees awarded, respectively (National Center for Education Statistics, U.S. Department of Education, 1992), despite the fact that these groups combined are approximately 25 percent of the total population.

A majority of doctoral degrees were awarded to students pursuing graduate studies in education, engineering, and the physical and life sciences. Eight percent of doctoral degrees were awarded to students in the social sciences (National Center for Education Statistics, U.S. Department of Education, 1992) and only 1 percent were received by sociologists.

The small proportion of minorities who received doctoral degrees has resulted in their small proportion as professors.

Among professors, 90 percent are white, 4.2 percent are Asian, 3.2 percent are African American, 2.3 percent are Latino, and less than 1 percent (0.7 percent) are Native American. Together, minorities are approximately 10 percent of all full-time faculty members in the United States (National Center for Education Statistics, U.S. Department of Education, 1992). Whites are overrepresented compared to their proportion in the total population.

This overview provides a clear message. If we wish to increase the number and proportion of minorities who teach in institutions of higher education, our society must increase the number and proportion of minorities who receive doctoral degrees. James Blackwell's (1987, p. 359) study indicates that this connection is direct; he found that "the most powerful predictor of enrollment and graduation of blacks from professional school" is the presence of black faculty on the campus where they study. This holds for other minorities as well.

Increasing Minority Presence: A Minority Fellowship Program

The limited participation of minority scholars in the affairs of the American Sociological Association is symbolized by the small number who have been elected to high office. Founded in 1905, only two minorities have served as president—E. Franklin Frazier in 1947 and William Julius Wilson in 1990. Both are African American. Thus far, the association has not elevated to its highest office an Asian, Latino, or Native American, although individuals from these and other minority groups have served as elected members of its governing council.

To overcome their limited involvement in the affairs of the association, members of the Caucus of Black Sociologists (now the Association of Black Sociologists) petitioned and pressured the ASA to redress their grievances and to take affirmative action on behalf of all minorities. The pressure began in 1968 and continued until the association recognized programs designed to increase the number of minority sociologists and their participation in organizational activities as a high priority.

A tangible effort toward increasing the number of minority

sociologists was the Minority Fellowship Program (MFP). With funding from the Minority Groups Mental Health Center of the National Institute of Mental Health, ASA launched the MFP in 1973. The program was funded to increase the number of trained minority investigators prepared to conduct research on issues of mental health, generally, and minority health, specifically. In existence now for approximately two decades, this program has sponsored minority students in leading graduate schools throughout the nation. Of the 312 students supported between 1974 and 1993, 29 percent are Latino, 17 percent Asian American, 7 percent Native American, and 47 percent African American. Fully 54 percent of the program's participants have earned doctoral degrees. Several have made significant contributions to the discipline and have received awards and recognition for their excellent work. The dropout rate has been small—only about 10 percent.

A review of data prepared by the National Research Council indicates how desperately needed a program like the Minority Fellowship Program is (Table 14.1). Between 1977 and 1990, there was a 41 percent decline in the number of doctoral degrees awarded in the United States. But the drop in terminal degrees awarded to minorities in this field was only 9 percent during this period. If a special program had not been in place and the proportion of doctoral degrees awarded to minorities in 1990 had remained the same as in 1977 (that is, 9 percent), only about forty degrees would have gone to them. But because of the MFP and other grant programs stimulated by the ASA effort, the actual number of doctoral degrees awarded in sociology to minorities held steady during the period of retrenchment and continued at the level of about sixty per year. Moreover, as implied by the figures just cited, special fellowship programs targeted on minorities helped them to improve their share of doctoral degrees in sociology, from 9 percent in 1977 to 15 percent in 1990. While this proportion is less than that of minorities in the population at large (which is about 25 percent), it nonetheless moves closer to their fair share.

The Minority Fellowship Program helped the discipline as well as its minority members. Between 1977 and 1990, when the production of doctoral degrees in sociology was shrinking,

Table 14.1. Doctorates in Sociology by Race or Ethnicity, 1977–1991.

Year	Total (N)	Non-U.S. (%)	Minority (%)	American Indian	Asian	Black	Puerto Rican	Mexican	Other Latinos
1977	725	09.1	09.5	08	15	33		13[b]	
1978	610	09.0	09.6	04	16	29		13[b]	
1979	632	09.5	11.2	05	21	30		15[b]	
1980	602	10.6	09.5	03	14	24	01	04	11
1981	603	11.4	12.6	00	18	25	02	11	02
1982	568	09.5	12.0	02	19	29	06	07	05
1983	525	12.1	08.9	00	10	26	05	04	02
1984	515	12.0	11.1	01	11	28	04	06	07
1985	461	13.0	11.1	00	08	26	05	07	05
1986	492	13.8	10.9	04	11	25	03	04	07
1987	423	12.7	09.9	02	18	12	02	04	04
1988	449	15.1	11.8	02	13	22	02	06	08
1989	435	21.1	14.2	01	13	26	05	07	10
1990	427	21.8	14.8	01	15	20	06	06	15
1991	466		14.6	02	17	26	06	07	10
1992	495	23.8	13.1	06	22	25	04	03	05
Total									
N	8,428								
%		13.6	11.3	0.5	2.9	4.8			3.1[c]
Population proportions[a]		0.8		0.8	2.9	12.1	8.9		8.9

[a]Figures are from 1990 census.
[b]Latino data are not disaggregated in 1979 and earlier; figures from 1977–1979 are for all Latinos.
[c]Figure is for all Latinos.

Source: National Research Council, 1977–1992.

the number of doctoral degrees awarded in some other fields was increasing. By increasing educational programs for minorities who tend to specialize in the social sciences, sociology was able to check the damage of the downward plunge in degrees granted. Without the MFP and other financial assistance for minority students, the drop in doctoral degrees awarded to sociologists would have exceeded the 41 percent figure noted above for this period.

In addition to its success in the recruitment, retention, and career attainments of talented minorities, the MFP has played a key role in the psychic support of minority students, in graduate school and in their careers. Evidence of this is provided from a survey of MFP Fellows carried out in 1985. Fellows who had completed the Ph.D. were surveyed about the impact the MFP had on them as graduate students and in their careers. Responses to this open-ended query were subjected to content analysis.

Perhaps respondents' own words are the best indicators of how the program helped minority graduate students financially, in marketing their talents after graduation, and in their socialization process in becoming a professional.

Financial Support
In the words of one Fellow:

> The MFP Fellowship and the Spivack Grant (the latter a supplement to help meet extraordinary expenses associated with dissertation research) alleviated some of the financial burdens I faced in graduate school. The MFP contributed toward my tuition (at an elite private university) and also allowed me to devote a nice block of time toward my dissertation.

Another noted that

> it provided me an adequate stipend that freed me from basic financial worries.

A third offered that

it provided me with a source of financial support, which was critical for the prompt completion of my Ph.D. The Fellowship allowed me to resign from my position doing biological research for the Marine Review Committee . . . and to devote my full attention to the . . . dissertation. Without that support, I would have toiled much longer writing my dissertation. . . .

Taking another tack, another Fellow noted that

the money . . . afforded me the chance to devote full time to my academic studies . . . ; this placed me in an advantageous position relative to other graduate students, since I was not as heavily burdened with the demands of graduate assistantships, which at times interfered with one's finishing a degree on time. Indeed, of my graduate cohort . . . , I was second to finish the Ph.D. degree requirements.

Another stated that

as a minority fellow, I was able to "vigorously" pursue my graduate degree without having to work a full-time job. As a mother of four children, working a full-time job and pursuing a graduate education would have been impossible.

Yet more on the value of the award:

They (MFP funds) helped to support me, gave me funds for books, xeroxing, and especially computer money, and in every way helped me to work and complete the dissertation. A typical University of Chicago tragedy was the ABD, since the University provided no support whatsoever for working on the thesis and working full time eroded most people's capacity to do all the work a really good dissertation requires. Since it is only a good dissertation that ultimately enables one to publish from it, support for the dissertation research is crucial.

In sum, the manifest goal of the MFP of providing a semblance of financial security in graduate school has several shades to it. First, it offers a sure income and helps meet a variety of academic expenses. Second, it frees recipients from other work responsibilities and tasks that often become obstacles to the completion of the degree. Third, it assists materially in the timely completion of the Ph.D. These elements bring us to another aspect to MFP support, also linked to finances.

Marketability

Associated with financial considerations, but still clearly distinct, the MFP helps make students more marketable. We see this in the following comments from Fellows:

> That dissertation which MFP supported was . . . the birth of my book (eventually published by a prestigious academic press).

> Without that support, I would have toiled much longer writing my dissertation, probably produced a less polished piece of research, and undoubtedly entered the job market in a less marketable position.

> With the award I was able to develop my dissertation research to a level that greatly enhanced my academic marketability.

These comments bring out two related, but analytically distinct, aspects flowing from the financial support by the MFP. The first is the direct benefit of providing the person with financial security. Such support can shorten a student's time in graduate school. The fellowship allows time for scholarly work free from many of the distractions faced by other students that cut into their study time. Second, the award helps the recipient become far more marketable with a higher-quality dissertation. This, in turn, often results in that first important job and provides a basis from which to launch publication efforts.

Networks and Sense of Community

There are other unanticipated results of an MFP award. One of these is the network linkages forged as a result of the program. These networks, in effect, create a supradepartmental experience for minority Fellows. It also is a means by which Fellows go through the rites of initiation, learning values, norms, and behaviors appropriate to the profession. It is a unique and necessary form of socialization. The following comments from Fellows illustrate these aspects of the MFP:

> For me, receiving the Fellowship provided, at a crucial stage, a sense of belonging to the sociological community. . . .

> Moreover, the MFP connected me with a group of stimulating peers who enriched my intellectual life. As an MFP Fellow, I interacted with a wide audience of young scholars unavailable to those whose contacts were limited to one department.

> The contact with other MFP Fellows, especially with [two other Fellows who also are American Indians and were in the same cohort], was also very beneficial. [We] have kept in touch over the years, and . . . have collaborated on a paper [presented at a professional meeting] and which we currently are revising for submission to a journal.

Regarding the practice of providing Fellows a small stipend to attend the ASA's annual meetings, one Fellow commented on the importance of attending professional meetings:

> At these meetings, I met many intellectual leaders in my field, as well as gaining new information and friends. . . . It was at one of these meetings that I was able to develop the ideas for my dissertation topic.

> Attending annual meetings (with funds from an MFP award) helped me get "socialized" into the discipline—by attending sessions, meeting established scholars.

> I do not think I would be where I am now without

the MFP, but it is difficult to know whether it was the financial support or the time and attention that the Directors [former directors of the MFP while this Fellow was a student] gave me that was more important.

In addition, the minority fellows met each year at the annual American Sociological Association meetings, where papers are presented, issues of mutual concern are discussed, and where faculty and other minority students can meet. These meetings were very helpful for getting to know other people in the discipline who shared similar interests and concerns. Often, minority students and faculty do not have personal access to some of the central activities of the discipline; these meetings helped ameliorate that condition.

The MFP was vital in my professional development for a number of reasons. First, the program provided a much needed network with other minority scholars and students. This was particularly important in my situation because there were no minorities on the faculty in the Department of Sociology. . . . In fact, when I entered the Ph.D. program there was only one other native-born minority in the program and he had been there four years before I arrived. Graduating in the same year, he and I became the first native-born minorities to complete the doctorate. So the MFP was my key to minority perspectives and the minority community in sociology.

Second, [the MFP director] and my advisor were in constant contact with each other regarding my progress. Moreover, my advisor provided funds to supplement my stipend so that I could attend and/or present papers at professional meetings. Consequently, I presented and published papers before earning my Ph.D.

Third, I have continued my communication with other Fellows (most of whom I met at MFP receptions).

Finally, the program's requirement on producing research on minority issues is still a large part of my research agenda.

It is evident from these excerpts that financial support is closely associated with enhancing the marketability of Fellows and with a timely attainment of the Ph.D. These are direct effects of the program. Furthermore, the MFP helps Fellows establish networks and contacts in the profession with established and emerging scholars. It functions to initiate Fellows into the norms and values of the profession. These result in a sense of community, solidarity, and identification that transcend a Fellow's particular department. These professional links and ties, furthermore, extend beyond Fellows' tenure in the program, carrying over to their professional careers.

Self-Worth and Self-Esteem

The program has other, more subtle effects. The subjective effects of providing a sense of self-worth and self-esteem are real and tangible. A Fellow's comments amply document these subtleties:

> There was nothing in my childhood that prepared me for college, and certainly not for graduate school. Neither of my parents had finished high school (my mother obtained her GED when I was a high school junior and now has an MA and teaches fifth grade), and whether I would attend college at all was a question.
>
> In fact, I dropped out of high school and tried to join the Marines in 1968. . . . My wife and I married on my 18th birthday, we had our first child when we were 19, and after my sophomore year I dropped out of college for 1 1/2 years. During this time, I built and installed septic tanks.
>
> There were two things that kept me going academically during this time. First, there were people who believed in me, or at least pretended to believe in me, even when I gave up on myself. Second, because I am an Indian, I qualified for special educational assistance that is available only to Indians due to treaties and agreements between the U.S. government and different Indian tribes. This aid, my wife working full-time, and my working 20 hours per week while

I attended school made it possible for me to finish under-graduate school.

When I was accepted at [an elite private university in the West] and was awarded an ASA Minority Fellowship, I was both excited and frightened. I had no idea what graduate school was going to be like, nor did I know what it would be like to compete with students whose academic backgrounds included Michigan, Stanford, Harvard and so forth. It did not help when one of my professors [in graduate school] said that I came from an "inferior institution." Once I got into my courses, though, I began to enjoy graduate school, and my initial performance convinced me that I was going to make it. During the first year, it was nice to talk with [the MFP director and members of the selection committee] on the phone and to have them visit me early during my first quarter. It was also great not to have to work 20 hours per week at an outside job.

Both awards (MFP and Spivack) lifted my declining self-esteem and were prime motivators in completing my doctoral program.

Intellectually, the MFP strengthened my confidence in a set of ideas because it was a competitive award that promoted academic excellence.

Second, and perhaps more importantly, the Fellowship provided me with a sense of self-worth as a legitimate sociologist. Graduate school, like most professional training programs, is a vulnerable time for us, a time in which we question our identities, worth, and competence. Caught between the comfortable routine of undergraduate days past and the discomforting prospects of an unknown future career as a sociologist, many graduate students fail to realize their potential because of anxiety and self-doubts. Such doubting is particularly acute for minority students. For me, receiving the Fellowship provided, at a crucial stage, a sense of belonging to the sociological community, enabling me to realize my potential and launch my career.

While the economic support was very important . . . , I feel that the fact the MFP had faith in me and my abilities, and that they trusted in me, gave me the necessary motivation and determination to successfully complete my graduate studies.

The MFP provided a sense of group membership that motivated me to finish my studies. The site visits by the director made me feel I belonged to a special group, and they indicated to the faculty [at an elite private university in the East] that our program was being monitored, as well as their commitment to help us.

These excerpts from Fellows' responses speak eloquently to the influence of the MFP in chasing away those blue devils of self-doubt and anxiety. They also illustrate how the program helps provide an induction into the folkways, mores, and values of the profession. The MFP helps deflect, and even counter, debilitating anxieties of graduate students by encompassing them in a supportive community, one that creates bonds linking Fellows to a larger organic whole.

The graduate fellowship program clearly has demonstrated its value in recruiting and retaining people of color in sociology. Fellows who complete their training are launched successfully into their careers. Most scholars enter the academy and progress through the academic ranks. They teach and do research in small liberal arts colleges, comprehensive colleges and universities, and research institutions. Their scholarship is proceeding apace, with significant numbers singled out by various organizations for their unique research contributions; several scholars have received competitive research grants from a range of funding agencies. A few have pursued careers in the private sector and in government.

Evidence that the MFP has been a success is its replication by other disciplines and the increased support that similar programs have received from foundations. Programs for the recruitment and retention of minorities are sponsored, for example, by the American Political Science Association, the American Psychological Association, the Council on Social Work Education, the American Nurses Association, and the American Psychiatric Association, among other professional groups. The largest of such programs is one sponsored by the National Consortium for Graduate Degrees for Minorities in Engineering and Science. It has eighty-four corporate sponsors. Sixty to seventy students annually receive fellowships for study in doctoral programs in science and engineering. In addition, the American Society for Engineering Education awards twenty fellowships annually for doctoral study. This program also has corporate sponsorship.

Foundations such as Lilly, Mellon, and Ford have funded doctoral programs for minorities in the social sciences, humanities, physical and life sciences, mathematics, and engineering. The Committee on Institutional Cooperation, for example, awards forty fellowships annually. The Ford and Spencer foundations offer postdoctoral and dissertation fellowships, respectively. Although these programs have provided valuable assistance and have enabled many minorities to receive doctoral degrees who otherwise would have been denied the opportunity of graduate study in the social sciences during the retrenchment era of the past two decades, the deficit and underrepresentation of minority scholars has not been erased. As noted earlier, Asians, African Americans, Latinos, and Native Americans received only about 9 percent of all doctoral degrees awarded in 1990 and filled only 10 percent of all full-time college faculty positions.

In spite of this clear record of need on the one hand, and of success in recruitment, retention, and completion of graduate studies on the other hand, federal funding for the MFP has declined. By 1985, the government had phased out one of the programs that helped fund the MFP and severely reduced the dollar-award amounts for the continuing grant. These fiscal constraints forced the association to seek cooperative funding arrangements with universities where Fellows were enrolled. Agreeing that the program was an unqualified success, many departments of sociology committed to varying levels of financial for MFP Fellows. Through these efforts, the program has continued to support almost as many Fellows annually as had been funded earlier from the two federal grants.

The federal government's interest in training programs during the 1980s shifted to engineering, mathematics, and the physical and biological sciences. A graduate research fellowship program for minorities was sponsored by the National Science Foundation for doctoral degrees in the fields mentioned above; 120 awards were made to Native Americans, African Americans, and Latinos in 1993. Support for study toward doctoral degrees in biomedical sciences is available through the Minority Access to Research Careers Program of the National Institute of General Medical Services. The bulk of federal funds for minority graduate education has encouraged study in mathematics and the physical and life sciences, but not in the social sciences.

To consolidate the gains of the MFP and to chart directions for the future, the American Sociological Association established a task force in 1985 to examine the MFP and to make recommendations regarding new initiatives, if any, that the association should take. The task force took note of the accelerated expansion of the formal curriculum in sociology (Blalock, 1991; Glenn, 1991) and the continuing concern within the discipline for a more systematic socialization of young sociologists into the norms and values of the profession, both as teachers and as researchers (Sullivan, 1991). The task force also tried to understand the meaning of the downward trend in graduate degree production in sociology during nearly a decade and a half while the overall rate of doctoral degrees was increasing.

The task force concluded that a longitudinal program was needed to begin the recruitment process for sociologists earlier in the pipeline, during undergraduate study. It recommended that the MFP should be continued and that an undergraduate recruitment program, the Minority Opportunity Summer Program (MOST), be established. The undergraduate program began in 1990. It was supported with a grant from the Ford Foundation.

The Undergraduate Recruitment Program

Minority students in their junior year of undergraduate studies were invited to participate in a summer curriculum of in-depth study; the program was modeled after honors courses. Two campuses—the University of Wisconsin and the University of Delaware—were designated as host sites. Students were given a choice of which site to attend. The curriculum included a specially structured course in the logic of social inquiry and a proseminar on the profession. Students were involved in research projects. A conscious and careful effort was made to match each student with a mentor at the summer site to help facilitate socialization into the discipline, including advice on graduate study. In addition to its academic content, the summer program was designed to reduce feelings of isolation and estrangement among students of color in predominantly white institutions.

During the first four years of this program, the number of applications has been extremely high—about 150 for each year's competition. Applications are received from students across the nation. The program is advertised in the association's monthly newsletter, *Footnotes,* and in mailings to all departments of sociology. Additional mailings are sent to historically black colleges and universities and campuses with large enrollments of Latinos and American Indians.

Thirty ($N = 30$) students were selected for each summer's institutes and divided between the sites. A list of students who could not be accommodated in the summer program because of space limitations was made available to all graduate programs of sociology. Departments were encouraged to recruit these students to their universities for graduate study. This technique gave talented minority students interested in graduate work in sociology wider recognition and visibility. It proved a good strategy; many of these students in fact were recruited into graduate studies in sociology.

The first summer institutes (1990 and 1991) were held at the University of Delaware and the University of Wisconsin at Madison. The next (1992 and 1993) were at the University of California at Berkeley and the University of Michigan at Ann Arbor.

Students received a $1,000 stipend, travel expenses, and room and board while at the summer institutes. The association used the Ford Foundation grant to pay tuition expenses and provide a book allowance. Host sites contributed faculty salaries and scheduled enrichment activities for their students. The institutes concentrated on providing information and experience that would create a strong foundation for a career in sociology.

The MOST program is having its intended effect. Information on the first two cohorts, for example, indicated that the majority had completed the B.A. or were making excellent progress toward completion. Most impressive, 44 percent of those who attended the MOST program in 1990 or 1991 were in graduate school, 39 percent in sociology departments. Another 39 percent planned to enter graduate school in sociology.

Preliminary results from the third and fourth cohorts suggest that the program increased its success in all areas: the number of students earning the B.A., aspiring to graduate studies in sociology, and applying for and gaining admission to graduate studies.

Summer institute site directors were required to submit summary reports on the institute's activities. They provided considerable detail on the individual programs, covering issues from dealing with students' initial loneliness to problems with required coursework. These reports support the continuing need to structure a close bond between protégés and mentors via academic activities, social events for the group, and one-on-one meetings.

Directors concluded that the summer program for undergraduates was a success. Most valuable was the presence of faculty and a support staff on location who offered students the opportunity for discussion and sympathetic introspection on alternative ways of dealing constructively with a myriad of student concerns. Site directors noted that their relationship with program participants did not end with the conclusion of the summer session. Students continue to call for advice, counseling, guidance, and information on innumerable topics: problems with projects; information about courses to take at their home institutions, graduate programs, and application procedures; requests for letters of recommendation; and so on. In this regard, MOST is achieving its goals of developing a community of scholars who help one another navigate the life course of a professional career.

Overall, students who participated in the summer institutes rated them very highly; 88 percent rated their experience as "very" or "quite" valuable. Many noted that the opportunity to establish ties with other minority students and faculty from other universities who shared an enthusiasm for and interest in sociology were noteworthy highlights. Academic aspirations and expectations clearly were enhanced by the summer program. The majority—nearly three-quarters of those who participated in the program's first three years—stated that they were more likely to go on to graduate school as a result of their experience.

A new grant from the Ford Foundation, based on the success of the initial MOST activity, calls for an intervention in undergraduate and graduate programs simultaneously. This is to be accomplished by having fifteen undergraduate departments commit to planned change over a three-year period. Each department will work with six students and their mentors, constituting a core group for rendering change at their institutions. Mentors and students will participate in activities at one of two graduate programs, with mentors involved in a week-long workshop and students in summer institutes. Host graduate programs will rotate annually. The objective is to increase the number of graduate departments involved in the overall program. As a condition for participation in the program, each graduate department must identify strategies for addressing diversity and inclusiveness issues.

Over a six-year period, a total of 180 students from thirty undergraduate campuses will work with faculty, graduate students, and administrators from six ($N = 6$) graduate programs. The structure of the activity calls for more intensive cooperation among programs focusing on a common problem. It also will be more extensive, reaching a larger number of individuals and departments.

Essential to the initiative is institutional change regarding the recruitment, retention, and training of minority sociologists. Participating undergraduate programs will seek to implement curriculum improvements and identify specific means of enhancing the academic and social climate for minority students. Individual students and faculty mentors will play key leadership roles as change agents.

The summer institutes will continue their emphasis on substantive issues relating to the logic of social inquiry, socialization into the profession, and professional and career development. Mentoring continues to command a central focus. The targeted training of specific students will be valuable not only to participants and faculty, but will constitute a key strategy for change at "sender" departments. Students will serve as undergraduate teaching assistants and peer mentors.

The Minority Affairs Program of the American Sociological Association has changed dramatically in its twenty-year history. It has evolved from a program aimed at individuals—a graduate fellowship program to increase the number of minorities with a Ph.D. in sociology—into a broad-based cooperative program designed to change institutions so that they may become more hospitable learning environments for minorities. The enlarged program extends its concern through the systematic inclusion of departments of sociology, both graduate and undergraduate, linking them more directly with the professional association and funding agencies. This more inclusive program has the objectives of continuing to increase the minority presence in sociology, enhancing its quality, and affecting long-term institutional change in higher education.

Conclusion

The findings of Willie, Grady, and Hope in *African Americans and the Doctoral Experience* (1991) indicate that attention must focus on the campus community as well as on minority individuals if efforts at achieving faculty diversity are to be realized. Their findings indicate that "opening predominantly white colleges and universities to African American students and to other racial minorities is essential if the increasing numbers of such students who wish to pursue higher education are to be accommodated. But whether or not they will stay the course and become credentialed with a . . . graduate degree . . . may depend a great deal on the campus experiences of these students" (p. 51). These researchers go on to note that students' negative experiences include the lack of opportunities to be involved in collaborative work with faculty and to serve as teaching and research assistants, as well as the absence of racial diversity among the faculty at predominantly white institutions.

Both minority recruitment and retention programs (MOST and MFP) of the American Sociological Association emphasize the significance of mentors in helping minority students make a good adaptation to their schools. Daniel Levinson (1978, p. 89) describes mentors as advocates for students who facilitate "the realization of [their] dreams." For minority students, mentors also often "provide a link of trust between individuals and institutions" (Willie, 1987, p. 99).

Because minority-group students tend to turn to faculty members of their own racial or ethnic origins for mentoring, a diversified faculty is essential for any school that wishes to recruit a diversified student body. Nevertheless, an additional finding of the study by Willie, Grady, and Hope (1991) is that cross-racial and cross-gender mentoring is possible and occurs to a degree at several colleges and universities. Thus, faculty members who want their departments to become a diversified community of scholars must find the will and the way to serve as mentors for all sorts and conditions of students.

American higher education has reason to be concerned about the multicultural attitudes and practices of many faculty and administrators. A survey of senior administrators conducted by the American Council on Education in 1989 revealed that diversity ranked ninth among thirteen issues administrators believed would be challenges to their institutions in years to come ("State Proportion . . . ," 1989). From the perspective of these senior administrators, maintaining enrollment levels and quality were more important challenges than achieving diversity. Focusing only on the responses of administrators at doctoral degree–granting institutions, survey results indicate that the perceived need to serve new populations is ranked near the bottom—twelfth—in the hierarchy of the thirteen issues. Regrettably, these administrators failed to recognize the linkage between diversity and quality. The ASA's dual programs offer a proven, effective, and constructive way of achieving diversity by linking it to an array of opportunities for a high-quality graduate education of talented minority scholars. This is possible by combining the resources of multiple organizations. Shown to be successful, it could be implemented by various disciplines and offers the potential for large-scale organizational change.

References

Blackwell, J. E. *Mainstreaming Outsiders.* New York: Dix Hills, 1987.

Blalock, H. M., Jr. "Providing Opportunities for Disciplined Creativity." *Teaching Sociology,* 1991, *19*(3), 403–407.

Glenn, N. D. "Some Troublesome Trends and Persisting Weaknesses in Sociology Graduate Education." *Teaching Sociology,* 1991, *19*(3), 445–446.

Levinson, D. J. *The Seasons of a Man's Life.* New York: Ballantine, 1978.

National Center for Education Statistics, U.S. Department of Education. *Digest of Education Statistics.* Washington, D.C.: U.S. Government Printing Office, 1992.

National Research Council. *Summary Reports: Doctorate Recipients from the United States.* Washington, D.C.: National Academy Press, 1977–1992.

Nelson, J. L. "Time in Place: The Increased Length of Time to Complete the Degree." *Teaching Sociology,* 1991, *19*(3), 441–443.

"State Proportion of Enrollment Made Up of Minority Students." *Chronicle of Higher Education Almanac,* Sept. 6, 1989.

Sullivan, T. A. "The Skimming Effect: Why Good Graduate Students are Unprepared for the Professoriate of Tomorrow" (pp. 24–28). In J. D. Nyquist and others (eds.), *Preparing the Professoriate of Tomorrow to Teach.* Dubuque, Iowa: Kendall/Hunt, 1991.

Willie, C. V. *Effective Education.* Westport, Conn.: Greenwood Press, 1987.

Willie, C. V., Grady, M., and Hope, R. *African Americans and the Doctoral Experience.* New York: Teachers College Press, 1991.

Chapter 15

Ensuring Campus Climates That Embrace Diversity

Shanette M. Harris, Michael T. Nettles

Both institutions and policy makers are being held accountable for educational outcomes—institutions for the goals and programs carried out by administrators and faculty, and policy makers for their allocation of taxes to colleges and universities. To eliminate differences in access and outcomes of education for minorities, institutional faculty and administrators, as well as policy makers, must consider the challenges that minority students confront on predominantly white campuses. This chapter describes some of the college experiences of minorities and focuses on methods to improve the predominantly white institutional climate for minority students, especially as it affects minority student outcomes. Methods for assessing student outcomes are suggested that focus on college and student characteristics throughout the college life cycle.

Minority Students on Predominantly White College Campuses

The college experiences of students have been explained by a combination of personal background characteristics, precollegiate experiences, and college environmental factors. Students typically enter colleges and universities with various characteristics and precollege experiences, and these interact with the characteristics of the institution to influence student affect and cognition, which in turn help to determine their behaviors (Bandura, 1986). The attitudes, behaviors, and precollege characteristics of students combine with the norms, ideologies, and values of their institutions to create a campus climate. The climate of an institution is therefore comprised of interactions between student characteristics and the characteristics of their institutions. Each one influences the other such that within the overall student population, students can perceive and experience the university system in dissimilar ways, depending on their backgrounds. Variations in student and institutional characteristics also make it likely that no two campus climates are the same. Even within a single institution, the climate may vary over time because of changes in student characteristics.

Relationship Between Students and Institutions

The bidirectional relationship that exists between students and their institutions becomes complex when student characteristics are found to be incongruent with the mores and values of the institution. Consequently, students whose characteristics are different from campus norms may be more likely to experience more difficulties than those whose characteristics are a better match with institutional values. Efforts to increase "nontraditional" student enrollment can lead to feelings of resentment on the part of traditional elements of the institution. These interactions provide opportunities for hostile climates to evolve as the presence of nontraditional students presents demands that institutions are unprepared to meet. This pattern of negative interactions is clearly illustrated by the enrollment of minority students in predominantly white colleges.

The culture of a college or university is comprised of concrete and observable qualities and less obvious and difficult-to-measure variables. Kuh (1993) discusses two properties that intricately relate to university climate: the institutional mission and philosophy. The mission is the broad justification for the existence of the institution that embodies historical aspirations and determines present and future university priorities. The philosophy consists of specific values and assumptions that guide the daily operations of the university and behaviors of institutional employees. Underlying assumptions that encompass issues such as the appropriateness of certain interpersonal relations, individual behaviors, standards of truth and reality, and the importance of certain assumptions relative to others comprise the philosophy. However, the values, beliefs, and assumptions that guide the operation of the university can be incongruent with the expectations represented in the mission statement. The mission and philosophies espoused or articulated can also differ from the behaviors actually enacted by university affiliates.

Collectively, the expectations for a university system and the values and assumptions that represent the philosophy interact to give rise to a specific culture. Culture is defined here as the reciprocally influencing relations among values, beliefs, assumptions, historical influences, expectations, and behaviors that are observed in traditions, rituals, norms, rules, policies, symbols, and campus artifacts. These variables serve as a baseline against which to gauge and determine the meaning of student situations, events, and behaviors. The observable evidence of the college culture consists of easily observable behaviors, structures, and symbols. For example, the presence or absence of American Indian, African American, or Hispanic American art may have a different meaning for nonminorities than for minorities. Whereas nonminorities may never notice the absence of minority art or the presence of European art, decor, and architecture, these images constantly remind nonminorities of their racial or ethnic status. The presence of the Confederate flag or swastikas in resident hall windows may also send chills down the spine of minority students but lead to feelings of pride among nonminorities. Whereas one group views the Confederate flag as evidence of a strong and forceful fight for values, dignity, and respect, another perceives this same fabric as an indication of servitude, oppression, and rejection as a human being. The presence of nonminority fraternity houses and sorority floors also gives different messages to students. While nonminority students expect that such structures and conveniences exist for socializing and partaking in the spirit of college, others question the absence of similar structures and places of pleasure for themselves. John Hope Franklin is quoted in an interview for the *Journal of Blacks in Higher Education* (Bliwise, 1993–94, p. 70) on campus integration as saying: "You drive on any major university campus today, and you will see fraternity row. It's lily white; oh, maybe the odd black, it's lily white. Imagine a black walking down fraternity row anywhere and confronting that all-white, arrogant, exclusive institution—it must be one awful experience."

The presence of a multicultural or black cultural center also triggers different feelings and thoughts. Minority students (especially African Americans) may experience feelings of security, safety, and comfort to know that this service exists. In contrast, nonminorities may view this structure as unnecessary and unavailable to them, as a way for minorities to isolate themselves from others, or as an inappropriate use of the institution's finances.

Campus rules, regulations, and policies also represent written institutional values and philosophies. An example is the requirement by many colleges and universities that students must take the Scholastic Aptitude Test or Graduate Record Examination before being admitted, even though the prevailing evidence is that the average scores of minority students are lower than those of nonminority students, and many relatively low performers are successful in college. Another example is the policy on some campuses that competency in Spanish does not fulfill the criterion for a foreign language in doctoral programs although German, French, or Russian are appropriate. Likewise, various institutional norms arise from values, assumptions, and traditions, despite recent evidence that refutes their validity. The tendency for nonminority students to challenge the competency and authority of minority faculty and the expectation that minority students will peform at lower levels than their nonminority peers are some of the institutional mores that negatively influence the predominantly white college climate.

Interaction of Students with Campus Culture and Environment

A variety of student personal and background characteristics interact with campus cultures and environments to deter the educational attainment of minorities. Minority students' socioeconomic status may influence the degree to which students are knowledgeable about nonminority norms and behaviors and may relate to their level of satisfaction with their undergraduate experience (Astin, 1992; Carter, 1990). Social status may also relate to educational aspirations, problem-solving abilities, interpersonal skills, and academic development (Allen, 1992; Astin, 1992). Irrespective of college preparedness or ability, students from low economic backgrounds encounter more negative experiences in college (Astin, 1992). Partly as a function of interactions between cultural assimilation and socioeconomic status, minority students experience more complications related to separation from previous environments (such as home, neighborhood, high school) to attend college than nonminority students do (Rendón, 1992; Terenzini and others, 1994). Whereas nonminority students' decisions to attend college often evolve from the values and life-styles of their parents, the decisions of minority students to pursue a college degree have been suspected of conflicting with the traditions, customs, and norms of their home community. Although college attendance is highly regarded and promoted among low socioeconomic group families as an opportunity for success, family members may experience ambivalence about the extent to which educational attainment will isolate their relatives from their home origins. Uncertainties about the appropriateness of possible changes in the family member may lead relatives to unknowingly give their student family member mixed messages about student educational endeavors. Indirect expressions of ambivalence generate feelings of anxiety that require energy to manage the resulting distress. Energy invested to cope with distress, avoid changes in family relations, and show loyalty to customs and traditions can interfere with college-related tasks.

Many minority students enter the white university with a history of few verbal and nonverbal rewards for academic performance. African American students have been found to receive more negative feedback about classroom behavior and academic performance than nonminorities (Aaron and Powell, 1982). Mexican American students also receive less positive feedback from teachers than do nonminority students (Buriel, 1983). Yet positive feedback about skills and talents is associated with high academic self-confidence. Studies of minority student and teacher interactions have also revealed that teachers have more negative beliefs and lower performance expectations for minority students than majority students (Simpson and Erickson, 1983). These beliefs and expectations for performance combine with lower standardized test scores to direct some well-intentioned high school counselors to guide potential college applicants away from four-year institutions and instead into community colleges.

Peer-Group Influences

Characteristics of the high school peer group influence the academic self-concept of minority college applicants. Oppositional values about academic achievement and educational advancement place minority students who plan to attend college in a double bind. Among high school peer groups in which social acceptance and approval are contingent on behaviors that indicate academic disinterest, students must choose between popularity or social support and academic achievement. Alternatively, they may become skilled in the creation of solutions to conceal academic-related behaviors (for example, by hiding books) (Steinberg, Dornbusch, and Brown, 1992). Such experiences contribute to student worries and feelings of academic self-doubt.

Peer groups formed in high school influence the transition to college in other ways. Results from focus groups conducted to investigate the transition process for college students reveal that high school friends who enter the same or different colleges offer invaluable support until new social networks are formed (Terenzini and others, 1994). However, the quality of the support received is as important as the quantity of support (for example, see Belsher and Costello, 1991). Certain sources of social support can introduce problems rather than reduce stress. Previous friendship circles may assist or deter the adjustment of minority students to college. Given the small percentage of minority students who attend college, it is likely that high school networks largely consist of non-college-bound students. Because of dissimilar future aspirations and fewer shared interests, some previous friends are unable to offer support for their college-bound friends, and may even exert negative influences on the process (Terenzini and others, 1994).

Academic Performance

Although some minority students outperform nonminorities with similar college entrance credentials, and some even outperform nonminorities with higher college entrance credentials, group comparisons show lower performance for minorities. Overall, non-Asian minority students receive lower college grade-point averages, progress more slowly through the curriculum, receive lower scores on outcome measures, receive lower graduate admissions test scores, and are less likely to attend graduate school than nonminority students (Harris and Nettles, 1991; Mow and Nettles, 1990). Even in instances in which entrance exam scores, high school averages, and personal characteristics are similar to those of nonminorities, some minority students are predicted to receive lower college grades (Nettles, 1988). However, in-college attitudes, behaviors, and experiences seem to better predict college performance than precollege characteristics (Nettles, 1988). In-college experiences can impede or enhance ethnic or racial disparities in academic performance. For example, alterations in the academic environment may moderate the effects of minority students' economically disadvantaged backgrounds. Hurtado (1994) conducted a longitudinal study and found that changes in the demands of the academic environment influenced academic self-concept such that background factors changed from having a direct to an indirect effect by graduation. Other studies also show academic self-images to become more positive over time (Pascarella and Terenzini, 1991).

Nonacademic Influences

Practical considerations and research findings suggest difficulties that extend beyond the academic arena. Increased racist acts on predominantly white campuses have brought national attention to environmental difficulties that haunt minorities (Goleman, 1990; National Institute Against Prejudice and Violence, 1987). The preponderance of the findings on minority student experiences indicate that the predominantly white climate is significantly more alienating and isolating than involving, facilitating, and validating (Allen, 1992; Bennett and Okinaka, 1984; Mow and Nettles, 1990; Suen, 1983; Tambe, 1984). For example, studies also show that minorities obtain few rewards from interpersonal relationships with nonminority peers (Allen, 1988; Madrazo-Peterson and Rodriquez, 1978).

Minority student efforts to cope with feelings of alienation and isolation take various forms. Many students withdraw psychologically from the university but continue to complete basic tasks in a perfunctory manner. Some withdraw both psychologically and physically, as evidenced by high attrition rates. Still others retain and increase contact with peers, organizations, and university systems of similar racial or ethnic backgrounds. Same-race or same-ethnic-group relations provide a context of safety by alleviating interracial tension, ambivalence related to assimilation and identity, and fear of rejection from nonminorities. Unfortunately, movement toward same-race or same-ethnic-group relations can lead to disengagement from other aspects of campus life. Perceptions of forced disconnection from university systems can induce feelings of resentment and frustration, which in turn thwart the completion of tasks associated with successful academic performance (Harris and Nettles, 1991).

Peers are related to social and academic well-being and exert the greatest influence on undergraduate student growth and development (Astin, 1992). Student values, beliefs, and goals also become more consistent with those that are most salient among peer-group members during the college years (Astin, 1992; Pascarella, 1980; Tinto, 1975). Interaction with peers of the same and other racial or ethnic groups is also associated with social involvement (Allen, 1992). On predominantly white campuses, however, minority and nonminority students engage in few cross-race interactions and segregate themselves for most social activities (Bourassa, 1991; Clark, 1988; Duster, 1991). The small percentage of cross-race friendships that do occur are usually initiated by minority students. McClelland and Auster (1990) examined peer-group relations on the campus of a small liberal arts institution and found no evidence of traditional racism (for example, negative affect, reported prejudice, interracial violence). However, the overt absence of traditional racism and prejudice gave the appearance of harmonious student relations, but covert domination and control, disguised as ideologies, exerted negative effects on cross-racial interactions and the experiences of minority students. Whereas African American students were willing to form relationships with nonminorities across levels of intimacy, nonminorities defined relationship boundaries for African Americans that differed from those desired for same-race peers. These findings suggest that segregation on the part of minority students is a defensive reaction to racial-group discrepancies in acceptable levels of friendship. Thus, nonminority student overtures to minorities are frequently met with suspicion and perceived as acts of "liberalism" that lack authenticity (Bourassa, 1991). For numerous reasons (such as racial anxiety or peer disapproval), the few cross-race friendships formed rarely continue for any length of time (Harris and Nettles, 1991).

Experiences with Faculty

Experiences with faculty on predominantly white campuses are related to social and academic integration. Satisfactory communication with faculty that occurs in informal and formal situations is important to student academic performance and social well-being (Nettles, Thoeny, and Gosman, 1986). Informal interactions with faculty seems especially important to engendering a sense of belonging for minority students who enter the university from strong kinship and extended family systems (Styles-Hughes, 1987). Although issues of causality remain questionable, a body of evidence exists to suggest that student-faculty social interactions also relate to educational aspirations and educational goal attainments (Pascarella and Terenzini, 1991). Many minority students believe, however, that nonminority faculty behave in a prejudiced manner toward them (Semmes, 1985). This perception influences students' behaviors toward nonminority faculty, which often affects the subsequent responses of the faculty. Nonminority faculty have also been reported to interact less frequently with minority than with nonminority students (Mingle, 1987). In addition, undergraduate African American students report that nonminority faculty are uncomfortable during interactions with them and seem to avoid them outside of class (Allen, 1981). The small number of minority faculty on predominantly white campuses and the difficulties that characterize relations between minority students and nonminority faculty have particular implications for the success of minority graduate students. Graduate training requires close faculty-student relationships, and the career and academic development of students depends on the quality of interactions with faculty. Positive relations with faculty can allow students to advance academically and economically. The presence of someone who is trusted to offer corrective feedback, interpret and impart institutional norms, and provide emotional and social support can increase the probability of a successful academic experience.

Financial Issues
Needs assessments conducted on predominantly white campuses indicate that minority students report more financial need than their nonminority counterparts (June, Curry, and Gear, 1990). This information is consistent with the reality that a greater percentage of minority students enter college from economically disadvantaged backgrounds. Receipt of financial aid provides a base for low socioeconomic students to attend college. Minorities, however, are less likely to receive merit-based scholarships than nonminorities (Kreuzer, 1993). Yet comparisons of scholarships with other forms of financial aid (such as loans and grants) reveal that scholarships have more positive effects on student persistence than other forms of assistance (Astin, 1992). To afford the costs of college, many of these students supplement financial assistance that usually consists of loans and grants with part-time employment. Because minority students require financial resources beyond loans, grants, and work-study, many seek off-campus employment. However, student employment off campus has more negative effects on persistence and graduation than

on-campus employment (Ehrenberg and Sherman, 1987). Pascarella and Terenzini (1991) attribute the negative impact of off-campus employment to the reduction in institutional involvement and inhibition of campus integration. Meeting the demands of employers can take important time away from studies and decrease the available time for social activities and result in less university involvement (Abrahamowicz, 1988).

Institutional Strategies and Programs

Based on these findings, factors specific to both the student and institutional level should be addressed to make the climate of predominantly white campuses more appropriate for minority students. An interactional model suggests that change at one level is likely to produce change in the other. Designing interventions for multiple levels is more likely to lead to hospitable environments for minorities than targeting either level alone.

Movement in this direction has been conceptualized as consisting of three stages: reactive, strategic, and adaptive (Richardson and Skinner, 1991). The reactive stage has traditionally focused on the goal of adherence to affirmative action regulations and includes behaviors such as modification of admissions standards, distribution of financial assistance, and participation in recruitment strategies. Movement to the second, or strategic, stage is facilitated by evidence in the reactive stage that increased access does not necessarily indicate successful academic and graduation outcomes. Responses of this stage are initiated to prepare newly recruited students to meet the norms, values, and ideologies of their institution. The development and implementation of programs and services for students characterize the strategic stage. Only with the recognition that strategic stage activities (which are unidirectional) are unable to resolve a dilemma arising from interactional causes can the institutional system move toward behaviors associated with the adaptive stage.

Various strategies and programs associated with student and institutional levels are recommended below. These recommendations are not exhaustive but include a sample of strategies to potentially enhance the climates of predominantly white campuses.

Institutional Commitment to Diversity

A commitment to diversity extends beyond state and federal government mandates and guarantees that students of various racial and ethnic backgrounds are supported at each institutional level. Attainment of this goal also requires the same degree of motivation and enthusiasm that has propelled institutional leaders to meet traditional university objectives (for example, obtaining funds from alumni). A strong commitment to a diverse university system also ensures that efforts in this direction will continue until success is achieved. Whether and when diversity is achieved, however, is difficult to determine and can give rise to a variety of opinions. A definition that appears to have face validity, reliability, and the potential for global acceptance has been offered to operationalize this standard. Based on a definition used by the Ohio Board of Regents (1988), Richardson and Skinner (1991) propose that proportionate enrollment *and* comparable achievement can serve as indicators of "success" for diversity efforts. The proportionate enrollment criterion is met when institutions enroll a percentage of students from each racial or ethnic group that is comparable to the actual number in the high school populations within a given state or service area. Success based on the comparable achievement criterion is attained when the percent of students of each race that receive an undergraduate degree from an institution reflects the percent of each racial and ethnic group actually enrolled in the institution.

Previous efforts to diversify predominantly white campuses have primarily concentrated on students. However, for many state institutions, governing boards (such as boards of trustees) are extremely important in the evolution of a college's mission statement. Because members of the university board of trustees are usually appointed by the governor, the climate of the university strongly reflects the political climate of the state at any given time. Major decisions are made by the board that affect policies about tenure, new degree programs, budgets, and the institutional president. The president, being elected by the board, also has the authority to make nonvoting appointments from among institutional faculty. Recognition of the types of power held by the board of trustees is important to efforts to increase diversity on state campuses. The ideologies, values, and philosophies of the board are *directly* transmitted to the campus in votes on certain institutional policies (like those affecting degree programs). *Indirect* influence is also transmitted through the selection of a particular president with certain personal values and educational philosophies. The philosophies, goals, and expectations of the board exert further influence on the campus by way of the president's power. For example, the appointment of college faculty to the board shapes the climate of the institution as a function of the criteria used to make the selections. In most cases, the behaviors of the president are likely to follow the expectations of the board. Likewise, faculty and occasional student appointments made by the president are likely to reiterate the themes of the board and president. This reinforcing flow of values, philosophies, and expectations between members of the board, the university president, and appointed faculty influence the operations and policies of the college, which in turn generalize to influence students.

A willingness to objectively appraise a university environment as it has traditionally existed is required for institutions to move from the strategic to the adaptive stage of evaluation. Internalization of institutional values and ideologies produces a type of blindness. That is, daily adherence to a system makes it difficult to see beyond the organizational structure. In many ways, faculty, administrators, and staff operate as though the institutional value system and their personal value system are one and the same. Because of expected discomfort and conflict, even institutional affiliates who maintain an awareness of climate deficiences often ignore the impact of traditional and symbolic university values on educational outcomes of minority students. Thus, a gradual but consistent effort to remove the layers that shield institutional members from recognition of the values and assumptions that comprise the culture of these institutions is needed.

This appraisal process should include an inventory of national and state as well as sociohistorical factors that preceded the founding and growth of the college or university. The primary objective of this assessment is to understand how the mission evolved from these events and its relevance to current institutional practices and student characteristics. Information that results from this process can serve as a base on which to conceptualize future university plans.

A related step is to determine the goals and standards of diversity. Usually, decisions that emerge from discussion at this level will relate strongly to previous university efforts and resultant successes. For example, a commitment to diversity should recognize and incorporate the roles of race and ethnicity within each hierarchy of the institution and include governing boards, administrators, faculty, staff, and students. University decisions and policies that involve hiring, promotion, admissions, recruitment, teaching, and community service should also reflect diversity efforts. Data should guide the implementation of new policies and procedures.

For instance, policies related to evaluations of teaching effectiveness should be guided by qualitative and quantitative studies conducted to obtain information about classroom dynamics when the teacher and students are of different racial or ethnic backgrounds. Another example relates to cross-race or cross-ethnic student interactions. For example, what is the nature of the relations between Hispanic and nonminority students? Do similar dynamics (such as distance) also characterize relations for American Indians and nonminorities? What is the quality of relations between Hispanic and African American students? How do these cross-race or cross-ethnic factors vary in general between different minority groups? Data should be obtained on these and other interactions that influence the atmosphere of the university and inhibit the successful integration of minorities.

Presence of Minority Faculty and Administrators
The presence of minorities in faculty and administrators is vitally important to institutions and students.

Faculty Presence. Faculty are the second most important influence on the development of students (Astin, 1992). Minority faculty introduce a multicultural experience for both nonminority faculty and students. The mere visibility of minority faculty may have positive effects on traditionally monocultural college climates that are being transformed. The presence of minority faculty may encourage nonminorities to reconsider stereotypes about culturally different groups and increase the likelihood of positive contact with culturally different individuals before encounters occur in the workplace. Negative student beliefs about ethnic and racial groups are also more easily dispelled when opportunities for interactions with and observations of minorities exist. Whereas interactions with ethnic or racial minority students are optional, class attendance and course activities make interactions at this level a more likely occurrence. The presence of minority faculty may also positively alter minority student perceptions of the climate. A significant representation of minority faculty can reduce feelings of social estrangement and alienation associated with enrolled minority students' dissatisfaction. The presence of satisfied minority faculty who support the university is also instrumental in attracting a larger number of minority students, faculty, and administrators.

Administrator Presence. A significant representation of minority administrators who identify with and relate to the culture of minority faculty enhances the climate in direct and indirect ways. The presence of minority administrators may benefit the level of satisfaction and well-being of minority faculty. The presence of minority administrators tends to provide a sense of security and helps to validate the university as an acceptable environment. Minority administrators tend to model for faculty the possibility of succeeding within a predominantly nonminority institution. The presence of this emotional support system is extremely valuable for new and untenured minority faculty. They can offer guidance with specific tasks as a function of their areas of expertise and promote camaraderie by linking faculty from different departments. Minority administrators also mediate relations between minority faculty and nonminority administrators on issues related to teaching, research, and service. For junior faculty, these administrators can offer feedback about behaviors and perceptions similar to tasks associated with the role of a mentor. In most instances, however, the presence of minority administrators offers more than behavioral assistance. Previous academic networks formed by minority administrators and their perceived ability to navigate the nonminority terrain may engender feelings of optimism and acceptance rather than helplessness and despair.

The commitment of minority administrators and their approval of an institution's values, philosophies, and assumptions enhance the trust and respect of minority faculty, which provides more comfort and satisfaction on which to draw for assisting students. Faculty who desire to hold administrative positions are also offered vicarious learning experiences. Minority faculty may look toward minority administrators to model ways of interfacing with nonminority networks, methods of coping with job-related dissatisfaction, and means of attaining career objectives in the face of conflict and difficulty.

Increasing the Pool of Faculty and Staff. Most institutions have few tenure track minority faculty, fewer tenured faculty, even fewer tenured faculty at the full professor rank, and racial or ethnic administrators are virtually absent. For example, 90 percent of full professors, 88 percent of associate professors, and 84 percent of assistant professors employed full time at 817 colleges and universities (public liberal arts, private two-year, and religious and other specialized colleges excluding medical schools) are white Americans (Wilson, 1994). The low representation of minority faculty and administrators on university campuses is usually attributed to a small pool of qualified candidates from which to draw, the inability to afford the high salaries demanded by applicants, and the inability to retain minority faculty because of their low rates of scholarly productivity.

Ambiguous messages are evident in some announcements used to recruit faculty. Employment notices that use subtle racist phrases reduce the likelihood that minorities will apply for university positions. Position announcements that read "seeking qualified minority" may arouse feelings of distrust and anxiety because of prejudicial overtones. Institutions must also move beyond recruitment strategies that rely on specific publications and bulletins. A most obvious pool of talent exists on campuses with strong doctoral programs. Minority students admitted into these programs can be mentored and encouraged to seek employment on graduation at the institution. "Grow Your Own" is a program based on this philosophy that exists at the University of Tennesse at Knoxville. Employees and students who enroll in graduate programs are offered financial incentives for educational study in exchange for a commitment to work at the university after receiving their doctorate. Duke University has attempted to reduce the difficulty of attracting minority professors by initiating the Preparing Minorities for Academic Careers program in conjunction with the Charles A. Dana Foundation. African American students from six historically black colleges spend the summer at the university with a faculty member who directs them in research and offers advice on graduate study.

Networking with certain foundations can also offer information about potential minority applicants for university faculty and administrator positions. For example, the Ford Foundation maintains a mailing list with names of hundreds of minorities who have received fellowship funding for research excellence at the predoctoral, doctoral, and postdoctoral levels. Efforts to attract minorities should also include building relationships between predominantly white institutions and faculty and administrators of traditionally minority institutions. In addition, the pipeline should be expanded to include relationships with minority community leaders, minority-owned businesses and organizations, and graduate programs with minority doctoral candidates.

Recruitment and employment of administrators as figureheads in order to display an adequate representation of minorities is a deterrent to climate change. The figure head image is promoted when minorities are sought for administrative roles that only supervise services linked to minority student and faculty populations (for instance, as director of multicultural center or vice president of minority affairs) and/or when institutions fail to bestow the range of privilege and power associated with a position on the minority administrator. It is not the presence of minorities in positions of power over minority campus concerns should not be the objective. Rather, it is eliminating the absence of minorities in positions that retain authority for nonminority *and* minority campus issues, policies, and regulations (as vice president for academic affairs or dean of liberal arts, for example) that should be the goal. The message transmitted to the university system is also suspect when the minority administrator with a similar title as a nonminority administrator (for instance, vice president of minority affairs versus vice president of student affairs) lacks the freedom to make decisions and handle the office in the same way without greater interference from higher-echelon administrators.

The literature on faculty in higher education and a review of two years of the *Chronicle of Higher Education* (1992 and 1993) reveals an absence of evidence to support the notion that minorities "expect" higher salaries than their nonminority counterparts. Yet many nonminority faculty and administrators offer this belief as justification for the failure to recruit and hire minorities. The finding that minority faculty are more likely than their nonminority colleagues to be found in junior faculty positions would suggest that their salaries are significantly less than those received by nonminorities, particularly nonminority males. However, institutions should willingly offer salaries and benefit packages that compare favorably to those of similar institutions in the same geographic regions. In addition, if minority faculty are expected to fulfill responsibilities beyond those specified for nonminorities (such as minority advising, minority campus workshops, minority community service), it seems logical that such efforts should receive recognition and appropriate compensation. At the University of Houston, for example, a Minority Faculty Recruitment Incentive Program was established in 1986 to recruit African American and Hispanic American faculty. An additional policy guarantees research funds to new faculty and supplements summer salaries to junior faculty. These supplementary funds provide release from teaching responsibilities and the opportunity to conduct research.

Effectiveness Standards
Approaches that recognize diversity should also influence standards for teaching, research, public service, promotion, and merit.

Teaching Effectiveness. Committees comprised of minority and nonminority tenured faculty should evaluate the teaching effectiveness of minority faculty. Student ratings of teaching also need examination in relation to the ethnic and racial context of the class and subject matter of the course. For example, racial or ethnic minority and female faculty (regardless of race or ethnicity) who teach "controversial" subjects (for example, Racism 101: Gender Role Behavior, Black Psychology) to predominantly nonminority students face numerous challenges (Harris, 1993). Negative student reactions to the content can influence the classroom atmosphere and course evaluations. In these instances, if students drop the course the reduced enrollment is viewed as negative. But if they remain, the negative atmosphere created because of their dissatisfaction may influence their faculty member's performance. Yet many institutions fail to understand the complexities of these classroom dynamics. Evaluations based on "liking" when cultural styles—such as degree of expressiveness—vary among racial and ethnic groups may not provide an adequate reflection of consumer views about teaching quality. If the objective of evaluations is to assess student feelings about faculty, then these measures are excellent. On the other hand, if the goal is to ascertain the degree to which the professor has influenced reasoning and writing skills and transmitted knowledge of a particular content area, it would seem that the course evaluations should focus on student outcomes. Evaluations that focus on student outcomes might also serve as an incentive for faculty to take more responsiblity for student performance (Phillips, Gouran, Kuehn, and Wood, 1994).

Research and Publishing. Aspects of minority faculty research are often misinterpreted and deemed to lack scholarship and intellectual development. This perception is usually associated with the value placed on conventionality. That is, the common tendency among minority faculty to provide a cultural context for basic research issues (for example, in a project exploring childrearing *and* cultural practices) is misconstrued as an inability or unwillingness to focus on traditional aspects of a particular topic. Thus, research content that focuses on concerns related to minorities may receive less positive evaluations than content perceived as "more scientifically worthy." The use of theories that are nontraditional—such as Afrocentric theories—is also less highly regarded than the use of an "objective" paradigm or framework (Phillips, Gouran, Kuehn, and Wood, 1994; West, 1993). Differences in the value assigned to the use of abstract theoretical ideas to prove or disprove existing notions versus the pursuit of research that has personal and group meaning can also differentiate the preferences of minority faculty from those of tenure committees.

This disagreement on what is acceptable scholarship arises from assumptions and philosophies that scientific inquiry must be proven through logical principles and the collection and analyses of data. Consistent with these themes is the tendency to give a higher comparative rank to journals that require conventional logic, content, theory, and methodology. Whereas more negative attributions about "nonconventional" research can stem from misinterpretations because of a lack of knowledge, nonminority chairpersons and faculty simply see these efforts as less valuable and behave according to this subjective yardstick. Yet research with nontraditional theory or content that is published in "acceptable" journals receives a higher subjective rating than similar research in nonconventional (that is, less acceptable) journals. Cornel West (1993, p. 43) speaks to the irony of the situation in the following way: "The academic system of rewards and status, prestige and influence puts a premium on those few black [minority] scholars who imitate the dominant paradigms elevated by fashionable Northeastern seaboard institutions of higher learning."

Differences in philosophical assumptions can be handled in numerous ways. First, minority faculty can be encouraged to study topics and use methods consistent with conventional standards. Second, minority faculty can be required to show expertise in conventional and "nontraditional" theoretical models and content areas. Finally, standards of campus departments can be altered to reflect the interests and research approaches of all faculty. Based on this preference, it follows that evaluative criteria should emphasize the significance of contributions that research activities make to particular areas of study, rather than the absence of multicultural or gender-related content and theory (Phillips, Gouran, Kuehn, and Wood, 1994). The distribution of names and editors of multicultural journals for various disciplines can increase a chairperson's familiarity with sources that some minority faculty use as publication avenues. Disseminating relevant information about minority-based journals to department heads on a regular basis may assist chairpersons with decisions about merit increases. This information could be especially helpful when personal beliefs or lack of knowledge about publications in minority and majority refereed and nonrefereed journals are issues of concern. Research issues related to participant samples, research theories, and methodologies also deserve clarification and discussion. These issues are especially pertinent for minority faculty employed in departments without institutional sanction to study Hispanic, African American, or American Indian culture as compared to faculty employed in Chicano/ Chicana or African American Studies Departments.

Service. Department chairpersons and faculty on predominantly white campuses often use dual sets of criteria to evaluate the service efforts of minority faculty. Expectations that minority faculty are to graciously serve the campus and surrounding minority communities are implied in the failure to recognize or financially compensate such efforts. An absence of a sufficient number of minority faculty often means that those affiliated with the university will serve on numerous departmental and university committees to provide the "minority voice." Minority faculty are frequently asked to participate in all minority programs and services, advise and counsel minority students, teach minority-related courses within and across departments, assist with minority student and faculty recruitment, mentor minority graduate students, and intervene in racial conflicts in addition to effectively meeting the usual expectations of institutional faculty for teaching, research, and service (Farmer, 1993; Moses, 1989). This list of tasks is further lengthened by the emotional and psychological stressors confronted on these campuses. For example, Moses (1989) found that African American women administrators and faculty were constantly challenged by students and nonminority faculty, closely monitored by students, peers, and superiors, and expected to perform at higher levels to obtain respect—but without support and access to necessary power sources.

To alleviate dual standards of performance, institutions must take a thorough inventory of their unacknowledged expectations of minority faculty based on the needs of a particular campus. From this perspective, position announcements should clearly reflect *all* that is required for a particular position. An honest appraisal of the position followed by clear and genuine communication of this information to interview candidates can prevent dissatisfaction and attrition. When numerous tasks are required, institutional search committees must also be willing to provide detailed and written indications of the weight assigned to each for merit and tenure purposes. This initial establishment of trust enhances the relationship between minority faculty and their institution. Tangible rewards should also be granted to minority faculty who have the energy and desire to extend themselves beyond the agreed-on position specifications. Thus, faculty who render invited and noninvited service to minority organizations and communities should receive recognition similar to that received for service offered to nonminority organizations of similar local, state, regional, or national rank. A paper presented at a predominantly minority state conference should be assigned the same value as a paper presented at a state nonminority conference. Evaluative criteria for service delivered to minority and nonminority university, community, and national organizations should also be similarly viewed. For example, the appointment to the office of president, vice president, or secretary on a national committee should receive the same weight as service on a nonminority national committee (so that a contribution to the National Black Psychological Association should be equated with a similar contribution to the American Psychological Association). Finally, internal and external tenure review committees should consist of nonminorities and minorities familiar with multicultural research topics, various types of methodological procedures, minority organizations, and pluralistic styles of teaching.

Officials sincere about attracting and retaining minority

faculty and administrators rather than just meeting affirmative action goals should expend the same effort to recruit minority faculty as athletic departments use to recruit African American athletes. As early as 1990, whereas African American students represented only about 6 percent of the total student population on predominantly white campuses, African American athletes comprised approximately 38 percent and 58 percent of Division 1 football and basketball teams, respectively, on the same campuses (Ashe, 1990).

Recruitment and Admissions

Central to a commitment to enhance the campus climate are successful recruitment and admission of minority students.

Minority Representation. An adequate representation—in other words, proportionate enrollment—of minority students in the campus population can reduce feelings of isolation and alienation. The presence of minority students can also modify the image that predominantly white campuses are unconcerned with the educational attainment of ethnic and racial minorities. The analogy "it takes money to make money" applies here. That is, existing percentages of enrolled minority students influence the degree to which other students will feel attracted to the campus.

Admissions Criteria. A continuing issue in the area of recruitment and acceptance is the reliance on SAT scores by most predominantly white institutions. Despite not producing sufficient evidence to show how these scores predict performance and attrition for minority students, colleges and universities use this criterion as a gatekeeper for minority access to higher education. To achieve increased credibility for the predictive validity of standardized tests on the performance of minorities, traditional admissions criteria like the SAT and moderator variables found effective as predictors of performance should be used in combination with other attributes. Research has consistently demonstrated the validity of seven factors, for example, that adequately predict the performance, progress, and graduation of minorities (including international students). Minority students most likely to experience academic success are those who have: (1) a positive self-concept, (2) skill for realistic self-appraisal, (3) an understanding of and ability to deal with racism, (4) a preference for long-term goals over short-term or immediate needs, (5) the availability of a strong support person, (6) a successful leadership experience, and (7) demonstrated community service (Tracey and Sedlacek, 1985; White and Sedlacek, 1986). Evidence also supports the importance of academic self-concept as a moderator variable for enhancing prediction of academic success.

Diversifying the Pool. Efforts should also focus on the recruitment of a heterogeneous population of American Indian, Hispanic American, and African American students. This heterogeneity should involve social class, academic performance, social experiences, career interests, and other factors related to intraracial and intraethnic differences (Tracey and Sedlacek, 1985; White and Sedlacek, 1986). Presently, many of these students elect to attend minority or predominantly nonminority institutions that offer attractive financial packages (Kreuzer, 1993). For instance, seventy-three African American National Achievement Scholars were attracted to Florida A&M University, a historically black institution, for the class of 1996. In addition, forty-nine and twenty-eight Achievement Scholars were attracted to Harvard and Stanford, respectively, for the class of 1996. Students with nationally recognized records of excellence can meet an important need in the minority peer group, nonminority peer group, and classroom environment. The presence of these students may influence nonminority students' and faculty members' views of minority enrollment as "affirmative action cases." Highly talented minority students also validate the value of academic performance and give credence to the truism that minorities perform at a high standard without ridicule. The presence of these students is particularly valuable for minorities who may experience conflict between ethnic or racial loyalties and academic standards of excellence (for example, the fear of becoming "too white").

Research has also shown that gender issues among the African American population affect outcomes and experiences for minority students. African American males are less likely than females to attend college in general (Marks, 1986). Beyond the great disservice to American society, imbalances in the ratio of African American males to females have implications for the psychosocial development of African American females on predominantly nonminority campuses. The low number of African American males reduces the opportunity to form male-female relations associated with intimacy at later stages of the college experience. Although evidence exists to suggest that African American females fare better academically than do their male counterparts, Harris and Nettles (1991) found African American females to report lower faculty involvement and lower grades than same-race males and nonminorities. African American females also seem more positively affected by attending traditionally black colleges and universities (Pascarella, Smart, and Stoecker, 1989).

Different levels of university integration related to the greater percentage of minority male than female athletes may account for gender differences in college experiences. Athletes are heavily recruited and enter universities with social support associated with the comaraderie of team members and other athletes. On the other hand, nonathlete females enter the system with fewer supports and more responsibility for finding a community within the campus student network. Because African American males on college campuses are more likely than females to participate in athletics, greater opportunities also exist for contact with coaches, and athletic personnel and fan clubs. Even when grades are not laudable, successful athletic participation maximizes the chances for rewards in the forms of verbal praise and campus media recognition. On many campuses, tutoring and advising services also exist for athletes that reinforce personal support and academic performance.

These findings suggest that recruiters should enhance attempts to identify and recruit balanced numbers of African American males and females. The "Black Male Initiative" located at Texas Southern University for four years is an academic and personal support program designed to increase the number of African American males who attend college to pursue professional careers. This program consists of tutoring, remedial assistance, conflict resolution and study skills, and sex education to enhance academic performance and self-confidence. During this experience, students are exposed to business leaders and community members and fulfill mentorship roles with disadvantaged children.

The diverse subgroups that comprise the Hispanic population also deserve attention in recruitment plans. Despite the commonalities in language, values, religion, and certain customs, Hispanic students are diverse and have distinct profiles that must be included in attempts to modify the college climate. Diversity mediators such as level of acculturation, gender, generational status, language preference, and political status are important. Efforts to attract students of Puerto Rican, Mexican American, and Cuban backgrounds in proportion to numbers actually present in a given geographic service area should be made. Students of Hispanic origin are also members of various racial and ethnic groups. This background information should also be considered in order to recruit members of student groups that are disproportionately underrepresented on predominantly white university campuses.

College Recruiters. Personal qualities of college recruiters are important in the attracting minority students. Individuals of diverse racial and ethnic backgrounds who are charismatic and comfortable in the presence of minority families, churches, and communities should be selected for these positions. Because recruiters who appear genuine and have a sincere commitment to increase minority representation are more likely to persuade students to attend a particular university, special attention should be given to qualities of recruiters that may inspire trust and rapport. Recruiters should also recognize and feel comfortable with intraracial and intraethnic differences in language, customs, and behaviors among minority groups. The same vigor and tenacity used to locate star athletes must also underlie efforts to recruit students. Recruiters should develop long-term strategies geared toward secondary and elementary schools. Community leaders within the Hispanic, African American, and American Indian populations can also be identified to participate in the identification of achievement-oriented students. Because the family is of primary importance in the college decisions of many minorities, establishing rapport with these individuals can increase the probability that a university will be considered. To develop relationships with these families, university recruiters can arrange programs and services for the parents of potential recruits and discuss the reasons their family members should attend the institution. Positive and warm relations between families and universities might also ease difficulties associated with student transition from community and family to college.

Financial Incentives

The issue of college cost has held and continues to hold primary significance for minority students. However, changes in the political tone of the country have directly affected the degree and type of assistance received by students. Although federal involvement in the process of education has existed for over 200 years, the role of the federal government expanded considerably during the 1960s. The Higher Education Act of 1965 was responsible for offering federal education grants to undergraduate students. Educational amendments during the administration of President Jimmy Carter also increased assistance for education by increasing the boundaries used to determine need and establishing loans for parents to assist with student expense. Ceilings were also advanced for Supplemental Educational Opportunity Grants, State Student Incentive Grants, and College Work Study programs (Eaton, 1991). Under the administration of President Ronald Reagan, however, a consistent decline in federal assistance was promoted for higher education initiatives. During this administration, involvement in education by schools, parents, students, and families was held to be more important than federal government commitments. Values that stressed individualism and competitiveness were also consistently emphasized during this period. Almost a 50 percent reduction in grant assistance occurred between 1977 and 1987 (Eaton, 1991).

A decrease in federal grants and college work-study and the elimination of social security benefits appears to have had significant implications for the enrollment, progress, retention, and graduation of minority students. The trend toward loan programs rather than grant assistance has been viewed as a major factor. According to Stampen and Fenske (1987, p. 17), "There is plausible evidence that minorities made impressive gains from the mid-1960s through the mid-1970s because student aid was growing and mainly composed of grants. However, by the 1980s the gains had turned into losses as student aid became less tailored to the needs of low income students and ultimately declined in purchasing power."

The impact of this change is further noted by the finding that 90 percent of low-income minority students rely on Pell Grants (originally Basic Educational Opportunity Grants) compared to 80 percent of low-income nonminority students (Miller and Hexter, 1985). Minorities and low-income students are also more likely to be enrolled in public than private institutions, although students who attended private institutions received more aid (Eaton, 1991). In addition, students of high ability from low-income backgrounds are less likely than those of similar ability from higher-income backrounds to attend college (Wilson and Justiz, 1987–1988).

Although the role of the federal government has changed with respect to financial aid, institutions can assist in several ways. They may initiate campaigns to seek funds from nonminority alumni to increase the number of merit-based scholarships offered to minority students. Institutional representatives may also encourage dedicated alumni to allot a portion of their yearly contributions to this campaign. A greater percent of funds received by alumni for other university purposes can also be used to pursue this purpose. Merit-based scholarships provide financial assistance and also contribute to the academic self-concept and well-being of minority students. High-ability minority students from families with relatively low incomes could especially benefit from this type of support.

Institutions can also designate a greater percentage of work-study positions for minority students. Given the positive relationship between on-campus employment and university involvement, minority students would benefit from campus positions that are closely related to future career plans and academic areas of study. To reduce the number of students who obtain non-career-related off-campus employment (for example, in fast food restaurants), staff of career planning and placement centers could develop relationships with local businesses to assist with students' needs for off-campus employment. These positions could be linked with course credit for practical experience in a specific major.

Research faculty could also assist in providing financial assistance for minority undergraduate and graduate students. For example, minority supplement awards can be obtained for major grants funded by the National Institute of Mental Health and the National Institutes of Health. These supplemental awards can be used to offer financial assistance to minority students who investigate a worthy research topic related to the parent grant project.

Retention Programs and Services

Some retention programs concentrate on reducing student deficiences during the summer that precedes fall enrollment (Garfield and Romano, 1983; White and Bigham, 1982). A few also offer courses previously determined to be problematic for minorities (Blanc, DeBuhr, and Martin, 1983). These programs usually consist of only the students identified as at risk for leaving the university because of academic difficulties. However, the social and emotional adjustment of minority students seems to be as important as academic adjustment in predicting persistence. Students who are incapable of forming social networks, regulating personal freedom and responsibilities, and managing emotional concerns related to the college transition process are inclined to leave the university before completing their degree (Hays and Oxley, 1986; Rich and Scovel, 1987).

Workshops and time-limited programs for enhancing study skills and coping with issues such as procrastination are also offered on some campuses (Abrams and Jernigan, 1984). In addition, most campuses offer individualized tutorial and writing skill services to assist students. These services are not mandatory and rely on students to evaluate their performance to determine when such services are needed. Because of unrealistically optimistic expectations about their ability to adjust to college (Plaud, Baker, and Groccia, 1990), many students may decide that such services are unnecessary. Some avoid these programs because of the stigma associated with having to admit academic troubles in an environment that is perceived as expecting them to fail (Gerdes and Mallinckrodt, 1994).

The retention, progression, and graduation of minority students is dependent on program conceptualizations that address potential difficulties in psychosocial, financial, and academic dimensions. Most universities offer services that concentrate on one or two of these concerns without considering the others. First and foremost, administrators must be willing to reorganize university finances to contribute funds to the retention of students. These resources should be used to conduct small-scale pilot programs from which the results can be applied to long-term programs and services. Campus programs are frequently hurriedly designed in reaction to glaring needs before obtaining an adequate understanding of the intricate relations among social, emotional, and academic aspects of students' lives. Prior to program and service development, pen-and-paper and focus-group needs assessments should be conducted with minority groups to obtain quantitative and qualitative data related to student perceptions of needs in each of the relevant areas. Student needs assessment data should be followed up with data from faculty and counseling service staff to determine differences and similarities in perceived student needs. Findings from these sources should be combined with existing institutional data related to the attrition and progress of minority students. Based on results, faculty and students should conceptualize services for minority students that meet needs in the academic, social, and emotional realms across the college life cycle. Formative evaluative data should be used to monitor and alter services delivered throughout the life of the program.

Given that students often prematurely leave college for other than academic reasons, effective programs must include components designed to improve minority student social wellbeing. Interventions that address the significance of positive interactions with nonminority faculty, as well as minority and nonminority students, can yield better outcomes than programs directed only at academic needs. For example, students could be matched with faculty and advanced student mentors at the beginning of their academic careers. Faculty mentors would be responsible for making student referrals to campus organizations, collaborating with relevant instructors about student performance, and offering encouragement and support. Advanced student mentors could assist by informing students about the courses offered by various instructors, helping them form study groups, and sharing personal experiences at the university. Another idea is to assign incoming minority students to mentoring teams consisting of a faculty member, graduate student, advanced undergraduate, and another first-year minority student. Each team would be assigned a number of students during their freshman and sophomore years and help promote the social integration of students. Minority students should have an opportunity to gradually interact with nonminority students prior to the start of their first semester. Forming interracial friendships during the beginning of the transition phase is more likely to lead to positive outcomes. Students of nonminority status should be involved in programs designed to meet social adjustment needs of minority students.

Counseling center and multicultural center staff and faculty members could also design preorientation services for family members of entering students that respond to emotionally laden issues such as separation from family, friends, and community. Participants could be provided with a cognitive framework and set of behavioral skills for reestablishing relations with those who have served in a supportive role prior to this transition. Outreach activities conducted by counseling center and multicultural center staff in conjunction with high school counselors might also be appropriate for parents who are unable to afford the cost of visiting the university. When possible, financial assistance could be offered for parents and students to visit the campus and meet other minority and nonminority faculty and staff. Orientation and preorientation programs should also include adjustment components related to skills required to function as a minority student on a predominantly white campus.

To address concerns related to academics, care should be taken to include at-risk nonminority students *and* minority students who have academic deficiencies. This approach to academics reduces the myth that only minority students need help and removes much of the stigma. Skills related to study habits, the selection of courses and credit hours, specific information about the meaning of unfamiliar academic jargon (for example, *drop-add deadline, withdrawal, syllabus*), ways to determine when to meet with a professor, how to schedule appointments with professors, the importance of a syllabus, class attendance policies, where to find assistance with writing skills, and effective ways to listen to lectures and to take notes are some of the numerous factors that could be included in this component. This information is likely to be more easily retained when the presentations involve the provision of factual information and an opportunity to actually engage in experiential tasks related to each topic. For example, information on study habits should involve a rationale for developing patterns of study and discussion of the usual number of hours necessary to prepare for each course. Students should also engage in practicing how to take notes during class, how to integrate reserved readings and textbook material, and how to read for exams rather than for entertainment.

Sensitization to Diversity

Many nonminority students enter universities with little awareness or understanding of how culturally different students or faculty view the world. The uncertainty and confusion generated by the presence of minority faculty or roommates may lead to behaviors such as avoidance or withdrawal and feelings of anger or frustration. In many instances, nonminority students suppress these feelings because of discomfort surrounding the acknowledgment of racial and ethnic differences. Feelings of anger and jealousy are also intensified because of student interpretations of government policies such as affirmative action to indicate that minorities receive favorable attention from administrators. Ironically, some nonminorities may also feel powerless and estranged as they are confronted for the first time with what it means to be nonminority in America. In addition, discoveries of how nonminorities are perceived by minorities can also lead to feelings of guilt and shame. These feelings may then lead to forms of self-protection manifested overtly as racist epithets and unkind gestures toward minority students and faculty.

Many universities have attempted to improve the college climate for minorities and nonminorities by teaching students to facilitate change. The National Coalition-Building Institute (NCBI), a nonprofit training organization, is one agency that provides assistance to colleges and universities with developing peer training teams. The model used by NCBI is based on theoretical principles that guide personal and small-group exploratory sessions. This model focuses on identifying and reducing stereotypical beliefs about other groups and one's own group, examining and discussing factors that contribute to behavioral mistreatment of others, sharing experiences of discrimination, providing training for coping with prejudicial remarks, and teaching skills to resolve intergroup conflicts (see Brown and Mazza, 1991).

Mann and Moser (1991) describe five programs on five different college campuses designed to promote racial and ethnic awareness and appreciation of diversity based on the stages of the Jackson and Hardiman Oppression/Liberation Development Model. This model consists of five stages ranging from an oppressed or oppressive consciousness to a liberated social consciousness and includes Naivete, Acceptance, Resistance, Redefinition, and Internalization.

Hate Busters is a student organization formed by Ed Chasteen at Jewell College in Liberty, Missouri, and is used to modify the worldviews of minority and nonminority students by teaching positive and caring feelings for oneself, positive and caring feelings for others who are similar to oneself, and positive and caring feelings for those unlike oneself. Students pledge to fight against and resist various forms of racism and bigotry. Racial Awareness Pilot Project (RAPP) and RAPPORT have been established at the University of Cincinnati. RAPP is a student-directed program that selects students interested in integrating gender, race, majors, and involvement in campus organizations.

Participants engage in workshops, movies, cultural events, sponsored programs, reading assignments, ongoing journal writing, and other activities. Hate Busters and RAPP confront students who are in the Acceptance stage of awareness. RAPPORT consists of RAPP alumni and members who primarily conduct educational programs related to racial awareness on campus (such as in residence halls) and for community organizations. This model is appropriate for students in the Acceptance and Resistance stages of development.

The Multicultural Program on the campus of the University of Texas at Austin is an example of a program that is appropriate for the Redefinition stage. This program familiarizes freshmen with diversity issues related to campus life and focuses on assisting students in developing a positive sense of identity within their own racial or ethnic group. Components of this program include viewing films on issues of racism—like *A Class Divided*—in a large-group format. Large-group interactions are followed by discussions of racial myths, stereotypes, and discrimination in small groups facilitated by students who have been trained in this capacity.

The goal of the Internalization stage is to increase student knowledge about similarities between racial and ethnic groups in order to integrate this knowledge into their behaviors and to avoid being drawn into previous prejudicial ways of relating. Programs designed to promote development at this stage encourage activities and services that applaud diversity of all types (including sexual orientation, race, ethnicity, and so on). Celebrating Our World (COW) is designed for this purpose and is found at the University of Wisconsin at Whitewater. Members of this committee promote self-worth by engaging in activities with an antimonocultural theme (for example, by holding an international food sampling event).

Methods of Assessment

Historically, educational assessment involving minorities referred to the development and administration of tests. Scores obtained have been assumed to reflect the ability or trait. Most often, assessment has focused on minority intellectual and cognitive performance. Thus, assessment has traditionally been viewed as synonymous with testing.

The interdependence of elementary, secondary, and college levels of education requires that assessment encompass variables specific to students and institutions at each stage of the educational process to determine the factors that promote or impede academic success. Of great importance to institutional administrators and policy makers is a national and state profile of the prospective college student population over an extended time period. Demographic information including racial and ethnic origin, gender, socioeconomic status, parental educational level, geographic origin, and the number of students can assist administrators at each educational stage to plan more effectively for predicted changes. This information can also provide an objective and detailed account of the consistency with which minorities enter elementary stages of education and progress to graduate from four-year colleges. Related factors such as the quality and type of education received and the degree to which prospective college students are academically and socially prepared before proceeding to the next educational stage are also important.

Surveys of student attitudes, opinions, behaviors, and perceived performance are also valuable sources of assessment data. The measurement of variables before college enrollment may identify cognitive factors that contribute to students' in-college behaviors and experiences. For example, student expectations of college performance could be assessed prior to enrolling and then be compared with actual evidence of college performance (in terms of grades, college progress, friendship networks, class participation, and writing skills) during each academic year. Results would indicate the extent to which such variables as knowledge of the college process affect actual performance. In addition, factors such as student study habits, satisfaction with faculty interactions, perceptions of services and programs, and participation in honors programs and student body organizations are important to the assessment of the college climate.

Assessment, however, should not end on graduation or departure from the university but continue intermittently throughout students' postcollegiate careers to shed light on the long-term impact of a particular university. For those who graduate, exit interviews as well as short- and long-term follow-ups should be conducted to obtain information about student perceptions of the university, the education received, future plans, and actual behavioral outcomes. For example, items such as satisfaction with the academic and social aspects of the college, perceptions of how the campus could have been more accommodating, changes they would have made in their behavior if they could relive the experience, and readiness for graduate school or the world of work are useful to faculty and administrators. Universities should also attempt to obtain data related to success in obtaining employment as measured by first-year salaries, promotions, the percent who apply and are actually accepted into graduate programs, among other things. Similar data should be obtained from students who leave the university to seek employment, join the military, or transfer to other institutions. In addition, demographic data should be recorded to account for the success of minority students who transfer from two- to four-year institutions.

Conclusion

This chapter presented a case for national goals to reflect a commitment to diversity in higher education. A national commitment to diversity, however, requires that institutions create environments conducive to the academic and psychosocial well-being of both minority and nonminority students. Predominantly white institutions have an obligation to maintain policies of nondiscrimination and to increase cultural and ethnic diversity among students, faculty, administrators, and staff. Thus, methods and strategies similar to those outlined above should be implemented on university campuses. A need also exists for ongoing assessment. Assessment efforts should aim to identify student and institutional objectives, gather information on the need for and implementation of various enhancement strategies, monitor the progress of strategies selected, and identify both positive and negative factors associated with attaining specified objectives.

References

Aaron, R., and Powell, G. "Feedback Practices as a Function of Teacher and Pupil Race During Reading Groups Instruction." *Journal of Negro Education,* 1982, *51,* 50–59.

Abrams, H. G., and Jernigan, L. P. "Academic Support Services and the Success of High Risk College Students." *American Educational Research Journal,* 1984, *21,* 261–274.

Abrahamowicz, D. "College Involvement, Perceptions, and Satisfaction: A Study of Membership in Student Organizations." *Journal of College Student Development,* 1988, *29,* 233–238.

Allen, W. R. *Study of Black Undergraduate Students Attending Predominantly White State-Supported Universities: Preliminary Report.* Ann Arbor: Center for Afro-American and African Studies, University of Michigan, 1981.

Allen, W. R. *National Study of Black College Students.* Ann Arbor: Department of Sociology, University of Michigan, 1982.

Allen, W. R. "The Education of Black Students on White College Campuses: What Quality the Experience?" In M. T. Nettles (ed.), *Toward Black Undergraduate Student Equality in American Higher Education.* Westport, Conn.: Greenwood Press, 1988.

Allen, W. R. "The Color of Success: African-American College Student Outcomes at Predominantly White and Historically Black Public Colleges and Universities." *Harvard Educational Review,* 1992, *62,* 26–44.

Ashe, A. "NCAA Propositions Itself over Proposition 42." *Washington Post,* Jan. 20, 1990, pp. D1, D5.

Astin, A. W. *What Matters in College? Four Critical Years Revisited.* San Francisco: Jossey-Bass, 1992.

Bandura, A. *Social Foundations of Thought and Action: A Social Cognitive Theory.* Englewood Cliffs, N.J.: Prentice Hall, 1986.

Belsher, G., and Costello, C. G. "Do Confidants of Depressed Women Provide Less Social Support Than Confidants of Nondepressed Women?" *Journal of Abnormal Psychology,* 1991, *100,* 516–525.

Bennett, C., and Okinaka, A. "Explanations of Black Student Attrition in Predominantly White and Predominantly Black Universities." Paper presented at the annual meeting of the

American Educational Research Association, New Orleans, La., Apr. 1984.

Blanc, R. A., DeBuhr, L. E., and Martin, D. C. "Breaking the Attrition Cycle: The Effect of Supplemental Instruction on Undergraduate Performance and Attrition." *Journal of Higher Education,* 1983, *54,* 80–90.

Bliwise, R. J. "Reflections of John Hope Franklin." *Journal of Blacks in Higher Education,* 1993–94, (2), 68–72.

Bourassa, D. M. "How White Students and Students of Color Organize and Interact on Campus." In J. C. Dalton (ed.), *Racism on Campus: Confronting Racial Bias Through Peer Interventions.* New Directions for Student Services, no. 56. San Francisco: Jossey Bass, 1991.

Brown, C. R., and Mazza, G. J. "Peer Training Strategies for Welcoming Diversity." In J. C. Dalton (ed.), *Racism on Campus: Confronting Racial Bias Through Peer Interventions.* New Directions for Student Services, no. 56. San Francisco: Jossey-Bass, 1991.

Buriel, R. "Teacher-Student Interactions and Their Relationship to Student Achievement: A Comparison of Mexican-American and Anglo-American Children." *Journal of Educational Psychology,* 1983, *75,* 889–897.

Carter, R. T. "Cultural Value Differences Between African-Americans and White Americans." *Journal of College Student Development,* 1990, *31,* 71–79.

Clark, M. L. "The Status of Interethnic Contact and Ethnocentrism Among White, Hispanic, and Black Students." Paper presented at the annual meeting of the American Educational Research Association, San Francisco, Apr. 1988.

Duster, T. *The Diversity Project: Final Report.* Berkeley: Institute for the Study of Social Change, University of California, 1991.

Eaton, J. S. *The Unfinished Agenda: Higher Education and the 1980s.* New York: Macmillan, 1991.

Ehrenberg, R., and Sherman, D. "Employment While in College, Academic Achievement, and Postcollege Outcomes: A Summary of Results." *Journal of Human Resources,* 1987, *22,* 1–23.

Farmer, R. "Place But Not Importance: The Race for Inclusion in Academe." In J. James and R. Farmer (eds.), *Spirit, Space, and Survival: African-American Women in (White) Academe* (pp. 196–217). New York: Routledge, 1993.

Garfield, J. B., and Romano, J. L. *Retention and Academic Achievement in Higher Education: The General College PEP Program,* 1983. (PEP I, II, and III.) (ED 235 743)

Gerdes, H., and Mallinckrodt, B. "Emotional, Social, and Academic Adjustment of College Students: A Longitudinal Study of Retention." *Journal of Counseling and Development,* 1994, *72,* 281–288.

Goleman, D. "As Bias Crime Seems to Rise, Scientists Study Roots of Racism." *New York Times,* May 29, 1990, pp. B8, B10.

Harris, S. M. "Women of Color in the Classroom: Satisfaction on the Predominantly Euro-American College Campus." Paper presented at the National Conference of the Association of Women in Psychology, Atlanta, Ga., Mar. 1993.

Harris, S. M., and Nettles, M. T. "Racial Differences in Students' Experiences and Attitudes." In J. C. Dalton (ed.), *Racism on Campus: Confronting Racial Bias Through Peer Interventions.* New Directions for Student Services, no. 56. San Francisco: Jossey-Bass, 1991.

Hays, R. B., and Oxley, D. "Social Network Development and Functioning During a Life Transition." *Journal of Personality and Social Psychology,* 1986, *50,* 305–313.

Hurtado, S. "Graduate School Racial Climates and Academic Self-Concept Among Minority Graduate Students in the 1970s." *American Journal of Education,* 1994, *102,* 330–351.

June, L. N., Curry, B. P., and Gear, C. L. "An 11-Year Analysis of Black Students' Experience of Problems and Use of Services: Implications of Counseling Professionals." *Journal of Counseling Psychology,* 1990, *37,* 178–184.

Kreuzer, T. L. "The Bidding War for Top Black Students." *Journal of Blacks in Higher Education,* 1993, (2), 114–118.

Kuh, G. D. "Appraising the Character of a College." *Journal of Counseling and Development,* 1993, *71,* 661-668.

McClelland, R. E., and Auster, C. J. "Public Platitudes and Hidden Tensions: Racial Climates at Predominantly White Liberal Arts Colleges." *Journal of Higher Education,* 1990, *61,* 607–640.

Madrazo-Peterson, R., and Rodriquez, M. "Minority Students: Perceptions of a University Environment." *Journal of College Student Personnel,* 1978, *19,* 259–263.

Mann, B. A, and Moser, R. M. "A Model for Designing Peer-Initiated Activities to Promote Racial Awareness and an Appreciation of Differences." In J. C. Dalton (ed.), *Racism on Campus: Confronting Racial Bias Through Peer Interventions.* New Directions for Student Services, no. 56. San Francisco: Jossey-Bass, 1991.

Marks, J. L. *The Enrollment of Black Students in Education: Can Declines Be Prevented?* Atlanta, Ga.: Southern Regional Conference Board, 1986.

Miller, S. E., and Hexter, H. *How Low Income Families Pay for College.* Washington, D.C.: American Council on Education, 1985.

Mingle, J. "Faculty and Departmental Response to Increased Black Student Enrollment." *Journal of Higher Education,* 1987, *49,* 201–217.

Moses, Y. T. *Black Women in Academe: Issues and Strategies.* Baltimore, Md.: Project on the Status of Education of Women, Association of American Colleges, 1989.

Mow, S. L., and Nettles, M. T. "Minority Student Access to, and Persistence and Performance in, College: A Review of the Trends and Research Literature." In J. Smart (ed.), *The Handbook of Higher Education* (pp. 35–105). New York: Agathon Press, 1990.

National Institute Against Prejudice and Violence. *Ethnoviolence on Campus: The UMBC Study.* Institute Report No. 2. Baltimore, Md.: National Institute Against Prejudice and Violence, 1987.

Nettles, M. T. "Introduction: Contemporary Barriers to Black Student Equality in Higher Education." In M. T. Nettles (ed.), *Toward Black Undergraduate Student Equality in American Higher Education.* Westport, Conn.: Greenwood Press, 1988.

Nettles, M. T., Thoeny, A. R., and Gosman, E. J. "Comparative and Predictive Analyses of Black and White Students' College Achievement and Experiences." *Journal of Higher Education,* 1986, *57,* 289–318.

Ohio Board of Regents. *Student Access and Success in Ohio's Higher Education System.* Columbus: Ohio Board of Regents, 1988.

Pascarella, E. T. "Student-Faculty Informal Contact and College Outcomes." *Review of Educational Research,* 1980, *50,* 545–595.

Pascarella, E. T., Smart, J. C., and Stoecker, J. "College Race and the Early Status Attainment of Black Students." *Journal of Higher Education,* 1989, *60,* 82–107.

Pascarella, E. T., and Terenzini, P. T. *How College Affects Students: Findings and Insights from Twenty Years of Research.* San Francisco: Jossey-Bass, 1991.

Phillips, G. M., Gouran, D. S., Kuehn, S. A., and Wood, J. T. *Survival in the Academy: A Guide for Beginning Academics.* Cresskill, N.J.: Hampton Press, 1994.

Plaud, J. J., Baker, R. W., and Groccia, J. E. "Freshman Decidedness Regarding Academic Major and Anticipated and Actual Adjustment to an Engineering College." *National Academic Advising Association,* 1990, *10*(2), 20–27.

Rendón, L. I. "From the Barrio to the Academy: Revelations of a Mexican American Scholarship Girl." In L. S. Zwerling and H. B. London (eds.), *First Generation Students: Confronting the Cultural Issues.* New Directions for Community Colleges, no. 80. San Francisco: Jossey-Bass, 1992.

Rich, A. R., and Scovel, M. "Causes of Depression in College Students: A Cross-Lagged Panel Correlational Analysis." *Psychological Reports,* 1987, *60,* 27–30.

Richardson, R. C., Jr., and Skinner, E. F. *Achieving Quality and Diversity: Universities in a Multicultural Society.* New York: Macmillan, 1991.

Semmes, C. E. "Minority Status and the Problem of Legitimacy." *Journal of Black Studies,* 1985, *15,* 259–275.

Simpson, A., and Erickson, M. "Teachers' Verbal and Nonverbal Communication Patterns as a Function of Teacher Race, Student Gender, and Student Race." *American Research Journal,* 1983, *20,* 183–198.

Stampen, J. O., and Fenske, R. A. *Financial Aid and Ethnic Minorities.* Paper presented at From Access to Achievement: Strategies for Urban Institutions Conference, Los Angeles, Nov. 1987.

Steinberg, L., Dornbusch, S. M., and Brown, B. B. "Ethnic Differences in Adolescent Achievement: An Ecological Perspective." *American Psychologist,* 1992, *47*(6) 723–729.

Styles-Hughes, M. "Black Students' Participation in Higher Education." *Journal of College Student Personnel,* 1987, *28,* 532–545.

Suen, H. K. "Alienation and Attrition of Black College Students on a Predominantly White Campus." *Journal of College Student Personnel,* 1983, *24,* 117–121.

Tambe, J. T. "Predicting Persistence and Withdrawal of Open Admissions for Students at Virginia State University." *Journal of Negro Education,* 1984, *53,* 406–417.

Terenzini, P. T., and others. "The Transition to College: Diverse Students, Diverse Stories." *Research in Higher Education,* 1994, *35,* 57–73.

Tinto, V. "Dropout from Higher Education: A Theoretical Synthesis of Recent Research." *Review of Educational Research,* 1975, *45,* 89–125.

Tracey, T. J., and Sedlacek, W. E. "The Relationship of Noncognitive Variables to Academic Success by Race over Four Years." *Journal of College Student Personnel,* 1985, *25,* 405–410.

West, C. *Race Matters.* Boston: Beacon Press, 1993.

White, W., and Bigham, W. "Information Systems Approach to Admissions, Instruction, and Retention of College Students with Developmental Lag." *Journal of Research and Development in Education,* 1982, *15,* 16–26.

White, T. J., and Sedlacek, W. E. "Noncognitive Predictors: Grades and Retention of Specially-Admitted Students." *Journal of College Admissions,* 1986, *3,* 20–23.

Wilson, R. "Education Department Study of Faculty Members Finds Most Have Full-Time Appointments." *Chronicle of Higher Education,* Nov. 23, 1994, p. A16.

Wilson, R., and Justiz, M. "Minorities in Higher Education: Confronting a Time Bomb." *Educational Record,* 1987–1988, *68,* 9–14.

Chapter 16

Expanding External Support for At-Risk Students

L. Steven Zwerling

We are currently witnessing a concerted attack on the university. The assault threatens the very fabric of the institution and access to those who seek to enter it, especially those who have historically been excluded from higher education. The thesis of this chapter is that foundations have played and must continue to play a critical role in helping schools and colleges provide access to at-risk students and facilitate their success once they are enrolled. The chapter begins with a historical account of how liberal and conservative agendas have impacted education and concludes with a case study of how one foundation—the Ford Foundation—has attempted to assist schools and colleges in enhancing their commitment to preserving access for at-risk students.

Anyone who lived through the 1960s and 1970s may feel this era is a case of déjà vu all over again. In fact, though the intensity of the assault against the university is familiar, its content and direction are new. But the stakes are just as high. Nothing less than the mission, leadership, curriculum, and faculty of the university are threatened. Those laying siege know well the history of those earlier decades, when the university as we currently know it was shaped. They now see an equivalent opportunity to take control of higher education, shaping it to their purposes and influencing the university's agenda for at least the next quarter of a century. As in the 1960s, when the growth in student enrollments was virtually exponential and colleges and universities needed to quadruple their faculties and staff, in this era of static or declining numbers, as the result of inevitable upcoming retirements, there is a chance to reconstitute the faculty and administration. And since those to be hired will control the shape of the curriculum, admission and scholarship policies, and direction of research, there is the concomitant opportunity to put an indelible mark on the ways the young and their part-time adult counterparts are educated.

Conservatives claim that liberal and "radical" faculty, especially minorities and women, in a nihilistic impulse to overthrow the traditional Western canon and replace it with a new orthodoxy centered around ethnic, gender, and non-Western studies, have imposed a new collegiate culture. These critics argue that in this effort, politically correct thought and modes of expression and discourse stifle critical and analytical thought.

The liberal professors and their administrative apologists, it is also asserted, hypocritically rail against materialistic and capitalistic values, attacking the government and the corporations that support it, while skimming off the overhead of government and foundation grants to support their own opulent life-styles: trips via business class, well-stocked bars in presidents' houses, reduced workloads and "released" time for faculty that make them unavailable to the students they profess to nurture.

And then, closer to the themes of this chapter, the same critics—in trying to revive a particular vision of academic excellence—heap equal scorn on colleges' and universities' affirmative action efforts—from who is hired to join the faculty or administration to who will be admitted to the student body. Thus, they question the consensus that began to take shape as far back as the end of the Second World War, when millions of veterans enrolled in college via the G.I. Bill (the precursor to current admissions practices at open-door institutions), that everyone has the right to an undergraduate education. Financial aid policies based on who has the right to benefit require that federal support be available only to students who can demonstrate, prior to instruction, that they can succeed. Restrictions on minority scholarship programs are imposed, without even a hint of mischieviousness, as a way to avoid the desegregation of higher education—though athletic scholarships that support the academically unfit remain largely untouched. Dual-track or preferential admissions policies are claimed to be nothing less than reverse discrimination—though preferential treatment for the children of alumni "legacies" remain sacred.

All the progressive achievements of decades are being challenged—and, in truth, quite effectively. The critics write and speak in quotable sound bites, finding themselves in demand on the lecture circuit and talk shows. On the other hand, the proponents of diversity and access have been slow to rise to the defense, reluctant to respond in kind, perhaps because some abuses have occurred that are difficult to deny and embarrassing to concede.

Other forces have been at work that have rent the fabric of the progressive consensus. We should examine this process in some detail before proceeding to talk about ways that external agencies can expand their support for at-risk students in higher education and simultaneously counter the assault on the university.

The Conservative Restoration

The principles of access and equity find their roots in the nation's long-standing belief that a democratic and just society can only be achieved where all are educated broadly. From this perspective, the purpose of education in a free society is to ensure that all citizens, regardless of accidents of birth, are equipped to participate fully in the civic dialogue characteristic of democratic societies. Increasingly, over the last forty years, it has also been recognized that access to advanced education—an important prerequisite to economic success and leadership—must also be available without regard to class, race, gender, or other social factors.

By the mid 1960s, a loose coalition of Congress, the federal government, colleges and universities, and national foundations became concerned about the effectiveness of the nation's rapidly expanding system of higher education in providing appropriate levels of access for minority communities. Their concern grew out of the realization that between 1945 and 1965, the college entrance rate of minority high school graduates had fallen steadily behind that of their white counterparts. Whereas the gap in the college-going rate separating minority and white high school graduates had been only 3 percent as late as 1947, by 1966 the difference had increased to 21 percent. It was also recognized that isolated actions could do little to reverse this trend, so that a broadly conceived response was required. Members of this coalition sought to minimize many of the barriers limiting access to higher education for the nation's disadvantaged through a variety of strategies. These strategies included the expansion of targeted fellowships and scholarships, the opening of community colleges in proximity to minority students, and the active enforcement of civil rights legislation.

This coalition, while never formally organized, proved remarkably successful in improving the college entrance rates of minority students in a relatively few years. In 1967, for example, only 13 percent of blacks between the ages of eighteen and twenty-four enrolled in institutions of higher education. Largely as the result of the infusion of substantial new support for disadvantaged students (and a smaller but no less critical sum for institutions serving large numbers of such students) the percentage of eighteen- to twenty-four-year-old blacks attending college increased steadily until 1976, when 22.6 percent enrolled in higher education. The experience of Hispanics was much the same. In 1972 (the first year for which data are available), only 13.4 percent of Hispanics between eighteen and twenty-four years old entered college. By 1976, the rate had grown to 19.9 percent (National Center for Education Statistics, U.S. Department of Education, 1988; Carter and Wilson, 1991).

However, for all its success in promoting access to higher education, this broad-based effort was one of the first victims of what has been characterized as America's conservative restoration of the early 1980s. As Harold Howe (1984) has observed, the neoconservative movement succeeded in discrediting those who argued for greater access and equity in higher education by simply ignoring the real progress that had been made toward these ends over the previous decades. The advocates of America's new conservatism instead focused public attention and debate on the perceived threat to the nation's economic and cultural well-being posed by a "rising tide of mediocrity"—a threat they attributed directly to the coalition's efforts to promote greater access and equity within education.

That a system of higher education dedicated to the values of access and equity would be among the first targets of America's resurgent conservatism should come as no surprise, since this form of conservatism gains its particular force and direction from an uncompromising individualism. As traditionally conceived in a liberal democracy, education functions as a fundamental public good. Through education, one generation meets its obligations to the next by providing all youth with general knowledge and occupational preparation to ensure their full participation in the civic and economic life of the nation. From the perspective of the modern conservative, however, formal education is essentially a vehicle for self-advancement. Moreover, because it serves primarily as a means of obtaining future self-advantage, it is viewed from the conservative perspective as a private benefit. Rather than an obligation of one generation to the next, and the means by which democratic values and individual freedoms are transferred between generations, formal education is a commodity to be sought by the individual out of self-interest.

Yet, as Gary Orfield and others have argued, in this drive to promote excellence among the few, the nation seems increasingly unwilling to address the fundamental injustices in American society—for example, the inequities by which its core cities and their communities are burdened (Orfield and Ashkinaze, 1991). The repeated calls by national leaders for higher standards, in a country increasingly marked by diversity, without providing the vision or resources to reach such standards, blindly ignore the fundamental differences in the conditions of American schools, colleges, and their students. Such calls simply disregard the basic inequities inherent in the day-to-day life of America's youth and the inevitable impact of these inequities on their performance and persistence.

The Federal Government and Shifting Values

Under the leadership of presidents Kennedy, Johnson, and Nixon, the federal government played a central role in the national effort to promote access to higher education among the nation's disadvantaged. This support not only took the form of direct aid to students and significant grants to a variety of developing institutions, but also included the adoption of civil rights legislation and aggressive court challenges to state-sanctioned discrimination. However, during the 1980s, under the influence of a resurgent individualism, the federal government employed its leverage in a concerted effort to reverse the noteworthy gains made by minority and other disadvantaged Americans in realizing their hope of a postsecondary education.

The groundwork for this fundamental reversal in federal policy was laid by a series of widely publicized national studies either sponsored by the federal government or appropriated to its purposes. A number of major reports, all issued within a relatively brief period, established a new context for the debate over the purpose and direction of the federal government's role in higher education.

While its stated focus was elementary and secondary education, the report that held the greatest significance for higher education was *A Nation at Risk* (National Commission on Excellence in Education, 1983). It provided a clear statement of the values underlying the new conservatism's view of America's educational system. It was a system, to quote the report, that accepted "lower standards and expectations" and that seemed only able to "spawn illiterates." Of little concern were the widely differing needs of increasingly diverse students; of great concern was the threat to the nation's security and economic well-being posed by the alleged failure of schools and colleges to promote "excellence."

A distinguishing feature of *A Nation at Risk* and the other reports of this period was not so much what was said as what was ignored. Neither access nor equity, long at the center of public

policy debate and action in higher education, was emphasized.
Also overlooked were the effects on student achievement of the
growing concentration of minorities and other disadvantaged
Americans in decaying core cities. Stedman and Smith's (1983,
p. 94) assessment of *A Nation at Risk* is equally applicable to the
other reports: "Yet even though the rhetoric is egalitarian, the
analysis and the recommendations failed to address the needs
of the poor, the minorities, and the inner city youth." What one
finds, instead, is a highly charged rhetoric informed by vaguely
conceived concerns about the nation's future. In the face of
these concerns, there is a call for classroom discipline, a narrowing of the curriculum, and a disregard for local interests, all in
the service of national workforce and security concerns.

       An important theme common to the reports is their dis-
crediting of the values of access and equity. They uniformly argue that a concern for access and the demand for equity have
undermined excellence in America's schools. Indeed, in their
view—which they back up with little substantial evidence—excellence has been neither valued nor attained by any segment of
American public education. Indeed, a number of the reports
suggest that educational "standards" have been intentionally de-
based to allow the traditional rewards of formal education (di-
plomas, degrees, and certificates) to be distributed more broadly
among the population.

       The rash of school reports appearing during the first
years of the Reagan administration created a rationale for a
broad retreat from the nation's long-standing public policy commitment to access and equity. Some have noted that spreading
disinterest in equity considerations was quickly reflected by the
Reagan administration through a virtual abandonment of civil
rights enforcement. Others have suggested that this was based
on a decision to restrict the access of the nation's underserved
to higher education in order to eliminate a potential source of
competition for the privileged. "As higher education became
more crucial to individual success," observed Orfield and Ashkinaze (1991, p. 171), "colleges became less accessible to blacks,
and external pressure for civil rights compliance disappeared.
And as blacks moved backward, white access increased."

Since the 1960s, the cornerstone of the federal commitment to promote access to higher education has been a system of need-based grants and loans. And it was in changes to this system during the 1980s that the federal government most clearly signaled its growing disinterest in issues of access and equity. Since 1982, two disturbing trends have become apparent: an overall reduction in the funding of student aid programs, despite significant increases in the cost of college attendance, and a pronounced shift in the source of aid from direct grants to loans. When measured in constant 1982 dollars, total student aid actually fell from $16.02 billion to $15.37 billion by 1987. Further, while in 1982 more than 4.2 million grants had been made by the federal government through the Pell, Supplemental Educational Opportunity Grants, and College Work Study programs against $3.7 million loans, by 1987 slightly more loans ($4.34 million) were made than grants ($4.26 million) (Giley, 1990).

As many have noted, what has made the recent shift in federal student aid policy so threatening to the ideals of access and equity is that this weakening federal commitment has come at a time of rapidly increasing tuition and other costs. While overall federal aid fell by 4.1 percent between 1982 and 1987, the cost of attending a private college rose by 41 percent and the cost of attending a public college increased by 22 percent. And families, particularly those of low and moderate income, could not be expected to bridge the growing affordability gap, since family income for the period increased by just 5 percent. As Giley (1990, p. 49) sums up, "A growing gap exists between costs of higher education and available funding sources—both public and private—to close that gap."

The significant decline during the 1980s in minority student persistence to the baccalaureate described above may have its primary sources in these shifting patterns of student aid. One might describe the consequence of this shift in federal policy as a rationing of access by price, with obvious consequences for minority and underclass communities.

Something else that may turn out to have an even greater impact on access to higher education for the nation's underclass is the federally inspired call for outcome documentation by colleges and universities. This requires institutions to report publicly the academic progress and graduation rates of their students, with the clear implication that colleges and universities with low rates will risk their eligibility for federal support.

Whereas the 1980s saw a concern with individual excellence supersede the values of access and equity at the core of public education's values, we are increasingly likely to see this commitment to individual achievement institutionalized into mandatory systems of student outcome assessment. This requirement for colleges and universities to establish programs of narrowly defined student outcome assessment may provide clear incentives for schools to shun the underserved, the disabled, and those at high risk in order to protect their data. As Cynthia Brown (1985, p. 300) has pointed out, "In the search for excellence, incentives to segregate and track students are tempting."

The North Central Association of Colleges and Schools (1990, p. 391) has called attention to the dangers to access and equity inherent in outcome measurement programs and has sternly warned its member colleges not to abandon their commitments to students at risk: "An overemphasis on student achievement and excellence may have a negative influence on the national commitment to access and equity. This must not occur." However, in many states, the impact of the developing emphasis on outcome measurement has been strengthened by legislated "report card" mandates that devolve into interinstitutional comparisons, thereby penalizing institutions that actively seek out high-risk students.

Restoring Egalitarian Values and Democratic Ideals

The costs of the nation's long embrace of the conservative agenda and its unqualified individualism are becoming more and more apparent. Whether we consider the devastation of the cities, and their growing underclass communities, or the erosion of egalitarian values as the basis for public policy, we find that not only have those trapped in the nation's inner cities paid a terrible price—so has the national spirit.

But even as these costs become clear, a revival of more

democratic beliefs seems uncertain. The coalition of government, schools, colleges, and private foundations that proved so effective in the 1960s and 1970s in promoting access to higher education has been weakened by the reduction in the role of the federal government as a partner. Only by building new coalitions, drawing together not only public sector agencies but the private sector and the resources of community-based organizations as well, will those committed to the enduring values of access and equity find a way of restoring hope and opportunity for the nation's underserved communities.

Major foundations have played a significant role at least since the 1960s in helping at-risk students enter college and succeed once enrolled. The role that these institutions have played has shifted during these years as the various coalition partners have either expanded or reduced their participation. Foundations continually reassess their funding priorities, in part in response to what they sense to be movement on the agenda of either the government or the schools themselves. When government policy is seen to be complementary to the overarching goals of a particular foundation, the foundation is comfortable playing a supporting role. At other times, if dissonance exists between federal and foundation policy, the foundation may find itself articulating priorities on its own or in concert with nongovernment agencies such as corporations and community-based organizations.

In all of this, it should be understood that the major foundations pursue at least three simultaneous agendas. First and most basic, in their work with schools, foundations attempt to support programs that will be of direct benefit to students—for example, in helping more underrepresented students enter college after graduating from high school. Second, foundations try to support programs within institutions that contribute to institutional change and benefit the institutions themselves—assisting colleges, for instance, in revising and diversifying their undergraduate curricula in ways that reflect and include more of the recent scholarship on women and ethnic minorities. Third and most ambitious, through their programming, foundations attempt to affect the field itself—for example, through their work in helping individual community colleges improve their transfer programs, foundations attempt to influence the community college movement to re-embrace the transfer mission, seeing this to be its central function and as a result provide leadership and resources to make it more effective in this role.

The Ford Foundation's Community College Program: A Case Study

It may now be timely to describe how one foundation—the Ford Foundation—carried out its work with two-year colleges over the years while shifting the focus of its programming to reflect the shifting commitments of its traditional coalition partners. This case study is presented to document how this foundation has played a continuing role in expanding opportunities for access to higher education for underrepesented minorities.

First, why has the Ford Foundation provided so much support for the nation's community colleges? And why has the foundation set the strengthening of the transfer function as the priority guiding its grantmaking? When looking at the data on higher education, foundation staff saw that the community college was an important institution for the populations they wished to serve. Fully 51 percent of all first-time freshmen were and are found at two-year colleges, and they are disproportionately African American (43 percent of all black college students are enrolled in two-year institutions), Hispanic (55 percent), Native American (56 percent), and low income (44 percent of all poverty-level freshmen are found at community colleges). And though most community colleges stress vocational education as their central function, up to two-thirds of their first-time students aspire to baccalaureates. These transfer-oriented students, however, transfer to senior institutions at rates that are up to half that of their more affluent classmates. In California, for example, with nearly 90 percent of all minority students enrolled in college found at two-year colleges, only 5 to 10 percent transfer to four-year institutions.

These institutions not only provide access to the kinds of students with which the foundation wishes to work, but as their mission statements indicate, they see potential in everyone and are committed to helping everyone realize this potential. And during times when the costs of higher education are rising far faster than either aid or disposable income, community colleges provide a reasonably affordable opportunity to the underserved.

For these reasons, the Ford Foundation has chosen to work closely with these institutions of opportunity, the "people's colleges." And that work has evolved over the years as the commitments of others have shifted and waned: the foundation's community college program during the 1970s, when its priorities were consistent with the federal government's, was very different than it is now that the government has reduced its commitment to access and equity in higher education. It may therefore be instructive to trace this evolution as a case study of how external support programs are shaped over time in their efforts to help at-risk students enter and succeed in school.

During the 1970s, the foundation could assume that many of its efforts on behalf of the underserved would be carried out in a sympathetic context. It could focus its initiatives on specific programs with the understanding that their impact would be reinforced by other mutually supportive activities undertaken by the federal government and other partners in the broad national coalition committed to enhancing access and equity.

At that time, it was felt that the major impediment preventing more at-risk students from entering and succeeding in college was their lack of financial resources. The structures were in place: two-year colleges had greatly expanded both in number and size so that one was located at a commuting distance for the vast majority of potential students, open admissions policies allowed even the marginally prepared to enroll, articulation agreements linking the academic programs of junior and senior institutions seemed to ensure that credits earned by transferring students would be accepted, federal policy channeled money to the states in ways that enabled them to support campus expansion and the development of new vocational and academic programs, and both federal and state subsides began to make it possible for even the lowest-income students to pursue a college education. In this climate of mutual support for access and equity programming, the Ford Foundation saw its work as complementary. It thus launched its Upper Division Scholars Program (UDSP) in 1971 as a way of enriching and expanding what was then a national, loosely coordinated commitment to helping at-risk students attain bachelor's degrees. The UDSP was an enrichment program, since it made scholarship money available to a select group of graduating community college students transferring to four-year institutions. During the 1970s, nearly 4,000 of these scholarships were awarded, covering most of the cost of tuition, room, and board. This was a remarkably successful program. More than 90 percent of the scholars earned undergraduate degrees, while nearly 60 percent completed advanced degrees. It was the right kind of program for its time, in truth a rather generous program, fully in concert with the social policy of the day that provided an agenda and support for the basic efforts to foster access and equity in higher education.

There was, however, a disappointing side to this concerted effort. The data at the time revealed that in spite of the activities of the federal and state governments and the external founders, few at-risk students were succeeding in transferring from two- to four-year colleges. To help understand this lack of progress, officials at the Ford Foundation turned to the work of a number of scholars who were calling into question the community colleges' commitment to their academic or transfer function (Karabel, 1972; Zwerling, 1976). They criticized the national leadership of the community college movement, namely the founders and subsequent heads of the American Association of Community and Junior Colleges, for devaluing the transfer function in favor of the vocational function as one way of defining a unique mission for the two-year college. In addition, these writers claimed, as more and more new and nontraditional students demanded access to higher education as a way of preparing themselves for careers in the rapidly transforming economy, the community colleges took on the role of diverting these students away from senior institutions so that they could continue to limit admission to the academically most successful. Observers pointed to recommendations to redirect students in statewide master plans for higher education to support this assertion. In addition, at about this time, in the late 1970s and early 1980s, the deepening recession of the Carter years and the conservative restoration of the Reagan era saw a marked shift in federal higher education policy, including a retreat from its long-standing commitment to programs that contributed to access to higher education.

In this changing demographic and policy environment, the leadership of the Ford Foundation concluded that it needed to move beyond a complementary role and assume a more active role in support of the community colleges' transfer programs. Thus, the early 1980s saw a dramatic shift away from the scholarship approach of direct assistance to students to one that focused on the institutions themselves. It was felt that a revitalization of the collegiate function, in which the nation's community colleges would reassert the centrality of transfer, was essential if the growing percentage of at-risk students attending these institutions would have any real hope of gaining the baccalaureate and assuming leadership roles within their communities.

To that end, in 1983, the foundation began its Urban Community College Transfer Opportunities Program (UCC/TOP). UCC/TOP offered grants directly to individual community colleges to support their efforts to address the structural barriers to transfer. Twenty-four urban two-year colleges participated in the first round of grants by developing programs to enhance the transfer-oriented climate on campus through efforts designed to improve instructional practices, counseling services, and articulation policies with senior institutions.

This work continues to this day in various forms with ongoing Ford Foundation support. But in addition, as a way of affecting the field itself, in consistent attempts through the years to encourage higher education practitioners and leaders to join in this effort to revitalize the two-year college's transfer function, the foundation has sponsored policy research and dissemination activities in order to learn more about the structural impediments to transfer and to communicate to the field practices that work.

Some of this research and some of the efforts at dissemination, all felt to be vital in the continuing public policy environment unresponsive to issues of access and equity, led staff at the foundation more recently to continue to shift programmatic priorities in an effort to keep these issues before the higher education community. Based on the evidence of a steady decline in the number of community college students transferring, scholars such as Cohen and Brawer (1984) and Richardson and Bender (1985) called attention to what they described as a fundamental breakdown in the academic or collegiate culture that had once been characteristic of community colleges. Based on a study of the projects supported by the original twenty-four UCC/TOP participants, Donovan and Schaier-Peleg (1987) concluded that the most effective way to reinvigorate the transfer function was through programs that linked high schools with community colleges and community colleges with the senior institutions that received transferring students, particularly those efforts that focused on strategies for academic enrichment.

Thus, as the result of the prompting of these and related findings, the Ford Foundation again refocused its community college programming—this time to sponsor activities across the tiers of educational systems, activities that concentrated primarily on structural innovations and curricular and faculty development. Large grants were made to establish the Center for Academic Achievement and Transfer at the American Council on Education and the sixteen-city Urban Partnerships Program. The city partnerships are attempting to foster collaborations within citywide settings that cut across all parts of the educational continuum, making enriched academic programs and support services available to students as they move from kindergarten through college.

Much is known about sector-specific programs that work. The foundation and participating institutions and cities are cooperating to fuse these interventions into a seamless array of interlinked programs available to students as they progress through the schools. This advances the programming beyond the traditional approach that holds that moving a cohort of students through a specific program for a finite period of time provides so much benefit that additional interventions are unnecessary. This has proven not to be the case: at-risk students need more than short doses of quick-fix programming in order to be helped to succeed. In addition, these sector-specific programs have tended to serve limited numbers of students and therefore affect only a small portion of the population that requires assistance. These newer, cross-institutional, citywide approaches hold the promise that larger numbers of at-risk students than in the past will be assisted over longer periods of time. The foundation is committed to supporting the work of citywide teams for a ten-year period, at which time it is expected that systemic change, in its diverse forms, will have occurred, and that students in the sixteen participating cities will be on their way to academic success.

Conclusion

Particularly in a policy climate that no longer sees higher education to be effective in reducing social inequality, when much, to the contrary, is known about the ways schools can contribute to equity, external funders have an increasing obligation to build new partnerships among themselves via the cosponsorship of progressive practices. In recent years, to complete the story of the Ford Foundation's work with community colleges, there have been examples of such cooperative ventures. The Urban Partnerships Program has been cofunded by Ford and the Fund for the Improvement of Postsecondary Education, and some of the most extensive transfer-related programming in citywide settings has been undertaken collaboratively by Ford and the Pew Charitable Trusts. Many feel that if we are asking the critical institutions within cities to combine their expertise and resources to help at-risk students, the external funding community has a similar obligation to seek ways to link some of their own resources in a coordinated effort to help more of the underserved succeed. They also need to speak with a forceful voice to policy makers and the public, reminding them that the democratic goals that characterized the coalition during the 1960s and 1970s have not gone away and that even in the face of the conservative ascendancy these values are worth asserting and pursuing. Ironically, since these are the very values embedded in our founding documents and institutions, one would not expect that "liberals" would have to remind "conservatives" of the meaning of our shared history.

References

Brown, C. "Is 'Excellence' a Threat to Equality?" In B. Gross and R. Gross (eds.), *The Great School Debate.* New York: Simon & Schuster, 1985.

Carter, D. J., and Wilson, R. *Ninth Annual Status Report: Minorities in Higher Education.* Washington, D.C.: American Council on Education, 1991.

Cohen, A. M., and Brawer, F. B. *The American Community College.* San Francisco: Jossey-Bass, 1984.

Donovan, R., and Schaier-Peleg, B. *Transfer: Making It Work.* Washington, D.C.: American Association of Community and Junior Colleges, 1987.

Giley, J. W. *The Interactive University.* Washington, D.C.: American Association of State Colleges and Universities, 1990.

Howe, H. II. "Giving Equity a Chance in the Excellence Game." Paper presented at the Martin Buskin Memorial Lecture, Apr. 1984.

Karabel, J. "Community Colleges and Social Stratification." *Harvard Educational Review,* 1972, *42,* 521–562.

Mortenson, T. G. "Equity of Higher Educational Opportunity for Women, Black, Hispanic, and Low Income Students." ACT Student Financial Aid Research Report Series, no. 91-1. Iowa City: American College Testing Program, 1991.

National Center for Education Statistics, U.S. Department of Education. *Digest of Education Statistics.* Washington, D.C.: U.S. Government Printing Office, 1988.

National Commission on Excellence in Education. *A Nation at Risk: The Imperative for Educational Reform.* Washington, D.C.: U.S. Government Printing Office, 1983.

North Central Association of Colleges and Schools. *NCA Quarterly,* 1990, *65*(2).

Orfield, G., and Ashkinaze, C. *The Closing Door.* Chicago: University of Chicago Press, 1991.

Richardson, R. C., Jr., and Bender, L. W. *Students in Urban Settings.* ASHE-ERIC Higher Education Report No. 6. Washington, D.C.: Association for the Study of Higher Education, 1985.

Stedman, L. C., and Smith, M. S. "Recent Reform Proposals for American Education." *Contemporary Education Review*, 1983, 2(2).

Zwerling, L. S. *Second Best: The Crisis of the Community College.* New York: McGraw-Hill, 1976.

Chapter 17 ──────────────

Revitalizing Minority Colleges and Universities

Richard O. Hope

The history of minority higher education in the United States reflects the role of this country as a host to oppressed people. Minority colleges and universities have existed in the United States since the nineteenth century as institutions arising from the absence of more general higher education opportunities for African Americans, Hispanic Americans, and Native Americans. Thus, they evolved as a response to the need for education that originally was not available to these populations because of slavery, racism, isolation, segregation, and discrimination.

Minority colleges and universities arose to fulfill the need for the education of ex-slaves who were denied other educational opportunities, Latinos who were forced to "speak English," or Native American Indians who were made to feel ashamed of their cultural traditions and life-styles. These institutions have had similar functional origins and continue their essential character, but possess differences that reflect their unique histories.

Minority educational institutions play an important role in representing the collective concerns of minority students by serving as repositories for cultural, political, and socioeconomic achievement. The positive self-esteem derived from interacting with people of similar traditions, culture, language, and racial heritage is the foundation for the effective mentoring and peer relationships that are so essential for educational achievement and other forms of success. This discussion will be limited to three minority groups and their respective institutions of higher education: historically black colleges and universities (HBCUs), tribally controlled colleges (TCC), and the Hispanic Association of Colleges and Universities (HACU). After describing the past and present circumstance of each of these groups, this chapter will address the future of these institutions, separate yet integral parts of the educational system of the United States.

Historically Black Colleges and Universities

The history of many HBCUs begins in the basement of black churches across the country. The black church was the only independent institution allowed any autonomy after African Americans came to the United States in 1619. It was the only logical source for promoting education, which was prohibited during slavery. Slaves and their teachers were punished for simply learning or teaching how to read and write. Thus, education for blacks began as an illicit act done under the cloak of secrecy, and the small churches that were permitted then became safe havens for educational enterprise. Christianity was encouraged during slavery by masters who frequently saw it as a means of social control. After the Civil War, higher education for African Americans gradually came under the sponsorship of such national organizations as the African Methodist Episcopal Church, American Baptist Home Missionary Society, Baptist Missionary Convention, American Missionary Association, and African Methodist Episcopal Zion Church. These institutions created church-affiliated schools that adhered to the religious teachings of their sponsors. Daily chapel services were held on the campuses of these schools, and religion was a required part of the educational curriculum.

Most of these schools began as primary and secondary academies since there was no public education in the South available to freed slaves after the Civil War. These "normal

schools" became the bedrock for the development of black higher education. Some of these early schools began as trade schools
for freedmen and Indians. They were typically administered and
supported by Northern white abolitionists with the tacit and se-
cret support of some Southern whites who sympathized with the
goal of educating free blacks. For decades, these schools were
the only source for primary, secondary, and later higher education for freed blacks: "Prior to 1945, almost 90 percent of all
blacks in college attended historically black colleges and universities, institutions located primarily in the South and founded
after the Civil War for the express purpose of educating blacks"
(Willie, Grady, and Hope, 1991, p. 93).

    According to William Gray, (1993, p. 62), president of the
United Negro College Fund, "Black colleges have had a tremendous increase in enrollment—a 25 percent increase in the last
five years. That's twice the national average." HBCUs continue
to be a vital force in the education of African Americans with
approximately 107 two- and four-year schools in operation today.
About 40 percent are public institutions and 60 percent are private. In the fall of 1992, there were 277,261 students at these
schools—59 percent at women's colleges and 41 percent at
men's. The racial composition is as follows: 77 percent African
American, 13 percent Caucasian American, 1.8 percent Hispanic
American, 0.8 percent Asian American, and 0.2 percent American Indian/Alaska Native (National Association for Equal Opportunity in Education, 1993).

    Despite numerous obstacles, such as minuscule budgets,
lack of facilities, and constant pressure by the white community
to close HBCUs, these colleges have graduated men and women
who have become leaders in the United States as judges, doctors, engineers, scholars, teachers, and elected legislators and
other officials. According to the 1993 chair of the board of the
National Association for Equal Opportunity in Higher Education, Arthur E. Thomas, "HBCUs continue to outpace all other
institutions in the production of African American undergraduates. In such fields as medicine, pharmacy, law, veterinary medicine, and dentistry, HBCUs lead the nation in conferring first-
professional degrees for black graduates."

Like other minority institutions, HBCUs are constantly plagued with threats of extinction and closure. From their very inception, these institutions were targets of violent reaction— for example, during the Atlanta riots—and they frequently faced legal and legislative threats of annihilation. Recent lawsuits, such as *Ayers* v. *Fordice,* threaten Alcorn State and Mississippi Valley State with closure in Mississippi, and similar desegregation cases are being waged in Alabama, Louisiana, Maryland, and Tennessee. Benjamin E. Mays, past president of Morehouse College, stated before his death:

> If America allows black colleges to die, it will be the worst kind of discrimination and denigration known in history. To decree that colleges born to serve Negroes are not worthy of surviving now that white colleges accept Negroes would be a damnable act. No one has ever said that Catholic colleges should be abolished because they are Catholic. Nobody says that Brandeis and Albert Einstein must die because they are Jewish. Nobody says that Lutheran and Episcopalian Schools should go because they are Lutheran or Episcopalian. Why should Howard University be abolished because it is known as a Black University? Why pick out Negro colleges and say they must die? Blot out these colleges: You blot out the image of black men and women in education [Willie and Edmonds, 1978, pp. 19–20].

Native American Tribally Controlled Colleges

American Indians have been a marginal part of American higher education since the creation of colleges in the United States. Harvard College, founded in 1636, listed among its goals "the education of the English and Indian youth of this country in knowledge and goodness." According to Ernest Boyer (1989, p. 8), Harvard's response was "disappointing." He continues that "few young Indians ever went to Harvard and many of those who did enter the college did not stay." Dartmouth College, as well as the College of William and Mary, were designated in their original charters as schools for the education of American Indians.

The goal of most early education efforts was "assimilation" and seldom the enhancement of Indian students or of their tribal communities.

The history of Indian education is replete with numerous obstacles limiting educational opportunities at all levels, somewhat echoing the experiences of HBCUs. As a result, "Many HBCU's, in their earliest years, offered programs specifically geared to the education of American Indians. Hampton University, for example, had more than 1,300 American Indians from 65 tribes attending its institution between 1878 and 1923. In fact, some HBCUs, such as Tuskegee, were given Indian names" (Alexander, 1993, p. 13).

Today, less than 1 percent of those enrolling in postsecondary education are Indians. From 1976 through 1990, the National Center for Education Statistics lists a consistent "0.7 percent attendance" (National Center for Education Statistics, U.S. Department of Education, 1992, p. 106). This enrollment rate is dismal in comparison to that of other student groups in 1990: whites, 77.9 percent; blacks, 8.9 percent; and Hispanics, 5.5 percent. Primary and secondary schools are not adequately preparing these students to take advantage of postsecondary opportunities. The test scores of Indian students are lower than those of most other minority groups (U.S. Department of Education, 1991, p. 6). Unfortunately, as many as 35 percent, and in some instances 50 to 60 percent, of American Indian and Alaska Native students leave school early. There are approximately 1.9 million American Indians and Alaska Natives in the United States, with about 400,000 of both groups in the school-age population. A majority (roughly 85 to 90 percent) of these students attend public school, contrary to popular belief. Only 13 percent (or 50,000) attend schools on reservations operated by the Bureau of Indian Affairs.

Native American students frequently encounter a curriculum that is insensitive to their linguistic and cultural needs. Tribal leaders and native communities are concerned that the ability to learn from the elders, the music and art forms, the historical and practical knowledge, and the traditional social and cultural practices must not be lost to the tribes and the nation as a whole.

To ensure the cultural integrity of Indian postsecondary education, tribally controlled colleges (TCCs) were formed in the mid 1970s. There are twenty-four institutions of higher education founded and controlled by Indians. Just as the HBCUs began with humble resources and facilities, TCCs frequently hold classes in modest facilities, and some students are hampered by outdated textbooks and obsolete laboratory equipment. Nevertheless, TCCs offer vital community services, family counseling, alcohol abuse programs, and job training, with limited financial or administrative support. Boyer (1989, pp. 4–5) suggests that TCCs are essential for Indian communities:

- First, tribal colleges establish a learning environment that encourages participation by and builds self-confidence in students who have come to view failure as the norm.
- Second, tribal colleges celebrate and help sustain the rich Native American traditions.
- Third, tribal colleges provide essential services that enrich the communities surrounding them.
- Fourth, the colleges are often centers for research and scholarship.

Hispanic Colleges and Universities

The Hispanic Association of Colleges and Universities (HACU), which began in 1986, was created to promote the development of colleges and universities with 25 percent or more enrolled Hispanic students, improve access to postsecondary opportunities for Hispanic students, and assist faculty and administrators at these institutions. About 3 percent of all institutions of higher education in the United States are Hispanic-serving institutions (59 two-year colleges and 62 four-year universities) representing over 45 percent of all Hispanic college and university students. Unlike the HBCUs, HACU schools were not started for the primary purpose of educating Hispanic students. Instead, in the past several decades there has been a dramatic increase in the number of Hispanic students at general institutions of higher education, with more than 390,000 students enrolled in schools with over 25 percent Hispanic undergraduates or graduates.

Michael Olivas (1986, p. 3) expresses precisely why there is a need for a Hispanic association of colleges and universities to produce more leaders to fill the void found in higher education:

> In the summer of 1985, there were six Hispanic four-year college presidents and twenty Hispanic two-year-college presidents. A survey of two-year college trustees revealed that only 0.6 percent were Hispanic, while a study of postsecondary coordinating boards found 1.1 percent of the commissioners to be Hispanic. At another level of leadership, there is little evidence to suggest that significant leadership will be drawn from faculty ranks, because only 1.4 percent of all faculty (and 1.1 percent of all tenured professors) are Hispanics, including faculty members in Spanish and bilingual education departments. . . . Confronted with these data, one is forced to concede that Hispanics have not entered American institutions of higher education in any significant fashion.

The number of Hispanics enrolled in higher education has been increasing at a higher rate than other student populations. From 1980 to 1990, the proportion of Hispanic students rose from 3.9 to 5.5 percent, while that of African Americans decreased slightly from 9.2 to 8.9 percent and the percentage of American Indian students remained roughly the same at 0.7 percent. The proportion of white students declined from 81.4 to 77.9 percent in the same period. HACU membership is at an all-time high, reports Chuck Rodriquez, vice president for the Office of Advancement: "From its modest beginning in 1987 with 18 institutions, HACU's membership has grown to 127 institutions." Of this number, 85 are Hispanic-serving institutions and 46 are associate members. HACU members are located in fifteen states and Puerto Rico ("HACU Ends Year with Record Membership Numbers," 1994, p. 3). Given the continuing increase in Hispanic students, it is estimated that by the year 2000, 150 colleges and universities will have more than a 25 percent Hispanic student population.

The Survival of Minority Colleges and Universities

Implicit in the development of these minority-oriented institutions is the assumption that minority students share similar concerns about preserving and incorporating their history and culture into the curriculum. These minority schools were created because majority institutions were not necessarily providing for the educational and cultural needs of minority students.

It is the thesis of this chapter that quality schools are necessary and should be available to minority students, including the major nonminority colleges and universities. Predominantly minority schools must also be available to ensure the full range of higher educational experiences for minority and majority students.

The newspapers and educational journals are replete with articles about colleges and universities experiencing racial problems and having curricula that either ignore or provide little information regarding the unique contributions and characteristics of minorities. The ubiquitous discussions of "diversity" and code phrases such as "politically correct" speak directly to the concerns of minority students and reflect the racial climate on some university campuses (American Council on Education, 1993).

Institutional survival is not sufficient in and of itself as an issue for minority institutions of higher education without considering the issues of academic quality and the place of these institutions in the pantheon of colleges and universities. Likewise, to generalize about these schools as though they were monolithic is to ignore the diversity among them. But survivability is a key issue.

The debate regarding the survival of minority institutions seems to involve at least five arguments. First, minority schools provide a campus climate, atmosphere, and set of experiences rarely available to students at majority institutions. This explains why minority students are returning to these schools even though their primary and secondary educational experiences and test scores make them perfect candidates for Ivy League and other majority schools. Since many minority institutions are relatively small, they can provide special attention, one-on-one counseling, and mentoring that nurture and motivate students. Teachers at these schools are successful and positive role models who are available and willing to take the time to work with students.

Second, these institutions have pioneered innovative educational methods, demonstrating that students of varying cultural and educational backgrounds can learn with an effective instructional program. As Willie suggests, "Many of their practices and procedures offer useful models for all institutions of higher education" (Willie and Edmonds, 1978, p. 263). They have demonstrated a unique ability to "take a student where he or she is" and provide the kind of education that has consistently produced successful business and professional leaders. In some cases, students enter minority schools with educational deficits produced by segregated secondary education, and they are not permitted to graduate until the vestiges of these poor educational experiences are replaced with a positive and fundamental liberal education.

Third, minority institutions, at their very core, provide a sense of history and appreciation of the culture of minority groups. They instill pride in the students and appreciation for the legacy of their ancestors.

Fourth, these schools have produced a disproportionate share of the minority professionals in the United States. Even when they are confronted by integrated educational opportunity, the sons and daughters of minority professionals seek out these minority institutions.

Finally, these institutions of higher education contribute to the vast mosaic of diverse postsecondary schools that are part of a rich balance of institutions. Schools with specific ethnic, gender, or religious focus are part of the rich educational tradition in the United States.

Harold Howe, Jr., in his monograph titled *Black Colleges and the Continuing Dream* (1976, pp. 8–9), suggests that black colleges, and presumably all minority schools, will be needed as long as equal opportunity remains a dream:

I hope that those who emphasize the positive trends are indeed correct and that the present disadvantage of blacks as compared to whites in higher education will steadily diminish. But my hopes would be more firmly held if I had confidence that the forces which have sustained progress in the last fifteen years would continue to be exerted. Attempting to look at realities rather than hopes leads me to believe that these forces are losing strength and that the spearhead of that progress is at least blunted if not stopped. . . . It is precisely because I detect a loss of national leadership and a weakening of the commitment to equality that I see the black college as having a special role in the coming years.

In *Private Black Colleges at the Crossroads* (1973), Daniel Thompson reviews rationales and strategies for the survival of HBCUs. He summarizes one position as follows:

Some educators, who are essentially defenders of the status quo, contend that these colleges will continue to be needed in more or less their present form for the next few decades. They would like to see these colleges receive the level of financial support necessary to make them truly sound institutions. They hold that instead of providing higher education for Blacks who are systematically excluded from white colleges, as was the case until a decade ago, these colleges should now provide educational opportunities for Black students who lack academic and financial qualifications for admission to white colleges. They would have private Black colleges specialize in the education of the so-called culturally disadvantaged, assuming the educational role now primarily associated with the experimental colleges which are cropping up in certain urban Black ghettos, particularly outside the South [pp. 11–12].

While Thompson agrees that minority youth should have equal access to college education, he insists that "it is the public education system which has illegally shortchanged most black youth" (p. 270). Public schools, he continues, have never provided these students with the facilities or the quality of teachers and rich programs needed to prepare them to compete for entrance into, and adequate performance in, the most academically rigorous schools: "Educating those deliberately disadvantaged by this nation's neglect is logically the problem of the nation at large and should not be the exclusive domain of Black colleges. Certainly the problem itself is too complex and the solution far too expensive to be assumed primarily by private Black colleges" (p. 270).

Another solution is advocated by some individuals who accuse these colleges of perpetuating de facto racial segregation, since HBCUs enroll only a small number of nonblacks. These critics usually suggest that HBCUs be phased out or merged to produce quality and integrated education. This process is already under way. For example, Atlanta University has merged with Clark College. Other colleges are being threatened with closure because of the absence of financial resources.

Thompson's solution for minority institutions is that they become an "Island of Excellence." In the early 1970s, Willa B. Player, then president of Bennett College, recommended several ways that minority colleges could be restructured. Her perceptive suggestions remain vitally relevant and can be summarized as follows:

1. Specialize in one or a few interdisciplinary academic areas instead of offering the full range of such fields as liberal arts, business, education, and so on, while offering the strong general education program needed to undergird such specialization.
2. Attract a larger proportion of students with superior academic potential through wider recruitment programs.
3. Make curricula more relevant to the specific needs of the black community as well as the purely academic demands of graduate schools.
4. Recruit the very best teachers dedicated to addressing the special needs of minority students.
5. Establish channels of communication between minority

colleges and other top colleges and universities as well as the world of business and government.

Today, increasing numbers of HBCUs, Native American colleges, and Hispanic-serving colleges appear to be following these five suggestions. Specialization is occurring among these schools in formal academic curricula, while at the same time they are placing greater emphasis on meeting community needs. These schools deliberately focus on teaching the culture, language, history, and life-styles of the groups they represent. The result is increased enrollment of minority students seeking a solid academic experience along with programs making them more intimately aware of their ethnic and racial histories. This process produces a synergy that leads illustrious alumni to return to the larger nonminority universities as teachers. Finally, many minority schools are establishing both formal and informal relationships with majority universities, given the desire of the latter to attract talented minority students and teachers and the desire of the former to attract resources needed to upgrade laboratories, curricular materials, and courses.

Conclusion

Dramatic changes are taking place in minority colleges and universities today. These changes, occurring in the context of major shifts in higher education, are needed to compensate for the deficits many minority students have faced and are still facing. One is reminded of a commencement address of President Lyndon Johnson at Howard University, where he said: "You do not take a person who for years has been hobbled by chains and liberate him, bring him to the starting line of a race and say, 'you're free to compete with others, and justly believe that you have been completely fair.' "

References

Alexander, B. "Righting a Historic Wrong: 75 American Indian Educators," *Black Issues in Higher Education*, 1993, *9*(26), 12–15.

American Council on Education. "Student Interest in Racial Issues Increases." *Higher Education and National Affairs,* 1993, *42*(1).

Boyer, E. L. *Tribal Colleges: Shaping the Future of Native America.* Princeton, N.J.: Carnegie Foundation for the Advancement of Teaching, 1989.

Carter, D., and Wilson, R. *Tenth Annual Status Report on Minorities in Higher Education.* Washington, D.C.: American Council on Education, 1992.

Egerton, J. *The Black Public Colleges: Integration and Disintegration.* Nashville, Tenn.: Race Relations Information Center, 1971.

Garibaldi, A. *Black Colleges and Universities: Challenges for the Future.* New York: Praeger, 1984.

Gray, W. "On the Superiority of Black Colleges." *Journal of Blacks in Higher Education,* 1993, *1,* 60–66.

"HACU Ends Year with Record Membership Number." *HACU Newsletter,* 1994, *2*(5), 3.

Howe, H. *Black Colleges and the Continuing Dream.* 1976. (Reprint available from Ford Foundation, 320 East 43rd Street, New York, NY.)

National Association for Equal Opportunity in Higher Education, *NAFEO Inroads,* 1993, *7*(5–6), 1.

National Center for Education Statistics, U.S. Department of Education. *Digest of Education Statistics.* Washington, D.C.: U.S. Government Printing Office, 1992.

Olivas, M. (ed.). *Latino College Students.* New York: Teachers College Press, 1986.

Thompson, D. *Private Black Colleges at the Crossroads.* Westport, Conn.: Greenwood Press, 1973.

U.S. Department of Education. *Indian Nations at Risk: An Educational Strategy for Action.* Final report of the Indian Nations at Risk Task Force. Washington, D.C.: U.S. Government Printing Office, 1991.

Willie, C. V., and Edmonds, R. (eds.). *Black Colleges in America.* New York: Teachers College Press, 1978.

Willie, C. V., Grady, M., and Hope, R. *African Americans and the Doctoral Experience.* New York: Teachers College Press, 1991.

PART FOUR

Leadership Imperatives for Educating a New Majority

In the previous sections, we have presented the compelling economic, demographic, and social rationale for the systemic reform of education in order to clear the educational pathway of barriers hampering the advancement of low-income and minority students. We have also highlighted numerous strategies and policies designed to improve both the K–12 system and two- and four-year colleges and universities. In this concluding section, we focus on the key players that can and must provide leadership to effect change that will create new and better schools and colleges of the future.

In Chapter Eighteen, Tony Cippolone, Michael K. Grady, and Warren Simmons maintain that the full force of the social service system must now be joined with schools to provide comprehensive and coordinated services for children at risk. The authors review the Annie E. Casey Foundation's principles of school restructuring and provide case illustrations of the most promising examples enacted in states that have incorporated these principles.

Next, in Chapter Nineteen, Blandina Cardenas Ramírez provides perspectives on the development, characteristics, and behaviors of new leaders in colleges and universities who are trying to find ways of responding to increased diversity. In the context of what is needed to create institutional capacity for diversity, the author elaborates on leadership development, self-invention, organizational culture, assessment of organizational contexts, team building, the use of ritual, tradition, and symbol, as well as the incorporation of internal and external constituencies to develop an organizational culture that engages diversity.

In the book's concluding chapter, Richard O. Hope and Laura I. Rendón use the issues raised in this book as a context for providing a new vision of our nation's educational system, offering a mandate for the nation's leaders to take the necessary steps to educate a new student majority.

Chapter 18

Creating Schools for *All* Learners

Tony Cipollone, Michael K. Grady, Warren Simmons

Throughout its history, the urban public school in America has been called on to play a pivotal, often compensatory role in the face of major transformations in U.S. society. These developments are familiar to observers of American history—the shift in population from farms to cities; the industrialization of the Northeast, Mid-Atlantic, and Great Lakes regions of the late nineteenth and early twentieth centuries; waves of immigration, the first originating in Europe, more recently from Asia, Central America, and the Caribbean, bringing to the urban schools children who often have had little or no formal education. Each of these social transformations challenged the schools to reorient themselves to better meet the needs of the new arrivals. Notwithstanding heroic early successes in which the schools responded effectively to changes in urban society—for example, facilitating the assimilation of European immigrants and preparing a workforce for the factories and foundries of the early twentieth century—in general, poor and minority children have not been well served by the public schools. As David Tyack (1974, p. 11) has observed, "Schools have rarely taught the children of the poor effectively—[and] this failure has been systematic, not idiosyncratic."

The large-scale disintegration of the American family, a problem that many observers believe has reached crisis proportions, has been the most recent and perhaps most profound challenge facing the American school. In the 1980s we witnessed a 50 percent increase in the rate of single-parent families, the vast majority of these families being headed by working females. While some of these families managed to overcome hardships, the incidence of poverty for this group is three times that of families where both parents are in the home. These sweeping changes in family composition during this period corresponded to increases in child poverty. The poverty rate for Americans under the age of eighteen rose from 17 percent in 1979 to 20 percent by the end of the 1980s. While overall this means that poverty afflicts one child in five, the rates for African American and Latino children are 44 and 38 percent, respectively.

This rise in child poverty parallels a significant increase in family risk. The 1993 edition of the Annie E. Casey Foundation's *Kids Count Data Book: State Profiles of Child Well-Being* reports that three demographic factors place a new mother at substantially greater risk of poverty—being under age twenty at the time her first child is born, being a single parent, and lacking a high school degree (Annie E. Casey Foundation and Center for the Study of Social Policy, 1992). *Kids Count* reports that 45 percent of all new families formed in 1990 featured at least one of these three characteristics, 24 percent had two of the three risk factors, and 11 percent were saddled with all three. As alluded to above, data on family risk are far more disturbing when reported separately for racial and ethnic groups: 78 percent of newly formed African American families had one of these risk factors, as did 69 percent of new Latino families. These poverty and family risk data underscore the need for a social policy response that is purposeful, comprehensive, and immediate. To meet this challenge, educational institutions, together with other social and human service agencies, must rethink their approach to serving children and families at risk.

The Annie E. Casey Foundation, in partnership with a

group of urban school systems, is preparing a long-term initiative that promotes the comprehensive reform of selected large-city school systems. This effort will build on lessons from the thirty-year history of educational reform, together with research on human cognition, educational equity, curriculum and instruction, school governance, and other recent innovations in education and related fields. This chapter presents the context for the Casey educational reform initiative by describing how the stress on families living in urban areas has increased in recent years, the general failure of schools to prepare poor and minority students for success in mainstream society, and the strengths and shortcomings of previous attempts to reform schools serving large populations of disadvantaged children. The final section of the chapter lays out the guiding questions that will frame the Casey Urban Education Reform Initiative designed to advance the comprehensive reform of school systems with the overall goal of improving outcomes for disadvantaged students.

The Changing Face of Poverty in America's Cities

In today's society, the probability of being raised in a poor family is significantly greater for children living in single-parent households and for children in African American and Latino families. The growing nexus between child poverty, single-parent households, and minority status is a by-product of social and economic forces that have wrenched the structure of American families over the past thirty years. This period has witnessed a doubling of the divorce rate, which in turn has spawned both an increase in the number of children living with a single parent and a drop in the standard of living for families led by women recently divorced (Marshall and Tucker, 1992). During the same time span, the strength of American families has been weakened by economic restructuring and a series of recessions that have heightened the level and duration of unemployment among men (especially young adults between the ages of eighteen and twenty-four) and placed marriage and the formation of a family beyond the reach of many young men and women (Jencks, 1992; Wilson, 1987).

These economic and social forces have created a sea change in the family experience of children. In 1990, 8.6 million households with children under age eighteen were headed by single parents, an increase of 46 percent since 1980 (Children's Defense Fund, 1985, p. 2). Moreover, a staggering 82 percent of these households (7 million out of 8.6 million) were headed by women. Stated more simply, one in four children in America is now reared in a single-parent family headed by a female (Annie E. Casey Foundation and Center for the Study of Social Policy, 1992). Among African Americans and Hispanics, single-parent families now represent six in ten (African American) and one in three (Hispanic) families with children (Children's Defense Fund, 1985; Annie E. Casey Foundation and Center for Study of Social Policy, 1992).

While many single parents provide healthy, loving environments for their children, all too many struggle financially and emotionally at a time when it takes two incomes for a family to survive. As a consequence, in 1990 the poverty rate for households headed by single women was almost triple that for married-couple families in almost every major racial and ethnic group.

The dramatic rise in family poverty has occurred at a time when there are serious weaknesses in society's safety net, especially for families living in our nation's deteriorating cities. During the latter stages of the nineteenth century and for the first third of this century, poor children and families lived without the social safety net created later by social security, Medicaid, subsidized housing, public assistance, unemployment insurance, child labor laws, and a variety of other supports provided or insured by the federal government. As a result, poor children and their parents were often exposed to harsh and life-threatening working conditions and bound to jobs whose wages made life mean at best. Despite these hardships, the aspirations of many poor families were fulfilled over time by an industrial expansion that produced massive numbers of jobs requiring few skills other than a strong back and a willingness to use it. The industrial revolution, which continued almost unabated into the 1960s, combined with the creation of the first strands of the social safety net (social security, unemployment insurance, Aid to Families with

Dependent Children, Medicaid and Medicare) by the Roosevelt and Johnson administrations, helped reduce the harmful effects of poverty on children and families and shorten its duration.

Poor children and families in today's cities face social and economic conditions that are comparatively bleak. An exodus of businesses and middle-class families from the nation's cities has increased the levels and concentration of urban poverty, particularly among children. During the 1980s child poverty rose in 84 of the 100 largest cities in the United States (Ascher and Burnett, 1993). The loss of businesses and jobs in urban areas, however, has not stemmed the tide of immigration. America's cities continue to attract immigrants from around the globe, though the vast majority of new immigrants come from Latin America, Asia, Africa, and the Caribbean as opposed to Europe (Ascher and Burnett, 1993). This shift has created a cultural brew that has engendered new conflicts over language, religion, and behavioral norms along with heightened competition for a diminishing pool of jobs and services.

The restructuring of America's businesses and their migration, along with middle-class and white families to the suburbs, then, has left poor families in our nation's cities without the economic, social, and educational means needed to combat poverty, crime, and shrinking job markets. Such changes demand a fundamental rethinking of the purpose of schools in the lives of children and of how schools connect with other community agencies with whom they share the essential purpose of preserving the vitality and well-being of families. Unfortunately, recent descriptions of conditions in urban schools indicate that they have not grasped the challenge for change.

The Condition of Public Education in Urban America

By and large, urban schools are failing to bolster the achievement of poor students, a fact that undermines the well-being of disadvantaged families and the development of the cities themselves. Urban educational systems are characterized by large central bureaucracies that stymie innovation and flexibility, inadequate budgets that have been slashed dramatically over the past five years, union contracts that place rigid restrictions on the roles and assignment of teachers and other school personnel, curricula and instructional strategies that limit learning opportunities for students who desperately need them, and student performance that falls well short of new standards (Carnegie Foundation for the Advancement of Teaching, 1988; Hill, 1993).

The problems plaguing urban schools are seen most directly in the performance of students who attend them. Many big-city high schools are beset by four-year dropout rates that exceed 40 percent (U.S. Department of Education, 1988), while those who remain in school often perform well below established norms represented by grades, promotion rates, and test results. Much of the data on achievement in urban schools, though discouraging, actually masks the true extent of students' deficiencies because letter grades and numerical test scores obscure what students can actually accomplish. The exception to this general rule lies in the results from the National Assessment of Educational Progress (NAEP).

NAEP data paint a distressing picture because they indicate that, on average, poor and minority children are failing to acquire the very skills needed to succeed in the emerging economy. These "new age" skills place a premium on oral and written communication, critical thinking and problem solving, and advanced expertise in mathematics, science, and technology (Commission on Skills of the American Workforce, 1990; Marshall and Tucker, 1992). The NAEP performance of poor and minority youth reveals that they are being educated for basic skills jobs that are fast becoming extinct, a trend that will only hasten the demise of urban communities and heighten the poverty, social conflicts, and violence that threaten to rend our cities.

While the minority student achievement gaps revealed in NAEP surveys and other test results are often attributed to social and economic forces beyond the control of schools, there is substantial evidence that schools help produce the gaps they decry by treating poor and minority students differently from others. In comparison to students from advantaged and white families, for instance, poor and minority students:

- Take fewer advanced mathematics courses such as algebra and geometry (American Association for the Advancement of Science, 1984; Pelavin and Kane, 1991)
- Are retained in grade more frequently
- Are taught using outmoded instructional strategies and materials that emphasize basic skills (Cole, Griffin, and Laboratory of Comparative Human Cognition, 1987)
- Have less access to technology and software applications that support critical thinking, problem solving, and extended learning activities (Simmons, 1985)
- Drop out of school earlier and in greater numbers
- Receive lower grades and report receiving less counseling (National Research Council, 1989)
- Are overrepresented in low-ability groups and curricular tracks (Wheelock, 1992)

Despite abundant evidence of the harmful effects of practices like tracking and ability grouping, these approaches continue to flourish in urban schools due to centralized bureaucracies that resist change and because of political pressures brought by parents whose children are well served by the current system. Students in advanced academic groups tend to outperform students in other groups and have parents who are better off economically, more knowledgeable about schooling, and more powerful politically. Attempts to alter programs for gifted and talented students or to adopt more heterogeneous forms of grouping often spark fierce opposition from middle-class and affluent parents whom school boards are loathe to cross because of their political clout and the threat that they will send their children to private schools. Practices such as tracking and ability grouping, then, get preserved by virtue of tradition and efforts to appease middle-class parents who have the option to remove their children from the public schools.

The continued existence of questionable school practices, such as tracking, is also reinforced by the zero-sum mentality regarding school finances. Chronic underfunding of schools has led parents and entire communities to fight for resources for individual schools and programs rather than systems as a whole. This pattern has pitted magnet schools against neighborhood schools, advanced placement courses against general ones, dropout prevention and special education programs against mainstream classes, and bilingual education against Chapter 1 programs (Simmons and Grady, 1990). The bevy of suits against states for school funding inequities, however, offers some hope that the battle for adequate school resources will be broadened in the future to encompass districts and states and thus reduce rivalries between individual schools and communities (Odden, 1991). The recent attention given school funding has also fostered a new emphasis on standards for student learning and for instructional opportunities that guarantee that each child will meet them. School reforms pursued in Kentucky and plans being developed in Alabama, New Jersey, Texas, and Michigan bear watching to see if reforms driven by a set of high standards will address the needs of all students or be bent by political pressures brought by parents and communities threatened by change.

While litigation focused on school funding inequities promises to direct more attention to outcomes, school restructuring, and the equitable allocation of resources, the impact of these initiatives on disadvantaged children rests on a better understanding of the academic and nonacademic scaffolds these students require to succeed in school and in life. With the exception of the Kentucky reforms, most national and state reform efforts have given more thought to defining academic outcomes than to considering the strategies and resources needed to help disadvantaged students attain them. Even less thought has been given to the nature and levels of supports needed to achieve nonacademic outcomes. Tremendous controversies surrounding issues such as sex education, sexual orientation, teen pregnancy and parenting, multicultural education, ethical citizenship, and the place of religion in schools have caused many state and local education officials to defer or avoid efforts to address these concerns. Recent statistics on pregnancy, alcohol and drug use, and crime and violence among our nation's youth, however, indicate that these problems will not disappear of their own accord (Annie E. Casey Foundation and Center for the Study of Social Policy, 1992; National Commission on Children and Families, 1991). Schools must fashion strategies for attaining public support to help children develop socially as well as academically. School reforms that ignore the nonacademic needs of students have little chance to succeed, particularly where disadvantaged students are concerned.

Part of the challenge of any significant investment in education reform such as that proposed by Casey is to heed the lessons of previous attempts to improve schools, many of which failed to achieve their original aims. In addition to awareness of the lessons of history, renewed efforts to improve schools serving large populations of poor children must be grounded both in the best available knowledge about teaching, learning, and the nature of families, schools and communities to promote success for disadvantaged children. The Casey educational reform initiative will be grounded in lessons from recent attempts to reform urban schools and in evidence of effective practice from educational research, both of which are treated in the following section.

Recent Waves of Educational Reform

Educational reforms enacted over the past thirty years have taught us a great deal about the academic needs of students but precious little about factors influencing successful psychosocial development of children and youth. This disparity in focus and knowledge results from the tendency historically to view school achievement as a derivative of general ability, which, in turn, has been viewed as determined by some combination of "nature and nurture." The ability ethic has led to educational reforms that stressed cognitive and/or academic outcomes over social ones. Even when factors such as early child care and nutrition have been considered, their significance has usually been linked to their impact on cognitive rather than social development (Hunt, 1961).

Compensatory Education Programs

Two of the earliest efforts to improve the education of disadvantaged students were founded in the mid 1960s when Congress authorized the Head Start program and Title I of the Elementary and Secondary Education Act (ESEA). Both programs sought to break the link between poverty and low student achievement by providing supplemental assistance to children from disadvantaged families. Head Start and Title I—which subsequently became Chapter 1—were fueled by research suggesting that the school success of low-income children was undermined by cognitive and biological deficiencies that appear early in life (for example, Bronfenbrenner, 1979; Wachs, Uzgiris, and Hunt, 1971; Zigler, 1970). Head Start sought to remedy this problem by providing comprehensive services—including nutrition and health care as well as early preschool education—to low-income children. By contrast, Title I/Chapter 1 limited its attention to providing supplemental academic assistance to poor students in kindergarten through grade twelve who were diagnosed as at risk of failing in school. Despite the K–12 scope of the program, most schools continue to concentrate their Chapter 1 resources at the elementary level in keeping with the "critical period" notion spawned by the early childhood research.

As with most compensatory education programs authorized by the ESEA, Head Start and Title I/Chapter 1 have traditionally sought to change the learner—as opposed to the school—as the primary strategy for narrowing achievement gaps between advantaged and disadvantaged students. This approach is typical of programs initiated during the early 1960s, when research pointed to early cultural and/or cognitive deficits as the major source of low achievement on the part of poor and minority children (Ginsberg, 1972; Silverstein and Krate, 1975; Simmons, 1979). Consequently, many educators and researchers failed to consider how teacher, classroom, and school characteristics might contribute to the deficits in question.

The Cultural Difference Model

In the early 1970s, social scientists such as Michael Cole (Cole, Gay, Glick, and Sharp, 1971), Edmund Gordon (1970), and Joan Baratz (Baratz and Baratz, 1970) began to argue that group differences in school performance owed more to mismatches between the cultural and school experiences of certain groups than to purported cognitive or cultural deficits. This line of reasoning suggested that the academic problems encountered by poor and minority students were heightened by schools that were ill equipped to educate students from subcultural groups. These arguments broadened the focus of school reform to include an examination of the characteristics of teachers, classrooms, materials (texts and tests), and schools, and inspired efforts to create culturally appropriate curricula, assessments, and methods of instruction—though rarely were these adopted on a broad scale (Hilliard, 1991; Tharp, 1982).

Back to the Basics

By the late 1970s, education innovations initiated early in the decade were being linked to growing rates of youth and adult illiteracy (Hunter and Harman, 1979) and a steady decline in Scholastic Aptitude Test results. This alarm marshaled in another wave of school reform, whose manifesto was outlined in *A Nation at Risk*—the report issued by the National Commission on Excellence in Education (1983). The commission sought to define a "new" basics or core curriculum as a remedy for the declining performance of American students. Unfortunately, their description of the "new basics" was clearer about time requirements than about the content of learning. For example, the commission called for the completion of four years of English, three years of mathematics, three years of science, three years of social studies, and one-half year of computer science in high school and argued for schools to adopt a seven-hour day and a 200- to 250-day school year. In addition to being vague about content, the commission also skirted how equity might be defined and achieved.

Creating Effective Schools

As states and school districts began to tighten graduation requirements and underscore the importance of basic skills, an influential set of studies by the late Ron Edmunds and his colleagues (Edmonds, 1979) brought attention to the features of schools where disadvantaged children experienced success. Edmunds's work was a rejoinder to Coleman's findings questioning the potential of schools to overcome the effects of poverty on disadvantaged children. Edmunds illuminated several characteristics of successful schools that became benchmarks for the effective schools movement. These characteristics generally included instructional leadership from principals, safe and orderly environments, parent involvement, regular monitoring of student performance, high expectations for students, and a rich, challenging curriculum. The effective schools movement helped educators remain focused on school change at a time when governors, presidents, business leaders, and legislators were becoming intrigued by policies aimed at systemic reform. On the down side, proponents of effective schools contributed to the lack of clarity about curriculum and instruction by highlighting the process of school change more than its content. Moreover, the effective schools model showed a surprising disregard for the role of administrators and policy makers beyond the school principal—that is, school boards, superintendents, and the central office administration. A vestige of this shortcoming is exemplified by the number of districts that have implemented school-based management without redefining the role of the central office (Bryk, 1993).

Fixing the System

In the years following *A Nation at Risk,* several reports issued calls for broad reforms in education that would benefit poor and minority students. These reports usually couched school failure as a threat to the nation's economy (Commission on Minority Participation in Education and American Life, 1988; Carnegie Foundation for the Advancement of Teaching, 1988; Commission on Skills of the American Workforce, 1990). This was a questionable strategy given the short-lived economic expansion that occurred during the 1980s, but one that was, nonetheless, designed to mobilize important segments of the population, including the business and political community at the national and state levels. These reports frequently called for a national educational reform strategy that would unify efforts to transform schools across the nation.

The major underpinnings for a national educational re-

form movement were in fact created by the six national education goals set at the 1989 Education Summit involving former
President Bush and the nation's governors. The summit also produced a consensus about the broad goals of school restructuring—that is, obtaining "fundamental changes in expectations for
student learning, in the practice of teaching, and in the organization and management of public schools" (Elmore, 1990). Subsequently, educators, business leaders, legislators, community
leaders, and advocates have addressed issues as diverse as decentralized decision making, school-linked services, alternative methods of assessment, curriculum standards, school finance equity,
high-performance management, and public engagement—all
under the all-purpose rubric of school restructuring.

Goals 2000/Educate America Act

Although much of the initial work and thinking about standards
and assessments occurred under the Bush administration, this
orientation has also been a key part of the Clinton administration's educational reform strategy. This administration's Goals
2000 Bill would authorize the national education goals and the
Goals Panel, which would establish a council to coordinate and
certify the development of voluntary standards and assessments;
create a national board to oversee the development and certification of occupational skills standards; and provide funds for
state restructuring efforts aligned with new outcomes. New standards and forms of assessment are also a central component of
the administration's proposal for the Reauthorization of Title I,
which reflects (with regard to Chapter 1) the recommendations
of the Commission on Chapter 1 (1992).

New standards, assessment, and work readiness, however,
do not comprise the whole of the school restructuring agenda.
Over thirty-five states are grappling with the complex issue of
school finance equity as a result of legal and/or legislative challenges to existing state education funding formulas. On average,
states provide about 45 percent of the funding for local school
districts with the federal government contributing approximately 7 percent (Odden, 1991). Most states allocate funds to counties, which in turn distribute them to school districts on the basis

of complex formulas that consider local enrollment, local tax base, and local tax burden, among other factors. These funding formulas traditionally have slighted urban and poor communities, which ordinarily must tax businesses and individual property owners at a much higher rate to compensate for properties that usually have lower assessed values. Urban-suburban-rural differences in assessed property values and tax burdens have fostered gross inequities in school funding that have led many states—such as Kentucky, Michigan, and New Jersey—to search for more equitable ways to finance schools.

In places like Kentucky and Alabama, efforts to create a more equitable basis for school funding have led policy makers to redesign entire state educational systems. This process has generally resulted in the devolution of authority and decision making from state and local school districts to individual schools and communities. Operating under the broad headings of school-based management or school-community empowerment, many states and districts have transferred greater responsibility for budgeting, staffing, curriculum, and other aspects of schooling to school councils composed of teachers, administrators, parents, and members of the wider community. The creation of local school councils in Chicago represents the latest and most widely publicized attempt on the part of districts to radically change the ways schools are governed (Bryk, 1993).

But with the exception of Kentucky, a recurring flaw in national and state school restructuring activities is the paucity of detailed discussion about the needs of disadvantaged children and how they will be served by new standards, new forms of assessment, and new forms of school governance. How, in fact, does decentralized decision making address the needs of poor and minority children when school communities begin at different points with respect to the quality of school buildings and school personnel, and the amount of knowledge and other resources parents and community members possess related to teaching and learning? Will schools serving students who require educational, health, and other human services receive more resources than those serving students with fewer needs? Given the high mobility rates of students in many school systems, how will districts ensure that equity exists across schools in the areas of curriculum, student assessment, and placement? And finally, how will districts prevent local community politics and cultural conflicts from impinging on decisions made in individual schools? One is hard pressed to even find these questions posed—no less answered—in existing debates about school restructuring at the national and state levels.

One source of this shortcoming lies with the composition of the groups that have shaped the national and state restructuring agenda. Many of these groups have been led by the federal department of education, governors, chief state school officers, and business leaders who, though concerned about equity, are more inclined to look at the whole of the educational system rather than at a critical and underserved component or constituency. Traditional advocates for equity and the needs of the disadvantaged (for example, the Children's Defense Fund, the Mexican American Legal Defense Fund, the National Association for the Advancement of Colored People, the National Council of La Raza, the Urban League, and so on) have played a limited role in these discussions, in part because of their tendency to treat school funding as the primary impediment to success. As a result, the national and state restructuring agenda has been formed without much involvement from the advocates and groups most concerned with disadvantaged children.

In contrast, the urban school reform movement has focused largely on issues such as school desegregation, violence reduction, increased funding, dropout prevention, multicultural education, alcohol and drug abuse prevention, sex education, and expanded human services, which, though critical, often sidestep the need for comprehensive systemic reform. Urban schools typically take a program-based approach to problems like high dropout rates and alcohol and drug abuse prevention that results in new programs that compete with old ones for scarce resources. While the national and state restructuring agenda needs to speak louder and more directly to the circumstances of urban schools and the needs of disadvantaged students, urban schools must recognize that in addition to fighting for more resources, they must transform the way they do business.

Urban school reform efforts must become more and more grounded in basic and applied research highlighting effective practice for disadvantaged students. In addition, national/state and urban policy makers must find ways to integrate their respective reform agendas to avoid working at cross-purposes.

Fortunately, the foundation for building an integrated and research-based reform agenda lies in the experiences and achievements of school reform networks such as the Coalition of Essential Schools, the Accelerated Schools Program, the Performance Assessment Collaborative for Education (PACE), Project Zero, the Kamehameha Early Education Program (KEEP), the Comer School Development Program, the National Alliance for Restructuring Education, and Quasar, to name a few. Without exception, these school reform networks use approaches that place students and their experiences at the center of learning activities. For example, learning activities used by schools in Project Zero and KEEP address curricular outcomes by involving students in tasks that make connections between students' knowledge and experiences and the skills and content emphasized in school curricula. In addition, these networks usually engage students in tasks that integrate reading, writing, mathematics, and science; require students to formulate their own solutions; depend on primary materials (as opposed to textbooks); and require students to attend to the process as well as the product of their work. This new, constructive approach to learning represents a fundamental departure from traditional teacher- and textbook-centered school practices that stress products over processes, emphasize a single correct response, and place students in a passive role as learners. Moreover, this constructive approach reflects the influence of cognitive science, which has demonstrated that competence is context specific—for example, linked to specific knowledge, activities, and experiences (Laboratory of Comparative Human Cognition, 1988).

Psychologists, anthropologists, and other social scientists who defy easy description have shown that there are sharp differences between the way learning and performance occurs in school as compared to community and work settings (Cole, Gay,

Glick, and Sharp, 1971; Simmons, 1985). In school, teachers and textbooks define tasks and limit the resources and strategies students use in their work. Unlike schoolwork, tasks found in the community and workplace are usually more open ended—allowing individuals to use multiple resources and strategies, to work alone and/or in groups, and to choose the best solution from an array of correct responses. These contrasts between school and nonschool tasks have led many business leaders and social scientists to conclude that schools must incorporate more "authentic" learning activities to heighten students' interest and to prepare them for the cognitive demands of life outside the classroom (Marshall and Tucker, 1992; Resnick and Resnick, 1989; Lave, 1984; Laboratory of Comparative Human Cognition, 1988). As a result, educators are paying more attention to helping students understand how skills and knowledge learned as part of academic tasks are germane to real-life problems and situations. The attention being paid to applying academic skills to "real" tasks and problems has also led educators to develop more authentic forms of assessments. The significance of contextual relevance or specificity also undergirds the attention devoted to authentic assessment in many of the school reform networks.

Cooperative or Collaborative Learning

Cooperative or collaborative learning, heterogeneous grouping, and other alternative forms of instruction represent another set of strategies employed by many school reform networks. Despite research showing the positive benefits of cooperative learning and heterogeneous grouping—particularly for low- and moderate-achieving students (Slavin, 1987)—widespread adoption of these practices is often opposed by parents of advanced students seeking to preserve gifted and talented classes and other programs that group students by ability. Thus, the adoption of alternative forms of grouping has political as well as educational overtones. Notwithstanding the politics of this issue, which often pit different social-class and ethnic groups against each other, school reform networks such as the

Accelerated Schools Program and the Coalition manage to make cooperative learning and heterogeneous grouping central to their work.

Factors Outside of School
One of the most powerful barriers to school reform is the belief that the achievement problems of poor and minority students are largely caused by factors outside the school. While many students in urban schools come to school hungry, suffering from emotional and/or physical abuse, having severe health problems, and facing homelessness and despair, the school networks that are the subject of this section seek to address these problems by promoting collaboration among health and other human service agencies to provide medical care, counseling, job training, housing assistance, and other services in a coordinated manner. Led by the Casey Foundation's New Futures Initiative, these evolving collaborations have sparked a movement to integrate human services and link them to institutions, such as schools, that have the greatest access to families (see Schorr, 1988, for a description of exemplary programs).

Parental and Community Involvement
Many of the school networks have also developed more effective ways to involve parents and the broader community in the work of the school and, most important, its students. The Comer School Development Program has led the way in developing a model that fuses the integrated service approach with strategies that enhance parental involvement in schools. The Comer program focuses attention on the social, emotional, and cognitive/linguistic needs of children, and establishes school teams that enable parents, teachers, principals, psychologists, and other human service providers to collaborate in the design and delivery of school programs and student/family/community supports (Anson and others, 1991). Thus far, the program has been used by schools serving disadvantaged children in ten school districts and has resulted in significant improvements in school-community relations and student involvement in school. While there is some evidence that School Development has had a pos-

itive impact on student achievement, important research on this specific question continues (Haynes, 1993).

Professional Development

This section on the cornerstones of successful school reform networks would not be complete without discussing the need for sustained and targeted professional development. Each of the school reform networks mentioned makes a significant and sustained investment in the professional development of teachers and administrators. Most of the networks convene teachers at the school, regional, and national levels and employ strategies that result in teachers themselves becoming technical assistance providers. Moreover, each network emphasizes professional development that is tied directly to concerns emanating from the classroom and that results in the development of tools and approaches relevant to the classroom. Finally, teachers in these networks often work in local teams that provide a ready source of support and ideas on an ongoing basis.

General Accomplishments of School Reform Networks

These urban school reform networks have produced a cohort of flagship schools that are archetypes of practice for disadvantaged children, and increasingly, the researchers and educators involved in these efforts provide leadership and technical assistance to schools and school districts committed to reform. Why, then, aren't more schools and school districts in urban areas following their lead? While providing models for change at the school level, these same initiatives have been less successful and concerned with bringing about comprehensive reform at the central office or district level. The restricted scope of the school reform networks is due partly to limited resources and skepticism about the willingness and capacity of central offices, superintendents, and school boards to change on a large scale. At the district level, the schools involved in reform networks often become reform ornaments attached to a larger system that remains unaltered. This trend must change if urban school systems hope to survive pressures for vouchers and the dismantling of public education. Given what we know about effective practice for poor and minority students, urban school systems must take a comprehensive approach to transforming schools on the scale required to affect the vast majority of schools and students. The Annie E. Casey Foundation's Urban Education Reform Initiative seeks to advance efforts in urban communities and school systems with large concentrations of disadvantaged students that are committed to this type of reform. The final section of this chapter describes the core principles of the initiative and the strategies underlying its design and implementation.

Core Principles and Guiding Questions of the Casey Education Reform Agenda

In sum, local and state educators must learn to use lessons of the school reform networks and related knowledge to create urban school systems where the vast majority of schools and students function at high levels. We believe that this transformation will occur when school districts and entire communities become leaders of reform rather than participants in efforts designed and led by policy-making organizations and university-based groups. For school districts to become the center of the reform movement, they must move beyond the project or program stage to school change that encompasses much of what goes on in the name of school restructuring. To maximize the ability of schools to help students and families fulfill their educational aspirations, school systems should not seek solutions in new programs but should reexamine their existing approaches to school governance and finance; curriculum, instruction, and family support; personnel hiring and placement; professional development; information use and management; and public engagement. In our view, the bottom-up approach to school reform taken by many of the school reform networks must be complemented by central office and school board reforms that extend and support successful innovations to all schools.

While school districts must take more leadership and responsibility in bringing about these changes, they cannot and should not work in isolation. Alliances between schools, businesses, higher education, think tanks, community groups, and government agencies are essential for school systems to acquire the expertise and resources needed to make significant change. But in our judgment, alliances driven primarily by universities and think tanks—rather than schools and communities—do little to engender the ownership and commitment needed to make the far-reaching changes necessary. To the contrary, restructuring efforts led by university groups and nonprofit organizations usually end with the last grant dollar and often fail to transform school systems in fundamental ways.

The Annie E. Casey Foundation believes that alliances of schools, communities, and outside agents can alter the direction and outcomes of urban schools when the community and school system play a leading rather than supporting role in seeking comprehensive educational reform. The foundation is committed to aiding this kind of effort and is establishing a multiyear Urban Education Reform Initiative to enhance the achievement of all students—but particularly those from disadvantaged families and communities.

Conceptual Questions Framing the Initiative

We believe the foundation's principles cross at least five streams of concern: school governance; curriculum, pedagogy, and assessment; family support; public awareness and engagement; and capacity building.

School Governance. Historically, education has been a state and local concern, with the federal government providing targeted support for special populations such as the educationally disadvantaged. Many states organize schools in districts that, for the most part, coincide with town, county, or city boundaries and that are governed chiefly by elected or appointed school boards. On paper, most school boards set broad policies concerning curriculum, instruction, staff compensation, and the allocation of funds for these matters—policies then carried out by superintendents and central office administration. This process places school-based staff in the position of front-line workers who have little control over the content and resources they must use to advance student achievement. Following the lead of high-performance companies in business, many school districts have begun to place more authority and responsibility for decision making into the hands of school-based staff who, like the front-line workers in industry, are closest to the work that counts, which in education means teaching and learning. But devolving responsibility and authority to schools through decentralization means that boards of education and their central offices must be restructured along with individual schools in order to support local school improvement. Thus far, more attention has been given to the latter than the former. Given this shortcoming, the foundation is particularly interested in advancing efforts that think seriously about how the governance of schools might be changed to facilitate decentralization while ensuring accountability and support for achieving equity and excellence. We are interested in communities willing to pursue answers to questions like the following:

- How should the role of school boards change to make decentralization work to achieve the ends of both equity and excellence, and what kinds of training and support should school board members receive to carry out these new roles?
- What is the appropriate role of the central office in a decentralized system and how should the central administration be redesigned to give technical assistance and support to local schools while monitoring their progress in maintaining high standards and equity along with other systemwide criteria?
- How much and what kinds of training do school-based planning teams or local school councils require to make informed decisions about curriculum, instruction, community relations, and the use of fiscal and human resources?
- How much flexibility should schools have in determining curriculum, instruction, staffing, and school organization in light of local, state, and federal guidelines concerning curriculum or content standards, the length of the school

year, specific graduation requirements, teacher certification criteria, school desegregation agreements, Chapter 1
guidelines, and other external mandates?
*   What does decentralization in large urban school districts
    augur for the role and function of state departments of
    education?
*   What kinds of support and technical assistance should
    states offer to support comprehensive reform at the local
    level—particularly in large central city school districts that
    have not typically looked to the state for help?

Curriculum, Pedagogy, and Assessment. Out of necessity, the mission of many urban schools has been broadened to include alcohol and drug abuse prevention, violence prevention, parenting
skills, and pregnancy prevention. Teaching and learning, however, continue to be the core of an expanded mission—a core
that is being transformed as a changing society and world place
greater demands on students. These new demands are being
articulated in curriculum standards that are playing a prominent
role in the approach that many states and the federal government are taking to school reform. In essence, schools are being
given more authority and flexibility in exchange for their adherence to common standards influenced by business groups, disciplinary organizations, and communities themselves. Urban
schools face the difficult challenge of developing a core set of
standards that are both rich and challenging and reflect concerns for diversity expressed by the various cultural communities they serve. Comprehensive reform in urban schools, then,
must resolve student and school outcome issues that reside in
the following questions:

*   How can school districts and communities ensure that
    comprehensive reform is guided, first and foremost, by the
    need to enhance teaching and learning in the classroom to
    improve student outcomes?
*   How can the community be organized to reach a consen-
    sus about standards for student and school performance
    that reflect concerns for equity and excellence?

- How much leeway should individual schools and communities have to develop curricula in light of pressure for national, state, and local standards aligned with demands for global competitiveness?
- What is the range and best mix of tools (for example, assessments, information management systems, school/district report cards, public campaigns, and so on) needed to satisfy national, state, district, and school-building requirements for coherent information about student and school progress in a restructured system?
- How can professional development be provided to teachers, administrators, and others in a manner that honors individual school priorities, yet is consistent with systemwide goals and standards?
- What combination of resources and incentives should districts produce to ensure that schools with large concentrations of disadvantaged students obtain the support they need (for example, professional development, qualified teachers and counselors, school-linked services) to ensure success for the vast majority of their students?

Family Support. Both research and experience tell us that comprehensive reforms that improve outcomes for disadvantaged children work best when support is also provided for their families and communities. Although educators cannot do this work alone, schools can become a powerful lever for strengthening families and communities when allied with other human service providers and community groups. These types of alliances have traditionally been difficult to establish because of limited conceptions of parental and community involvement mixed with the existence of organizational cultures that target individuals and discourage collaboration. Comprehensive reform in urban school districts provides a window for creating a family-focused agenda that fosters collaboration within and between communities and agencies that impact the welfare of disadvantaged children and families (health, child welfare, juvenile justice, housing, employment, and so on). The groundwork for this agenda, in our view, lies in the response to the following questions:

- What kinds of groups should school systems and/or communities establish to plan and collaborate across agencies and communities to provide support for families that results in improved school achievement for disadvantaged students?
- Whose involvement is essential to the successful development and implementation of plans that bring the resources of schools and other human service providers to bear on the needs of families and communities?
- What kinds of information and expertise do collaborative efforts require to build and manage a system of family-focused services?
- How must policies governing eligibility criteria, the allocation of funds and other resources (equipment, space, time, and so on), personnel use and training, and public accountability be changed to facilitate collaborative planning and service linkage that is family focused?
- What unique roles and functions can school-based and central office staff play in this process?
- What conditions make schools, community groups, or other agencies the best anchors for school-linked or integrated services?
- What types of training and support do school staff and other service professionals require to work in a collaborative and sustained fashion?

Public Awareness and Engagement. Several surveys have reported that the public maintains conflicting beliefs about the need for school reform. People appear to be deeply troubled about the quality of school systems, while believing that their local school is just fine. This finding suggests that urban leaders have a good deal of work to do to convince the public that comprehensive reform is in the best interests of all students, not just those that are advantaged or disadvantaged. Raising the public's awareness of and support for comprehensive urban education reform requires a willingness on the part of educators to listen as well as talk, and to follow as well as lead. Urban educators must develop strategies and tools that allow them to discern the answers to the following questions:

- What are the public's views about the strengths and weaknesses of urban schools and school systems?
- What sources and types of information does the public use to make judgments about the quality of individual schools and the system as a whole?
- In the public's view, what roles should schools play in the lives of families and communities?
- What differences, if any, exist between the public's views about the need for and nature of new standards versus those held by states and national organizations, and where differences exist, how can they be reconciled?
- What is the public's level of understanding of and support for various elements of reform (such as new forms of school governance, enhanced curriculum standards and pedagogy, family-focused and school-linked services, intensive and sustained professional development, increased resources for schools, new roles for central office and school-based staff, and so on), and how can their support and understanding be strengthened and marshaled?

Capacity Building. The success of even the most thoughtful plans for comprehensive reform relies on the capacity of those charged with its implementation to carry it out successfully. The education world is rife with excellent plans that fall short of expectations because of a lack of experience or buy-in on the part of school and central office staff. Despite this fact, professional development and other aspects of capacity building are among the most underdeveloped components of the reform movement. States and school districts continue to build complex reform on a foundation of fragmented one-day workshops for educators that provide little time for reflection, planning, and practice. Somehow, our notions about how to promote learning for children—that they should be actively engaged, have time for reflection, and solve problems based on authentic tasks and materials—have not been extended to how we treat the adults who are expected to create these new kinds of learning opportunities. In most school districts, classroom teachers play a minimal role in planning and delivering professional development, or in developing the knowledge base that extends our understanding of teaching and learning. The professionalization of teachers, a critical element of school reform, will remain a distant goal as long as professional development remains the purview of outside experts.

School districts that are serious about comprehensive reform, then, must find ways to build the capacity of school and central office staff, parents, and members of the broader community to understand and actively participate in the school restructuring. The foundation believes that effective professional development and other forms of capacity building should follow a set of principles presented in a paper by Judith Warren Little (Little and McLaughlin, 1992, pp. 5–6):

1. Professional development should offer meaningful intellectual, social, and emotional engagement with ideas, with materials, and with colleagues both in and out of teaching.
2. Professional development should incorporate an explicit historical and contextual sensitivity: a means of locating new ideas in relation to individual and institutional histories, practices, and circumstances.
3. Professional development should offer support for principled and informed dissent.
4. Professional development should be grounded in a "big picture" perspective on the purposes and practices of schooling, and should provide a means of seeing and acting upon the connections among students' experiences, teachers' classroom practice, and school-wide structures and cultures.
5. Professional development should prepare teachers (as well as students and parents) to employ the techniques and perspectives of inquiry.

6. The governance of professional development should
    ensure bureaucratic restraint and a balance between the
    interests of individuals and the interests of institutions.

    We believe that capacity-building activities that follow
these principles can yield the kinds of expertise and ownership
needed to take comprehensive reform from paper to practice.
But while these principles provide sound directions, they still
leave several questions unaddressed:

-   How should school systems change their current profes-
    sional development paradigms to encourage the active
    involvement and participation of teachers and other pro-
    fessionals in the construction and delivery of knowledge
    and information relevant to the goals of reform?
-   How can schools and school systems work to build the capac-
    ity of parents and other community members to understand
    and participate in comprehensive educational reform?
-   How can the organization of the school day and year be
    altered to give teachers and other educators more time for
    planning, reflection, and practice?
-   What can schools and school systems do to create more
    coherence and balance between the professional develop-
    ment interests of individual schools/communities with
    those associated with systemwide goals and priorities?
-   What new strategies and technologies might be used to
    deliver professional development on time—as problems or
    questions arise during the course of classroom activity—
    and in a sustained manner?
-   How can resources in the community (for example, local
    businesses, colleges and universities, government agencies,
    community groups, and so on) be used as resources for
    professional development?
-   What role can states play to promote professional develop-
    ment that mirrors Little's principles and serves the aims of
    state and district priorities?
-   What lessons can we learn from the professional develop-
    ment activities of successful school reform networks?

Conclusion

The Annie E. Casey Foundation seeks to advance comprehensive educational reform efforts in several urban communities that serve large concentrations of disadvantaged students. While mindful that school restructuring must be grounded in the needs and aspirations of the community, we are also committed to supporting reforms that are consistent with the foundation's mission and principles and that address major questions having to do with school governance; curriculum, pedagogy, and assessment; family support; public awareness and engagement; and capacity building.

Much of the past thirty-five years in the history of American education has been characterized by the development of models of school improvement or reform by, for the most part, university researchers, government agencies, or private firms. These approaches, which have been mounted, tested, and proven effective in selected schools throughout the country, have aimed to enhance school instruction, curriculum, governance, assessment, parent involvement, and professional development. The purpose of the Casey Urban Education Reform Initiative is to challenge participating school districts to draw on the reservoir of existing knowledge about effective practice to design and embrace a strategy that raises the achievement of all the system's schools—with a special focus on the needs of the community's most disadvantaged children, youth, and families.

References

American Association for the Advancement of Science. *Equity and Excellence: Compatible Goals.* Washington, D.C.: American Association for the Advancement of Science, 1984.

Annie E. Casey Foundation and Center for the Study of Social Policy. *Kids Count Data Book: State Profiles of Child Well-Being.* Washington, D.C.: Center for the Study of Social Policy, 1992.

Anson, A., and others. "The Comer School Development Program: A Theoretical Analysis." *Urban Education,* 1991, *26*(1), 56–82.

Ascher, C., and Burnett, G. *Current Trends and Issues in Urban Education.* New York: Clearinghouse on Urban Education, Teachers College, Columbia University, 1993.

Baratz, S. S., and Baratz, J. S. "Early Childhood Intervention: The Social Science Base of Institutional Racism." *Harvard Educational Review,* 1970, *40,* 29–50.

Bronfenbrenner, U. *The Ecology of Human Development.* Cambridge, Mass.: Harvard University Press, 1979.

Bryk, A. *A View from the Elementary School: The State of Reform in Chicago.* Chicago: Consortium on Chicago School Reform, 1993.

Carnegie Foundation for the Advancement of Teaching. *An Imperiled Generation: Saving Urban Schools.* Lawrenceville, N.J.: Princeton University Press, 1988.

Children's Defense Fund. *Black and White Children in America.* Washington, D.C.: Children's Defense Fund, 1985.

Cole, M., Gay, J., Glick, J. A., and Sharp, D. W. *The Cultural Context of Learning and Thinking.* New York: Basic Books, 1971.

Cole, M., Griffin, P., and Laboratory of Comparative Human Cognition. *Contextual Factors in Education.* Madison: Wisconsin Center for Education Research, School of Education, University of Wisconsin, 1987.

Commission on Chapter 1. *Making Schools Work for Children in Poverty.* Washington, D.C.: American Association for Higher Education, 1992.

Commission on Minority Participation in Education and American Life. *One-Third of a Nation.* Washington, D.C.: American Council on Education, 1988.

Commission on Skills of the American Workforce. *America's Choice: High Skills or Low Wages.* Rochester, N.Y.: National Center on Education and the Economy, 1990.

Edmunds, R. "Some Schools Work and More Can." *Social Policy,* 1979, *9,* 28–32.

Elmore, R. F. "Toward a Transformation of Public Schooling." In R. F. Elmore and Associates, *Restructuring Schools: The Next Generation of Educational Reform.* San Francisco: Jossey-Bass, 1990.

Gardner, H. *Frames of Mind: The Theory of Multiple Intelligences.* New York: Basic Books, 1985.

Ginsberg, H. *The Myth of the Deprived Child: Poor Children's Intellect and Education.* Englewood Cliffs, N.J.: Prentice Hall, 1972.

Gordon, E. W. "Problems in the Determination of Educability in Populations with Differential Characteristics." In J. Hellmuth (ed.), *Disadvantaged Child.* Vol. 3. New York: Brunner/Mazel, 1970.

Hacker, A. *Two Nations: Black and White, Separate, Hostile, and Unequal.* New York: Charles Scribner's Sons, 1992.

Haynes, N. *The Comer School Development Program: A Summary of Research Findings.* New Haven, Conn.: Yale Child Study Center, 1993.

Heath, S. B. *Ways with Words: Language, Life, and Work in Communities and Classrooms.* Cambridge, England: Cambridge University Press, 1983.

Hill, P. T. *Urban Education.* Santa Monica, Calif.: RAND Institute on Education and Training, 1993.

Hilliard, A. G. *Testing African American Students.* Morristown, N.J.: Aaron Press, 1991.

Hunt, J. McV. *Intelligence and Experience.* New York: Ronald Press, 1961.

Hunter, S., and Harman, D. *Adult Illiteracy in the United States.* New York: Basic Books, 1979.

Jencks, C. *Rethinking Social Policy: Race, Poverty, and the Underclass.* Cambridge, Mass.: Harvard University Press, 1992.

Kozol, J. *Savage Inequalities: Children in America's Schools.* New York: Crown, 1991.

Laboratory of Comparative Human Cognition. *Culture and Intelligence.* New York: Cambridge University Press, 1988.

Lave, J. "Ideology and Disjunctive Practice: Arithmetic in School and Craft Apprenticeship." Unpublished manuscript, University of California at Irvine, 1984.

Lezotte, L. W., and others. *School Learning Climate and Student Achievement: A Social Systems Approach to Increased Student Learning.* Tallahassee, Fla.: National Teacher Corps, Florida State University Foundation, 1980.

Little, J., and McLaughlin, M. (eds.). *Teachers' Work: Individuals, Colleagues, and Contexts.* New York: Teachers College Press, 1993.

Marshall, R., and Tucker, M. *Thinking for a Living: Education and the Wealth of Nations.* New York: Basic Books, 1992.

National Center for Educational Statistics, U.S. Department of Education. *Longitudinal Study: High School and Beyond Survey.* Washington, D.C.: U.S. Government Printing Office, 1988.

National Commission on Children and Families. *Beyond Rhetoric: A New Agenda for Children and Families.* Washington, D.C.: National Commission on Children and Families, 1991.

National Commission on Excellence in Education. *A Nation at Risk.* Washington, D.C.: U.S. Government Printing Office, 1983.

National Research Council. *A Common Destiny: Blacks and American Society.* Washington, D.C.: National Academy Press, 1989.

Oakes, J. *Keeping Track: How Schools Structure Inequality.* New Haven, Conn.: Yale University Press, 1985.

Odden, A. *Education Policy Administration.* Albany: State University of New York Press, 1991.

Pelavin, S. H., and Kane, M. *Changing the Odds: Factors Increasing Access to College.* New York: College Entrance Examination Board, 1991.

Resnick, D. P., and Resnick, L. B. "Varieties of Literacy." In A. E. Barnes and P. N. Stearn (eds.), *Social History and Issues in Human Consciousness: Some Interdisciplinary Connections* (pp. 171–196). New York: New York University Press, 1989.

Schorr, L. B., with Schorr, D. *Within Our Reach: Breaking the Cycle of Disadvantage.* New York: Doubleday, 1988.

Silverstein, B., and Krate, R. *Children of the Dark Ghetto: A Developmental Psychology.* New York: Praeger, 1975.

Simmons, W. "The Effects of the Cultural Salience of Test Materials on Social Class and Ethnic Differences in Cognitive Performance." *Quarterly Newsletter of the Laboratory of Comparative Human Cognition,* 1979, *1*(3), 43–47.

Simmons, W. "Social Class and Ethnic Differences in Cognition: A Cultural Practice Perspective." In S. W. Chipman, J. W. Segal, and R. Glaser (eds.), *Thinking and Learning Skills.* Vol. 2. Hillsdale, N.J.: Erlbaum, 1985.

Simmons, W., and Grady, M. *From Peril to Promise: A Study of the Academic Achievement of African-American Males in the Prince George's County (Maryland) Public Schools.* A report to the Maryland Board of Education, 1990.

Slavin, R. "Making Chapter One Make a Difference." *Phi Delta Kappan,* 1987, *69,* 110–119.

Tharp, R. G. "The Effective Instruction of Comprehension: Results and Description of the Kahehameha Early Education Program." *Reading Research Quarterly,* 1982, *17*(4), 501–527.

Tyack, D. *The One Best System.* Cambridge, Mass.: Harvard University Press, 1974.

Wachs, T. D., Uzgiris, I. E., and Hunt, J. McV. "Cognitive Development in Infants of Different Age Levels and from Different Environmental Backgrounds: An Exploratory Investigation." *Merrill-Palmer Quarterly,* 1971.

Wheelock, A. *Crossing the Tracks: How Untracking Can Save America's Schools.* New York: New Press, 1992.

Wilson, W. J. *The Truly Disadvantaged: The Inner City, the Underclass, and Public Policy.* Chicago: University of Chicago Press, 1987.

Zigler, E. "The Environmental Mystique: Training the Intellect Versus the Development of the Child." *Childhood Education,* 1970, *46,* 402–412.

Chapter 19

Creating a New Kind of Leadership for Campus Diversity

Blandina Cárdenas Ramírez

Over the course of the next several decades, American higher education institutions will be called on to serve an unprecedented configuration of race and culture, gender and age, and individuals with special needs. Moreover, colleges and universities will be required to prepare those they serve to function as professionals and scholars in what may be the most culturally and racially complex society since the creation of the modern nation state. Creating institutional capacity for the diversity represented by these changes will require authentic leadership with the integrity and the vision, indeed the creativity and staying power, to accomplish four distinct but interrelated tasks.

1. To eliminate the gap in the participation, persistence, and success of members of underrepresented groups as students, faculty, and leaders in higher education institutions
2. To prepare students for cross-cultural transactions born out of tolerance, respect, and appreciation for individuals and groups unlike themselves
3. To promote scholarship among faculty and students that

will develop and apply a more complete and accurate body of knowledge necessary to the society's ability to solve problems rooted in the persistent effects of historical inequities, understand the opportunities inherent in diversity, and develop the full range of creative and productive capacities in a diverse population
4. To engage the institution's diverse constituencies, both internal and external, in the activities, rituals, and symbols that will develop the capacity of students to create community in the context of diversity, define a common stake, and envision a common future

Few individuals who currently make up the leadership pool in American higher education have had either the training or experiences necessary to provide leadership for the diversity that is beginning to characterize their institutions today and will constitute a central characteristic in the future. At best, the last several decades in American higher education have been characterized by additive responses to diversity or inequity—seldom by transformative ones. While institutions have generally turned away from the policies of de jure and de facto exclusion that characterized the period before 1950, and although most institutions embrace diversity as a goal, few understand the scope of the change required, and the challenge of developing a well-planned strategy to build institutional capacity for diversity remains unclear for many. The development of leaders and leadership strategies to guide institutions to and through these change processes is imperative. In *On Becoming a Leader,* Bennis (1989) cites John W. Gardner's description of the power of leadership: " 'Leaders have a significant role in creating the state of mind that is the society. They can serve as symbols of the moral unity of the society. They can express values that hold the society together. Most important they can conceive and articulate the goals that lift people out of their petty preoccupations, carry them above the conflicts that tear a society apart, and unite them in pursuit of objectives worthy of their best efforts' " (p. 13).

If we substitute the terms *institution, school, department, board of trustees, students, faculty,* and *staff* where Gardner has used *society,* we begin to understand the crucial need for leadership on diversity, not only at the top of institutional hierarchies but throughout the academic community.

Diversity presents formidable challenges in capacity building for institutions, but it is the historical separateness and inequality that have characterized American society that make the challenge of leadership for diversity exponentially more demanding. Since World War II, institutions of higher education have experienced formidable growth and success while operating with little if any consideration for issues of diversity or equity. Individual faculty careers, departments, research units, and schools have acquired resources, recognition, and prestige by concentrating on matters other than diversity. Issues of intergroup understanding and tolerance have been marginal, at best. Moreover, the reluctance of the academy to engage issues of differences and inequality has been strongly reinforced by a society that has great difficulty talking openly about race, culture, gender, sexual orientation, or conditions of disability. Leadership for diversity, then, must be prepared to deal with several layers of values, attitudes, and feelings in addition to the ones encountered in the pursuit of innovation and change in general.

Leadership Development for Diversity

If the complexity of diversity in our society is unprecedented and likely to increase and if the instrumentalities by which we develop leaders for our institutions have paid little attention to diversity until now, how then do we develop leadership for diversity and how can individuals currently in leadership positions become more authentic and effective as they confront the challenges in this arena?

Diversity, like leadership, does not lend itself to neat formulas, weekend workshops, or summer institutes where leadership skills for diversity may be modulized and acquired. Diversity calls up the most deeply felt passions about who we are, as individuals and as members of multiple groups, and about the kind of society we aspire to shape. The stakes associated with engaging diversity are high. One can begin to understand the complexities associated with diversity and acquire the strength to lead for diversity only if one recognizes and accepts the limited understandings of diversity acquired in contemporary life and contemporary education.

There are no all-knowing leaders in the struggle for equity and community in the face of diversity, but not knowing what to do to respond creatively to diversity in every instance is not an indication of either stupidity, apathy, racism, or sexism. It is a reflection of the failure of our society to value diversity sufficiently to incorporate it into the many processes by which we are educated. But accepting our limitations and therefore our fallibility is only half the equation; the potential leader for diversity must also be able to see possibilities. And the vision of those possibilities must serve as passionate motivation to embark on and persist in a journey in search of a deeper understanding of self as a cultural being in a diverse and often unequal society.

In this chapter, I will explore the development of leadership for diversity from two different perspectives. The first has to do with the individual journey on which anyone who pretends to lead in contemporary culturally and racially complex organizations must embark: *the journey of leadership and self-invention.* The second has to do with the *leader's role in shaping organizational culture in the face of diversity and inequality.*

Leadership and Self-Invention

In the early 1980s, when most of the nation was being led to retreat from efforts to reverse the persistent effects of discrimination, American higher education saw itself coming face to face with the demographic reshaping of the United States. The fact that students from groups that today we call minority would make up a rapidly increasing share of the market from which colleges would draw their students was accompanied by the realization that unless colleges and universities became far more proactive, too few minority students would be prepared to knock on the college door, much less walk in and stay in. Moreover, racial and gender tensions on college campuses were escalating as students who had lived largely segregated lives came in contact with students culturally, racially, and often socioeconomically different from themselves.

Given the political climate of the times, the response of the organized higher education community and of individual higher education leaders was heroic. It was grossly insufficient, however, in that the attempted solutions were often simplistic and almost always far too limited in scope. The result was that many college and university leaders found themselves in lose-lose situations. Confident in the rightness of their cause and their intentions and accustomed to solving problems with direct action, they prescribed responses to issues of underrepresentation and tensions associated with race, gender, and sexual preference that almost always put them at the center of backlashes from every direction. For some constituencies, nothing was ever enough; for others, anything was too much. And it was often the best of these leaders who suffered the greatest personal pain in the face of this turbulence.

Turbulence is inevitable in the face of the massive changes that U.S. higher education institutions will face in the next several decades. The polarization of the population on the basis of age, race, and ethnicity as well as socioeconomic groups will exacerbate the competition for resources and directly affect what happens on college campuses. The men and women who would effect leadership in those institutions—whether as faculty, staff, administrators, or members of a governance team—will have to draw on the resources of their *authentic* self to dare to shape answers to questions few have framed before.

Bennis identifies the basic ingredients of leadership as a guiding vision that clearly projects what the leader wants to do: an underlying passion for the promise of life and a course of action; integrity that proceeds from self-knowledge, candor, and maturity; trust that is earned and not acquired; and curiosity and daring that result in risk taking, experimentation, and learning from adversity.

While Bennis (1989, p. 50) does not address diversity, he describes the essential task of becoming a leader in terms that precisely frame the challenge of diversity for individuals, groups, and the whole of society:

I cannot stress too much the need for self-invention. To be authentic is literally to be your own author (the words derive from the same Greek root), to discover your own native energies and desires, and then to find your own way of acting on them. When you've done that, you are not existing simply in order to live up to an image posited by the culture or by some other authority or by a family tradition. When you write your own life, then no matter what happens, you have played the game that was natural for you to play.

To develop the authentic self on which to draw in exercising leadership on issues of diversity, however, it is necessary to risk learning in multiple modes. One must be willing to design a personal course of study and exploration that will enable one to learn not only facts but *truths, feelings, and interpretations*. Learning must be intellectual, but it must also be experiential, physical, and emotional. The journey to self-knowledge in the context of diversity can at times be undertaken with the aid of a teacher or in partnership with a peer and can be strengthened by group experiences, but ultimately it requires that one make time and space to make the journey in the company of one's self, with time for reflection, again and again and again.

The Journey to Self-Invention

On a recent visit to a community college in a small Texas city, I encountered a woman for whom the quest to understand diversity was providing the capacity to write her own life. A single white woman, born and raised in East Texas and the only daughter of only children, she retained the speech patterns that were the only clue to an upbringing marked by absolute separation of the races. It did not take long to see that she clearly loved teaching English to the African American and Hispanic students who made up a majority of the campus population. Her examination of gender issues in the curriculum had led her in turn to initiate a number of faculty development efforts to increase the faculty's understanding of multiculturalism, and she was clearly hungry for any insight that would strengthen her ability to understand and teach in the context of diversity. Our conversation flowed easily from the professional to the personal.

As she and my African American hostess drove me to several functions, I began to notice the absolute absence of subtle affectation or hidden strain in her manner or conversation. Somehow she was breaking all the bonds that maintain distance between African Americans, Hispanics, and non-Hispanic whites in Texas, particularly when race and culture are the topic. She was "discovering her own native energies and desires and finding her own way of acting on them."

In later conversation, my new friend revealed "her curiosity and daring which resulted in risk taking, experimentation, and learning from adversity." She told me about a summer-long immersion in Hispanic studies she had developed with colleagues and about a life-changing trip to Africa. "When I arrived in Africa, I felt as if I had arrived where I belonged. The people were warm and accepting and I was happier than I had ever been. When I came home, I found myself missing the people in Africa more than I had ever missed anyone with whom I had grown up." "I don't know exactly how," she said "but I know that I am going to find a way to make a difference."

Although she did not yet see herself as a formidable leader, my new friend was well on her way to becoming a strong leader for diversity. She had an underlying passion for the promise of life and for the broad outlines of a course of action and she was developing a guiding vision. Her self-invention radiated integrity and she was ready to take risks.

Indeed she was already, as a member of the faculty, exercising leadership among her peers and her students. In her enthusiastic search for understanding, she carried others along. In the discussion that followed my presentation on diversity, a young African American woman asserted the joy of her identity and two young Hispanic women kept repeating that they had never experienced an event that had such an impact. As an experienced lecturer, I knew that the students and I had both been led that evening by a white, Anglo-Saxon Protestant women born and raised in the separate and unequal world of East Texas who was in the process of inventing herself.

Of course few of us, regardless of gender, race, or culture, believe ourselves to be as free to self-invent as my East Texas friend. Family, children, community, and professional standing and relationships root us deeply in the investments we have made in shaping the self to the contours of tradition and safety. As academicians we are trained to search for new knowledge primarily in close proximity to the boundaries of existing knowledge. Moreover, we hold ourselves to a high standard of "objective" and "rational" understanding in the application of new knowledge.

Who then is a candidate for self-invention on issues of diversity? The answer is almost anyone who aspires to influence their environment. The journey to self-invention in the face of diversity is by definition never complete. While people who are members of groups for whom the effects of historical discrimination persist may have added insight into the experience that enables them to more easily understand groups other than their own, they too must seek out facts, truths, feelings, and interpretations about a configuration of culture and gender that neither their education nor their experience has prepared them for. Chauvinism is not the exclusive domain of any group.

As a Hispanic woman raised in Deep South Texas, my world was largely defined by people we called *Anglos* and people like me who called themselves *mexicanos*. While there were a few African American families in our communities, we led separate lives until after 1954, when the state's response to the Supreme Court mandate for integration was to integrate the African American children with the Mexican children. African Americans became our close friends, but they were few in number and for the most part adapted to us, speaking Spanish and even our brand of "Spanglish." We convinced ourselves that "they" were just like "us" and that this made them worthy of being our friends, except "of course" when it came to interracial dating. I grew up knowing little about African Americans.

An early interest in the history of civil rights policy in this country made me a student of African American history, but it was my immersion in civil rights that led to the experiences and relationships that began to deepen my understanding and

identification with the African American experience. The learning has taken many forms, but it must have been walking down
Auburn Avenue in Atlanta from the Martin Luther King Center
to the offices of the multigenerational African American newspaper that I finally felt the power of the African American struggle in this country. Just as sitting in the Longhouse on the
Orandaga Reservation listening to Chief Lloyd Elm's stories of
the teachings of his grandfather had connected me to the American Indian experience, it was being in the presence of three
African American women laughing about their adventures and
tribulations with demanding professors at Fisk University that
gave me a glimpse into the power and the lessons of this country's historically black colleges and universities. You can neither
"read" yourself nor "think" yourself into competence on issues
of diversity; when it comes to diversity, self-invention requires a
willingness to "experience."

But my journey to self-invention in the light of diversity is
far from over. Indeed it has come full circle. One of the major
cultural forces in Central Texas is Christian fundamentalism. For
years I have known of its existence, but my understanding of
what is clearly a culture has been minimal. It took less than a few
weeks of teaching a graduate course in education for me to realize that as many as half my students were products of homes
where Christian fundamentalism was a central focus in the development of cognition, language, problem-solving strategies,
worldviews, and values. And if these professionals were at least
one-third of my class, they would be at least one-third of the educational settings I was trying to affect. I would need to learn, to
reinvent my biases, to allow the experience of Christian fundamentalists to reach deep into my understandings. I began by
going to Christian bookstores. I sought out Christian fundamen-
talist ministers, trying to understand the origins of the questions
posed by my students. I listened to the ministers on Sunday
morning television. I do not know that I will ever be able to
identify with fundamentalists in the way I can with the African
Americans, but I have found much to value in the lives of my students and my understanding is growing. Most important, I have
examined myself in relation to this group of people and I will

never again think about educational reform in Central Texas without considering the role of Christian fundamentalism in the culture of the area.

When we search for an understanding of the culture of others, we cannot help but begin to identify the power of culture in our own formation. It is as an aid to self-knowledge that cultural exploration holds the greatest promise for members of the dominant culture. Just as my well-to-do Mexican cousins do not need to assert their cultural identity and probably seldom think about it, many members of the dominant culture in the United States find it bothersome and even difficult to define their own cultural identity. But we are all a product of the strengths and frailties, enlightenment and ignorance, struggles, defeats, victories, and guiding values of the generations that have gone before us. When we can understand and appreciate the ways others have been formed by their own unique cultural tradition, we can begin to appreciate the power and the sanctity of the cultural traditions that have formed ourselves, and from self-knowledge can come self-invention.

Leadership, Diversity, and Organizational Culture

In the course of the last quarter of a century, this country has invested billions of dollars in developing, implementing, and evaluating educational strategies designed to reverse historical inequality in educational opportunity. Substantial scholarly and leadership resources have also been focused on the development of knowledge emerging from the history and contemporary experiences of populations largely ignored by traditional scholarship.

Whether at the elementary, secondary, or higher education level, these strategies and research recommendations have shown at least modest short-term benefit to the participants and many have proven highly successful. But in spite of their success, all but a few of these strategies and scholarly works that have explicitly built on experience and perspectives based on race, culture, and gender remain at the margin of institutional life. Attempts to weave these strategies and scholarly works into the core of institutional practices have usually met with great resistance, often generating hostility toward the leadership, faculty, staff, and students involved in the innovation. Building the capacity of the academic culture to recognize, learn from, and incorporate diversity at its core remains a daunting task.

Higher education leaders, whether president or department chairperson, know that their success in meeting any goal is dependent on realities that flow from the history, personalities, long-standing as well as emerging formal and informal power structures, and comprehensive and inclusive planning processes. These realities—the "politics" of the organization—can make or break any initiative. Even in the best of circumstances, initiatives that focus on the building of institutional capacity for diversity enjoy a fragile configuration of support from the status quo culture of the institution.

The leader who would increase capacity for diversity must develop a two-pronged strategy for the exercise of leadership. First, the leader must develop specific strategic objectives that are doable, measurable and time specific, and that have the potential for demonstrating that commitment can lead to results. Such strategies may proceed from comprehensive institutional planning, as recommended by the American Council on Education in its *Handbook on Diversity* (1989), or may proceed from an "innovation incubator" approach in which diversity initiatives receive adequate fiscal and administrative support as the critical mass of institutional capacity necessary for comprehensive planning is developed.

There is no lack of models for adapting institutional practices to the needs of an increasingly diverse student population. Some models are merely collections of projects, others are more systemic. In *Sources: Diversity Initiatives in Higher Education* (1993), the Office of Minorities in Higher Education of the American Council on Education has compiled an exhaustive collection of diversity initiatives in higher education. The Association of Governing Boards has collected best practices in prekindergarten through graduate education programs in *Power in the Pipeline* (1992), the American Council on Education and the Council of Graduate Schools have examined the increased participation of diverse populations in graduate education, the National Association of Student Personnel Administrators has documented early outreach programs across the country, and the Education Commission of the States has done the same. The National Association of Independent Colleges and Universities, the American Association of Community Colleges, the American Association of State Colleges and Universities, and virtually every other higher education organization have published either collections of best practices by their member institutions or recommendations for action.

What is missing is not sufficient thinking on what needs to be done, but sufficient will and resources to do things on a scale broad enough to affect the numbers of students necessary to reduce the gap between groups. Higher education leaders must become advocates for private and public support of policies that will lead to the resources necessary to bring members of under-represented group to a level of parity in higher education.

The second imperative for diversity focuses on the development of an institutional culture that can recognize, learn from, support, and incorporate diversity at its core. The leader's fundamental challenge is to understand the institutional culture and to marshal the resources necessary to shape it to a new vision.

Deal and Peterson (1990) see the term *institutional culture* as describing the "character of a school as it reflects deep patterns of values, beliefs, traditions that have been formed over the course of its history." The authors state: "Beneath the conscious awareness of everyday life in any organization there is a stream of thought, sentiment and activity. This invisible, taken for granted flow of beliefs and assumptions gives meaning to what people say and do. It shapes how they interpret hundreds of daily transactions. This deeper structure of life in organizations is reflected and transmitted through symbolic language and expressive action. Culture consists of the stable, underlying social meanings that shape beliefs and behavior over time" (pp. 9–10).

This "invisible, taken for granted flow of beliefs and assumptions" is also the greatest challenge for leaders who would address diversity. It is into this substratum of beliefs and assumptions that the status quo has dug its strongest roots, nurtured on a daily basis by the success experiences of those individuals,

departments, research units, and formal and informal governance units for whom the status quo works well. Groups formerly
excluded from both the set of beliefs and assumptions and the
success experiences that nurture them tend to see the resistance
to diversity aimed primarily at "keeping them out," when the
aims are more likely to be "keeping us in" and "keeping things
as they have worked for years." As one particularly candid corporate executive said to a feminist activist, "The purpose of the
glass ceiling is not to keep you down, it is to keep me up."

But even when individual interests are not the only consideration, it is not easy to convince members of a culture that
has worked well for them and for the institution, to change the
culture by incorporating individuals and ideas that are genuinely different.

On matters of diversity, however, the essential leadership
task is to penetrate the beliefs and assumptions maintaining that
the mission of the institution can only be achieved when things
remain as they have always been. The leader for diversity must
bring to the institution her or his own vision of an institution,
school, or department carrying out its mission in a changing
world—one that demands a more complete and accurate picture of our history, contemporary condition, and future as that
reflects the totality of the human experience, one that demands
the intentional inclusion of a different configuration of individuals who can define problems and opportunities within a broader context. It is only when the leader can first envision and then
communicate—through word, symbol, ritual, and action—the
melding of the institution's mission with the social challenges
posed by diversity and equity that balkanization can be avoided.
It is in the formulation of this vision and its articulation that the
leader must be able to call up both the courage and creativity
that can only be earned through a process of self-knowledge and
self-invention in the light of diversity.

Knowing the context in which change is to occur is an important tool for leadership in any situation, but it is an absolute
prerequisite for leadership on diversity. The context must be understood on two levels. First, it is necessary to understand that
the higher education experience with diversity is in many ways

generationally determined. That is, higher education has been both influenced and defined by consecutive iterations of the nation's attempts to deal with exclusion and inequality. In a sense, much of the ethos relative to diversity in any institution is shaped by the particular level of intensity with which it has selectively engaged those iterations over time. If an institution's best memories of its engagement with exclusion and inequality are set in the 1960s, the people in the institution are likely to approach diversity first from a bipolar perspective (that is, black and white) and from a benevolent integrationist perspective (that is, "we will let you in so that you can become more like us because you are already enough like us to make you deserving of being let in"). The individuals who hold this ethos are not necessarily racist or sexist; they simply have not been able to progress in their thinking beyond that which was their noblest moment. Often individuals who were the most courageous in those prior periods of integration have the greatest difficulty in dealing with efforts to incorporate diversity into the institution at its core simply because they have invested much in their mid 1960s perspective on inclusion.

Subsequent generations of members of the academy have experienced the struggle for inclusion in diverse ways. The reaction to affirmative action, for example, will vary between and among members of diverse groups, depending on the historical period in which they engaged the practice as well as on the way practice has affected them or those close to them.

A second force affecting the leader's efforts to reshape organizational culture in the face of diversity is generated by a fundamental difference between members of the dominant culture and members of historically excluded groups in their approach to issues of *group identification* versus *individualism.*

Generally speaking, Americans of European origin have profited from an identity based on individualism. While every immigrant group initially experienced group-based discrimination and severe hardship, thinking of themselves as individuals allowed European Americans, usually within one to one and a half generations of immigration, to take full advantage of the promise of the country's expanding territory and economy.

Indeed individualism was the epitome of the "American identity." Extolled in popular culture, it was the common person's greatest weapon against the bonds of centuries of feudalism and class-based societies. It also served as a psychological buffer for any conscious responsibility for the historical treatment of other Americans on the basis of group identity.

Cultural diversity, by definition, is antithetical to this construct of an American identity. The individuals who gave up their claim to a cultural and linguistic connectedness to the generations that preceded them—whether willingly or by force—have for the most part extinguished the memory of the loss and focused on its benefits and utility. The process is locked deep in the milieu of beliefs and values of most individuals in the dominant culture and the institutions they control. Indeed, individualism is so deeply held a belief that non-Hispanic whites often seem incapable of recognizing the many ways in which their behavior is group based.

In contrast, generally speaking, members of historically excluded groups continue to struggle with the competing values of an identity based on individualism and one based on group membership. The promise of individualism was never an option for members of groups historically excluded de jure from the rights and privileges of full citizenship. While individual resiliency was critical to survival and heroic individual effort was necessary for success, it was the collective experience and the group's struggle and adaptation to its condition that defined the values that shape identity.

Regardless of educational or economic status, members of historically excluded groups continue to experience at least occasional treatment based on group membership. It is inevitable; just when you think you have gotten through any experience, something or someone reminds you that you are not an individual, you are a member of a group. In most cases, this intermittent reinforcement of a group identity keeps most members of historically discriminated groups connected to the group experience and to the persistent effects of historical discrimination that define contemporary conditions for the group. Struggle for the group, moreover, is a value deeply embedded in many families from groups that today we call minority. It is the stuff of which family myths and heroes are made, passed down in oral histories from generation to generation, and it is, for many the source of most individual achievement.

Whereas successful Americans of European origin have essentially separated their individual realization from that of members of their group, successful Americans who are members of historically excluded groups may chafe at the diminution of their individual effort or achievement, but they are far more likely to invest themselves heavily in the advancement of the group as a whole and to continue to struggle against the exclusion or devaluing of the group. This latter identity is not ambiguous, it is simply complex.

Understanding organizational culture as it engages, for better or worse, the challenge of diversity is but the base of leadership. The leader must be able to marshal the resources for shaping the culture to meet new realities. These resources include: the leader's vision; the administrative, faculty, and staff resources as these are augmented, deployed, and developed over time; the rituals, traditions, and symbols that give meaning to the institution; and the internal and external constituencies that influence the institution.

Identifying, recruiting, and incorporating individuals who can understand and support the leader's vision for an institution that engages the challenges and promise of diversity is essential to the leader's chances of success. In this regard, it is critical that the goal of the leader should be well thought out and go beyond efforts to recruit, hire, and retain minorities and women in an affirmative action mode. Indeed, the whole of the human resource identification, hiring, training, and rewards and punishment system requires adaptation to the demands of creating institutional capacity for diversity. The leader must understand that it is in adding and redeploying individuals within the organization that he or she wishes to shape, that an organizational culture capable of dealing positively with diversity will be strengthened or weakened. The organization must have as a goal the creation of a leadership team that reflects the diversity of the populations that are of central concern, and such a team must have the capacity to focus on a common stake and a common vision for the institution.

Sustaining the focus of the institution on a vision that engages the challenge and promise of diversity is infinitely more difficult than formulating and communicating one. Not only is it essential for the leader to create the mechanisms, events, and decisions that continue to communicate the vision; the leader must also ensure that diversity is at the center of institutional goals as additional innovation and improvement initiatives demand institutional attention. Total Quality Management, Community Engagement, Initiatives to Improve Teaching, Assessment, and other initiatives must incorporate diversity efforts, not replace them.

Conclusion

Dealing with issues of diversity will be one of the central themes in American higher education for the foreseeable future. Institutions will be either enhanced by the process or debilitated by it; they cannot avoid it. How well institutions fare in the face of diversity depends on the quality of leadership not only at the top of the organizational hierarchy, but throughout the organization. Leadership for diversity by definition implies leadership that is inspired, shared, and cohesive. It is leadership that is focused not only on strategies, projects, and programs but that entails the development of a new organizational culture. The leader who would embrace diversity is playing out a journey to self-knowledge and self-invention with ever-expanding possibilities.

References

American Council on Education. *Sources: Diversity Initiatives in Higher Education*. Washington, D.C.: Office of Minorities in Higher Education, 1993.
American Council on Education, Office of Minorities in Higher Education. *Handbook on Diversity*. Washington, D.C.: American Council on Education, 1989.
Association of Governing Boards of Universities and Colleges.

Power in the Pipeline. Washington, D.C.: Association of Governing Boards of Universities and Colleges, 1992.

Bennis, W. *On Becoming a Leader.* Reading, Mass.: Addison-Wesley, 1989.

Deal, T. E., and Peterson, K. D. *The Principal's Role in Shaping School Culture.* Office of Educational Research and Improvement, U.S. Department of Education. Washington, D.C.: U.S. Government Printing Office, 1990.

Chapter 20

Educating a New Majority: Mandate for the New Century

Richard O. Hope, Laura I. Rendón

John Paulos (1993, p. 14) asked the question: "If Everybody Knows So Much About Education, Why Doesn't Education Work?" This perennial question has been raised in numerous journals by those concerned about the state of education in the United States. From the point of view of minorities, this has proven a major frustration for those who have been taught that education is a ticket out of the ghetto or barrio. Hundreds of studies and research papers have been written to answer this question. Furthermore, resources exist to solve this problem. The answers are available and the knowledge base exists. We simply lack the will to ensure quality education for all minorities. Together with Robert W. Glover, Ray Marshall provides a basis for this discussion in Chapter Two of this book; with another colleague, he pursues the same issues in *Thinking for a Living: Education and the Wealth of Nations* (1992). He provides a major set of recommendations to garner fiscal support for education in the United States.

Recommendations for how to improve minority education are legion. Two classic sets of proposals were provided some thirty years apart. In 1960, educational performance data on

African American and Hispanic students were collected and analyzed by experts, resulting in a report titled *A Study of the Consequences of Powerlessness: Youth and the Ghetto* (Harlem Youth Opportunities Unlimited, 1962). This revolutionary document
brought together the best minds to ameliorate the social, educational, and housing deprivation experienced every day by Harlem children. Its suggestions are appropriate today because its
comprehensiveness brings all institutions of the community to
bear in solving the plight of Harlem youth. The most significant
aspect of this report, however, was not its high quality or its comprehensiveness, but its relative lack of impact in permanently
improving the lives of Harlem youth.

Some thirty years later, a similar project addressed the
problem of minority education and reached a similar conclusion in a report titled *Education That Works: An Action Plan for the
Education of Minorities.* (Quality Education for Minorities Project,
1990). Important, creative, and concrete actions were suggested
by experts, though with few practical results in permanently improving the education of minorities. The report argued that the
United States could no longer afford to ignore recommendations for fundamental change in the education of minority children. What makes *Education That Works* unique is its firm grounding in the political, social, and economic realities facing minority
students seeking quality education, and its recognition of the
peril awaiting the United States if these educational needs are
not met.

As a general statement, the *Workforce 2000* ((Johnston and
Parker, 1987) study postulates that the labor force will grow more
slowly, become older, more female, and more nonwhite. By the
year 2000, only 15 percent of new entrants into the workforce will
be white males, compared to 47 percent in that category in 1987.
As stated earlier in this book, we will become a nation progres-
sively more minority, and this "browning of America" will significantly alter every institution in our society from politics and education, the economy and industry, to national values and culture.
Ray Marshall and Robert Glover remind us that America is
changing rapidly, and the rapidity and necessity for that change
is one of the perils we face as a nation. As the need for techno-

logically competent workers increases, will America's schools, colleges, and universities be able to deliver teaching and learning of acceptable quality over the next several decades? These perils have been fully discussed in previous chapters, making the inevitable point that improving minority education is no longer an option for America if it is to remain competitive in the world economy. Developing the highest-quality education for minorities is a guarantee that excellence in education for all Americans is assured.

The Clinton administration recognized this fact when issuing "Goals 2000," sponsored by both the United States Departments of Education and Labor. Embracing a much more expanded mission than the Bush Administration's "Goals 2000," it proposes to move from "A Nation at Risk" to a "A Nation on the Move" by:

- Embracing new, world class learning standards
- Enriching course content so students can reach challenging goals
- Improving the training for quality teaching
- Promoting parental involvement
- Challenging all schools to show real results
- Encouraging reform from the bottom up, not the top down
- Underscoring the link between education and employment

According to President Clinton and his Secretary of Education, Richard Riley, accomplishment of these goals requires a partnership between local, state, and national governments, parents, educators, community groups, business and labor leaders, and citizens to reinvent our nation's education and training system. As former governors, Clinton and Riley feel strongly that education is primarily a state and local responsibility. In addition, the Clinton administration is proposing a $393 million bill to encourage bottom-up reform. Goals 2000 will provide information to educators, parents, businesses, and students so they will know exactly what world-class standards are, what they have to do to reach them, and how much progress they are making.

Caution must be exercised before handing responsibility

for improving and restructuring education to local authorities, given past segregation policies that denied quality education to minorities. Strict federal monitoring is necessary to ensure fair application of federal resources. One safeguard suggested by Floraline I. Stevens focuses on what teachers do in their classrooms. She suggests a more sensitive barometer to measure the extent of Opportunity-to-Learn (National Center for Education Statistics, U.S. Department of Education, 1993, p. 4):

- How time is spent in the classroom
- How learning is organized
- What curriculum materials are used
- What attitudes are reinforced
- What beliefs and values are operant
- How supportive are the conditions for teaching and learning

Secretary of Education Riley suggests that Opportunity-to-Learn standards be employed to include: quality and availability of curriculum, instructional materials and technologies, the capacity of teachers to provide quality instruction in each content area, and access to professional development for teachers and administrators. All of these measures bear directly on student learning especially for minorities. All suggestions for improving minority education inevitably become recommendations for upgrading the general educational system. To bring forward the organizing principles for making the education of a new majority in our schools a national responsibility, we must return to fundamental values.

Pride in Education

At the base of the specific recommendations discussed in *Education That Works* is pride, which must be the framework and central theme that holds the concepts of quality minority education together. Pride defines respect for the educational enterprise. Pride is respect for self and others arising from understanding of accomplishments, knowledge of the dignity of others, and gratification arising from association with a school. To have pride in something does not require one to diminish the value or quality of others. From the kindergarten through high school, all schools must be world class and supported to ensure the principle that these will be educational institutions chosen and preferred by the neighborhood. The single characteristic most common to schools that have been successful in serving low income and minority communities has been pride instilled in the educational enterprise. Four areas should be considered: school pride, teacher pride, student pride, and community pride.

School Pride

School pride encompasses leadership, vision, respect, organization, structure, and support given to teachers, students, and parents. The educational leader provides a positive atmosphere that allows for creative and enthusiastic teaching and learning. Even in times of low budgets and significant cuts in spending, schools can be clean, well lit, and open facilities supported by parents, teachers, and community. There are excellent examples of principals who organized campaigns to paint the school, fix the furniture, and clean the halls and restrooms, and by their leadership received the support of the teachers, students, parents, and even the unionized custodians (see Winerip, 1994). Educational leaders must ensure that the schools meet national standards, sets standards for teaching, and ensure compliance with these requirements. Schools must encourage high expectations for students' performance that conform to national standards in specific disciplines. They must provide the services of social workers, counselors, psychologists, and teacher aides, reduced class size, time for planning and coordination of shared resources and classes, and discipline for students.

Schools must establish linkages along the educational pathway at both the entry and exit points. Prekindergarten centers can serve as umbilical links to prepare students to learn, and schools must have reciprocal relationships between principals, teachers, students, and parents to make this a seamless web. Likewise, schools must have strong programs bridging higher education with reciprocal agreements linking colleges and universities with public secondary education.

Since all students will not go on to college, there must be strong "school-to-work" programs that allow students to prepare for the workplaces of the twenty-first century. The skills needed must be taught in close coordination with the future requirements of business and industry. Schools must begin to include corporate representatives on its curriculum planning committees.

School pride begins with respect and understanding between the educator and the consumer of the product of this education. The greater the fit between these two, the greater will be the resources available to the educational enterprise.

Teacher Pride

Teachers are responsible for the transference of culture, knowledge, and skills from one generation to another. This profession is less respected today and, as a consequence, there is increased violence against teachers, the loss of qualified teachers to other careers, and fear and loss of respect for students by teachers. This cycle of fear and lack of pride in the profession has a dramatic effect on the educational process.

Much of urban and rural public education has become a holding action to keep students off the streets during the work day. Thus educational standards centered around the ability of the teacher to maintain class decorum and order become the standard for measuring the quality of teaching. The educational profession cannot maintain high standards when those who utilize its services view it as pacifiers and warehousers of students.

Teachers must strive to eliminate remedial education and focus instead on: cognitive development—that is, abstract thinking, critical thinking, and problem solving. Accelerated learning should be emphasized in conjunction with language development, mathematics and science competencies, and employment of educational technologies such as computer skills to improve oral and written communication. Cooperative learning is an effective medium in the teacher's arsenal to promote efficient education, as well as teamwork and teaching personal responsibility and respect for others.

Teachers must respect and support each other as professionals, which begins in their training and continues throughout their career. Teacher education must establish the highest standards, incorporate new teaching strategies, and reinforce high expectations for all students regardless of background or circumstance. It is essential to revitalize curriculum and instruction; eliminate "tracking"; reconceptualize the use of tests, student assessments, and the learning environment; and rethink ways for teachers and counselors to interact with students. There must be a clear vision for training and retraining educational personnel (that is, teachers, counselors, superintendents, principals, and other administrators) in cultural diversity and multiculturalism. Teacher recruitment must encourage minority students to consider the teaching profession and emphasize fellowships and grants to support these students through college and graduate school.

Student Pride

School and teacher pride is a prerequisite for student success, which comes from the services, support, and hard work of an environment that motivates, cajoles, stimulates, pushes, and encourages the highest level of performance. The resulting confidence and self-respect ultimately translates into respect for the school, teachers, and the community.

The student is the client driving this system and must, therefore, be the focus for all other educational activity. Union rules and regulations, the professionalization of teachers, and the career enhancing activities of principals and other support staff are important but not as crucial as putting the student first. If students are made to feel that they are primary, much disruptive behavior might not exist, student retention and academic performance would also increase. However, this should not be viewed as a panacea or total solution to our educational problems.

Students themselves have a responsibility to respect teachers and appreciate the tremendous burdens placed on the school system. They should understand the personal sacrifice teachers often make in the face of scarce resources, such as having to mop the classroom floor when there is not enough staff to keep the school clean, class preparation not paid for by the system, hours spent after school calling parents to encourage family support for the student, and endless meetings to coordinate services to meet the unique needs of individual students. They should see education as an opportunity for personal success and improvement of society in general. This perception is hindered by violence gripping our schools today. The causes of school violence are complex and, therefore, the solutions are elusive.

Nevertheless, a massive movement against violence in schools must be launched and discussions should include all major sectors of the educational system: students, teachers, parents, community representatives, and professional research and support staff members in the primary, secondary, and higher education establishments. Deborah Prothrow-Stith's research demonstrates that violence can be curbed by developing mechanisms for disagreement that eliminate the feeling of personal affront. These mechanisms require significant focus on improving self-esteem and respect for the cultural background of others. Beyond efforts that the school can address, the community becomes pivotal in eliminating violence and its causes.

Community Pride

Neighborhoods and families shape student belief systems and behavior. Just as schools have an independent influence on students, so too does the community. Research indicates that youngsters in the first through third grades experience normal increases in academic performance that gradually diminish as twelfth grade approaches. This has been interpreted to suggest that the school does a poor job of educating given the existence of the community or environment as constant throughout the educational process. However, this does not absolve the community of responsibility for the education of its youth.

Communities must take responsibility for their youth and provide the protection and resources needed to obtain quality education. Education must be community based with parents and community leaders actively involved in all aspects of the educational process. Parents need the assistance of community leaders to create after-school homework study programs in churches and other neighborhood facilities. "Saturday academies" for the enrichment of students exist in communities and have had great success in developing basic skills, providing mentoring, and creating positive role models, as well as opportunities to observe educational activities in the community.

Prekindergarten centers and Head Start programs are effective readiness educational programs, and they can be linked with human service organizations including school-based health clinics. This provides an incentive for parents to participate in these programs where the needs of the family can be met while young children receive day-care services.

Alternative forms of education must be considered that allow for the support of youngsters who have little or no family support. Many become wards of the state because of absent parents or families that are dysfunctional. These youth have committed no crimes, broken no laws, but very often they are placed in "youth detention homes" along with troubled children who have criminal records. There are few options currently available to provide these youngsters with a loving and supportive atmosphere. But there are several promising options to remedy the situation: urban academies, residential day-time school environments, and the use of vacant buildings or closed military bases that could be converted to provide homelike settings for these unparented children. The Clinton administration's community "service corp" could support these installations by drawing upon individuals affected by corporate and government personnel reductions in force as well as college students who possess the nurturing, technical, and educational skills to assist these youth immediately.

Early intervention in the education of minority youth along the educational pathway ensures that our children will learn and perform well. Respect starts the process by establishing pride in the school, teacher, community, and, most important, the student. This internal process is not directly linked to federal, state, or local funds but starts with the community and infuses pride into the four groups noted above. It does not stop at high school; rather, it becomes part of lifelong learning that connects to higher education.

Higher Education's Role

Much has been said about the participation of minority students at the college and university levels. The bottom line to all the statistics is clear: there are not enough minorities opting for college, disproportionately low number of minorities receive the baccalaureate degree and a paltry number obtain graduate degrees. As recommended in the recent report of the Wingspread Group on Higher Education (1993), we must create a nation of learners:

> All of us, from pre-school to post-graduate, are in this together. It is not enough to complain about each other's failings. It is time to stop addressing the problem piecemeal. We must begin to work collaboratively on the system as a whole. It is no longer tolerable for so many in higher education to complain about the quality of those they admit, but do nothing to set higher standards and work with colleagues in K–12 schools to help students attain those standards. Our educational system is in crisis; business-as-usual is a formula for national disaster.

Transforming Higher Education

Creating a nation of learners requires changing the flawed paradigm in which higher education presently operates. Traditional program planning, teaching, advising, and retention are based on theories derived from research based on middle- and upper-class, predominantly white, male student populations that have limited utility for students of color. It cannot be assumed that a new student majority can become involved and socialized in a college environment that is vastly different from their home/community realities. It cannot be assumed that students of color will learn the same as white students or that they can find success in lecture halls where they passively study, read, and write about a white culture that has nothing to do with their experiences. It cannot be assumed that students will want to assimilate and shed or mask their culture and language in order to fit into an institutional culture that is more readily negotiable for white students. It is no longer enough to create "special programs," successful as they may be, that target only a few students and do little or nothing to impact the mainstream academic program. And we cannot expect that minority faculty and staff take on the responsibility for students of color by themselves. We know that there are not enough of them and that they are usually overburdened with additional responsibilities. Instead, what is needed is for the *entire* higher education community to view the education of students of color as a shared responsibility.

It is time that the higher education community engage in a national dialogue about what it is going to take to *transform* higher education in order to accommodate a coming new student majority that is presently in the K–12 system. Reports that have been issued about the reform of higher education such as *Involvement in Learning* (Study Group . . . , 1984) and *An American Imperative* (Wingspread Group on Higher Education, 1993) pay little to no attention to the issues of students of color. We call on the Secretary of Education, foundations, college presidents, and faculty and researchers that have specifically examined minorities in higher education, as well as state and national higher education associations, to lead the nation in a dialogue and a plan of action that addresses the issues put forth in this book.

Becoming a Vital Part of the Educational Pathway

Higher education must view itself as an integral part of the education continuum for a new student majority. These institutions must play a central role in helping students, whether black, brown, red, and yellow, to consider college a realistic option. Higher education, in conjunction with the K–12 system, must instill the vision that college begins in kindergarten. Without this vision, students can become disillusioned and potentially a part of the urban pathology being witnessed today. A much stronger link must also be developed between two- and four-year institutions, to ensure that the educational pathway toward the baccalaureate is cleared of pernicious barriers that have precluded students from transferring and earning bachelor's degrees.

Forging Partnerships with External Constituencies

Higher education institutions must also participate in educational partnerships with community-based organizations and human services agencies, such as health providers and the criminal justice system. In addition, they must develop a partnership with industry to develop curricula to equip students with the skills needed in the twenty-first century world of work.

Majority institutions need to create stronger partnerships with minority institutions—that is, specifically historically black colleges and universities (HBCUs), Hispanic Association of Colleges and Universities (HACUs), and tribally controlled colleges. Reciprocal relationships or pairings are already established providing for the exchange of students, faculty, curriculum materials, seminars, workshops, and fiscal resources. Partnerships between predominantly majority and minority institutions can significantly improve the racial atmosphere by thorough planning, discussing, and developing cooperative activities. These partnerships can ensure a more inclusive curriculum and a faculty that is more aware and sensitive to the needs of minority students.

Making the Curriculum Culturally Responsive to New Students

Several of this book's authors, notably Mildred García and Daryl Smith, provide a rational for the need to create a new paradigm for teaching and learning. New majority students do not get involved easily; they do not learn in the same way that whites learn; they do not find the predominant Eurocentric curriculum reflective of their realities. The time has come to totally redesign and rethink what we know about teaching and learning because most of the research that drove the present classroom paradigm is outdated and based on white male students. Along these lines, it is time to think of reconceptualizing the role of faculty and the rewards that lead to promotion and tenure.

Instituting a New System of Faculty Rewards

Many faculty, sensitive to the concerns of minority students, are actively developing inclusive curricular materials, and teaching and serving as mentors, but they are not receiving any rewards for their important contributions. We must put students first and provide a reward system that encourages promotion and tenure for faculty who are actively and effectively:

- Mentoring at-risk students
- Engaging in community service and field work
- Promoting affirmative action recruitment and retention
- Transforming the curriculum
- Building positive campus climate

Diversifying, Increasing, and Retaining the Pool of Faculty and Staff

Priority must be given to the recruitment, retention, and support of minority faculty, as well as to significantly increase the number of minorities who receive the doctorate. While funding is available for doctoral education, a major hindrance is the absence of mentors who can provide the advice and counsel necessary for the successful completion of the Ph.D.

John Hope Franklin (1993) is widely acclaimed for his mentorship of many minorities receiving the doctorate in the social sciences and humanities. He states that "the inclusive university must be an institution which accepts the responsibility of providing equal access and opportunity and an accommodating environment for all members of the academic community regardless of racial, ethnic, social, or economic background" (p. viii).

The academy must restructure its reward system to encourage mentors, increase contact time with students, and provide a more supportive campus climate for minority students. This cannot be done in a vacuum, however. Colleges and universities will require a major infusion of funds and heightened awareness on the national level to propel these issues to a wider audience. This requires federal and state government support and, most important, the president of the United States speaking about these concerns as strategic to our national interest.

A National Call to Leadership

We issue a clarion call for the nation's leaders to mobilize the will, strength, and resources of our country to solve the problem of poor quality minority education. After twenty years of educational reform, relatively little has changed in the lives of minority students. Unfortunately, in many areas of the country, the problem has gone from bad to worse. Our country has responded to crises before with resounding success. The New Deal, Marshall Plan, and G.I. Bill are but a few examples of our ability to solve problems. In each case, the United States took action because of strong and courageous leadership, which saw a problem and mobilized to solve it without testing the political environment or conducting a political pool to determine "political correctness."

The problem of poor-quality minority education represents a crisis in leadership. Our country is crying out for effective leaders who will not provide simple palliatives but more decisively to improve the quality of life. The November 1994, election represents this cry of desperation. If little action is taken in two years, the electorate will speak again with another dramatic change in leadership. The time has come for our nation's most prominent leaders to issue a national call for educating poor, minority, and other at-risk students. Absent from federal and state reform initiatives has been a new vision of America's educational system that incorporates the whole notion of educating a new majority and a new minority. It is time for our country's president, as well as for state governors to build a national movement to eradicate the barriers faced by minority students at every step of the educational pathway.

The Goals 2000/Educate America Act—President Clinton's comprehensive national response to reclaiming our children's future—is a very general document that lacks specific prescriptions and targeted assistance available to at-risk minority students along the entire educational pathway. Actions of the federal government must be done in conjunction with state agencies to set specific standards of appropriate behavior for complete equality of education. The president can encourage the states to restructure the educational systems by focusing on: computational literacy; institutional and student performance criteria; coordination of K–12 and higher education; transfer policies from two- to four-year colleges; the school-to-work transition; and creating and sustaining hospitable campus climates. As a previous governor of Arkansas, President Clinton should encourage the National Governors Association to sponsor a national conference addressing "The Education of Minorities at Risk."

The neglect of minority education is a barrier preventing the United States from maintaining its leadership in the world. Changes made to improve the quality of minority education will directly impact the effectiveness of education for all U.S. citizens. The 1990s are a time both of great peril and enormous opportunity. It is a time when fear, misinformation, and frustration guide and propel the passage of Proposition 187, intolerance and hostility toward nontraditional populations, increased attention to the needs of the affluent (at the expense of the poor and the victims of neglect), a focus on individualism and self-centeredness, racial riots, campus unrest, and the egregiously dangerous and damaging notion that people of color possess limited intellectual capacity.

Yet, even in the face of these perilous social developments, we believe that the vast majority of the American people do care about the welfare of this nation and all, not just some, of its citizens. The 1990s present us with the opportunity to welcome and celebrate the presence of a new student majority, along with their new languages and cultures that enrich our collective lives. We need new policies to transform educational institutions employing research-based facts, along with the habits of compassion, respect, and concern for those who have less. We call on our nation's leaders to heed our clarion call and lead this nation in instituting a new vision for the America of tomorrow.

References

Franklin, J. H. "Preface." In Joint Center for Political and Economic Studies, *The Inclusive University: A New Environment for Higher Education.* Washington, D.C.: Joint Center for Political and Economic Studies Press, 1993.

Harlem Youth Opportunities Unlimited. *A Study of the Consequences of Powerlessness: Youth and the Ghetto.* New York: Harlem Youth Opportunities Unlimited, 1962.

Johnston, W. B., and Parker, A. H. *Workforce 2000: Work and Workers for the 21st Century.* Indianapolis, Ind.: Hudson Institute, 1987.

Marshall, R., and Tucker, M. *Thinking for a Living: Education and the Wealth of the Economy.* New York: Basic Books, 1992.

National Center for Education Statistics, U.S. Department of Education. *Opportunity to Learn: Issues of Equity for Poor and Minority Students.* Washington, D.C.: U.S. Government Printing Office, 1993.

Paulos, J. "If Everybody Knows So Much About Education, Why Doesn't Education Work?" *New York Times Book Review,* Nov. 14, 1993, p. 14.

Quality Education for Minorities Project. *Education That Works: An Action Plan for the Education of Minorities.* Cambridge, Mass.: Quality Education for Minorities Project, 1990.

Study Group on the Condition of Excellence in Higher Education. *Involvement in Learning.* Washington, D.C.: National Institute of Education, 1984.

Winerip, M. "A Public School in Harlem That Takes the Time, and the Trouble, to Be Family." *New York Times,* Jan. 26, 1994, p. A19.

Wingspread Group on Higher Education. *An American Imperative: Higher Expectations for Higher Education.* Washington, D.C.: Johnson Foundation, 1993.

Name Index

Subject Index

A

A Nation at Risk, 377–378, 415, 416

Academic Champions of Excellence (ACE), 154

Accelerated Schools Program, 420

Accelerated Schools Project, Stanford University, 188–189, 192

Access: coalitions for, 374–376; to mathematics/science education, 61–62, 210; and multicultural education, 163; and neoconservative policy, 376–380

Accountability: in Native education, 260; performance-based, 143–144; for student learning, 128–129

Admissions: and gender issues, 353–354; minority student, 25, 352–353. *See also* Enrollment

African Americans: birth rate of, 3; college enrollment of, 21–22, 101, 354–355, 375; colleges of, 391–393; community college enrollment of, 290–291; diversity among, 4; doctoral degrees of, 310; educational level of, 74–75; and gender issues, 353–354; historical background on, 4; income of, 73; mathematics skills of, 203; and racism, 4; risk factors for, 406; scholarships for, 24; student demonstrations of, 22; as teachers, 18; and tracking/testing, 168, 170, 172, 174–175, 177, 182; as U.S. population group, 4; in workforce, 35–36

Alabama, school financing in, 418

Alaska Natives: college enrollment of, 394; and Eskimos/Aleuts, 5; historical background on, 5; subgroups of, 5; as U.S. population group, 4–5. *See also* American Natives; Native education

America. *See* United States

America 2000 Plan, 15

American Association for the Advancement of Science, 222–224

American Association of Colleges for Teacher Education (AACTE), 151, 157

American Association of Community Colleges, 449

American Association of State Colleges and Universities, 449

American Council on Education, 328, 386, 448

American Indian and Alaska Native Education Goals, 248

American Indians: and campus climate, 26; college population of, 21–22, 394; community college enrollment of, 290; educational level of, 74–75; as faculty, 24; historical background on, 5; income of, 73; mathematics skills of, 203; subgroups of, 5; as U.S. population group, 4–5. *See also* American Natives; Native education

American Natives: as at risk, 237–238; community self-sufficiency of, 243; defined, 231; doctoral degrees of, 310; government relationship/responsibility to, 231–232; national priorities for, 244; and racism, 240; school population of, 232, 239–240, 256; social/economic context of, 238; traditional culture of, 238–239; tribally controlled colleges of, 393–395.

478

tual questions of, 425–432; and curriculum/pedagogy; and family support, 428–429; principles of, 424–432; and public awareness, 429–430; and school governance, 425–427; and student outcomes, 407

Urban Partnerships Program, 386, 387

Urban Systemic Initiative, National Science Foundation, 13

Urban Teacher Program (UTP) (Mich.), 212–213

U.S. Department of Education, 232, 235, 248, 256, 258

W

Wayne County Community College (Mich.), 213

Wayne State University (Mich.), 213

Wesleyan University (Conn.), 281–282

Western New England College, 277–278

White House Conference on Indian Education, 252

Whites: discrimination against, 25; and racial tension, 9–10; in workforce, 35

William Penn Foundation, 215

Women: and curriculum transformation, 24; graduate degrees of, 81–82; in higher education, 71–72; hostility toward, 26;

Women's studies, 270, 273, 279–280

Workers: front-line, 42–43; high quality, 43–44; higher-order thinking skills of, 39; learning/training opportunities of, 46; least-skilled, 44; technology skills of, 41; wage decline of, 37–38

Workforce: advanced education of, 29; aging of, 47–48; and educational reform, 87–88; educational training for, 46, 101; mathematical skills of, 121–122, 203; minorities in, 29, 35–36, 47, 101, 398; and new world economy, 36–37; and schooling, 43; women in, 35

Workplace: and competitiveness, 39–41, 101; learning, 421; mass production in, 38–39; mathematics skills of, 203; participatory management in, 40–41; technological innovation in, 39